Susan Glaspell: Essays on Her Theater and Fiction

THEATER: Theory/Text/Performance

Enoch Brater, Series Editor

Susan Glaspell

Essays on Her Theater and Fiction

Edited by Linda Ben-Zvi

Ann Arbor

THE UNIVERSITY OF MICHIGAN PRESS

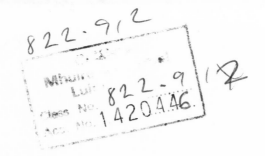
Copyright © by the University of Michigan 1995
All rights reserved
Published in the United States of America by
The University of Michigan Press
Manufactured in the United States of America

1998   1997   1996   1995   4   3   2   1

A CIP catalogue record for this book is available from the British Library.

Library of Congress Cataloging-in-Publication Data

Susan Glaspell : essays on her theater and fiction / edited by Linda Ben-Zvi.
    p.   cm. — (Theater : Theory/text/performance)
Includes bibliographical references.
ISBN 0-472-10549-3 (alk. paper)
  1. Glaspell, Susan, 1882–1948—Criticism and interpretation.
2. Women and literature—United States—History—20th century.
I. Ben-Zvi, Linda, 1939–   II. Series: Theater—theory/text/performance.
PS3513.L35Z86   1995
818'.5209—dc20   94-49647
                                                                CIP

For all those who have helped recover Susan Glaspell
and her work, especially Arthur Waterman, Gerhard Bach,
Marcia Noe, and Mary Papke.

Contents

Introduction

Linda Ben-Zvi

The career of Susan Glaspell (1876–1948), the American playwright and novelist, follows closely the trajectory of other "reclaimed" American women writers of the century such as Kate Chopin, Charlotte Perkins Gilman, and Zora Neale Hurston: well known in her time, effaced from canonical consideration after her death, and rediscovered years later through the surfacing of one work, around which critical attention has focused.

"In her time," for Glaspell, was the first decades of the century, in Greenwich Village, New York, and Provincetown, Massachusetts, when she—along with her husband George Cram Cook, and, later, Eugene O'Neill—established the Provincetown Players, the first modern American theater company, which put on one hundred plays by fifty-two playwrights in the seven years of its existence.[1] Dedicated "to giving American playwrights a chance to work out their ideas in freedom," the Provincetown Players became the place in which indigenous American drama took root; and Glaspell and O'Neill became the progenitors of the form, O'Neill writing fourteen plays under the aegis of the group, Glaspell eleven.

For Isaac Goldberg, Heywood Broun, Ludwig Lewisohn, and other eminent theater critics of the period, O'Neill was the undisputed father of American drama, Glaspell the mother, the pair initiating "the entrance of the United States into the deeper currents of continental waters," as Goldberg described their epochal work.[2] Both expanded the possibilities of what could be shown and discussed on the stage, offering glimpses of a theater to come; both experimented with new dramatic forms, stage language, and subject matter, since few American models existed; and, for their work, both were honored, Glaspell receiving the Pulitzer Prize in 1931 for her play *Alison's House.*

Yet while O'Neill's work survived his death, Glaspell's did not, and her plays and fiction were allowed to go out of print after 1948.[3] In post–World War II America, with women's lives no longer riveting but routine, and traditional roles refigured in the society and in the literature of the time, works as decidedly feminist as those Glaspell had written in the 1910s and 1920s were as out of fashion as the overalls Rosie had worn to work.

Susan Glaspell's writing is marked by strong women, personae whose consciousness of themselves and their world shape her plays and fiction. The plots invariably turn on their experiences, relationships, and attempts to wrest at least a modicum of self-expression and fulfillment in societies that impede, if not prohibit, such possibilities. Cutting across geographical and class lines, Glaspell's women display what Carolyn Heilbrun has noted as "the major, perhaps single, mark of a feminist life: resistance to socialization."[4] It takes a period not threatened by suggestions of cultural change to apprise such writing, such ideas, and such women adequately. The 1950s in the United States was not such a time.

The 1970s was, and, therefore, it is not surprising that among the first works to be critiqued by nascent feminist theory was Glaspell's 1916 one-act play, *Trifles,* and its short story offshoot, "A Jury of Her Peers." The first edition of Mary Anne Ferguson's 1973 ground-breaking text *Images of Women in Literature* introduced *Trifles* and has continued to alternate the play and short story through five editions. *Trifles* was also included in Judith E. Barlow's collection *Plays by American Women: The Early Years,* and "A Jury of Her Peers" became the focus of Annette Kolodny's influential 1980 essay entitled "A Map for Rereading: Or, Gender and the Interpretation of Literary Texts." The works have also made their way into the classroom, appearing in widely used introductory anthologies of literature and drama, included in response to demands to open up the canon to women writers.

The story of two virtually inarticulate women who, in the process of accompanying their husbands to an isolated farmhouse in which a woman has been accused of murdering her husband, read the signs of her thwarted life, motives for murder, and their own constricted existences and potential for violence—all writ clearly among the kitchen things the men dismiss as "trifles"—has become a feminist classic. The very simplicity of the tale, balancing male and female "readings" of the events of the case and offering up, as it does, questions about gender difference and communication across class lines, has also made *Trifles* and "Jury" palimpsests for evolving issues in contemporary feminist theory, worked out in the considerable body of criticism on Glaspell that has emerged. In the past twenty years over fifty articles and several doctoral dissertations have discussed her writing.[5]

Glaspell criticism, which began in the 1970s with discussions of *Trifles* and "Jury," moved in the late 1980s into a second period, in which critical attention began focusing on the retrieval of other works from her extensive, and still untapped, literary horde: fifty short stories, nine novels, and fourteen plays. Like *Trifles* and "Jury," these works speak directly to contemporary audiences, since they foreground female personae and issues of gender, class, and societal restrictions. In them Glaspell continues her radical revisions of literary forms, paring stories of their sentimentality; experimenting with voice, diction, idiom, and imagery in her novels; introducing expressionism, historical narratives, and symbolism on her stage. The works also serve as a repository for the social and political issues that concerned Glaspell during a forty-year career that began in 1902, with the publication of her first short stories in popular journals, and continued unabated until the publication of her last novel, *Judd Rankin's Daughter,* in 1945, three years before her death. A study of this rich oeuvre therefore offers more than a retrieval of a forgotten literary figure; it also offers an important means of reassessing the leading debates of the first half of the century, seen through the eyes of a woman directly involved with the shaping of modernist writing and modern social structures.

Born in Davenport, Iowa, on July 1, 1876—four days before the country's centennial celebrations—Glaspell experienced and reacted to many of the social upheavals that shaped the beginnings of the second century in America. A granddaughter of the earliest pioneers in Davenport, she witnessed the changes wrought by the second generation. Those who "began life there in a society unconscious of social distinctions, built for themselves big square ugly expensive brick houses painted slate gray, with towers and mansard roofs, 'small servants' rooms and big brick stables for their horses and carriages.' "[6] In a town in which her contemporaries began dynasties—the Deeres were just starting their fledgling equipment factory—her family went in a different direction. The first Glaspell farm was one of the largest in the new community; her own life began forty years later in a clapboard house, under the Davenport bluffs, in the undesirable part of the city, fronting the Mississippi River. Although family fortunes dissipated over time, and both her grandfather Glaspell and father ended their lives as invalids, suffering from extensive periods of depression before their deaths, the women in her life—grandmother Glaspell, who lived with Susan for twenty years, and her own mother, a schoolteacher who gave up her work when she married at twenty-five and in immediate succession had Susan and her two brothers—provided role models for the strong female figures who would appear in her writing.

As early as eighteen, writing a column in the local paper, under the byline Susie Glaspell, Glaspell had begun critiquing what passed for genteel life for young women. Writing about teas, dances, the latest sports crazes, or the current fashion, she was the outsider looking in, but one who increasingly eschewed what she saw in favor of a different life-style. In a period in which few women went to college and fewer pursued a career, Susan Glaspell did both: entering Drake University at the age of twenty-one, in 1897, studying philosophy, and—like her contemporary Willa Cather—excelling in debate and pursuing journalism after graduation, turning her newspaper material into short stories and later into novels. Her first stories won prestigious prizes;[7] her first novel, *The Glory of the Conquered*, was recognized by the *New York Times* for "bringing forward a new author of fine and notable gifts."[8] By 1913, when she married George Cram Cook, a fellow Davenport iconoclast and the twice-married son of one of the leading families in town, she had already achieved literary prominence, published two novels, a collection of short stories, traveled widely for a year in Europe, and established herself among the literary community in Chicago and New York.

The scandal the marriage caused follows precisely the model that Carolyn Heilbrun describes in *Writing a Woman's Life:* an act near middle age that would thrust the woman out of society but would also free her from further restrictions that residual conservatism might still exact. Like Heilbrun's examples—Colette, Dorothy Sayers, and George Eliot— Glaspell, at thirty-seven, was able to begin a new life, one still grounded in her Iowa heritage but cut loose from second generation sterility and fixity.

Together with Cook and Floyd Dell, another resident of Davenport, she retraced the direction of her antecedents, joining the swell of other Midwest writers—Sherwood Anderson, Theodore Dreiser, Sinclair Lewis, Edna Ferber, and Josephine Herbst—moving eastward, first to Chicago, during its short-lived Renaissance, and then to New York. A decade later midwestern writers would cross the Atlantic in their search for new forms and new experiences; this group congregated primarily in Greenwich Village and created one of the most exciting and fertile periods in American culture. It rivaled fin-de-siècle France and Vienna as a time of change, a decade after those European upheavals and less encumbered by the weight of the forms it was smashing.

Susan Glaspell figured prominently in this cultural and literary ferment. She was at home in the social haunts of Greenwich Village: the Liberal Club, a meeting place for intellectuals and political figures; Mabel Dodge's weekly salons; the office of *The Masses,* the radical magazine edited by Dell and Max Eastman. And just as the articles in *The Masses* chronicled the major issues of the period, such as women's suffrage, birth control, the "new woman," and "companionate marriage," and those *isms* that presaged the coming of a new societal order—socialism, pacifism, unionism, Darwinism, Freudianism—Glaspell's plays covered similar subjects and provided another bellwether for innovation and change.

The arguments embedded in her plays, however, were never essentialist, too wary was she of anything already foreclosed by the addition of a suffix. Sharing with her last persona, Francis, in *Judd Rankin's Daughter,* an abhorrence of closure, she sidestepped too rigid an adherence to any social movements. What she says of Francis could apply to Glaspell: "[She] had not long remained a Socialist. It was too all-settled, the air got a little stale, a room where you mustn't open the window; if you opened the window a breeze might come in to disturb what was now all tidily arranged. A belief should be—nascent, more true this moment than ever before, because of this moment of newly discovered truth."[9] A social critic who recognized the dangers in substituting one political correctness for another, Glaspell was that special kind of ideological writer: one wary of ideology. The forms of her writing attest to the drive to unfix both ideas and art.

Writing that assiduously works to evade categorization requires a particular kind of criticism, one attuned to the nuances between the lines. It also requires a sense of the historical forces that the works were attempting to deconstruct. New Criticism, which began to hold sway soon after Glaspell's death, was not well suited for such analysis, and its adherence to dehistoricized close textual readings may help explain why Glaspell's works were overlooked. There were no adequate means for assessing their radical departures, experimentation, and gendered voice.

Claire Archer, the hero of *The Verge*, Glaspell's most radical and challenging work, inveighs against "the old pattern, done again, again, and again. So long done it doesn't even know itself for a pattern."[10] Claire is talking about plants, but Glaspell may also have had literature in mind. "We need not be held in forms molded for us," Claire says. Her words could well be a motto for Glaspell criticism and for this book: the first collection of essays devoted to a study of her writing. It could also serve as a cautionary note to critics working with any noncanonical writing, particularly writing by women. So unused are we to devoting attention to a female oeuvre that often the very framing of the discussions illustrates the dearth of critical language and the tendency to relapse into traditional categorizations, to domesticate what is new and different, to fix the nascent by aligning it with the familiar.

It is not enough, I would argue, to reintroduce the works of Susan Glaspell into discussions of American drama, theater, and fiction; the critic must also use critical approaches that allow the works to emerge, as Claire would argue, in all their "otherness," not as "more of the same," bearing a certificate of approval granted in the past. "It's hard to get past what we've done. Our own dead things—block the way," Claire recognizes (54). The same could be said for any attempts to reach beyond the familiar, beyond the canon, to what lies outside it. This collection makes the attempt.

The purpose of this book is to explore the works of Susan Glaspell, the richness and diversity of her writing, the ways in which she has developed her art and pushed forward the boundaries of drama, theater, and fiction for others to follow. As a "first," it seeks to whet the critical appetite by suggesting the range of Glaspell's writing, both her dramas and her fiction, so that those with no knowledge of her work will make her acquaintance and those already familiar with *Trifles* and "Jury" will learn of the extensive body of material still awaiting critical attention. In keeping with the diversity of her genres, the critics assembled for this book come from a variety of disciplines: American drama, history of theater, feminist theater theory, American studies, American fiction, and women's studies. Most are academics; two are playwrights themselves; one is a poet. All first met Glaspell through *Trifles* and "Jury" and, impressed with the power of these works, sought out her other writings, not an easy task due to their inaccessibility in print.[11] Besides providing introductions and readings of these texts, the essays also reflect the social, cultural, and political forces that shaped the works and illustrate the ways in which a variety of contemporary critical approaches can provide the needed tools for a new appreciation of a writer, overlooked, in part, because we, as critics and as readers, did not know how to address her writing.

The collection opens with the words of one American woman playwright to another, Megan Terry to Susan Glaspell: Terry because her career has certain parallels with Glaspell's. Begun in an experimental theater company, the Open Stage, dedicated to finding an indigenous American theater form, her work has been concerned with ways in which social and political issues inform and shape her writing; and it has located in, and taken its impetus from, the Midwest, the region that gave birth to Glaspell and her art and which she never totally abandoned. Terry's greeting to Glaspell as "a contemporary, courageous, brilliant good friend" reinforces, yet again, a difference between literary forefathers, which J. Hillis Miller described as, "a long chain of parasitical presences" and Harold Bloom labeled as causing an "anxiety of influence,"[12] and foremothers, who can be greeted as "friends," since they provide, through their works and their lives, the possibility of, and models for, female authorship and survival. Glaspell behind Terry, just as behind Glaspell, still unacknowledged, is the writing of Alice Gerstenberg, Anna Cora Mowatt, and the first American woman playwright, Mercy Otis Warren.

Terry's comments open the section on *Trifles* and "A Jury of Her Peers." The following essays in part 1 provide new material and critical means for approaching these familiar texts. My essay offers a different historical avenue into the works by presenting, for the first time, details about the actual murder case upon which *Trifles* was based and the newspaper reports covering the investigation and trial, which Glaspell filed for the *Des Moines Daily News* in 1900 and 1901. By studying materials related to the Hossack murder case, in which a farm woman from Indianola, Iowa, was accused of hatcheting her husband to death while he slept in bed next to her, critics can gain insights into the ways Glaspell refigured and revised the material in her fictionalized versions. Elaine Hedges, in an award-winning essay, also historicizes *Trifles* and "Jury," providing background on the lives of prairie women and, particularly, the function of quilting as solace against loneliness. By so doing, she extends "the story's accessibility, making it more possible for contemporary readers to enter into and respond to the symbolic meanings of the details on which it is so crucially based." Revision is the theme of the two essays that follow, each offering new approaches to *Trifles* and "Jury." Karen Alkalay-Gut and Liza Maeve Nelligan, in different ways, question those first readings of the play and short story that were based, to a large degree, on essentialist concepts of women and gender that privileged sexual difference and female victimization.

Nelligan suggests that a far more representative Glaspell work, and one that more directly addresses 1990s feminist issues, is *The Verge*. She, and those discussing this play in part 2—Karen Malpede, Barbara Ozieblo, and Marcia Noe—seek to reposition interest in Glaspell's writing, arguing that it is *The Verge*, even more than *Trifles*, that marks the high point of Glaspell's feminist aesthetic and provides a model for playwrights to come, both in its subject matter and in its radical language experiments. For these critics, and for Gerhard Bach later in the collection, this play is one of the central dramas of the modern period. They share with C. W. E. Bigsby the belief that "few writers before or since would have attempted such a radical revisioning of all aspects of theatre";[13] however, they deny his obviously masculinist reading of the work—"Clearly Glaspell is critical of Claire"[14]—taking the position that Glaspell, in her portrayal of Claire, critiques the society, not the woman.

Part 2, like part 1, includes the words of a contemporary playwright. Karen Malpede responds to *The Verge*, comparing its persona Claire Archer with that other "nasty woman in modern drama," Hedda Gabler. Yet unlike Hedda, who at least "atones for the 'sin of being' by killing herself," Claire attempts to create—and to create herself—apart from the control of Tom, Dick, and Harry, the men who circle around her. Malpede eloquently interprets Claire's cries "You are too much" as "I cannot be myself" and "You are not enough" as "I cannot find myself in you." For her Claire is not an aberrant woman—crazy, as critics of the 1920s and certain contemporary critics still argue—but too much aware of the forces that limit women artists and all women seeking selfhood and love, a familiar figure whose final madness is all too explicable.

The other essays in this section approach *The Verge* through a variety of critical paths. Barbara Ozieblo traces Glaspell's continuing preoccupation with Freudianism, and with questions of repression and suppression of individual desires, handled humorously in the parodic *Suppressed Desires,* the first American play to introduce Freud on the stage, and starkly in *The Verge*. Marcia Noe indicates the ways in which *The Verge,* as early as 1921, fulfilled the call by contemporary French feminist theoretician Hélène Cixous for an *écriture féminine* arising from a woman's struggle and shaped by a woman's words. Glaspell's radical destruction of language and form in this play, Noe argues, replicates feminist struggles for individuation, sundering both the words of patriarchy and the literary patterns such forms impose. The play falls prey, however, to what Noe sees as the dangers endemic in the kind of writing Cixous and other feminist theoreticians call for: an obscurantist form, embodied in Claire's final utterances and in her madness.

Part 3, "Full-length Female Figures," moves beyond *The Verge* to other Glaspell plays. This section begins with Jackie Czerepinski's exploration of the device of the absent female figure, which Glaspell introduced in *Trifles* and continued to employ in *Bernice* and in her Pulitzer Prize–winning *Alison's House*. These absent central characters, Czerepinski argues, are not so much effaced as they are removed, in order that their position can be marked and taken up by an audience of women, who see the conditions of the absent protagonist conflated with their own lives. Un-figured, the character is universalized, a pervading presence not limited by physical representation and thereby able to represent the situation of all women. Sharon Friedman approaches *Bernice* from a different direction, seeing it as a work "poised between the feminist awakening in *Trifles* and the modernist revolt in *The Verge*," which attempts to navigate its particular, idiosyncratic way between conventional roles accorded women: the self-sacrificing wife, the inspiring muse, the angel in the house. J. Ellen Gainor studies another Glaspell play, *Chains of Dew*, the only produced play a woman wrote during the period that deals with that most controversial subject of the time: birth control. Gainor's extensive study breaks new ground by drawing together, for the first time, the unproduced plays on birth control that address the question and offer a historical contextualization for Glaspell's work. She also indicates how *Chains of Dew* influenced the debate and illustrated the possibilities of a polemical, feminist theater.

The plays discussed above were all written from 1916 to 1922, during Glaspell's Provincetown Players years. The two essays that conclude the section focus on Glaspell's *Alison's House*, written in 1931 and produced by Eva LeGallienne's Civic Repertory Company. The play, part of the centennial fervor surrounding Emily Dickinson's birth, is based on the Dickinson biography written by Genevieve Taggard. Glaspell changes the name of the protagonist in order to comply with the wishes of the Dickinson estate. Katharine Rodier, in her prize-winning essay, traces the public attention given to Dickinson's life and poetry at the time Glaspell wrote her play and the ways in which Glaspell fashions the available biographical information, and hearsay, to create a work that speaks to issues beyond the life of a single woman artist. Karen Laughlin, building on the work of Rodier, argues against the notion, expressed by critics in 1931 and today, that the play is one of the weakest of Glaspell's writings and not deserving of the Pulitzer Prize. She makes a case for it as a powerful transgressive study of the dilemma of the female artist, presented in a work that explores the very basis of the naturalistic theater Glaspell is attempting to sunder.

The last two essays to discuss drama appear in part 4, "Re-Visioning the Dramatic Canon." They open up the discussion beyond Glaspell, focusing on other women writers whose works may be seen in the context of Glaspell's writings and the ways in which the entire body of American drama will have to be rethought in light of the reintroduction of Glaspell and these women writers of the period. Taking Glaspell's plays as a point of reference, Judith E. Barlow, in her essay "Susan's Sisters," explores the plays of the other women who wrote for the Provincetown Players. Ferreting out these unpublished plays—including works by Djuna Barnes, Neith Boyce, Rita Wellman, and Alice Rostetter—Barlow illustrates the richness of the material and the diversity of the forms these playwrights employed. Her essay breaks new ground in American dramatic studies by presenting this literary trove that awaits future scholarship and productions. Critics will cite this essay as an epochal work. The final article on Glaspell is written by Gerhard Bach, who, in the 1970s, was one of the first critics to reclaim Glaspell for contemporary readers through his early studies of her work. Here he questions the entire method of American canon formation that would exclude this significant writer and the ways in which Glaspell's plays will reshape the long-held notions of dramatic invention and form.

Much of this collection is devoted to Susan Glaspell as playwright because this is the area first studied by contemporary critics and now available in print and because this is the genre in which her most radical experiments took place.[15] Yet she is also a writer of fiction and, in fact, in her own period was as well known for these works as she was for her plays. Certainly, an entire study could be done on her extensive fictional output.[16] In this book I thought it helpful to suggest the subject matter and general outlines of her fiction. Part 5, "Novel Women," includes two essays that study her short stories and novels. In the first Colette Lindroth concentrates on Glaspell's first collection of short stories, *Lifted Masks*, and illustrates the ways in which these stories markedly alter the popular short story form by making it responsive to social and political issues of the period and by introducing colloquial imagery and language, the better to promulgate the embedded ideas. Next, Veronica Makowsky moves to Glaspell's novels, offering exegeses of three representative ones—*Fidelity, Fugitive's Return,* and *Norma Ashe*—culled from three different periods in Glaspell's career, each reflecting her growing narrative power.

Just as this section cannot hope to be anything more than introductory, so, in a way, the entire book is a beginning, opening the critical discussion of Glaspell's writing by making available historical, cultural, and critical

tools through which her works may be read. The collection of essays should, however, firmly establish the significance of Susan Glaspell in American letters, the need for more studies of her writings, and the necessity of making her plays, novels, and short stories available to a new audience ready to receive them and in need of what they have to say. It should also assault traditional myths of canon formation. "The Big Bang Theory," which Bach names, exposes, and explodes, is predicated on the belief that American drama began with one man, Eugene O'Neill. These essays consign such creation myths to that same cultural refuse heap to which similar theories of the settlement of the American West were directed by historian Patricia Limerick and critic Annette Kolodny.[17]

Just as no social or historical movement springs completely from the imagination of one individual, no literary movement comes, Zeus-like, out of the head of one writer. It is certainly time to lay aside this outdated idea of literary genesis. The perpetuation of such a theory helps explain the central misogyny endemic in American drama from its beginnings. If this movement is seen as emerging fully formed from the pen of Eugene O'Neill, it is no wonder that the favored progeny have all been sons, created in their father's image. So few American women playwrights have been able to assault the critical headlands because they did not sound like Dad! If the voice of Glaspell had not been silenced, those who followed, like Lillian Hellman and, later, Marsha Norman, might have been freer to use their own registers and to use new forms. And those who have dared to do so—like Megan Terry, Karen Malpede, Maria Irene Fornes, Adrienne Kennedy, Joan Schenkar, Wendy Kesselman, and Holly Hughes— might have been heard more distinctly because the critical ear had grown accustomed to their voices.

NOTES

1. There has been some confusion about the exact number of plays staged by the Provincetown Players and the dates the group functioned. I date the beginning of the theater, July 15 (?) 1915, when *Suppressed Desire* by Susan Glaspell and her husband George Cram Cook, and *Constancy* by Neith Boyce were presented in Boyce's home at 621 Commercial Street, Provincetown and the concluding date the

production of Glaspell's *Chains of Dew* (April 27–May 15, 1922), the last play staged before the group reorganized. Using these dates and the chronology of plays which Robert Károly Sarlós provides in Appendix A of *Jig Cook and the Provincetown Players*, the Provincetown Players produced one hundred plays by fifty-two playwrights in seven years. Since the Provincetown Players was committed to the production of American writers, critics sometimes also omit *Last Masks* by Arthur Schnitzler, (March 26–April 8, 1920) and *Autumn Fires* by Gustav Wied (June 8–July 1, 1921), the two works by non-Americans. Omitting Schnitzler and Wied, the number would be ninety-eight plays by fifty playwrights, beginning in 1915. This includes three plays that were part of the Other Players' Bill and that do not appear on the list supplied by Helen Deutsch and Stella Hanau in *The Provincetown: A Story of the Theatre: Manikin and Minikin* and *Jack's House*, both by Alfred Kreymborg, and *Two Slatterns and a King* by Edna St. Vincent Millay. The group produced fourteen plays by nine playwrights—including a Children's Bill, *Mother Carey's Chickens* by Henry Marion Hall—in the summers of 1915 and 1916, five of which were not repeated in the schedule beginning in New York in 1916. If one uses, as Sarlós does, the fall 1916 date as the official opening of the group, omitting the works of Schnitzler and Wied and the five plays not repeated in the official seasons, but including the plays by Kreymborg and Millay, the number of plays produced by the Provincetown in six seasons is ninety-three plays by forty-nine playwrights. Sarlós in his book gives the number in six seasons as ninety-seven plays by forty-seven American playwrights (5), which does not conform with his list. For another partial list of plays presented by the Provincetown, see the unpublished manuscript of Edna Kenton on the history of the Provincetown Players, Fales Collection, New York University.

2. Isaac Goldberg, *The Drama of Transition* (Cincinnati: Stewart Kidd, 1922), 471.

3. Nine months after Eugene O'Neill's death, on November 27, 1953, the Random House Edition of O'Neill's plays was also allowed to go out of print. Carlotta Monterey bemoaned the fact that O'Neill's works might be forgotten. With the posthumous production of *Long Day's Journey into Night* in 1955 in Stockholm and the revival of *The Iceman Cometh* in 1956 in New York, however, O'Neill's reputation was secured.

4. Carolyn Heilbrun, "Letter," *New York Review of Books*, March 1992, 5.

5. See the bibliography at the end of this book for a complete listing of recent Glaspell criticism.

6. Susan Glaspell, *The Road to the Temple* (New York: Frederick Stokes, 1927), 4.

7. In 1902 Glaspell was awarded a prize of $150 from *Black Cat* magazine

for her short story "The Work of the Unloved Libby"; in 1904 she received a prize of $500, the highest prize the magazine gave, for her story "For the Love of the Hills."

8. *New York Times,* March 13, 1909.

9. Susan Glaspell, *Judd Rankin's Daughter* (Philadelphia: J. B. Lippincott, 1945), 14.

10. Susan Glaspell, *The Verge* (Boston: Small, Maynard, 1922), 52. All further references to the work will appear in the text.

11. Although it was possible to discover a few of Glaspell's plays among anthologies of one-acts and Pulitzer Prize–winning plays, it was not until 1987 and the publication of *Plays by Susan Glaspell,* edited by C. W. E. Bigsby, that critics were able to find four of Glaspell's plays in one edition. The rest of her plays are still out of print at this time. The University of Michigan Press, however, will soon be publishing the complete edition of Glaspell's plays, edited by Linda Ben-Zvi and J. Ellen Gainor.

12. As quoted in Sandra M. Gilbert and Susan Gubar, *The Madwoman in the Attic: A Study of Women and the Literary Imagination in the Nineteenth Century* (New Haven: Yale University Press, 1979), 46.

13. C. W. E. Bigsby, *Plays by Susan Glaspell* (London: Cambridge University Press, 1987), 19.

14. C. W. E. Bigsby, *Twentieth Century Drama: Volume One, 1900–1940* (London: Cambridge University Press, 1982), 32.

15. University of Michigan Press, which has become a center for Glaspell studies, has recently reprinted a collection of Glaspell's short stories, *Lifted Masks and Other Works,* edited and with an introduction by Eric S. Rabkin (Ann Arbor: University of Michigan Press, 1993).

16. Glaspell also broke new ground for the biographical form in *The Road to the Temple,* her monument to the life of her husband, George Cram Cook. Glaspell as biographer and the implications of the woman biographer is a study that awaits attention.

17. See Patricia Nelson Limerick, *The Legacy of Conquest: The Unbroken Path of the American West* (New York: Norton, 1987); and Annette Kolodny, *The Lay of the Land: Metaphor as Experience and History in American Life and Letters* (Chapel Hill: University of North Carolina Press, 1975); and *The Land before Her: Fantasy and Experience of the American Frontiers, 1630–1860* (Chapel Hill: University of North Carolina Press, 1984).

Part 1
Trifles and "A Jury of Her Peers": Lifelines

I admire the control, the precision and the power of *Trifles*. I've just read it again, three times. It never tires. It seems to be a perfect play and accomplishes all the playwright's intentions. It is a model of subtlety and understatement. I marvel at its compactness and perfection, and the satisfaction it conveys to the reader or audience in the sure achievement of its creator. The play is more than an inspiration, it's a quiet, firm and constant standard to match. The wry warmth of her mind, the compassion of her heart combine with the architecture of her play to give you a total feeling of these Mid-West people. The work is suffused with the sense of justice, wit, and fairness Glaspell must have possessed as a person. She lives in this work, so much so that you can clasp her presence to you as you would that of a contemporary, courageous, brilliant good friend.

—Megan Terry

"Murder, She Wrote": The Genesis of Susan Glaspell's *Trifles*

Linda Ben-Zvi

In the preface to her book *Women Who Kill* Ann Jones explains that her massive study of women murderers began with a quip. After working through a reading list that included *The Awakening, The House of Mirth,* and *The Bell Jar,* a student asked: "Isn't there anything a woman can do but kill herself?" Jones responded, "She can always kill somebody else" (xv).

Women killing somebody else, especially when that somebody is male, has fascinated criminologists, lawyers, psychologists, and writers. Fascinated and frightened them. Fear is the subtext of Jones's book: "The fears of men who, even as they shape society, are desperately afraid of women, and so have fashioned a world in which women come and go only in certain rooms; and about the fears of those women who, finding the rooms too narrow and the door still locked, lie in wait or set the place afire" (xvi). Or kill.

Women who kill evoke fear because they challenge societal constructs of femininity—passivity, restraint, and nurture—thus the rush to isolate and label the female offender, to cauterize the act. Her behavior *must* be aberrant, or crazed, if it is to be explicable. And explicable it must be; her crime cannot be seen as societally driven if the cultural stereotypes are to remain unchallenged.[1]

Theater loves a good murder story: violence, passion, and purpose. The stuff of tragedy is the stuff of the whodunit; *Oedipus* is, among other things, the Ur-detective story. Therefore, it is not surprising that contemporary dramatists should turn to murder—specifically, murder by women—as sources for plays. And following the thesis of Jones's book, it is also not surprising that the most powerful of the dramas—those that are more than exempla, docudramas, or hysterogenic flights—should be written by women who share with Jones an awareness that often the murderer, like the feminist, in her own way, "tests society's established boundaries" (13).

Three plays of this century, based on murder cases and written by American women, are Sophie Treadwell's *Machinal,* Wendy Kesselman's *My Sister in This House,* and Susan Glaspell's *Trifles.* All do more than rework a tale of murder; they reveal in the telling the lineaments of the society that spawned the crime.

Machinal, written in 1928 and successfully revived in New York in 1990, is loosely based on one of the most sensational murder cases of the 1920s: Ruth Snyder and Judd Gray's killing of Snyder's husband. Diverting attention from that other case of 1927—Sacco and Vanzetti—headlines had blazed, "If Ruth Snyder is a woman then, by God! you must find some other name for my mother, wife or sister" (Jones 257). Treadwell turns this tabloid hysteria on its head. Her Ruth is neither aberrant or insane; she is ordinary, unexceptional, exactly someone's mother, wife, or sister, worn down by the societal machine of the title.

More disturbing because less easily domesticated is the equally famous 1933 murder case, in Le Mans, France, in which two maids, the sisters Christine and Lea Papin, bludgeoned, stabbed, and mutilated the bodies of their employer and her daughter: Mme and Mlle Lancelin. The crime was directed against women; however, the two plays that have sprung from the murder—Jean Genet's *The Maids* and Kesselman's *My Sister in This House*—focus on repressed sexuality and its relation to power, victimization, and enforced gender roles, Kesselman's version moving beyond the acts of horror to implicate "the rage of all women condensed to the point of explosion" (Hart 145).

While Treadwell and Kesselman reconstitute celebrated murder cases and alter the historicity to shape their readings of female experience, Glaspell's *Trifles* takes its leave from a previously unknown source, and, therefore, until now it has been impossible to determine what contextual material she employs and how she reworks it in order to create her one-act masterpiece and its fictional offshoot, "A Jury of Her Peers."[2]

In *The Road to the Temple,* her biography of her husband, George Cram "Jig" Cook, she offers a brief comment on the conditions under which the play was written and its genesis. In the summer of 1916 she, Cook, and other transplanted Greenwich Village writers, artists, and political activists were summering in Provincetown, Massachusetts, and, for the second season, were amusing themselves by putting on their own plays on a fishing wharf, converted at night to a makeshift theater. At the end of July Glaspell had brought Eugene O'Neill to the group, and they had staged his play *Bound East for Cardiff*. They now needed a play for their third bill. As Glaspell tells the story, it was Cook who urged her to supply one:

> I protested. I did not know how to write a play. I had never "studied it."
>
> "Nonsense," said Jig. "You've got a stage, haven't you?"
>
> So I went out on the wharf, sat alone on one of our wooden benches without a back, and looked a long time at that bare little stage. After a time the stage became a kitchen—a kitchen there all by itself. . . . Then the door at the back opened, and people all bundled up came in—two or three men, I wasn't sure which, but sure enough about the two women, who hung back, reluctant to enter that kitchen. (255–56)[3]

Whenever she became stuck at a certain point in the writing Glaspell would walk across the narrow street that separated the wharf from her own home and sit once more in the theater until she could visualize the scene; after structuring it on paper, she would test it in the actual space where it would be played. And so *Trifles* was written under conditions many playwrights would envy.[4]

As for its genesis, she claimed it was based on an actual murder case: "When I was a newspaper reporter out in Iowa, I was sent down-state to do a murder trial, and I never forgot going into the kitchen of a woman locked up in town" (256). In numerous interviews throughout her life she offered variations on this memory, but she never provided the name of the murderer or the details of the trial.

In the process of completing research for a biography of Susan Glaspell, I discovered the historical source upon which *Trifles* and "Jury" are based: the murder of a sixty-year-old farmer named John Hossack on December 2, 1900, in Indianola, Iowa. Glaspell covered the case and the subsequent trial when she was a reporter for the *Des Moines Daily News,* a position she began full-time the day after she graduated from Drake University in June 1899, a twenty-four-year-old woman with a bachelor of philosophy (Ph.B.) degree and several years of newspaper work in Davenport and Des Moines behind her.[5] Although her general beat was the Iowa statehouse, and she would later say that the experiences there provided her with sufficient material to quit her job a year later and turn to fiction, it was the Hossack murder case that was the central story of her brief journalistic career.

Although not as sensational as the Snyder or as horrific as the Papin case, the Hossack killing also focuses on a woman accused of murder, and the investigation and subsequent trial offer one more example of what Jones so graphically details in her book: the process by which juridical attitudes toward, and prosecution of, women are shaped by societal concepts of female behavior, the same concepts that may have motivated the act of murder. A difference among the plays, however, is the position of the author in relation to the material. While Treadwell probably attended the Snyder trial, she was not an active participant in the situations she recasts. Glaspell was. And while Kesselman could make a thorough, dispassionate investigation of the commentary and reactions that surrounded the history of the Papin case, Glaspell was actually a primary contributor to the shaping of public opinion about the woman being tried. The news accounts Glaspell filed, therefore, offer more than an important contextual basis for approaching the fictional texts; they also provide important biographical information about the author and her own personal and artistic evolution and document the cultural shifts that took place between 1900, when the murder took place, and 1916, when Glaspell wrote her play.

The case at first glance seemed simple. Sometime after midnight on December 2, 1900, John Hossack, a well-to-do farmer, was struck twice on the head with an ax while he slept in bed. Margaret Hossack, his wife of thirty-three years, who was sleeping beside him, reported that a strange sound, "like two pieces of wood striking," wakened her; she jumped out of bed, went into the adjoining sitting room, saw a light shining on a wall, and heard the door to the front porch slowly closing. Only then did she hear her husband's groans. Assembling the five of her nine children who were still residing at home, she lit a lamp, reentered the bedroom, and discovered Hossack bleeding profusely, the walls and bedsheets spattered, brain matter oozing from a five-inch gash, his head crushed. One of his sons claimed that the mortally injured man was still able to speak. When he said to his father, "Well pa, you are badly hurt," Hossack replied, "No, I'm not hurt, but I'm not feeling well" (Dec. 4).

It was assumed that prowlers must have committed the crime, but, when a search of the farmhouse failed to reveal any missing items, a coroner's inquest was called. Its findings were inconclusive. However, after discovering the presumed murder weapon smeared with blood under the family corn crib, and listening to reports and innuendos from neighbors, who hinted at a history of marital and family trouble, the sheriff arrested Mrs. Hossack, "as a matter of precaution" (Dec. 5), while the funeral was still in progress, or, as Glaspell would more vividly report, "just as the sexton was throwing the last clods on the grave of her murdered husband" (Jan. 14).

There was really nothing unique about such a murder in the Iowa of 1900, which, if no more violent than it is today, was certainly no less so. Sandwiched between ubiquitous advertisements for "Female Nerve Cures" and romantic accounts of the courtships of Vanderbilts and Rockefellers are a whole range of lurid tales that would keep a contemporary tabloid busy—and happy: reports of a woman being set on fire, a farmhand murdering another man with a neck yoke, a young man attempting to kill his parents, and a garden-variety assortment of rural knifings, insanity, and violence.[6] What makes the Hossack case stand out are the extended length of the coverage and the vivid style of the reporter. Her paper seems to have charged Glaspell with two tasks: rousing the readership and insuring that the story stay on the first page. She accomplished both.

Employing the techniques of "Gonzo" journalism sixty years before Hunter Thompson, Glaspell filed twenty-six stories on the Hossack case, from the fifteen-line item on page 3, dated December 3, 1900, that summarily described the event of the murder, to the page 1, full-column story on April 11, 1901, that reported the jury's decision at the trial. Most are indistinguishable from her own unsigned "Newsgirl" features running in the paper at the time. They make ready use of hyperbole, invention, and supposition, all filtered through one of Glaspell's common devices in her column: a lively, often opinionated persona. Whether labeled "your correspondent," "a representative from the *News*," or "a member of the press," she is a constructed presence who invites the reader to share some privileged information, intriguing rumor, and running assessment of the case and of the guilt or innocence of the accused.

In her first extended coverage of the crime, under the headline "Coroner's Jury Returns Its Verdict This Morning—Mrs. Hossack Thought to Be Crazy," Glaspell announces the imminent arrest of the woman, a fact "secretly revealed to your correspondent." She also provides the first of many rumors that become increasingly more prominent in her coverage although never attributed to specific sources: "Friends of Mrs. Hossack are beginning to suggest that she is insane, and that she has been in this condition for a year and a half, under the constant surveillance of members of the family," and "the members of the Hossack family were not on pleasant relations with each other," information that comes as "a complete surprise, as Hossack was not supposed to have an enemy in the world." She concludes by citing the most damaging evidence used against the accused woman throughout her trial: Mrs. Hossack's claim that she lay asleep beside her husband and was not awakened while the murder was taking place (Dec. 5).

Glaspell continues to mix fact, rumor, and commentary with a superfluity of rousing language and imagery, opening her next report with the reminder that Mrs. Hossack has been arrested for the death of her husband, "on charge of having beaten out his brains with an axe"; that the accused woman has employed the legal services of Mr. Henderson and State Senator Berry; that when arrested she showed no emotion and absolutely declined to make any statement concerning her guilt or innocence; and that, while her family supported her, "the public sentiment is overwhelming against her." How she gleaned this information or arrived at these conclusions Glaspell does not say. She does, however, provide her first description of the accused woman: "Though past 50 years of age, she is tall and powerful and looks like she would be dangerous if aroused to a point of hatred." She again repeats the rumors of domestic tensions and quotes a neighbor named Haines, a witness at the inquest, who implied that Mrs. Hossack had years before asked him to get her husband "out of the way" (Dec. 6).

"Public sentiment is still very much against the prisoner," the December 8 news story begins, reiterating the claim that Mrs. Hossack wanted "to get rid of her husband" and adding that she was willing to pay liberally for the services of anyone undertaking the task—a story "the public generally accepts" and will, therefore, "sympathize with the county attorney in his efforts to convict the woman." In an added development Glaspell reports that Mrs. Hossack had left home a year before but had been persuaded to return "with the idea of securing a division of the property, but this division had never been made." Although the sheriff had refused all requests to see photographs of the murdered man, Glaspell announces, "a representative of the *News* was accorded this privilege though it must be confessed there is little satisfaction in it" (Dec. 8).

Waiving a preliminary hearing, Mrs. Hossack's attorneys decided to take the case directly to the grand jury, which bound her over for trial in April. In the interim the defendant requested and was given bail. The story Glaspell files immediately prior to the release contains a new element. The reporter, who only days before had described Mrs. Hossack as cold, calm, and menacing, now describes her as "worn and emaciated" as she was led from her jail, with "red and swollen eyelids indicating that she had been weeping" (Dec. 11). Since Mrs. Hossack was immediately released after this date and remained in her home until the trial, it is likely that what caused Glaspell to alter her description was her own visit to the Hossack farm, the event she uses as the basis for *Trifles*. From this point on in her reporting, Glaspell's references to the accused woman become more benign, the "powerful" murderer becoming, with each story, older, frailer, and more maternal.[7]

Glaspell was probably at the farmhouse gathering material for the front page, double-column feature that appeared on December 12, the most extensive coverage of the pretrial events. It began with the headline "Mrs Hossack May Yet Be Proven Innocent," followed by the subheadings "Tide of Sentiment Turns Slightly in Her Favor—Notified Today That She Will Soon Be Released—First Photographs Bearing on the Tragedy." The photographs turn out to be three simple pencil drawings: one of Mrs. Hossack, sitting in a rocking chair, her head bent down, her eyes

closed; one of her dead husband with the two gashes to his head; and one of the ax, complete with four dots of blood. Captions indicate that the first is "sketched from life," the second "from flashlight photograph of the dead man" that "others tried to obtain access to . . . but failed." In more detail Glaspell describes her revisionary image of Mrs. Hossack: "The aged prisoner . . . looked up into the officer's face, smiled and remarked that she would be glad to get home again with her children but did not manifest any great degree of joy at the news." Bail, the reader is told, will not be excessive because the accused "is an aged woman and one who would not try in any manner to escape."

As much as she may have altered her own perceptions of Mrs. Hossack and may have tried to influence her readers, Glaspell still had the job of keeping them interested in the case. Borrowing devices from popular

detective fiction of the time (see Jones 111–16), she dangles tantalizing questions: the test on the murder weapon may now be known, but the readers will have to wait until the trial to learn the results; the same for the blood stains on Mrs. Hossack's clothing. Glaspell does hint that the results substantiate the claim that the blood on the ax comes from slaughtered fowl and continues: "If that is true one of the strongest links in the chain of circumstantial evidence is broken. If the blood is human, it will look bad for the accused." If still not intrigued, the reader is given a gruesome detail—a "substance resembling brains" has also been found on the ax—and a rumor: that the defense will enter a plea of insanity if their efforts on behalf of their client fail. She must be crazy or innocent, "the best people of Indianola" surmise, since visits to the home in the past few months did not indicate problems, the wife attentive to her husband's needs, seeing "that he lacked for nothing." Of Mrs. Hossack's character these unnamed sources reveal, "She is said to be a woman who is quick tempered, high strung, like all Scotch women, but of a deeply religious turn of mind" (Dec. 12).

In the months before the trial Glaspell filed only three small articles about the case, each one using the opportunity of a new piece of news to summarize the details of the murder, the grisly events becoming more grisly with the retelling. On March 23 she reports that new evidence has emerged "and that in all probability it would result in Mrs. Hossack's acquittal at an early date." She does not say what the evidence is, but she offers an important turn in the case. Mr. Haines, the primary source of information about trouble in the Hossack home and the party to whom, it is believed, Mrs. Hossack turned to get rid of her husband, "had gone insane brooding over the tragedy, and was yesterday sentenced to the insane asylum."

Although there had been talk of moving the venue of the trial because of the strong feelings against Margaret Hossack and the fear that an impartial jury could not be found (Jan. 14), the trial finally began in the Polk County Courthouse on April 1, 1901, and was held every day except Sundays for the next ten days. Glaspell had apparently been successful in stirring public interest because she reports that on the first day over twelve hundred people attended, far more than the tiny rural court could accommodate, and that on the day the jury returned its verdict more than two thousand were present. Noting the composition of the observers, she says: "The conspicuous feature so far is the large attendance of women in court. Over half of the spectators present today belong to the gentler sex. The bright array of Easter hats lent a novelty to the scene, giving it much the appearance of some social function" (Apr. 2).[8]

The seventy-eight witnesses, fifty-three for the prosecution and twenty-five for the defense, focused on seven specific questions during the trial: (1) Would it have been possible, as his son testified, for John Hossack, who had sustained two traumatic blows—one made with the ax head, the second with the blunt handle—to talk and call for his wife and children? (2) Were the blood found on the ax and the hairs later discovered nearby human, or were they, as claimed by the family, the residue of the turkey killed two days earlier for Thanksgiving? (3) How had the ax, which the youngest son said he placed inside the corn crib after killing the turkey, come to be found under it, in its usual place? (4) Had the ax and Mrs. Hossack's nightclothes been washed to remove incriminating stains of blood? (5) Was the dog, who always barked when strangers appeared, drugged on the night of the crime, as family members testified? (6) Had earlier domestic troubles in the Hossack house been resolved and all dissension ceased for over a year before the murder, as the family stated? and (7) Would it have been possible for an intruder or intruders to enter the house through the bedroom window, stand at the foot of the bed, and reach up to strike the fatal blows without rousing the woman who slept by her husband's side? An eighth question—what prompted Mrs. Hossack to leave home and wish her husband "out of the way"?—only entered the testimony twice. One neighbor, the wife of Mr. Haines, stated that she and her husband had come to aid Mrs. Hossack, who thought her husband would kill the family (Apr. 3). Another neighbor testified that he had to act as protector when Mrs. Hossack returned to her home "in case her husband again maltreated her as she had reason for believing" (Apr. 2).

Glaspell's reports do not suggest that the prosecution or the defense pursued the possibility of violence in the home, and she does not broach the subject herself. Instead, her stories of the trial tend to be summaries of testimony by experts and lay people who describe the structure of the brain, the disposition of the body in the bed, and the configuration of the blood spots on the walls. She does pause to describe the shock caused when the Hossack bed was brought into the courtroom, complete with bloodstained bedding, and when two vials of hairs were displayed—one found near the ax, the other obtained by exhuming John Hossack.

Interspersed between these accounts are her descriptions of the accused and of those attending the trial. During day one, for example, Glaspell describes Mrs. Hossack's reaction to the recital of counts against her: "Her eyes frequently filled with tears and her frame shook with emotion" (Apr. 2). On the next day, when the murder scene was again invoked, she notes that Mrs. Hossack, who occupied a seat by the sheriff's wife, surrounded by three of her daughters and all but one of her sons, broke down and wept bitterly: "Grief was not confined to her alone, it spread until the weeping group embraced the family and the sympathetic wife of Sheriff Hodson who frequently applied her handker-chief to her eyes" (Apr. 3).

Since there were no witnesses to the crime, the prosecution's case was based entirely on circumstantial evidence, and Glaspell often stops in her narration of testimony to weigh the success of the unsubstantiated argu-ments and to prod her readers to keep following the case. After one lengthy argument about how well Mrs. Hossack was able to wield an ax, Glaspell comments: "It must be admitted, however, that the prosecution has not thus far furnished any direct evidence and it is extremely doubtful if the chain of circumstantial evidence thus far offered will be sufficient to eliminate all doubt of the defendant's guilt from the minds of the ju-rors . . . on the other hand it is claimed by the prosecution attorney that the best evidence is yet to come" (Apr. 4). When Mrs. Hossack took the stand in her own defense and repeated the story she had held since the inquest, describing how she and her husband had spent a typical evening together the night of the crime—"He sat in the kitchen reading . . . later played with his whip . . . [while] I was patching and darning"—Glaspell observes, "When she left the stand, there seemed to be the impression on the audience that she had told the truth" (Apr. 8). Earlier questions of Mrs. Hossack's sanity apparently were dispelled by her composed appear-ance in court.

Like the novelist she would soon become, Glaspell saves her most impassioned descriptions for the climax of the trial, the summations by the lawyers. Of State Senator Berry, the defense counsel, she writes:

> It is said to be the master effort of his life . . . at times the jury without an exception was moved to tears. Strong men who had not shed a tear in years sat in their seats mopping their eyes and compressing their lips in a vain effort to suppress the emotion caused by the Senator's elo-quent pleas. (Apr. 9)

This lachrymose display, she says, even extended to the prosecution attor-neys, who were "seen to turn away their heads fearful lest the anguish of the family would unman them and the jury would have an impression which they could not afterward remove." The spectators were also moved. When the court was adjourned at noon, she writes, "fully two thousand people went out in the sunshine, their faces stained by the tears which had coursed down their cheeks."

Aside from tears Berry's chief strategy was to charge that Mr. Haines, "the insane man," was the real murderer. When he had been asked by the Hossack children to come to the house on the night of the murder, he had refused, saying that there were tramps about. It was he who had first implicated Mrs. Hossack by suggesting that she had wanted her husband dead and had sought his aid. And it was Mrs. Haines who had provided some of the most damning evidence about dissension in the Hossack home.

As successful as Berry may have been in concluding for the defense, Glaspell warns her readers that "it is certain that when attorney McNeal closes the argument for the prosecution the effect of Senator Berry's eloquence will have been lost and the verdict, if any at all is reached, can hardly be acquittal" (Apr. 9). Why, she does not say.

On the last day of the trial County Attorney Clammer and Mr. Mc-Neal summarized for the prosecution, and, as Glaspell predicted, McNeal was able to rouse the audience with his indictment—"She did it, gentlemen, and I ask you to return it to her in kind . . . she has forfeited her right to live and she should be as John Hossack, who lies rotting beneath the ground." He, too, had his own bombshell: Margaret Hossack had been pregnant and given birth to a child before their marriage. This, McNeal claimed, was the dark secret often referred to in the trial, the story Hossack said he would take to his grave, and the reason for the unhappiness in the Hossack home. Just how a pregnancy thirty-three years earlier could have been the sole cause of trouble in the marriage and how it proved Mrs. Hossack's guilt in the murder of her husband was not clear, but, as Glaspell reports, it provided the jury with the impression that she was a woman who could not be trusted. It was with this revelation that the trial ended (Apr. 10).

The case went to the jury on April 10, the judge presenting the following charge: "When evidence consists of a chain of well authenticated circumstances, it is often more convincing and satisfactory and gives a stronger ground of assurance of the defendant's guilt than the direct testimony of witnesses unconfirmed by circumstances" (Apr. 11). In less than twenty-four hours the jury returned its verdict. Margaret Hossack was found guilty as charged and was sentenced to life imprisonment at hard labor. Glaspell reported the outcome but made no comment on the finding.

It was the last story she filed in the case; it was also the last story she filed as a reporter for the *Des Moines Daily News*. Immediately after the trial she resigned and returned home to Davenport to begin writing fiction, and by the summer of 1901 she had moved to Chicago and enrolled in the graduate English program at the University of Chicago. Therefore, she may never have learned the final disposition of the Hossack case, for the story was not yet over. In April 1901 Lawyers Henderson and Berry lost an appeal with a lower court, but in April 1902 the Supreme Court of the State of Iowa agreed to hear the case. Citing several instances in which the trial judge had ruled incorrectly on the evidence, the higher court overturned the original conviction and requested a new trial.[9] A second trial took place in Madison County in February 1903. This time the jury, after twenty-seven hours of deliberation, was unable to reach a verdict: nine voting for conviction and three for acquittal. In papers filed in April 1903 the prosecutor stated that, since no further information had surfaced, it would be a waste of taxpayers' money to ask a third jury to hear the case. Mrs. Hossack, then near sixty and in failing health, was ordered released and was allowed to return to her home, her guilt or innocence still in question.

Eight years earlier a court in Fall River, Massachusetts, had freed Lizzie Borden because they could not imagine that a refined, New England "maiden" who wore demure silk, carried flowers, and wept copiously in court could wield the ax that slew her family. So strong were the prevailing views about femininity that even the prosecuting attorney found it hard "to *conceive*" of the guilt of "one of that sex that all high-minded men revere, that all generous men love, that all wise men acknowledge their indebtedness to" (Jones 231).

What is striking in the Hossack case is how ready the community was to assume the guilt of "one of that sex." Unlike Lizzie, who quickly read the signs of the time and played the part that was demanded of her—she learned to cry in court—Margaret Hossack, for all her tears and Glaspell's mid-course correction and subsequent, embellished descriptions of "the frail mother of nine," did not win over the jury. They may not have been convinced that she was guilty of murder, but she certainly was guilty of questionable female behavior: she had left her husband, discussed her marital troubles with neighbors, and, most damaging, had been pregnant before marriage. To have found such a woman innocent or to have explored the question of justifiable homicide would have been unthinkable in the Iowa court of 1901. Such a direction in the trial would have necessitated an investigation of the family, the power wielded by the husband, his physical abuse over a long period, and the circumscribed lives of the wife and children; both the prosecution and, tellingly, the defense seemed loath to pursue such investigations. Instead, as Glaspell's accounts indicate, their cases were each discourses in evasion, argued on small, tangential points, few of which addressed the central issue of motive. Even the Supreme Court ruling, which acknowledged John Hossack's repeated beatings of his wife—with his hands and with a stove lid—couched its findings: "The family life of the Hossacks had not been pleasant perhaps [*sic*] the husband was most to blame. He seems to have been somewhat narrow minded and quite stern in his determination to control all family matters." Absent from the seven points on which it reversed the lower court decision, however, was abuse. In fact, the court argued that prior relations in the family should not have been introduced in the original trial since harmony had been established for over a year. Domestic life thus remained untarnished for the record.

Why such juridical sidestepping? Because John Hossack was a pillar of the society, he had been nominated "for some of the highest offices in Warren County" (Dec. 12), and "the twelve good men" Glaspell describes sitting in judgment of Mrs. Hossack were all men who knew him well and who had a vested interest in protecting his name, if they could no longer protect his person. The women attending the trial in their Easter finery—perhaps even the sympathetic sheriff's wife—might have been able to offer a different reading of the case, but they were not accorded the opportunity in the court or in the newspaper accounts Glaspell filed. Sixteen years later, in her play, Glaspell offered them the opportunity to be heard.

Trifles begins at home. A murder has been committed—a man strangled while he slept—and his wife, who claimed to be sleeping beside him at the time, has been accused of the crime and been taken to jail to await trial. Those prosecuting the case, County Attorney Henderson and Sheriff Peters, have returned to the scene to search for clues that will provide "a motive; something to show anger, or—sudden feeling" and explain "the funny way" the man was murdered, "rigging it all up like that." Accompanying them are Mr. Hale, who found the body; Mrs. Peters, the sheriff's wife, charged with bringing the accused woman some of her things; and Mrs. Hale, who keeps her company in the kitchen below while the men move around the upstairs bedroom and perimeter of the farmhouse searching for clues.

In the absence of the wife the women, like quilters, patch together the scenario of her life and of her guilt. As they imagine her, Minnie Foster Wright is a lonely, childless woman, married to a taciturn husband, isolated from neighbors because of the rigors of farm life. When they discover a bird cage, its door ripped off and a canary, its neck wrung, they have no trouble making the connection. The husband has killed the bird, the wife's only comfort, as he killed the birdlike spirit of the woman. The motive and method of murder become as clear to them as the signs of sudden anger they infer from the half-wiped kitchen table and Minnie's erratic quilt stitching. Based on such circumstantial evidence, the women try the case, find the accused guilty, but dismiss the charge, recognizing the exigencies that led her to the act. In the process of judging they become compeers, Mrs. Peters recognizing her own disenfranchisement under the law and her own potential for violence, Mrs. Hale recognizing her failure to sustain her neighbor and thus her culpability in driving the desperate woman to kill.

This brief summary indicates how few specific details remain in Glaspell's re-visioning of the Hossack case. There is mention of "that man who went crazy," but he is not named or connected to the events.[10] Of the names of the participants only Henderson is used, assigned to the county attorney rather than the defense lawyer. Margaret Hossack has been renamed Minnie Foster Wright, the pun on the surname marking her lack of "rights" and implying her right to free herself against the societally sanctioned right of her husband to control the family, a right implicit in the Hossack case.

Glaspell's most striking alterations are her excision of Minnie and the change of venue. The accused woman has been taken away to jail before

Trifles begins, her place signified by the empty rocking chair that remains in her kitchen. By not physically representing Minnie on the stage, the playwright is able to focus on issues that move beyond the guilt or innocence of one person. Since the audience never actually sees Minnie, it is not swayed by her person but, instead, by her condition, a condition shared by other women who can be imagined in the empty subject position. And by situating her play in the kitchen not the court, in the private space in which Minnie lived rather than the public space in which she will be tried, Glaspell is able to offer the audience a composite picture of the life of Minnie Wright, Margaret Hossack, and countless women whose experiences were not represented in court because their lives were not deemed relevant to the adjudication of their cases. Most important in her shift of venue, Glaspell can focus on the central question never asked in the original Hossack case, that concerning the motives for murder: Why do women kill?

Motives are writ large in *Trifles*. The mise-en-scène suggests the harshness of Minnie's life. The house is isolated, "down in a hollow and you don't see the road"—dark, foreboding, a kind of rural, Gothic scene. The interior of the kitchen replicates this barrenness and the commensurate disjunctions in the family, as the woman experienced them. Things are broken, cold, imprisoning; they are also violent. "Preserves" explode from lack of heat, a punning reminder of the causal relationship between isolation and violence. The mutilated cage and bird signify the brutal nature of Wright and the physical abuse the wife has borne. Employing expressionistic techniques, Glaspell externalizes Minnie's desperation and the conditions that caused it.[11] She also finds the dramatic correlative for revenge. Rather than use an ax, this abused wife strangles her husband: a punishment to fit his crime. So powerfully does Glaspell marshal the evidence of Minnie's strangled life that the jury on the stage and the jury who observe them from the audience presume the wife's right to take violent action in the face of the violence done to her. They see what might cause women to kill.

When Glaspell turns to the characters in her play she again reworks the figures from the Hossack case, offering a revisionary reading of their roles in the original trial. The lawmen in *Trifles* bear traces of the original investigators, the county attorney and the sheriff. Mr. Hale is Glaspell's invention, a composite of the Indianola farmers who testified at the Hossack trial, his name possibly derived from Mr. Haines. By introducing a man not directly charged with prosecution of the case, Glaspell is able to show patriarchal power and privilege, the united front that judged Margaret Hossack. She also illustrates the process through which an individual joins the ranks.

In "A Jury of Her Peers" she goes to great lengths to indicate Mr. Hale's awkwardness at the beginning of the story, as he relates the details of the case, and how easily he is intimidated by the county attorney. Yet when he is allowed—by virtue of his gender—to go upstairs with the men of law, it is Hale, not they, who directly taunts the women: "But would the women know a clue if they did come upon it?" It is also he whom Glaspell ironically says speaks "with good natured superiority" when he declares that "women are used to worrying over trifles." Gender tran-scends class here, as it did in the original trial, in which the farmers, jurors, and lawyers had a common connection: they were male, and, as such, they were in control of the court and the direction of the testimony. She also indicates, however, that the privileged club does have a pecking order. Mr. Hale is recently admitted—or, more likely, only temporarily admitted—and, therefore, more likely to chide those below him in order to gain favor with those above. A similar desire to ingratiate themselves with the law and to establish a camaraderie that temporarily suspended class was clearly apparent among the farmers of Indianola, eager to play a part in convicting Mrs. Hossack, some so ready that their zeal in intruding themselves into the investigation was cited in the Supreme Court reversal.

Constructing her category of men across class lines, establishing their connectedness based on legal empowerment and rights, Glaspell sum-marily dismisses them to roam about on the periphery of the tale, their presence theatrically marked by shuffling sounds above the heads of the women and occasional appearances as they scurry out to the barn. With her deft parody Glaspell undercuts the authority they wielded in the original case and throws into question their sanctioned preserve of power. They physically crisscross the stage as they verbally crisscross the details of the crime, both actions leading nowhere, staged to show ineffec-tuality and incompetence.

In her version of the Hossack case it is the women, also drawn across class lines, who occupy their place, standing in stage center and functioning as the composite shaping consciousness that structures the play.[12] Glaspell carefully chooses the two women who will usurp legal agency. Mrs. Peters is the wife of the sheriff, patterned after Sheriff's Hodson's wife, whose acts of kindness to Margaret Hossack seem to have stayed in Glaspell's memory. At first Mrs. Peters parrots the masculinist view and voice of her husband, defending the search of the home as men's "duty." She gradually comes to recognize, however, that marital designation— wife of the sheriff—offers her no more freedom than it does Minnie; in fact, it completely effaces her as an individual. Glaspell illustrates this condition by having the women identified only by their surnames, while, at the same time, they seek to particularize Minnie, referring to her by both her first and her maiden name.[13]

To the men, however, Minnie is John Wright's wife, just as Mrs. Peters is the sheriff's wife: "married to the law," "one of us," "not in need of supervision." Even Mrs. Hale, at the beginning of "Jury," assumes that Mrs. Peters will be an extension of her husband and will share his views of the murder. Yet as Mrs. Peters slowly ferrets out the facts of Minnie's life—the childlessness, the isolation—and conflates the experiences with her own early married days, she begins to identify with Minnie. It is when she comes upon the bird cage and the dead canary that she makes the most important connection: an understanding of female violence in the face of male brutality: "When I was a girl—my kitten—there was a boy took a hatchet, and before my eyes—and before I could get there— (*covers her face an instant*) If they hadn't held me back I would have— (*catches herself, looks upstairs where steps are heard, falters weakly*)— hurt him."

It is significant that Glaspell attributes to Mrs. Peters, the sheriff's wife, the memory of a murder with an ax, the murder weapon in the Hossack case, and offers as sign of brutality the dismemberment of an animal, a trace, perhaps, of the turkey in the original case. In the reversal of roles that Glaspell stages—in having Mrs. Peters act in lieu of her husband, dispensing her verdict based on her reading of the case and the motives for murder—she destroys the notion that a woman is her husband. She also stages what a woman may become when given legal

power: a subject acting under her own volition, her decisions not necessarily coinciding with her husband's or with the male hegemony. She becomes self-deputized.

If Mrs. Peters is taken from life, so too is Mrs. Hale, a possible surrogate for the young reporter Susan Glaspell.[14] Just as Mrs. Peters recognizes her own potential for murder in the face of powerlessness, and this recognition motivates her to act and to seize the juridical position, Mrs. Hale comes to her own awareness in the course of the play. What she discovers in the kitchen of the Wright home is her own complicity in Minnie's situation, because of the aid she has withheld. "We live close together and we live far apart. We all go through the same thing, it's just a different kind of the same thing," she says, summarizing her insight about "how it is for women." In light of the Hossack case and Glaspell's role in sensationalizing the proceedings and in shaping public opinion, the lines appear to be confessional; thus, to her question "Who will punish that?" Mrs. Hale's words seem to indicate Glaspell's awareness in 1916 of her omissions and commissions in 1901, of her failure to act in Margaret Hossack's behalf, and of her failure to recognize the implications of the trial for her own life.

Given this awareness, it may seem strange that, when Glaspell has the opportunity to retry Margaret Hossack and change the outcome of the case, she does not acquit the woman, or, as Kayann Short argues, give her "her day in court" (9) to prove her innocence. Instead, she has Mrs. Peters and Mrs. Hale assume Minnie's guilt and, as in the original trial, base their findings on circumstantial evidence instead of incontrovertible proof. When approaching *Trifles* in relation to the Hossack case, however, it becomes clear that acquittal is not Glaspell's intention, not why she wrote the play. Whether Margaret Hossack or Minnie Wright committed murder is moot; what is incontrovertible is the brutality of their lives, the lack of options they had to redress grievances or to escape abusive husbands, and the complete disregard of their plight by the courts and by society. Instead of arguing their innocence, Glaspell concretizes the conditions under which these women live and the circumstances that might cause them to kill. She thus presents the subtext that was excised from the original trial and that undergirds so many of the cases cited in Ann Jones's study: men's fears of women who might kill and women's fears of the murder they might be forced to commit. In so doing, she stages one of the first modern arguments for justifiable homicide.[15] By having Mrs. Peters and Mrs. Hale unequivocally assume Minnie's guilt and also assume justification for her act, Glaspell presents her audience/jury with a defense that forces it to confront the central issues of female powerlessness and disenfranchisement and the need for laws to address such issues.[16]

Yet Glaspell does not actually present the victimization of women or the violent acts such treatment may engender; instead, she stages the potential for female action and the usurpation of power.[17] By having the women assume the central positions and conduct the investigation and the trial, she actualizes an empowerment that suggests that there are options short of murder that can be imagined for women. Mrs. Peters and Mrs. Hale may seem to conduct their trial sub rosa because they do not actively confront the men, but in Mrs. Hale's final words, "We call it— knot it," ostensibly referring to a form of quilting but clearly addressed to the actions the women have taken, they become both actors and namers. Even if the men do not understand the pun—either through ignorance or, as Judith Fetterley suggests, through self-preservation—the audience certainly does. It recognizes that the women have achieved an important political victory: they have wrested control of language, a first step in political ascendancy, and they have wrested control of the case and the stage. Not waiting to be given the vote or the right to serve on juries, Glaspell's women have taken the right for themselves. Her audience in 1916 would get the point. It would also understand that Glaspell is deconstructing the very assumptions about the incontrovertibility of the law and about its absolutist position. Mrs. Peters and Mrs. Hale, by suturing into their deliberations their own experiences and fears—just as the men in the Hossack case did—illustrate the subjective nature of the reading of evidence and, by implication, of all essentialist readings.

In 1916 it would be clearer than it often is to contemporary audiences that Glaspell is more concerned with legal and social empowerment than with replacing one hierarchy with another; that women acting surreptitiously may be less a comment on their natures than on the political systems that breed such behavior; not that women speak "in a different voice" but, rather, that they speak in a manner deriving from their different position under the law, from their common erasure. Her depiction of the conditions of her women is close to what Catherine MacKinnon describes in her book *Feminism Unmodified:* women's actions—their voices—deriving not from some innate nature but from the ways they have been forced to speak and to act. MacKinnon suggests that, if legal and social changes could occur, it would then be time to decide how a woman "talks."[18] When women are powerless, she argues, "you don't just speak differently. A lot, you don't speak. Your speech is not differently articulated, it is silenced" (39). In *Trifles* Glaspell, like MacKinnon, posits gender as a production of the inequality of power under law, "a social status based on who is permitted to do what to whom" (MacKinnon 8).

That Susan Glaspell was able to reshape the events of the Hossack case in order to focus on these issues can be attributable to at least two causes. The first is biographical. Glaspell herself had changed in the sixteen years that separate the trial from the composition of the play. When she covered the Hossack case she was twenty-four, right out of college; when she wrote *Trifles* she had just turned forty and had already published three well-received novels, thirty-one short stories, and a collection of short fiction, all focusing on the lives of women. She had also spent a year in Paris and lived in Chicago, Greenwich Village, and Provincetown, before her marriage, at the age of thirty-seven, to fellow Davenport native George Cram Cook.[19]

It is a mistake to claim that Glaspell was a slumbering midwestern woman until Cook brought her to life and political awareness when they married. Before her marriage, and even before her coverage of the Hossack case, she was already something of an iconoclast, aware of the imposition of cultural restrictions on women, at least as they had an impact on her own life and those of the women she observed as Susie Glaspell, the eighteen-year-old society editor of a local Davenport newspaper. Her nascent feminism was based, however, on the class structure of the city: she was poor in a town that valued wealth; she worked in a society in which women were expected to find others to work for them.

What she seems to have experienced for the first time in her coverage of the Hossack case was legal, rather than social, powerlessness that cut across class lines: the testimony of Mrs. Hossack, the ladies in their

Easter finery attending the trial, and even the sheriff's wife were equally silenced. While Glaspell may have felt sympathy, if not empathy, for Mrs. Hossack when she entered her kitchen in 1901, and while she may have been aware of the skewed nature of the trial, she was not able to translate this experience or insight into her writing, certainly not into her newspaper reports. As Ann Jones shows in her description of the coverage of a variety of murder trials of women during the period, the news accounts offer what the society will bear. The possibility of exploring the implications of the Hossack trial in terms of gender roles or of pursuing the question of justifiable homicide would have been unthinkable in Iowa in 1901, even if Glaspell had consciously been moved to do so.

In 1916 it was not. If Glaspell had changed, so had society. Although the general public might still resist such positions, the people for whom Glaspell fashioned her theater, if not her fiction, would certainly see the Hossack trial in light of their own agitation for the Nineteenth amendment, women's rights, and the dismantlement of absolutist thought in all areas.[20]

At the time she wrote *Trifles* Glaspell was living in a community passionately concerned with socialism and feminism; she herself was a founding member of Heterodoxy, the New York–based group of women whose numbers included activists Marie Jenny Howe, Crystal Eastman, Elizabeth Irwin, Mary Heaton Vorse, and, for a time, Charlotte Perkins Gilman.[21] The audience for the Provincetown Players was already a body of the committed, who in 1916 worked for suffrage and for social reform that would redress class distinctions in the United States and who, for the most part, were opposed to Wilson and the war. Unlike many suffragists, their arguments were usually posited on a materialist rather than an essentialist reading of gender, concerned either with class struggles of which gender limitations were part or enlightenment ideals of individualism applicable to both women and men. They did not romanticize femininity; most debunked the "cult of the home." Their major concern was in insuring "that women shall have the same right as man to be different, to be individuals, not merely a social unit," and that this individualism would manifest itself in legal and social freedom.[22] It was for this audience and at this time that Glaspell returned to the Hossack case.

Trifles, therefore, is grounded in a double-focused historical context:

the Iowa of 1901 and the Provincetown of 1916, the two periods leaving traces and providing many of the tensions and fissures that produce the contemporary feel to Glaspell's best works. Thus positioned, her writing acts as a palimpsest for the shifting roles of women in the early twentieth century and for her own shifts in attitudes toward the possibilities for women and for herself. It is either a testament to the skill with which Glaspell constructed *Trifles* and "A Jury of Her Peers" or proof of how little women's lives have changed since 1916 that contemporary feminist critics still use the play and story as palimpsests for their own readings of contemporary feminist issues, and these readings still point to some of the dilemmas that faced Glaspell and her personae in 1901 and in 1916: how to free women from the stereotypic roles into which they have been cast, how to articulate their lives and their rights without reinscribing them in the very roles against which they inveigh, how to represent female power not victimization—in short, how to represent Margaret Hossack. Yet in reading the works through a contemporary grid, critics should be careful of turning them into contemporary tracts, assuming that, just because Glaspell offers a picture of two women who bond, she is arguing for a higher moral ground for women, romanticizing femininity and home, arguing sexual difference, or the categorization of women under a fixed moral genus.[23] Given her own interests and concerns at the time, and her own relation to the Hossack case, it is more likely that her play and story are illustrating the need to provide both male and female voices in court—and in art—if human experience is not to be forever subsumed under the male pronoun and if women's voices are to be heard not as difference but as equally registered.

NOTES

Reprinted from *Theatre Journal* 44 (1992): 141–62.

1. At the turn of the century the father of modern criminology, Cesare Lombroso, offered a checklist of physical qualities that would identify women who might kill: "approximate more to males . . . than to normal women, especially in the superciliary arches in the seam of sutures, in the lower jaw-bones, and in peculiarities of the occipital region" (Jones 6).

2. Unless otherwise specified, when I mention *Trifles* I am also assuming "A Jury of Her Peers."

3. Glaspell's comments in *The Road to the Temple* are often misleading. The book is hagiography, and just as she constructed other scenes to make them more dramatic—and to dramatize the role of Cook—she may be doing so here. That she should want to portray his role in her shift to drama as that of a mentor encouraging his tutor is, however, revealing. It may be attributed to Cook's recent death in Greece, her return alone to Provincetown, and her immediate love affair with Norman Matson. (See Carroll and Larabee for other explanations.) Glaspell offers variations on this scene in notes for the book. In one version she writes: "I began writing plays because my hisband [*sic*] George Cram Cook made me [crossed out and replaced with 'forced me to']. 'I have announced a play of yours for the next bill,' he told me, soon after we started the Provincetown Players. I didn't want my marriage to break up so I wrote *Trifles* . . ." (Notes from Berg Collection, New York Public Library).

4. Judith E. Barlow, in "Susan's Sisters: The 'Other' Women Writers of the Provincetown Players" (this volume) suggests that Glaspell may have also been influenced by her friend Neith Boyce's play *White Nights,* a work produced by the group the year before that has as its theme a troubled marriage and a wife who wishes independence.

5. Glaspell first started writing for newspapers when she graduated from high school in Davenport, Iowa, in 1894. She covered local news and social events for the *Trident,* the *Davenport Morning Republican,* and the *Weekly Observer,* which listed her as society editor, under the name Susie Glaspell.

6. Glaspell may have covered the story about murder by a neck yoke, or at least read of it, because she appropriates the method for use in *Trifles.*

7. It is possible that Glaspell was actually accompanied to the Hossack house by the sheriff and the county attorney, who made several trips there during this period to gain evidence. One of the points cited by the Supreme Court of Iowa in their overturning of the initial conviction was the possible impropriety of having the same county attorney who would conduct the trial also gather the evidence. There is no indication, however, that the sheriff's wife also traveled to the Hossack farm, although the possibility is there.

8. The Hossack case was not unique in the number of women in attendance. Jones offers examples of irate ministers commenting on the large numbers of women who attended celebrated murder trials around the same period. In one case a minister comments that, "It is a strange thing that women, under no compulsion whatever, are found in large numbers in every notorious trial every-

where, and the dirtier the trial the more women usually will be found in attendance" (138). He does not conjecture about this phenomenon.

9. There were seven procedural points upon which the Supreme Court of
Iowa based its reversal, the most significant of which were the following: that the
hairs found under the corn crib were not proved to be from the murder weapon
and had been taken by the county attorney and given to the sheriff and could not,
therefore, be introduced as evidence; that the dissension in the Hossack house
had abated at least a year prior to the murder and could not, therefore, be
introduced in the case. See *State v. Hossack,* Supreme Court of Iowa, April 9,
1902, *Northwestern Reporter,* 1077–81.

10. See Hedges for a discussion of insanity in rural American life and the
practice by women on the plains of having canaries to provide them company.

11. Glaspell often used expressionistic techniques in her plays. See Ben-Zvi,
"Susan Glaspell and Eugene O'Neill (1982 and 1986), for a discussion of *The
Verge* as an expressionistic drama.

12. Mrs. Peters and Mrs. Hale are of different classes, a fact visually captured
by the filmmaker Sally Heckel in her version of "A Jury of Her Peers" (Texture
Films). Mrs. Hale wears a plain, cloth coat and head scarf; Mrs. Peters has a fur
tippet and large, feathered hat.

Their language also bears signs of their class, a technique Glaspell often repeats. In *Trifles* Mrs. Hale makes grammatical errors, has unfinished sentences,
drops letters. Mrs. Peters speaks in a grammatically correct manner befitting the
sheriff's wife. For example, Mrs. Hale's comment, "I wonder if she was goin' to
quilt it or just knot it" becomes Mrs. Peters's "We think she was going to—knot
it," the omitted *g* signifying for Glaspell different education and position. What
joins them is the men's categorization of them, predicated on gender, erasing
difference, dismissing individuality.

13. At the time Glaspell was writing the play, the question of women taking
their husbands' names was a political issue. One of Glaspell's friends, Ruth Hale,
launched a movement called the Lucy Stone League, which supported married
women who chose to keep their maiden names. (See Schwarz 14, 58, 83.) Glaspell, like her contemporaries Neith Boyce, Mary Heaton Vorse, and others, never
assumed her husband's name.

14. When the Provincetown Players staged the play Glaspell chose to play
Mrs. Hale and had her husband, George Cram Cook, play Hale.

15. One could argue that the precedent for staging a case of justifiable homicide for women was established in *The Oresteia,* in which the motives leading to
Clytemnestra's murder of Agamemnon are delineated, or would be if one affixed
to the work the murder of Iphigenia, as Ariane Mnouchkine did in a production

of the Aeschylus' trilogy at the Théâtre du Soleil that is prefaced by Euripides' *Iphigenia in Aulis.* (See *New York Times,* March 27, 1981, B3, for a description of this performance.) For a discussion of contemporary wife battering cases and the plea of justifiable homicide, see Jones (chap. 6).

16. In most of Glaspell's plays there is a political component directly connected to particular events of her period that would have been immediately evident to her audience but is often lost in contemporary discussions of her works. In *Suppressed Desires,* for instance, she takes on a noted antifeminist of the period, one Professor Sedwick, who had said, "All women were hens." In the play Glaspell and Cook play on the name Stephen (Step-hen), parodying both Freudianism and Cook's childhood pronunciation of the word (*Road* 25). Yet they also are answering Sedwick, a reference her audience would immediately have understood. Even more overtly, *Inheritors* challenges contemporary issues such as the Alien and Sedition laws and the Red Scare.

17. See Butler on the problems of staging victimization and thus representing the very condition the writer may wish to dismantle.

18. MacKinnon, while acknowledging the work of such people as Carol Gilligan, argues that Gilligan "achieves for moral reasoning what the special protection rule achieves in law: the affirmative rather than the negative valuation of that which has accurately distinguished women from men, by making it seem as though those attributes, with their consequences, really are somehow ours, rather than what male supremacy has attributed to us for its own use": "For women to affirm difference, when difference means dominance, as it does with gender, means to affirm the qualities and characteristics of powerlessness" (38–39). What is relevant about MacKinnon in relation to *Trifles* and "Jury" is her emphasis on law and enfranchisement. Reading Glaspell through MacKinnon allows the critic to move beyond the questions of "different voice" that were the critical bulwarks of the first moment of Glaspell criticism (see, e.g., Ben-Zvi, Stein, Alkalay-Gut, and Malpede) or critiqued in the more recent materialist readings (see Carroll, Hart, Nelligan [this volume], Short, Stephens, and Williams). It is hard to imagine, however, that Glaspell would have supported MacKinnon's stance on censorship as a way of alleviating pornography. Repeatedly in her writing, Glaspell objected to any form of censorship, for whatever reason.

19. Glaspell's marriage parallels almost exactly the paradigm Caroline Heilbrun presents in *Writing a Woman's Life:* a marriage near middle age that is scandal ridden and that both forces the woman out of society and allows her a freedom such societal marginalization provides.

20. It is important to note that *Trifles* and "A Jury of Her Peers" were written

for different audiences. The fiction, appearing in the popular magazine *Every-week*, stresses identification between the reader and Mrs. Hale, a familiar farm housewife, and leads to a reading that seems to romanticize housework and traditional feminine roles far more than *Trifles* does. For example, in the story version, Glaspell has Mrs. Hale say: "The Law is the law and a bad stove is a bad stove. How'd you'd like to cook on this?"—an image and a question with which her readers could identify, just as they could identify with Mrs. Hale's sudden call from her own kitchen to travel to the kitchen of Minnie Wright. One of the anomalies in the criticism of the two works is the failure of most critics to note that there are two versions of the same basic story and to take into consideration the differences in accordance with the nature of the audience and the differences implicit in the genre. Interestingly, two of the most influential essays on the works use "Jury" and make no reference to the more subtle and radical workings of *Trifles* (see Kolodny). When Williams compares the Dutch film *A Question of Silence* to Glaspell's work, she also uses "Jury," not *Trifles* (see Williams).

21. See Judith Schwarz's description of Heterodoxy, in which she lists Glaspell as a founding member; also see Nancy Cott's detailed study of the feminist movement in New York in the years 1910–20; and June Sochen's descriptions of the period and of Glaspell's relation to feminists in Greenwich Village. In *Women and American Socialism, 1870–1920* Buhle discusses how Glaspell "created female characters as working-class women with capacities to feel intensely, to understand injustice rather than internalizing oppression, and when conditions allowed to strike back at their oppressors" (203).

22. These quotations are taken from the same *New York Times* report (February 18, 1914) concerning a meeting organized by Heterodoxy president, Marie Jenny Howe, at Cooper Union, billed as "the first feminist meeting ever convened." At the time Glaspell was in Davenport, after suffering a miscarriage, but many of her friends were there, and she would most likely have been in the audience, if not on the dais. For other references to articles on feminism written between 1913–16, see Cott.

23. Five years later she would write *The Verge,* her most powerful and most feminist play. Her persona, Claire Archer, would demand a life not circumscribed by the traditional roles assigned to women—mother, caregiver, hostess—and would stand in juxtaposition to her daughter and her sister, who represent conventional women whose gender does not provide them with an insight into Claire's life or her aspiration. In *The Verge* Glaspell also pursues feminism as a "transvaluation of values" on a Nietzschean model. See Cott (296) in relation to Dora Marsden and a similar position; also see Carroll.

WORKS CITED

Alkalay-Gut, Karen. " 'A Jury of her Peers': The Importance of Trifles." *Studies in Short Fiction* 21 (1984): 3–11.

Barlow, Judith, ed. *Plays by American Women: 1900–1930.* New York: Applause Books, 1985.

Ben-Zvi, Linda. "Susan Glaspell and Eugene O'Neill." *Eugene O'Neill Newsletter* 6 (1982): 22–29.

———. "Susan Glaspell, Eugene O'Neill, and the Imagery of Gender." *Eugene O'Neill Newsletter* 10 (1986): 22–28.

———. "Susan Glaspell's Contributions to Contemporary Women Playwrights." In *Feminine Focus: The New Women Playwrights.* Ed. Enoch Brater, 147–66. New York: Oxford University Press, 1989.

Bigsby, C. W. E., ed. *Plays by Susan Glaspell.* Cambridge: Cambridge University Press, 1987.

Buhle, Mari Jo. *Women and American Socialism, 1870–1920.* Urbana: University of Illinois Press, 1981.

Butler, Judith. "Performing Acts and Gender Constitution: An Essay in Phenomenology and Feminist Theory." In *Performing Feminisms: Feminist Critical Theory and Theatre.* Ed. Sue-Ellen Case, 270–82. Baltimore: Johns Hopkins University Press, 1990.

Carroll, Kathleen. "Centering Women Onstage: Susan Glaspell's Dialogic Strategy of Resistance." Ph.D. diss. University of Maryland, 1990.

Cott, Nancy. *The Grounding of Modern Feminism.* New Haven: Yale University Press, 1987.

Gilligan, Carol. *In a Different Voice: Psychological Theory and Women's Development.* Cambridge: Harvard University Press, 1982.

Glaspell, Susan. "The Hossack Case." *Des Moines Daily News,* December 2, 1900–April 13, 1901.

———. "A Jury of Her Peers." *Everyweek,* March 5, 1917.

———. *Trifles.* New York: Frank Shay / Washington Square Players, 1916; rpt. in Bigsby.

Hart, Lynda. "They Don't Even Look like Maids Anymore: Wendy Kesselman's *My Sister in This House.*" In *Making a Spectacle.* Ed. Lynda Hart, 131–46. Ann Arbor: University of Michigan Press, 1989.

Hedges, Elaine. "Small Things Reconsidered: Susan Glaspell's 'A Jury of Her Peers.' " *Women's Studies* 12 (1986): 89–110.

Heilbrun, Carolyn. *Writing a Woman's Life.* New York: W. W. Norton, 1988.

Jones, Ann. *Women Who Kill.* New York: Holt, Rinehart and Winston, 1980.

Kolodny, Annette. "A Map for Re-Reading: Gender and the Interpretation of Literary Texts." In *The New Feminist Criticism.* Ed. Elaine Showalter, 46–62. New York: Pantheon, 1985.

Larabee, Ann. "Death in Delphi: Susan Glaspell and the Companionate Marriage." *Mid-American Review* 7, no. 2 (1987): 93–106.

MacKinnon, Catherine. *Feminism Unmodified: Discourses on Life and Law.* Cambridge: Harvard University Press, 1987.

Malpede, Karen. "Introduction." *Women in Theatre.* New York: Drama Books, 1983.

Murphy, Jeanette. *"A Question of Silence."* In *Films for Women.* Ed. Charlotte Brunsdon, 99–108. London: British Film Institute, 1986.

Noe, Marcia. *Susan Glaspell: Voice from the Heartland.* Macomb: Western Illinois Monograph Series, 1983.

Northwestern Reporter, April 9, 1902, 1077–81.

Polk County Transcripts of Court Records, case no. 805, April 2, 1901–March 3, 1903.

Rockwell, John. "An *Oresteia* Using Non-Western Techniques." *New York Times,* March 27, 1981.

Schwarz, Judith. *Radical Feminists of Heterodoxy: Greenwich Village, 1912–1940.* Lebanon, N.H.: New Victoria Publishers, 1982.

Short, Kayann. "A Different Kind of the Same Thing: The Erasure of Difference in 'A Jury of Her Peers.' " In *Trifles* and *"A Jury of Her Peers" Casebook.* Ed. Linda Ben-Zvi, forthcoming.

Sochen, June. *The New Woman in Greenwich Village, 1910–1920.* New York: Quadrangle, 1972.

Stein, Karen. "The Women's World of Glaspell's *Trifles.*" In *Women in American Theatre.* Ed. Helen Krich Chinoy and Linda Walsh Jenkins, 253–56. New York: Theatre Communications Group, 1987.

Stephens, Judith. "Gender Ideology and Dramatic Convention in Progressive Era Plays, 1890–1920." In *Performing Feminisms: Feminist Critical Theory and Theatre.* Ed. Sue-Ellen Case, 283–93. Baltimore: Johns Hopkins University Press, 1990.

Supreme Court of Iowa, April 9, 1902, *Northwestern Reporter:* 1077–81.

"Talk on Feminism Stirs Great Crowd." *New York Times,* February 18, 1914.

Warren County Court Records. Hossack trial, April 1903.

Williams, Linda. "A Jury of Their Peers: Marlene Gorris's 'A Question of Silence.' " In *Postmodernism and Its Discontents: Theories and Practices.* Ed. E. Ann Kaplan, 107–15. London: Verso, 1988.

Small Things Reconsidered:
"A Jury of Her Peers"

Elaine Hedges

Susan Glaspell's "A Jury of Her Peers" is by now a small feminist classic. Published in 1917, rediscovered in the early 1970s, and increasingly reprinted since then in anthologies and textbooks, it has become for both readers and critics a familiar and frequently revisited landmark on our "map of rereading." For Lee Edwards and Arlyn Diamond in 1973 it introduced us to the work of one of the important but forgotten women writers who were then being rediscovered, and its characters, "prairie matrons, bound by poverty and limited experience [who] fight heroic battles on tiny battlefields," provided examples of those ordinary or anonymous women whose voices were also being sought and reclaimed. For Mary Anne Ferguson, also in 1973, Glaspell's story was significant for its challenge to prevailing images or stereotypes of women—women as "fuzzy minded" and concerned only with "trifles," for example—and for its celebration of female sorority, of the power of sisterhood. More recently, in 1980, Annette Kolodny has read the story as exemplary of a female realm of meaning and symbolic signification, a realm ignored by mainstream critics and one, as she urges, that feminist critics must interpret and make available. Rediscovering lost women writers, reclaiming the experience of anonymous women, reexamining the image of women in literature, and rereading texts in order to discern and appreciate female symbol systems—many of the major approaches that have characterized feminist literacy criticism in the past decade have thus found generous validation in the text of "A Jury of Her Peers." The story has become a paradigmatic one for feminist criticism.[1]

Whatever their different emphases, all of these approaches, when applied to Glaspell's story, have in common their central reliance, for argument and evidence, on that set of small details describing women's daily, domestic lives that constitutes the story's core. These details—the "clues" through which in the story the two farm women, Mrs. Hale and Mrs. Peters, solve the mystery of the murder of John Wright—include such minutiae as a soiled roller towel, a broken stove, a cracked jar of preserves, and an erratically stitched quilt block. So central are these details not only to the story's plot but to its larger symbolic meanings that Glaspell gave them precedence in the title of the dramatic version she originally wrote, the one-act play *Trifles,* which she produced for the Provincetown Players in 1916. It is by decoding these "trifles," which the men ignore, that the two women not only solve the murder mystery but also develop their sense of identity as women with Minnie Wright and demonstrate their sisterhood with her by acting to protect her from male law and judgment. It is, therefore, essentially through these trifles that Glaspell creates in her story that female world of meaning and symbol that, as Kolodny says, feminist critics must recover and make accessible.

My interest here is in extending the story's accessibility, making it more possible for contemporary readers to enter into and respond to the symbolic meanings of the details on which it is so crucially based. Any symbol system, as Jean Kennard for one has shown in her discussion of literary conventions, is a shorthand, a script to which the reader must bring a great deal of knowledge not contained in the text.[2] Critical exegeses of the symbolic worlds of male writers—the forest, the river, the whaling ship—may by now have enabled us imaginatively to enter those worlds. But the same is not yet true for women writers. What is needed, as Kolodny says, is an understanding of the "unique and informing contexts" that underlie the symbol systems of women's writing. Only after these contexts are made accessible are we likely to be able to enjoy that "fund of shared recognitions" upon which, as Kolodny also notes, any viable symbol system depends.[3]

In Glaspell's story Mrs. Hale and Mrs. Peters constitute an ideal (if small) community of readers precisely because they are able to bring to the "trivia" of Minnie Wright's life just such a "unique and informing context." That context is their own experience as midwestern rural women. As a result, they can read Minnie's kitchen trifles with full "recog-

nition and acceptance of . . . their significance." For contemporary readers, however, who are historically removed from the way of life on which
Glaspell's story depends, such a reading is not so readily available. Superficially, we can of course comprehend the story's details, since women's
work of cooking, cleaning, and sewing is scarcely strange, or unfamiliar,
either to female or to male readers. But to appreciate the full resonance of
those details requires by now an act of historical reconstruction. Glaspell's details work so effectively as a symbol system because they are
carefully chosen reflectors of crucial realities in the lives of nineteenth-
and early-twentieth-century midwestern and western women. The themes,
the broader meanings of "A Jury of Her Peers," which are what encourage us to rediscover and reread it today, of course extend beyond its
regional and historical origins. Women's role, or "place," in society, their
confinement and isolation, the psychic violence wrought against them,
their power or powerlessness vis-à-vis men, are not concerns restricted to
Glaspell's time and place. But these concerns achieve their imaginative
force and conviction in her story by being firmly rooted in, and organi-
cally emerging from, the carefully observed, small details of a localized
way of life.

I would therefore like to reenter Glaspell's text by returning it to that
localized, past way of life. Such reentry is possible by now, given the
recent work of social historians in western women's history. The past six
to seven years, especially, have seen the publication of works on the lives
of western women by such historians as John Faragher, Julie Jeffrey,
Norton Juster, Sandra Myres, Glenda Riley, and Christine Stansell. And
the same years have seen a resurgence of interest in women's writings in
nontraditional forms—the diaries, letters, journals, and autobiographies
of nineteenth- and early-twentieth-century pioneer and farm women,
women less silenced than Minnie Wright in Glaspell's story—on which,
indeed, much of the published social history depends.[4] It is this body of
material, as well as my own researches into the autobiographical writings
of nineteenth-century women, on which I shall draw in order to recreate,
however imperfectly, some of the historical reality that informs the responses of Mrs. Hale and Mrs. Peters to Minnie Wright's life. Again and
again in "A Jury of Her Peers" Mrs. Hale and Mrs. Peters perform acts of
perception in which a literal object opens out for them into a larger world

of meaning. At one point in the story Glaspell describes these acts as a way of "seeing into things, of seeing through a thing to something else."[5] To uncover that "something else"—the dense, hidden background reality of rural women's lives—may enable us to participate more fully in those acts of perception and thus to appreciate Glaspell's achievement, the way in which, by concentrating on a small, carefully selected set of literal details, she communicates, in one very brief short story, an extraordinarily rich, multilayered sense of women's sociocultural place in late-nineteenth- and early-twentieth-century American society.

By the time she published "A Jury of Her Peers," in 1917, Susan Glaspell had been living in the east for several years, both in Greenwich Village and in Provincetown, Massachusetts. But she had been born and raised in Iowa, and her earliest fiction had dealt with the people of her native Midwest, and especially with the confined lives, whether on the isolated farm or in the midwestern small town or village, of women. In writing her play *Trifles,* and then her story, therefore, she was returning to her midwestern origins and to the lives of women of her mother's and grandmother's generations.

"A Jury of Her Peers" is set in the prairie and plains region of the United States. The story itself contains a reference to the county attorney's having just returned from Omaha, which would literally locate the action in Nebraska. And a further reference to "Dickson County," as the place where the characters live, might suggest Dixon County, an actual county in the northeastern corner of Nebraska where it borders on Iowa. In the narrowest sense, then, given Glaspell's own Iowa origins, the story can be said to refer to the prairie and plains country that stretches across Iowa into Nebraska—a country of open, level or rolling land, and few trees, which generations of pioneers encountered during successive waves of settlement throughout the nineteenth century. More broadly, the story reflects the lives of women across the entire span of prairie and plains country, and some of the circumstances of Minnie Wright's life were shared by women further west as well. While emphasizing Iowa and Nebraska, therefore, this essay will draw for evidence on the autobiographical writings by women from various western states.

Glaspell's references to the outdoor setting are few. As the story opens, she emphasizes the cold wintry day and the emptiness of the terrain through which the characters travel on their way to the Wright home-stead, where they are going to investigate the murder. But the very sparse-ness of her detail serves to suggest the spare, empty lives of her characters, and especially of Minnie Wright's. What Mrs. Hale notes as the group approaches the Wright farm is the "loneliness" both of the farmhouse and its surroundings. Three times in as many sentences she uses the words *lonely* or *lonesome* to describe the locale. (The road is lonely, and the farm, "down in a hollow," is surrounded by "lonesome looking poplar trees.") Kolodny has suggested that this sensitivity to place distinguishes the women in the story from the men, who confine their talk to the crime that was committed the day before. Whether or not one can generalize from this difference (as Kolodny does) to conclusions about gender-linked perceptions, it does seem to be the case that nineteenth-century pioneer women were more strongly affected than men by a sense of the loneliness of the landscape they encountered in the west.

In spring, when the wildflowers were in bloom, the western prairie might seem "a perfect garden of Eden," as it did to an Iowa woman in 1851. But frequently the women's voices that we hear from that pioneer past express dismay at what they saw when they arrived. A prairie burned by the autumn fires that regularly ravaged the land might understandably seem "black and dismal," as the Illinois prairie did to Christiana Tillson in 1822. Other women, however, even when viewing a less seared and searing landscape, found the prairie unsettling, especially as they moved farther west. "What solitude!" exclaimed the Swedish visitor Fredrika Bremer, arriving in Wisconsin in the 1850s. "I saw no habitation, except the little house at which I was staying; no human beings, no animals; nothing except heaven and the flower-strewn earth." And Mrs. Cecil Hall, visiting the northern territories in 1882, wrote: "O the prairie! I cannot describe to you our first impression. Its vastness, dreariness, and loneliness is [*sic*] appalling."[6]

When a male pioneer registered his sense of the land's emptiness it was often to recognize that the emptiness bore more heavily upon women. Seth K. Humphrey wrote of his father's and his own experiences, in the Minnesota territory in the 1850s and in the Middle Northwest in the 1870s, and he remembered that "the prairie has a solitude way beyond the mere absence of human beings." With no trees, no objects to engage or interrupt the glance, the eyes "stare, stare—and sometimes the prairie gets to staring back." Women, he observed, especially suffered. They "fled in terror" or "stayed until the prairie broke them." Women themselves reported that it was not unusual to spend five months in a log cabin without seeing another woman, as did a Marshall County, Iowa, woman in 1842, or to spend one and a half years after arriving before being able to take a trip to town, as did Luna Kellie in Nebraska in the 1870s. The absence both of human contact and of any ameliorating features in the landscape exacerbated the loneliness felt by women, who had often only reluctantly uprooted themselves from eastern homes and families in order to follow their husbands westward.[7]

Minnie Wright is not, of course, living in circumstances of such extreme geographical isolation. By the time of Glaspell's story established villages and towns have replaced the first scattered settlements, and networks of transportation and communication link people previously isolated from one another. But John Wright's farm, as we learn, is an isolated, outlying farm, separated from the town of which it is formally a part. Furthermore, he refuses to have a telephone, and, as we also learn, he has denied his wife access to even the minimal contacts that town life might afford women at that time, such as the church choir, in which Minnie had sung before her marriage. Minnie Wright's emotional and spiritual loneliness, the result of her isolation, is, in the final analysis, the reason for her murder of her husband. Through her brief opening description of the landscape Glaspell establishes the physical context for the loneliness and isolation, an isolation Minnie inherited from and shared with generations of pioneer and farm women before her.[8]

The full import of Minnie's isolation emerges only incrementally in Glaspell's story. Meanwhile, after the characters arrive at the Wright farm, the story confines itself to the narrow space of Minnie's kitchen—the limited and limiting space of her female sphere. Within that small space are revealed all the dimensions of the loneliness that is her mute message. And that message is, of course, conveyed through those "kitchen things," as the sheriff dismissively calls them, to which Mrs. Hale and Mrs. Peters respond with increasing comprehension and sympathy.

One of the first "kitchen things," or "trifles," to which Glaspell introduces us is the roller towel, on which the attorney condescendingly comments. Not considering, as the women do, that his own assistant, called in earlier that morning to make up a fire in Minnie's absence, had probably dirtied the towel, he decides that the soiled towel shows that Minnie lacked "the homemaking instinct." The recent researches of historians into the lives of nineteenth-century women allow us today to appreciate the full ironic force of Mrs. Hale's quietly understated reply: "There's a great deal of work to be done on a farm." One of the most important contributions of the new social history is its documentation of the amount of work that pioneer and farm women did. The work is, as one historian has said, "almost endless" and, over the course of a lifetime, usually consisted of tasks "more arduous and demanding than those performed by men." Indoors and out, the division of labor "favored men" and "exploited women." Sarah Brewer-Bonebright, recalling her life in Newcastle, Iowa in 1848, described the "routine" work of the "women-folk" as including "water carrying, cooking, churning, sausage making, berry picking, vegetable drying, sugar and soap boiling, hominy hulling, medicine brewing, washing, nursing, weaving, sewing, straw platting, wool picking, spinning, quilting, knitting, gardening and various other tasks." Workdays that began at 4:30 A.M. and didn't end until 11:30 P.M. were not unheard of. Jessamyn West's description of her Indiana grandmother—"She died saying, 'Hurry, hurry, hurry,' not to a nurse, not to anyone at her bedside, but to herself"—captures an essential reality of the lives of many nineteenth- and early-twentieth-century rural women.[9]

The work involved for Minnie Wright in preparing the clean towel that the attorney takes for granted is a case in point. Of all the tasks that nineteenth- and early-twentieth-century women commented on in their diaries, laundry was consistently described as the most onerous.

Friday   May 27   This is the dreaded washing day
Friday   June 23   To day Oh! horrors how shall I express it; is the dreaded washing day.

This entry from an 1853 diary is typical of what are often litanies of pain, ritualistically repeated in the records that nineteenth-century women have left us of their lives. In her recent study of housework, *Never Done,* Susan Strasser agrees that laundry was woman's "most hated task." Before the introduction of piped water it took staggering amounts of time and labor: "One wash, one boiling, and one rinse used about fifty gallons of water—or four hundred pounds—which had to be moved from pump or well or faucet to stove and tub, in buckets and wash boilers that might weigh as much as forty or fifty pounds." Then came rubbing, wringing, and lifting the wet clothing and linens and carrying them in heavy tubs and baskets outside to hang.[10] It is when Mrs. Peters looks from Minnie's inadequate stove, with its cracked lining, to the "pail of water carried in from outside" that she makes the crucial observation about "seeing into things . . . seeing through a thing to something else." What the women see, beyond the pail and the stove, are the hours of work it took Minnie to produce that one clean towel. To call Minnie's work "instinctual," as the attorney does (using a rationalization prevalent today as in the past) is to evade a whole world of domestic reality, a world of which Mrs. Hale and Mrs. Peters are acutely aware.

So too with the jars of preserves that the women find cracked and spoiled from the cold that has penetrated the house during the night. It is the preserves, about which Minnie has been worrying in jail, that lead Mr. Hale to make the comment Glaspell used for the title of the dramatic version of her work. "Held for murder, and worrying over her preserves . . . worrying over trifles." But here again, as they express their sympathy with Minnie's concern, the women are seeing through a thing to something else: in this case, to "all [Minnie's] work in the hot weather," as Mrs. Peters exclaims. Mrs. Hale and Mrs. Peters understand the physical labor involved in boiling fruit in Iowa heat that one historian has described as "oppressive and inescapable." By the same token they can appreciate the seriousness of the loss when that work is destroyed by the winter cold.[11]

The winter cold is, as has been said, one of the few references to outdoor setting that Glaspell includes in her story. When at the beginning of the story Mrs. Hale closes her storm door behind her to accompany the others to the Wright farm, it is a "cold March morning," with a north wind blowing. Later we are told that the temperature had fallen below zero the night before. Historians have described the prairie and plains winters, their interminable length, the ceaseless winds that whipped across the treeless spaces, the "infamous" blizzards peculiar to the region—storms not of snow but of ice particles that penetrated clothes and froze the eyes shut. Eliza Farnham, traveling through the prairie in 1846, described the cold in the uninsulated log cabins and frame houses: "The cups freeze to the saucers while [the family] are at table." And Mary Abell, living in Kansas in 1875, related how "my eyelids froze together so I picked off the ice, the tops of the sheets and quilts and all our beds were frozen stiff with the breath. The cold was so intense we could not breathe the air without pain."[12] Such weather demanded heroic maintenance efforts to keep a family warm and fed. Engaged as they were in just such maintenance efforts (at the beginning of the story Mrs. Hale is reluctant to leave her kitchen because her own work is unfinished) the women can appreciate the meaning of the loss of Minnie's laboriously prepared food.

Hard as the work was, that it went unacknowledged was often harder for women to bear. The first annual report of the Department of Agriculture in 1862 included a study of the situation of farm women, which concluded that they worked harder than men but were neither treated with respect as a result nor given full authority within their domestic sphere. And Norton Juster's study of farm women between 1865 and 1895 leads him to assert that women's work was seen merely as "the anonymous background for someone else's meaningful activity," never attaining "a recognition or dignity of its own." Indeed, he concludes, women's work was not only ignored; it was ridiculed, "often the object of derision."[13] Mr. Hale's remark about the preserves, that "women are used to worrying over trifles," is a mild example of this ridicule, as is the attorney's comment, intended to deflect that ridicule but itself patronizing: "Yet what would we do without the ladies." It is this ridicule to which Mrs. Hale and Mrs. Peters especially react. When Mr. Hale belittles women's work we are told that "the two women moved a little closer together," and when the attorney makes his seemingly conciliatory remark the women, we are further told, "did not speak, did not unbend." Mrs. Hale and Mrs. Peters, who at the beginning of the story are comparative strangers, here begin to establish their common bonds with each other and with Minnie. Their slight physical movement toward each other visually embodies that psychological and emotional separation from men that was encouraged by the nineteenth-century doctrine of separate spheres, a separation underscored throughout the story by the women's confinement to the kitchen, while the men range freely, upstairs and outside, bedroom to barn, in search of the "real" clues to the crime.

Women's confinement to the kitchen or to the private space of the home was a major source of their isolation. Men didn't appreciate how "their own toil is sweetened to them by the fact that it is out of doors," said one farm woman, and Juster has concluded that the lives of farm women in the second half of the nineteenth-century were lives "tied to house and children, lacking opportunity for outside contacts, stimulation, or variety of experience."[14] In Glaspell's story Mrs. Hale moves only from one kitchen to another. That she hasn't visited Minnie, whom she has known since girlhood, in over a year she guiltily attributes to her antipathy to the cheerlessness of the Wright farm. But there is truth in Mrs. Peters's attempt to assuage that guilt: "But of course you were awful busy . . . your house—and your children."

"A walking visit to neighbors was not a casual affair but could take an entire morning or afternoon," says Faragher in describing the settlement on separate farmsteads, often far distant from each other, and, like Juster, he concludes that "the single most important distinction between the social and cultural worlds of men and women was the isolation and immobility of wives compared to husbands." "Grandma Brown," whose one-hundred-year life span from 1827 to 1927 is recorded in her autobiography, lived on an Iowa farm for fourteen years, from 1856 to 1870. They were, she said, "the hardest years of my life. The drudgery was unending. The isolation was worse."[15] Both during the frontier stage and in later periods of village settlement men routinely enjoyed more opportunities for social life than women. They traveled to town with their farm produce, to have their grain and corn milled, to trade surpluses, to have wool carded or skins tanned. In "A Jury of Her Peers" John Wright's murder is discovered because Mr. Hale and his son stop at the Wright farm while traveling to town with their potato crop. Once in town men had places to congregate—the market, the country store, the blacksmith shop, the saloon. That "women really did little more than pass through the masculine haunts of the village," as Faragher concludes, was a reality to which at least one nineteenth-century male writer was sensitive. "The saloon-keepers, the politicians, and the grocers make it pleasant for the man," Hamlin Garland has a character comment in his story of midwestern rural life, "A Day's Pleasure"; "But the wife is left without a word." Garland wrote "A Day's Pleasure" to dramatize the plight of the farm wife, isolated at home, and desperate for diversion. Mrs. Markham has been six months without leaving the family farm. But when, over her husband's objections and by dint of sacrificed sleep and extra work to provide for her children while she is gone, she manages to get into town, she finds scant welcome and little to do. After overstaying her leave at the country store, she walks the streets for hours, in the "forlorn, aimless, pathetic wandering" that, Garland has the town grocer observe, is "a daily occurrence for the farm women he sees and one which had never possessed any special meaning to him."[16]

John Wright's insensitivity to his wife's needs parallels that of the men of Garland's story. Lacking decent clothes, Minnie doesn't travel into town. What she turns to in her isolation is a bird, a canary bought from a traveling peddler. It is after her husband strangles that surrogate voice that, in one of those "intermittent flare-ups of bizarre behavior," as one historian has described them, which afflicted rural women, she strangles him.[17]

Here again Glaspell's story reflects a larger truth about the lives of rural women. Their isolation induced madness in many. The rate of insanity in rural areas, especially for women, was a much-discussed subject in the second half of the nineteenth century. As early as 1868 Sarah Josepha Hale, editor of the influential *Godey's Lady's Book,* expressed her concern that the farm population supplied the largest proportion of inmates for the nation's insane asylums. By the 1880s and 1890s this concern was widespread. An article in 1882 noted that farmer's wives comprised the largest percentage of those in lunatic asylums. And a decade later the *Atlantic Monthly* was reporting "the alarming rate of insanity . . . in the new prairie States among farmers and their wives." Abigail McCarthy recalled in her autobiography stories she had heard as a girl in the 1930s about the first homesteaders in North Dakota, two generations earlier. Women could be heard, she wrote, "screaming all night long in the jail after the first spring thaw. Their husbands had brought them into town in wagons from the sod huts where they had spent the terrible Dakota winter; they were on their way to the insane asylum in Jamestown."[18]

That the loss of her music, in the shape of a bird, should have triggered murderous behavior in Minnie Wright is therefore neither gratuitous nor melodramatic, as is sometimes charged against Glaspell's story. In the monotonous expanses of the prairie and the plains the presence of one small spot of color, or a bit of music, might spell the difference between sanity and madness. Mari Sandoz, chronicler of the lives of Nebraska pioneers, describes in her short story "The Vine" a woman so desperate for some color in the brown, treeless expanse of the prairie that she uses precious water—scarce during a drought—to keep alive a trumpet vine outside the door of her sod house. When her husband, enraged at her wastefulness, uproots and kills the vine, she goes mad. In *Old Jules*, her account of the life of her homesteading father, Sandoz relates the true story of a farm wife who suddenly one afternoon killed herself and her three children. At her funeral a woman neighbor comments, "If she would a had even a geranium—but in that cold shell of a shack—." Again and again in their recollections of their lives on the prairie and plains women described the importance of a bit of color or music. The music might come, as it did for Minnie Wright, from a canary in a cage. Late-nineteenth-century photographs of families outside their Dakota and Nebraska sod huts routinely show the birdcage hung to one side of the front door. Indoors it was likely to be one of the deep windows carved into the thick sod walls that provided the "spot of beauty" so necessary to psychological survival. As late as 1957, the *Nebraska Farmer* published interviews it had secured with women who had experienced the conditions of pioneer settlement. The comment of Mrs. Orval Lookhart is typical of many the journal received. She remembered the special window in the prairie sod house that was invariably reserved for "flowers and plants . . . a place where the wife and mother could have one spot of beauty that the wind the cold or the dry weather couldnet [*sic*] touch."[19] There is no spot of beauty in Glaspell's description of Minnie's kitchen, which is presented as a drab and dreary space, dominated by the broken stove, and a rocking chair of "a dingy red, with wooden rungs up the back, and the middle rung was gone, and the chair sagged to one side." When the women collect some of Minnie's clothes to take to her in prison, the sight of "a shabby black skirt" painfully reminds Mrs. Hale by contrast of the "pretty clothes" that Minnie wore as a young girl before her marriage.

Unable to sing in the church choir, deprived of her surrogate voice in the bird, denied access to other people, and with no visible beauty in her surroundings, Minnie, almost inevitably one can say, turned in her loneliness to that final resource available to nineteenth- and early-twentieth-century women—quilting. Minnie's quilt blocks are the penultimate trifle in Glaspell's story. The discovery later of the strangled bird and broken bird cage explain the immediate provocation for Minnie's crime. But it is with the discovery of the quilt blocks, to which the women react more strongly than they have to any of the previously introduced "kitchen things," that a pivotal point in the story is reached.

The meaning of quilts in the lives of American women is complex, and Glaspell's story is a valuable contribution to the full account that remains to be written. Quilts were utilitarian in origin, three-layered bed coverings intended to protect against the cold weather. But they became in the course of the nineteenth century probably the major creative outlet for women—one patriarchically tolerated, and even "approved," for their use, but which women were able to transform to their own ends. Through quilting, through their stitches as well as through pattern and color, and through the institutions, such as the "bee," that grew up around it, women who were otherwise without expressive outlet were able to communicate their thoughts and feelings.

In *Trifles* Glaspell included a reference she omitted from "A Jury of Her Peers" but which is worth retrieving. In the play Mrs. Hale laments that, given her husband's parsimony, Minnie could never join the Ladies Aid. The Ladies Aid would have been a female society associated with the local church, in which women would have spent their time sewing, braiding carpets, and quilting, in order to raise money for foreign missionaries, for new flooring or carpets, chairs or curtains for the church or parish house, or to add to the minister's salary. Such societies, as Glenda Riley has observed, provided women with "a relief from the routine and monotony" of farm life. They also provided women with a public role, or place. And through the female friendships they fostered they helped women, as Julie Jeffrey has noted, to develop "feelings of control over their environment," mitigating that sense of powerlessness that domestic isolation could induce.[20]

Denied such associations, Minnie Wright worked on her quilt blocks alone, and it is the effect of that solitude that the women read in her blocks and that so profoundly moves them. It is, specifically, the stitches in Minnie's blocks that speak to them and, particularly, the "queer" stitches in one block, so unlike the "fine, even sewing," "dainty [and] accurate," that they observe in the others. Nineteenth-century women learned in childhood to take stitches so small that in the words of one woman, it "required a microscope to detect them."[21] Mothers were advised to teach their daughters to make small, exact stitches, not only for durability but as a way of instilling habits of patience, neatness, and diligence. But such stitches also became a badge of one's needlework skill, a source of self-esteem and of status, through the recognition and admiration of other women. Minnie's "crazy" or crooked stitches are a clear signal to the two women that something, for her, was very seriously wrong.

Mrs. Hale's reaction is immediate. Tampering with what is in fact evidence—for the badly stitched block is just such a clue as the men are seeking: "Something to show anger—or sudden feeling"—she replaces Minnie's crooked stitches with her own straight ones. The almost automatic act, so protective of Minnie, is both concealing and healing. To "replace bad sewing with good" is Mrs. Hale's symbolic gesture of affiliation with the damaged woman. It is also the story's first intimation of the more radical tampering with the evidence that the two women will later undertake.

In so quickly grasping the significance of Minnie's quilt stitches, Mrs. Hale is performing yet another of those acts of perception, of seeing through a detail or trifle to its larger meaning, on which Glaspell's dramatic effects depend throughout her story. As she holds the badly stitched block in her hand, Mrs. Hale, we are told, "feels queer, as if the distracted thoughts of the woman who had perhaps turned to it to try and quiet herself were communicating themselves to her." Resorting to needlework in order to "quiet oneself," to relieve distress or alleviate loneliness, was openly recognized and even encouraged throughout the nineteenth century, especially in the advice books that proliferated for women. One of the earliest and most popular of these was John Gregory's *A Father's Advice to His Daughters,* published in 1774 in England and widely read both there and in the United States well into the nineteenth century.

Gregory recommended needlework to his female readers "to enable you to fill up, in a tolerably agreeable way, some of the many solitary hours you must necessarily pass at home." By 1831, as advice manuals began to be produced in this country, Lydia Child in *The Mother's Book* urged mothers to teach their daughters needlework, such as knitting, as a way of dealing with the "depression of spirits" they would inevitably experience in later life. "Women," Child wrote, "in all situations in life, have so many lonely hours, that they cannot provide themselves with too many resources." And as late as 1885 popular writer Jane Croly introduced a book of needlework instructions with a parable in which an angel, foreseeing the "abuse" that woman would suffer from men, urged God not to create her. God refused. Out of pity, however, woman was given "two compensating gifts." These were "tears, and the love of needlework." Although one woman who read Croly's book tartly rejoined, in a letter to *The Housekeeper,* a magazine for women, that she would prefer to keep the tears and given men the needlework, for numbers of others needlework served, in Croly's words, as "that solace in sorrow—that helper in misfortune." That it might have so served Minnie Wright, Mrs. Hale can immediately appreciate.[22]

Minnie's stitches speak with equal directness to Mrs. Peters. It is she who first discovers the badly stitched block, and, as she holds it out to Mrs. Hale, we are told that "the women's eyes met—something flashed to life, passed between them." In contrast to the often outspoken Mrs. Hale, Mrs. Peters has been timid, self-effacing, and "indecisive," torn between sympathy for Minnie and resigned submission to the authority of the law, which her husband, the sheriff, represents. She has evaded Mrs. Hale's effort to get her more openly to choose sides. The flash of recognition between the two women, a moment of communication the more intense for being wordless, is, as one critic has said, "the metamorphizing spark of the story."[23] It presages Mrs. Peter's eventual revolt against male authority. That revolt occurs when she snatches the box containing the dead bird—the evidence that could condemn Minnie—in order to conceal it from the men. Her defiant act is, of course, the result of the effect on her of the accumulated weight of meaning of all of the so-called trifles she has perceived and interpreted throughout the story. But it is here, when she reads Minnie's stitches, that she is first released from her hesitancy into what will later become full conspiratorial complicity with Mrs. Hale.

In examining Minnie's quilt blocks, Mrs. Hale observes that she was making them in the "log cabin pattern." The log cabin pattern was one of the most popular in the second half of the nineteenth century, frequently chosen for its capacity to utilize in its construction small scraps of leftover fabric. For Minnie in her poverty it would have been a practical pattern choice. But there accrued to the pattern a rich symbolism that would not have escaped a farm woman like Mrs. Hale and that adds yet another rich layer of meaning to Glaspell's exploration of women's place. The log cabin quilt is constructed of repetitions of a basic block, which is built up of narrow overlapping strips of fabric, all emanating from a central square. That square, traditionally done in red cloth, came to represent the hearth fire within the cabin, with the strips surrounding it becoming the "logs" of which the cabin was built. As a replication of that most emotionally evocative of American dwelling types, the log cabin quilt came to symbolize both the hardships and the heroisms of pioneer life. More specifically, it became a celebration of women's civilizing role in the pioneering process: in the words of one researcher, "women's dogged determination to build a home, to replace a wilderness with a community."[24]

The nineteenth-century ideology of domesticity defined woman's sphere as that of the home, but within that home it gave her, in theory, a queenly role, as guardian and purveyor of the essential moral and cultural values of the society. That role was frequently symbolized, especially in the popular domestic fiction of the nineteenth century, by the hearth fire, over which the woman presided, ministering, in the light of its warm glow, to the physical and emotional needs of her family. Julie Jeffrey has demonstrated the willingness and even determination with which women resumed this domestic role upon their arrival in the trans-Mississippi west after the dislocations induced by the overland journey, their sense of themselves as the culture bearers and civilizers. And in her recent *The Land before Her: Fantasy and Experience of the American Frontiers, 1630–1860* Annette Kolodny shows that on the earlier Mississippi Valley frontier (and in Texas as well) women's dreams were above all domestic: to create a home as a paradise.

That Minnie is making a log cabin quilt—and the women find a roll of red cloth in her sewing basket—is, both in this historical context and in the context of her own life, both poignant and bitterly ironic. The center of her kitchen is not a hearth with an inviting open fire but, instead, that stove with its broken lining, the sight of which, earlier in the story, had "swept [Mrs. Hale] into her own thoughts, thinking of what it would mean, year after year, to have that stove to wrestle with." In Glaspell's story the cult of domesticity has become a trap; Minnie's home has become her prison. Minnie has asked Mrs. Peters to bring her an apron to wear in jail, a request the sheriff's wife at first finds "strange." But when Mrs. Peters decides that wearing the apron will perhaps make Minnie feel "more natural," we can only agree, since in moving from house to jail she has but exchanged one form of imprisonment for another.

In 1917, when Glaspell rewrote and retitled *Trifles,* feminists were engaged in their final years of effort to free women from at least one of the "imprisonments" to which they had been historically subject—the lack of the vote. Her change of title emphasized the story's contemporaneity, by calling attention to its references to the issue of woman's legal place in U.S. society. The denouement depends on that issue. It is immediately after the county attorney, patronizing as always, expresses his confidence that, in carrying things to Minnie in jail, Mrs. Peters will take nothing suspicious because she is "married to the law," that she proceeds to divorce herself from that law by abetting Mrs. Hale in concealing the dead bird. With that act the two women radically subvert the male legal system within which they have no viable place. Throughout much of the nineteenth century married women were defined under the law as "civilly dead," their legal existence subsumed within their husbands, their rights to their own property, wages, and children either nonexistent or severely circumscribed. Nor did they participate in the making and administering of the law. In 1873 Susan B. Anthony had challenged that legal situation, in a defense that was widely reprinted and that would have been available to Glaspell at the time of the final agitation for the vote. Arrested for having herself tried to vote, and judged guilty of having thereby committed a crime, Anthony had argued that the all-male jury that judged her did not constitute, as the Constitution guaranteed to each citizen, a "jury of her peers." So long, she argued, as women lacked the vote and other legal rights, men were not their peers but their superiors.[25] So, in Glaspell's story, Mrs. Hale and Mrs. Peters decide that they, and not the men, are Minnie's true peers. They take the law into their own hands, appoint themselves prosecuting and defense attorneys, judge and jury, and pass their merciful sentence.

In committing her "crime," Mrs. Peters resorts not to any constitutional justification but to a bit of sophistry cunningly based on the trivia that are the heart of Glaspell's story. Why reveal the dead bird to the men, she reasons, when they consider all of women's concerns insignificant? If the men could hear us, she suggests to Mrs. Hale, "getting all stirred up over a little thing like a—dead canary. . . . My, wouldn't they *laugh?*" But it is the women who have the last laugh (in a story in which potential tragedy has been transformed into comedy), and that laugh hinges upon a very "little thing" indeed. Glaspell gives literally the last word to one of the story's seemingly least significant details. As the characters prepare to leave the Wright farm, the county attorney facetiously asks the women whether Minnie was going to "quilt" or "knot" her blocks. In having Mrs. Hale suggest that she was probably going to knot them (that is, join the quilt layers via short lengths of yarn drawn through from the back and tied or knotted at wide intervals across the top surface, rather than stitch through the layers at closer intervals with needle and thread), Glaspell is using a technical term from the world of women's work in a way that provides a final triumphant vindication of her method throughout the story. If, like Mrs. Hale and Mrs. Peters, the reader can by now engage in those acts of perception whereby one sees "into things, [and] through a thing to something else," the humble task of knotting a quilt becomes resonant with meaning. Minnie has knotted a rope around her husband's neck, and Mrs. Hale and Mrs. Peters have "tied the men in knots." All three women have thus said "not," or "no," to male authority, and in so doing they have knotted or bonded themselves together. Knots can entangle and they can unite, and at the end of Glaspell's story both men and women are knotted, in separate and different ways, with the women having discovered through their interpretation of the trifles that constitute Minnie's world their ties to one another. One nineteenth-century woman described quilts as women's "hieroglyphics"—textile documents on which, with needle, thread, and bits of colored cloth, women inscribed a record of their lives.[26] All of the trifles in Glaspell's story together create such a set of hieroglyphics, but it is a language we should by now begin to be able to read.

NOTES

Reprinted from *Women's Studies* 12 (1986): 89–110. © 1986 Gordon and Breach Science Publishers, Inc.

1. Lee R. Edwards and Arlyn Diamond, eds., *American Voices, American Women* (New York: Avon, 1973), 17; Mary Anne Ferguson, *Images of Women in Literature* (New York: Houghton Mifflin, 1973), 390; Annette Kolodny, "A Map for Rereading: Or, Gender and the Interpretation of Literary Texts," *New Literary History,* 11 (1980): 451–67. The title of my article is indebted to James Deetz, *In Small Things Forgotten: The Archaeology of Early American Life* (Garden City, N.Y.: Anchor, 1977). Deetz, as historical archaeologist, demonstrates the value of investigating "forgotten" material objects as a way of understanding past human experience.

2. Jean E. Kennard, "Convention Coverage or How to Read Your Own Life," *New Literary History* (1981): 69–88.

3. Kolodny, "Map," 465, 463.

4. John Mack Faragher, *Women and Men on the Overland Trail* (New Haven: Yale University Press, 1979); Julie Roy Jeffrey, *Frontier Women: The Trans-Mississippi West, 1840–1880* (New York: Hill and Wang, 1979); Norton Juster, *So Sweet to Labor: Rural Women in America, 1865–1895* (New York: Viking Press, 1979); Sandra Myres, *Westering Women and the Frontier Experience, 1800–1915* (Albuquerque: University of New Mexico Press, 1982); Glenda Riley, *Frontierswomen: The Iowa Experience* (Ames: University of Iowa Press, 1981); Christine Stansell, "Women on the Great Plains, 1865–1890," *Women's Studies* 4 (1976): 87–98. For women's autobiographical accounts, see especially Lillian Schlissel, *Women's Diaries of the Westward Journey* (New York: Schocken Books, 1982); Joanna L. Stratton, *Pioneer Women: Voices from the Kansas Frontier* (New York: Simon and Schuster, 1981).

5. The complete text of "A Jury of Her Peers" is reprinted in Edwards and Diamond, *American Voices,* 359–81. Since the story is so short, I have omitted page references to the text in my discussion.

6. Riley, *Frontierswomen,* 27, 186; Christiana Tillson, *A Woman's Story of Pioneer Illinois,* ed. Milo Milton Quaife (Chicago: Lakeside Press, R.R. Donnelley and Sons, 1919); Fredrika Bremer, *The Homes of the New World* (London:

Arthur Hall, Virtue, 1853), 2:251; Mrs. Cecil Hall, *Farm Life in Manitoba* (London: W. H. Allen, 1884), 24. In *The Land before Her: Fantasy and Experience of the American Frontiers, 1630–1860* (Chapel Hill: University of North Carolina Press, 1984) Annette Kolodny argues that women were "more easily and immediately at home on the prairies" than they had been in the forested tracts of the Ohio Valley frontier earlier (106). Her study, however, is of women's experience on the "well-watered, tree lined, and rolling prairies of Wisconsin, Indiana, Illinois, and Texas" (129). Further west, where trees were scarcer, the sense of loneliness was more pronounced.

7. Seth K. Humphrey, *Following the Prairie Frontier* (Minneapolis: University of Minnesota Press, 1931), 131; Mary Ann Ferrin, "An Autobiography and a Reminiscence," *Annals of Iowa* 37, no. 4 (Spring 1964): 244–61; Luna E. Kellie, "Papers" (transcript), Manuscript Collection, Nebraska State Historical Society.

8. Glenda Riley disputes what she sees as an overemphasis by historians on women's loneliness and isolation on the prairie and plains frontiers (*Frontierswomen*, 30, 176), and women's isolation was, of course, relative—worse for those who arrived earliest in sparsely settled regions. But there remains more than enough testimony by pioneer women themselves to establish the historical context for the loneliness emphasized in Glaspell's story.

9. Carl Degler, *At Odds: Women and the Family in America from the Revolution to the Present* (New York: Oxford University Press, 1980), 363; Faragher, *Women and Men*, 61–62; Sarah Brewer-Bonebright, *Reminiscences of Newcastle, Iowa, 1848: A History of the Founding of Webster City, Iowa* (Des Moines: Historical Department of Iowa, 1921), 169–70; Juster, *So Sweet*, 145–47; Jessamyn West, *Hide and Seek: A Continuing Journey* (New York: Harcourt, Brace, Jovanovitch, 1973), 266.

10. "Mrs. Butler's 1853 Diary of Rogue River Valley," *Oregon Historical Quarterly* 41 (1940): 347; Susan Strasser, *Never Done: A History of American Housework* (New York: Pantheon, 1982), 105.

11. Riley, *Frontierswomen*, 45.

12. Riley, *Frontierswomen*, 44; Everett Dick, *The Sod-House Frontier, 1854–1890* (New York: D. Appleton-Century, 1937), 24; Eliza Farnham, *Life in Prairie Land* (New York: Arno Press, 1972), 199; Mary Chaffee Abell, quoted in *Victorian Women: A Documentary Account of Women's Lives in Nineteenth-Century England, France, and the United States*, ed. Erna Olafson Hellerstein, Leslie Parker Hume, and Karen M. Offen (Stanford: Stanford University Press, 1981), 316.

13. Faragher, *Women and Men*, 59–62; Juster, *So Sweet*, 9, 131, 158.

14. Juster, *So Sweet*, 159, 6.

15. Faragher, *Women and Men,* 112; Harriet Connor Brown, *Grandma Brown's Hundred Years, 1827–1927* (Boston: Little, Brown, 1929), 111.

16. Faragher, *Women and Men,* 115; Hamlin Garland, "A Day's Pleasure," *Main-Travelled Roads* (New York: Harper and Brothers, 1956), 168, 167.

17. Jeannie McKnight, "American Dream, Nightmare Underside: Diaries, Letters, and Fiction of Women on the American Frontier," in *Women, Women Writers, and the West,* ed. L. L. Lee and Merrill Lewis (Troy, N.Y.: Whitson Publishing Co., 1980), 27.

18. Sarah Josepha Hale, *Manners: or, Happy Homes and Good Society All the Year Round* (Boston: J. E. Tilton and Co., 1868), 119–20; Juster, *So Sweet,* 171; Abigail McCarthy, *Private Faces, Public Faces* (New York: Doubleday, 1972), 11. Stansell ("Women") also provides documentation for the psychological toll on women of the environment of Nebraska and the Dakotas.

19. Mari Sandoz, "The Vine," *Hostiles and Friendlies: Selected Short Writings* (Lincoln: University of Nebraska Press, 1959); *Old Jules* (New York: Hastings House, 1935), 83; Mrs. Orval Lookhart, "Letter," *Nebraska Farmer,* April 26, 1957, Manuscript Collection, Nebraska State Historical Society.

20. Riley, *American Voices,* 173; Jeffrey, *Frontier Women,* 86.

21. Clarissa Packard [Caroline Gilman], *Recollections of a Housekeeper* (New York: Harper and Brothers, 1834), 11.

22. John Gregory, *A Father's Advice to his Daughters,* as quoted in Jenni Calder, *Women and Marriage in Victorian Fiction* (New York: Oxford University Press, 1976), 20; Lydia Child, *The Mother's Book* (New York: Arno Press, 1972), 62; Mrs. [Jane] Croly [Jennie June], *Needle Work: A Manual of Stitches and Studies in Embroidery and Drawn Work* (New York: A. L. Burt, 1885), "Introduction," n.p.; Mrs. M. P. A. Crozier, "Household Decoration," *Housekeeper,* May 1876, 79.

23. Kathy Newman, "Susan Glaspell and 'Trifles': 'Nothing Here But Kitchen Things,' " *Trivia: A Journal of Ideas* (Fall 1983): 93.

24. Suellen Jackson-Meyer, "The Great American Quilt Classics: Log Cabin," *Quilters' Newsletter,* October 1979, 13.

25. Anthony's defense is reprinted in Miriam Schneir, ed., *Feminism: The Essential Historical Writings* (New York: Vintage Books, 1972), 134–36.

26. See also Susan Gubar and Anne Hedin, "A Jury of Her Peers: Teaching and Learning in the Indiana Women's Prison," *College English* 43, no. 8 (December 1981): 779–89, for a discussion of the pun in *knot;* Harriet Farley and Rebecca C. Thompson, "The Patchwork Quilt," *Lowell Offering* 5 (1845), as reprinted in Benita Eisler, ed., *The Lowell Offering: Writings by New England Mill Women, 1840–1845* (New York: Harper and Row, 1977), 150.

Murder and Marriage:
Another Look at *Trifles*

Karen Alkalay-Gut

The objective plot of Glaspell's most successful play, *Trifles,* is very much at odds with the triviality of the title.[1] The story is of the brutal murder by a wife of her husband, the evidence for which is covered up by other women almost unacquainted with the perpetrator. When even a sheriff's wife is willing to become an accessory after the fact to a murder because she seems to agree to its inevitability, it is necessary to ask some basic questions: What is it that the women perceive to have in common that necessitates this bond, and what do audiences generations after have in common with these women that this decision is accepted as inescapable?

It is certainly not the fidelity to truth that encourages identification. Some of the elements of the play were drawn from contemporary reality, but the others that were altered were basic. When Susan Glaspell covered the case of Margaret Hossack, who was charged with killing her husband with an ax while he was asleep in December, 1900, she discovered the inconsistency of the legal system that excluded women from judicial decisions but judged them nevertheless. It was not only Glaspell who found herself drawn to this case: the trial drew a crowd of up to two thousand people. But despite the many parallels in the case, including the "sympathetic wife of Sheriff Hodson," who sat with Margaret Hossack throughout the trial, in reality Hossack was convicted in her first trial.

Glaspell's need to change the ending of the trial, to empower women to rectify an apparently unjust situation, is both a criticism of the legal system and an indictment of the social and romantic conventions of society. The danger to women is not only in the legal system but also for those who do not run afoul of the law, in the very structure of marriage.

71

Women, in the context of *Trifles* and even more in the story "Jury of Her Peers," are trapped by a social system that may lead them into crime and punish them when they are forced to commit it. It is this situation of the double bind with which the women of the play identify and which readers and audiences continue to explore. "We all go through the same things— it's all just a different kind of the same thing" (*Trifles* 44), Mrs. Hale tells Mrs. Peters in the play and adds in the story: "If it weren't—why do you and I *understand?* Why do we *know*—what we know this minute?" ("Jury" 260)

The typical romantic background for the brutal murder is not explained onstage, but one need only examine the name of the protagonist, Minnie Foster, to understand its integrality with what goes on in the dreary farmhouse. The name Minnie is derived from the German word for *love;* this potential for love is nurtured and cherished in Minnie's maiden name, Foster; when she discovers her ideal man, Mr. Wright (Right), it is transferred to her husband. Mrs. Wright is then an emblematic romantic heroine of standard tales for women, whose potential is "fulfilled" through the right man, when she becomes acceptable as "Mrs. Right." Mrs. Hale and Mrs. Peters, the other women in the play, have also followed this pattern, fulfilling themselves as "wives" of men—and it is only in this capacity, as wives of the witness and of the sheriff, that they are invited to be present at the investigation at all.

As the emblematic woman, Mrs. Wright's own life becomes, of necessity, trivial. Her absence throughout the play emphasizes this tangentiality to existence. But it is also apparent in the position of the other women, who have, as Christine Dymkowski has pointed out, been confined to the least significant room of the house, the kitchen, for the duration of the investigation. And even that kitchen is available to the women only when it is vacated by the men. When the women remain by the door until the men leave, "the separateness of the female and male worlds is . . . immediately established visually and then reinforced by the dialogue" (Dymkowski 92).

For the significant world is elsewhere: the men search for clues in the barn, in the bedroom, in higher spheres—"upstairs"—and in the world outside the farmhouse, and they allow the women in the kitchen no relevance. The women are present only to collect Minnie Wright's trivial and unaccountably needed paraphernalia for her stay in jail. The apron that Mrs. Wright requests—irrelevant to her prison activities yet essential to her concept of self as practical and protected servant—would only be a further source of derision to the men, who are far too ready to laugh at any woman's request, even those that might appear to make sense. Not only Mrs. Wright's concern for the jars of fruit that might freeze in the unheated kitchen but also Mrs. Hale's apprehension about leaving her work undone and her curiosity about Mrs. Wright's sewing are at best causes for impatience on the part of the men.

And yet, of course, it is precisely their unwillingness to perceive the potential relevance of the kitchen, the world and pattern of the women, that excludes the men from understanding what has happened: they fail to comprehend the motivations for the events, and the method of uncovering the underlying pattern eludes them. The little squares of material being formed into a quilt that the women decide to bring to Mrs. Wright to "occupy her time" is ridiculed by the men but provides an unrecognized key to this male exclusion because this quilting method parallels the only way clues could form the truth: the joining together of scraps of details allow the women to comprehend the situation of Minnie Foster and her development from housewife to criminal. The "log cabin" patchwork the women discover in Minnie Foster's sewing basket is made exactly in this fashion: rectangular strips are sewn around the original square or rectangle, followed by a series of longer scraps, which are measured to the increasing size of the patch. Each patch has an individual entity, but its beauty (and meaning) is in relationship to the other patches formed with similar painstaking consideration. The colors are coordinated and contrasted by balance and relationship, but the general pattern is one that emerges with the quilt.

The significant world for the men is elsewhere, but for the women it is in the ordering of the scraps of information around the central "square" of marriage and the total dependence of the wife upon her husband for all physical, emotional, and spiritual fulfillment as well as validation as a human being. The shabbiness of the clothes that Mrs. Wright requests for her stay in jail, the broken rocker and the bad stove in the kitchen indicate John Wright's "stinginess," his unwillingness to provide basic warmth and shelter for his wife. Wright's objection to a telephone, Mr. Hale's initial reason for his visit and the reason for his discovery of the crime, are unquestionably further deterrences on the part of the husband to his wife's communication with the world and validation as an individual.

It is because she realizes that these details don't count to the men that her communication with the outside world will be deemed irrelevant, that Minnie Foster can retell her story with many particulars, the significance of which she can be certain will escape her interrogators. When asked about her husband's murder she explains, "He died of a rope round his neck." In retrospect it becomes clear that her explanation reflects her vision of the murder as a symbolic retribution, a revenge execution for the strangling of her canary (in itself a symbolic act).

Yet this is not all that Minnie explains in these lines. The physical complexity of this method of murder is apparent to Mrs. Peters, the sheriff's wife, who in the play puzzles, "They say it was such a—funny way to kill a man, rigging it all up like that" (*Trifles* 39), leaving the reader to interpret the action. For to Minnie this is an administered death and not a murder, and the husband is not a "victim" but, instead, dies as one would die of a long chronic illness, "of a rope around his neck." Mr. Hale, the one man who is not totally alienated from the world of women, seems momentarily to grasp the significance. "It looked . . . ," begins Mr. Hale, in both the story and the play, but is overcome by emotion and cannot continue, because this particular method of murder not only re-calls the woman next to him in bed to whom he too is bound but also the situation of marriage in general, in which the couple are bound together; and marriage for the husband is popularly referred to as a noose. Mrs. Wright's further description elaborates on this relationship: "Weren't you sleepin' in the bed with him?" Mrs. Hale's son, the only unmarried character, asks her. " 'Yes,' says she, 'but I was on the inside.' " Spatially, the couple slept in the same bed and should have defended each other against the world outside, but because the woman was "on the inside," in the protected and passive position, she claims to have been rendered helpless and even unconscious. Since the primary differences between men and women are described in spatial terms like this throughout the play as well as the story, with the "significant" events repeatedly placed on the outside and the "trivial" on the inside,[2] this detail is crucial and foreshadows the affected innocence of the wives at the end.

"If I am given no power," Minnie Foster seems to say, "then how can I claim to have any?" How can she claim to have murdered if she has always been on the "inside," where important things don't happen, and, if she has always been thought to know only trivia, why should she now claim to have known more? The women accept this premise and base their final decision on the same premises. Relegated to the kitchen, they do not point out that it is, ultimately, the most significant room in the house. Reduced to poking through a sewing kit while the men look for important clues, they do not reveal that in this inner sanctum is the secret that could validate the men's case.

This behavior alone does not simply illustrate the generally accepted feminist message that women must stick together. As Karen Stein argues: "The women here realize, through their involvement in the murder investigation, that only by joining together can they, isolated and insignificant in their society, obtain for themselves and extend to others the support and sympathy that will help them endure the loneliness and unceasing labor required of them."[3] Underlying Stein's attitude is the assumption that the women's lives are individually trivial and that their only strength and/or success can come from banding together. Triviality can be overcome by the unification of large numbers, by sewing together the scraps into a quilt.

There are two important problems with this assertion. First, it is only in the most limited sense that the women's lives can be seen to be occupied with trivia. And second, what brings the women together, what forces them to endanger themselves for a criminal, is the fact that they do not only sympathize but also *identify* with the murderess.

Trivia, the concerns of life that are weighed as insignificant when compared to more central and weighty interests, begin the story, although not the play. Mrs. Hale is compelled to leave her own kitchen, where she has been engaged in sifting flour, in order to participate in a murder investigation. But she finds the decision difficult to make: "It was no ordinary thing that called her away—it was probably farther from ordinary than anything that had ever happened in Dickson County. But what her eye took in was that her kitchen was in no shape for leaving: her bread all ready for mixing, half the flour sifted and half unsifted" ("Jury" 256). The kitchen is a world of simple imperatives—cleanliness, order, productivity, economy, and fruitfulness. Mrs. Hale's dilemma in leaving her kitchen might suggest her lack of hierarchy in values, her "typically feminine" concern for insignificant details, but although she keeps the investigators waiting out in the sleigh while she contemplates this scene, it is this contemplation that allows her later to comprehend the urgency of Minnie Foster's actions, for Mrs. Hale, like Mrs. Wright, was impelled by a "chill wind" to abandon the making of bread.

The detail assumes centrality, then, when the "important" clues fade, lead in the wrong direction, and/or disappear. This is something Mrs. Hale learns when the county attorney criticizes the dirty towel in the Wright kitchen. "Not much of a housekeeper, would you say Ladies?" he asks rhetorically, both in play and story, and Mrs. Hale feels moved to defend Mrs. Wright on the basis of her sympathy with the difficult life of farm wives, while accepting his conclusion from the evidence. Later, when her evaluations have assumed different proportions, she understands that the attorney's deduction was based upon the necessity to integrate the perceived details with the assumption of Minnie's guilt and her accompanying inevitable character flaws as a woman.[4] At that point she can release her observation from his psychological imperatives and realize that the towel is dirty because the deputy wiped his hands on it when he made the fire.

For the men details, then, are not trivial but become integrated into the male preexisting vision. The trivial minutiae in themselves cannot be examined because they are not conceived of as separate from a larger fabric, a more general theory, clues to support a thesis. It is this limitation that prevents the men from understanding the murder case, and it this same limitation that prevents them from comprehending their wives' situation, which in turn forces the wives to employ passivity and subterfuge. Mr. Hale, increasingly influenced by the demeaning attitude of the other men toward the women, asks "Would the women know a clue if they did come on it?" unaware that the approach of the women has been far more productive and also of the fact that his attitude has made it impossible for his wife to share vital information with him. His silence for the rest of the play is an indication of his inaccessibility to the women.[5]

The initial discriminatory division between the men and women of the play becomes one of choice. Women band together to protect one another from the evaluations of men because the men are simply not capable of understanding their situation, the same situation that led to the murder in the first place; and it is a political as well as a social condition.

The political nature of the situation is made clear by the title of the story, "Jury of Her Peers." Elizabeth Cady Stanton, in her address to the Legislature of the State of New York on February 14, 1854, used the term first:

> The most sacred of all rights, trial by a jury of our own peers. . . . [S]hall an erring woman be dragged before a bar of grim-visaged judges, lawyers, and jurors, there to be grossly questioned in public on subjects which most women scarce breathe in secret to one another? Shall the most sacred relations of life be called up and rudely scanned by men who, by their own admission, are so coarse that women could not meet them even at the polls without contamination? [And] yet shall she find there no woman's face or voice to pity and defend? Shall the frenzied mother, who to save herself and child from exposure and disgrace, ended the life that had but just begun, be dragged before such a tribunal to answer for her crime? How can man enter into the feelings of that mother?[6]

When *Trifles* and "Jury of Her Peers" were written, women in the state of Iowa did not have the right of which Stanton spoke. Women served in juries only in Utah, Washington, Kansas, and California (Kerber 16). Suffrage, of course, was in the future. This disenfranchisement makes inevitable a different perspective on justice and the concept of primary responsibility to the law. "The law is the law," Mrs. Peters first asserts, in the story version but not in *Trifles*, horrified by her gradual revelation that there may be something other than the law, and Mrs. Hale soon adds: "The law is the law—and a bad stove is a bad stove." The law just does not apply here—because women have nothing to say in matters that concern women and because the scale of values is simply different for men and women. Carol Gilligan has pointed out that this distinction is seen as a flaw in women's judgment. Freud, writing at the same time as Glaspell, noted that "for women the level of what is ethically normal is different from what it is in men . . . [and] concluded that women 'show less sense of justice than men, that they are less ready to submit to the great exigencies of life, that they are more often influenced in their judgments by feelings of affection or hostility' " (Gilligan 7).

My point here is that the problem is far more complex than that of loyalty to women rather than to men. Legally, the women who protect Minnie Wright are criminals, accessories after the fact, guilty of concealing evidence. If the legal system is right (Wright) then their crimes are plainly wrong, their sympathies allowing them (as often is the case with women in stereotypical situations, according to Freud and others) to ignore the higher significance of their actions as they allow their emotions to take over. The gradual process in which this incipient "criminality" develops could help to prove this argument. For as Weisbrod points out, the women progress in their deception from concealment to a lie. Beginning with the fruit that has been spoiled because the fire in the faulty stove went out (another obvious symbol of the thwarted fruition of Mrs. Wright's life due to an absence of warmth), when Mrs. Hale says: "If I was you I wouldn't *tell* her her fruit was gone! Tell her it ain't. . . . Here—take this [the one surviving jar] to prove it to her!" (*Trifles* 44), the progression is from concealment to a lie to, finally, a truth put forward to prove a lie, so that the woman in jail will not be further injured by the knowledge that her fruit has been ruined. "This scene anticipates the women's concealing the evidence" (Weisbrod 78 n. 67). Indeed, from lying about the fruit they move to a lie about the murder.

It is, however, only when they realize that the men are not capable of understanding the evidence before them, when they realize that there is no chance for a fair trial, that they resort to these deceptions. These are not deceptions of weakness or of emotions and sisterhood overriding logic and morality. They are calculated deceits that are only perpetrated upon those who have proven themselves blind to the clues, insensitive to the trivia that delineate the lives of all the women in the play, including Minnie Foster. For not only do all women share the loneliness of housewifery, each woman alone in her own house, not only do the women feel the potential for violence on the part of the men in their lives (as does Mrs. Peters, remembering her kitten playfully slaughtered like Mrs. Wright's canary), but they all suffer from the unwillingness or inability of the men to understand their situation of helpless isolation, their constrained passivity, their overwhelming enforced dependence. Mrs. Peters and Mrs. Hale know that, like Mrs. Wright, their identities, their lives, and their futures have been determined totally by the men they have married. Mrs. Hale's fortune is better than the rest, perhaps, and Mrs. Peters has been enlisted, by marriage, into a stable system of justice with which she need not argue. But had the situation been different, either of these women might have been in Mrs. Wright's bed and compelled to murder the man whose total control over her was, in this case, totally negative. "If they hadn't held me back," says Mrs. Peters, remembering her slaughtered kitten, "I would have—(*Catches herself, looks upstairs where steps are heard, falter weakly*)—hurt him" (*Trifles* 44). In this situation, in which the individual is not free to make decisions, to determine the consequences of actions, the legal concept of justice is simply not relevant. What would be murder to a free agent is here tyrannicide and/or justified revolution. The emotional responsibility of Mr. Wright to provide for his wife's needs was ignored by him and would be ignored by any all-male jury.

And yet the concluding scene is one of total feminine community, symbolized by the work of quilting. Not only is quilting a simple communal task in which the trivial becomes integrated vitally into a larger framework, but it also makes use of hidden patterns and significances. To quilt a blanket is to sew the joined patches to the lining all the way around the borders of the patch. It is to make a thin, flat quilt, in which all the thicknesses are equal. To knot a quilt is to sew the fabric together, generally through a thicker lining, only at the corners of each patch. Quilting equalizes the thickness of the blanket; knotting emphasizes the distinctions. When the women inform the men at the conclusion that Minnie was planning to knot the quilt, although they had not discussed this matter between them, they determine to differentiate between the legal definition of the crime, in which all considerations external to the act itself are meaningless and equal, and their moral definition of the crime, in which nothing is even and flat. Distinctions must be made, with the delicacy of a needle, and they have made them.

Patchworking is conceived as a collective activity, for, although it is the individual woman who determines the pattern, collects and cuts the scraps, and pieces them together, quilting work on an entire blanket is too arduous for a single person. Minnie's patchwork would have been knotted and not quilted because knotting is easier and can be worked alone. And the guilty-hearted Mrs. Hale knows this.

With her hand against the pocket of her coat, where the bird is hidden, Mrs. Hale emphasizes the additional meanings of the phrase "knot it"—meanings she is certain her investigators will overlook, as they have overlooked every other significant fact. "Knot it" conveys the sense of knotting the rope around the husband's neck: the women disclose the murderess. But they will "knot" tell. Mrs. Hale speaks a language understood now by Mrs. Peters but totally incomprehensible to those who cannot perceive the significance of trifles.

If the women "trifle" with the evidence, it is with the full recognition that they are meting out a different form of justice, the justice of women, the justice of those whose case could not be understood by anyone unwilling to proceed from details to an unprejudiced understanding of truth.

NOTES

1. I am particularly grateful to Aviam Soifer, Dean, Boston College Law School, who first helped me to see the legal issues of this play.

2. For an elaboration of this concept, see my article: "Jury of Her Peers: The Importance of *Trifles*," *Studies in Short Fiction* (Winter 1984): 1–9.

3. Karen Stein, "The Women's World of Glaspell's *Trifles*," *Women in American Theatre,* ed. Helen Krich Chinoy and Linda Walsh Jenkins (New York: Crown, 1981), 251–54.

4. The prevalent belief about women who murder at the time of this play seems to have been that only a depraved woman could murder. If a depraved person sins against society somehow, the fault lies in his or her mind, but, when a "normal" socialized person commits a murder, there is an implied criticism of society. Therefore it is necessary for the county attorney to understand Minnie as deviant as a housewife. This, of course, explains the general masculine criticism of Mrs. Wright's housekeeping as well as the attempts to perceive Mrs. Wright as out of her mind.

5. Speaking as a sign of empowerment has been noted and discussed by Marijane Camilleri, "Lessons in Law from Literature: A Look at the Movement and a Peer in Her Jury," *Catholic University Law Review* 39 (1990): 588. The

effect on the stage is the women's silence in the presence of the men, and, of course, the overwhelming pervasive silence of Minnie Wright.

6. I am indebted to note 46 in the article by Carol Weisbrod, "Images of the Woman Juror," *Harvard Women's Law Journal* 9 (1986): 59–82, for pointing out this passage. Elizabeth Cady Stanton's address has been reprinted in *History of Woman Suffrage, 1848–1861,* ed. E. C. Stanton, S. B. Anthony, and M. J. Gage, 2d ed., (New York: Arno Press, 1969): 595–98. Lucy Stone also used this phrase in an even more relevant context, pleading for a fair trial for Lizzie Borden ("A Flaw in the Jury System," *Women's Journal* [June 17, 1893]: 188).

WORKS CITED

Camilleri, Marijane. "Lessons in Law from Literature: A Look at the Movement and a Peer in Her Jury." *Catholic University Law Review* 39 (1990): 557–94.

Des Moines *Daily News.* 14 Jan. 1901.

Dymkowski, Christine. "On the Edge: The Plays of Susan Glaspell." *Modern Drama* 31 (March 1988): 91–105.

Gilligan, Carol. *In a Different Voice.* Cambridge: Harvard University Press, 1982.

Glaspell, Susan. *Trifles,* in *Plays by Susan Glaspell,* ed. C. W. E. Bigsby and Christine Dymkowski. Cambridge: Cambridge University Press, 1988.

Kerber, Linda. "The Case of the Broken Baseball Bat: Women and the Obligation of Jury Service. *Hoyt v. Florida* 368 U.S. 57 (1961)." Ms.

Stein, Karen. "The Women's World of Glaspell's *Trifles*." *Women in American Theatre,* ed. Helen Krich Chinoy and Linda Walsh Jenkins. 251–54. New York: Crown, 1981.

Weisbrod, Carol. "Images of the Woman Juror." *Harvard Women's Law Journal* (Spring 1986) 59–82.

Part 2
Toward *The Verge*

"The Haunting Beauty from the Life We've Left": A Contextual Reading of *Trifles* and *The Verge*

Liza Maeve Nelligan

In 1921, in response to a reporter's question, Susan Glaspell answered, "Of course I am interested in all progressive movements, whether feminist, social, or economic, but I can take no active part other than through my writing."[1] Indeed, she could hardly help being interested in the progressive movements of the early twentieth century, particularly the feminist movement. Susan Glaspell was not only historically situated in a major transformative moment for American women—politically, economically, and, most interesting to her, psychologically—but she was also literally surrounded by the feminist intelligentsia of her day. From the time Glaspell moved to Greenwich Village in 1913 until her departure for Greece in 1922 with her husband, George Cram Cook,[2] Glaspell was immersed in a radical social milieu that included such notable feminist thinkers and activists as Charlotte Perkins Gilman, Crystal Eastman, Havelock Ellis, Floyd Dell, Henrietta Rodman, and Elsie Clews Parson.[3] It should not then be surprising that her plays reflected the revolutionary qualities of feminist thought by privileging female experience in the dramatic context. As Linda Ben-Zvi writes:

> Glaspell saw that if the world portrayed is the world of women—if the locus of perception is female—then her plays would have to strive for a shape which reinforces this new vantage point and a language which articulates it.[4]

What makes Glaspell's plays so fascinating, however, is that the world of women she portrays is by no means a monolithic one; rather, it shifts

85

and transforms with the same speed that the world she herself inhabited did.

As the nineteenth century drew to a close, the separate male and female spheres that had shaped and defined both genders were beginning to dissolve, and by the late 1910s virtually every aspect of "womanhood" was under scrutiny. The previously fixed concepts of female sexuality, maternal responsibility, and sex-determined intellectual ability aroused considerable debate and decisively challenged nineteenth-century definitions of woman's natural place.[5] Perhaps most important, women were questioning the essentialist notion that "woman" was a unified subject with biologically determined characteristics. Many feminists turned to the Enlightenment ideals of individualism, long considered the province of men, to shape their politics, their activities, and their concepts of self.[6] In 1914 Henrietta Rodman, a colleague of Glaspell's and the founder of the Feminist Alliance, rejected the "special qualities" of women, such as moral purity, and argued instead for "the removal of all social, political, economic, and other discriminations which are based upon sex, and the award of all rights and duties in all fields on the basis of individual capacity alone."[7]

Glaspell's work, particularly the drama she produced for the Provincetown Players between 1916 and 1922, provocatively reproduce the nuances, contradictions, possibilities, and dangers of the feminist philosophies of this period. Thus, it might be worthwhile to examine her plays through the lenses of Glaspell's own historical context to illuminate further what Glaspell's drama meant to the audiences of her time and to complicate, and cross-pollinate, our own readings of her work.

The two plays that best reflect the dramatic developments in American feminist thought early in the century are *Trifles* and *The Verge*. The remarkable contrast between the female characters of these two plays, and the issues that define them, provide compelling insights into the political and psychological transformations that occurred in the feminist imagination of the 1910s and 1920s. While *Trifles* has as its premise the existence of a unified female morality and world, *The Verge* operates under an increasing emphasis on an individuality that rejects old notions of "femininity" and struggles to form a new definition of womanhood.

Glaspell's second play, *Trifles,* was produced in 1916. It has received more attention from contemporary feminist critics than any of her other plays, probably because it highlights the stark contrast between female and male ways of knowing the world—a subject of increasing interest to feminist scholars of the late twentieth century.[8] Several critics have argued that the play anticipates feminist thought of the 1970s and 1980s and have read the play from the standpoint of the contemporary women's movement. As one critic notes, "Feminist critics have praised Glaspell's recognition of female bonding":

> This play subtly explores such human experiences as disintegration of a marriage, bitter loss of innocence, psychological and physical spouse abuse, assault, breakdown of human communication, stress born of frustration and few alternatives, and bonding of individuals with shared experiences.[9]

While it is certainly true that *Trifles* does explore several of these themes, it is also true that Glaspell did not discover female bonding but was, in fact, drawing from a long tradition of powerful female-centered networks that are almost inconceivable to women of the late twentieth century.

Trifles neatly encapsulates what historians have named the "cult of domesticity" of the nineteenth century. Mary Beth Norton defines this concept as an ideology that insisted that "woman's proper sphere was the home":

> Females were uniquely suited to the creation of a nurturing home environment . . . women were inherently more pious, gentle, instinctive and submissive than men; therefore, they had no place in the public world outside the home.[10]

In other words, the essential nature of woman was virtually uncontested and fixed. This uncompromising division between the male public sphere and the female private sphere has generated a wide range of interpretations from various feminist scholars. One specific point of contention has been whether or not this exclusive female sphere was inherently oppressive to women. In her essay "The Cult of True Womanhood" Barbara Welter maintains that the four cardinal virtues of the "true woman"—

piety, purity, submission, and domesticity—effectively barred women from intellectual fulfillment by defining them solely in terms of the repressive roles of mother and wife. On the other hand, Carroll Smith-Rosenberg argues that the confinement of women to the private sphere led to complex female-centered networks that conferred a status and power on women unavailable to them in the public world of men.[11] *Trifles* nicely mirrors these diverse perspectives. Clearly, Glaspell intended to show that women in the domestic sphere were vulnerable to the brutality of men like John Wright, but she also dramatizes the powerful sense of solidarity women shared and assumes that this solidarity was somehow responsible for a superior female morality.

The action of *Trifles* takes place entirely in the kitchen of Minnie Foster Wright, who is being held for the murder of her husband. The play opens as three men enter the kitchen: Lewis Hale, the neighbor who discovered the crime, Henry Peters, the local sheriff, and George Henderson, the county attorney. The men are followed by two women, Mrs. Peters and Mrs. Hale, who have come to collect the jailed Minnie Wright's belongings. As the men futilely hunt the Wright house for clues that point to a motive, trying, as Mrs. Hale says, to get Minnie Wright's "own house to turn against her,"[12] the women examine the signs of the kitchen; half-done chores, errant stitches in a quilt, a broken bird cage, and, finally, a dead canary with a broken neck. Gradually, they uncover the evidence that suggests Minnie Wright's motive for killing her husband. The crucial action of the play, however, is in their joint decision to suppress, and partially destroy, the evidence they have pieced together and effectively to acquit Minnie Wright based on their own "female" understanding of justice.

From the beginning of the play Glaspell emphasizes the separate spheres of men and women. As the men briefly review the kitchen before deciding that there's "nothing here but kitchen things," their critical comments serve to remind the two women (and the audience) that the female sphere is insignificant and composed primarily of "trifles." But they also force the women to defend the values of the female world and to "move closer together." As the action of the play unfolds, we watch Mrs. Hale and Mrs. Peters expertly read the text of Minnie Wright's life and begin to piece together the clues revealing the terrible isolation and loneliness forced upon her by a cruel and malicious husband. The fact that these two women are so easily able to interpret the universe of Minnie Wright suggests that the female world described by Smith-Rosenberg is still intact; however, it is also losing its centrality in women's lives. Deeply felt same-sex relationships are the legacy of the women in *Trifles*, but not their reality. Mrs. Hale, Minnie's childhood friend, expresses extreme regret for her neighbor's isolation, crying out at one point: "Oh, I *wish* I'd come over here once in a while! That was a crime! That was a crime! Who's going to punish that?"

Several critics have agreed with Mrs. Hale and have argued that, along with Mrs. Peters, she is at least partly to blame for Minnie Wright's alienation. C. W. E. Bigsby argues that "the fact is that the women, too, have failed one another. They, too, have allowed trifles to come between them and their human responsibilities."[13] From a historical perspective, however, what came between Minnie Wright and the other women of the community can hardly be described as trifles. The disintegration of female relationships at the end of the nineteenth century occurred under the weight of enormous social change, including the increasing emphasis on "appropriate" heterosexual networks. As Elaine Showalter writes, "The traditional notion of sisterhood broke down . . . [because] women in the twentieth century learned that they were supposed to have emotional attachments to men."[14] In the last thirty years feminists have again begun to value a sense of sisterhood among women, but Glaspell's understanding of such allegiances in *Trifles* is less prophetic and more a remembrance of things past.

As Mrs. Hale and Mrs. Peters understand the implications of the evidence they have found, they begin a quiet struggle to decide what to do with it. Mrs. Peters, who is "married to the law," reaches her decision to acquit Minnie Wright through a series of insights into the parallels between her own life and Minnie Wright's, including the loss of a child. Here *Trifles* implicitly invokes maternity as a unifying theme among women, drawing from the suffrage movement's emphasis on the strong link between maternal sensibilities and women's inherent moral superiority. In the 1910s the moderate voices of the suffrage movement, including those of Carrie Chapman Catt and Jane Addams, argued that woman's special moral talents had the potential for exerting a purifying influence on the corrupt public sphere. This argument was related to woman's supposed maternal endowment, in addition to her sexual purity, or passionlessness. Glaspell certainly suggests that women are better prepared to make moral judgments; *Trifles* explicitly juxtaposes a male sense of justice with a female one, and the female view prevails.

Glaspell's depiction of the female sphere in this play is, then, relatively conservative. As Judith Stephens argues: *Trifles* "perpetuates the romantic notion that each woman can secretly and individually subvert the larger system, if she so desires. . . . *Trifles* both challenged and reinforced the dominant gender ideology of this period."[15] While this is an accurate criticism of the play, it is also true that Glaspell was celebrating the highly synthesized networks that the female sphere made possible, and in Carroll Smith-Rosenberg's words, demonstrated that "women's sphere had an essential integrity and dignity that grew out of women's shared experience and mutual affection."[16] This sphere was not long for the world, however, and Glaspell would soon explore what the world would look like without it.

The Verge was produced in 1921, less than five years after *Trifles,* yet the intervening years had seen monumental historical events that had profound impacts on the expression and interpretation of feminism in the early 1920s: World War I, the passage of the Nineteenth Amendment, the Bolshevik revolution in Russia, and the corresponding backlash (the "Red Scare") in the United States all contributed to feminism's entrance into a period of metamorphosis with a promise of boundless possibility for change.[17] As the historian Nancy Cott explains, feminists were

> conceding the revolutionary open-endedness and sometime internal contradictions of their project and making their formlessness, that lack of certain boundaries, that potential to encompass opposites, into virtues.[18]

Glaspell captures this mood of experimentation and "lack of certain boundaries" in the feminist imagination by creating a play that not only tests the boundaries of dramatic conventions but also centers on a feminist hero whose life's purpose is to create "something that has never been before"—an ambition not unlike feminism itself, which was then, as it is today, a movement dedicated to reconstituting the social order so that female human beings can be something that has never been before: unconditionally free to choose life's patterns. The question, though, and the one that *The Verge* is interested in asking is: What should the new social order look like?

The suffrage victory in 1920 was philosophically liberating to those feminists who had been struggling to articulate an analysis of women's oppression that was far more systematic than their exclusion from the voting booth. With the vote finally won feminists were in a position to formulate comprehensive strategies addressing the economic, political, and psychological boundaries that impeded women's ability to move freely within the social system. For many feminists this freedom could only be realized if women learned to see themselves not as women but, instead, as autonomous individuals with unique attributes and desires.

The organization that best characterized the feminism of this period was Heterodoxy. Based in Greenwich Village, the women's collective, whose membership is a Who's Who directory of the major feminist thinkers of the early twentieth century, reveled in unorthodox philosophies.[19] One Heterodoxy member described her friends as "the most unruly and individualistic females you ever fell upon."[20] Heterodoxy members understood individual self-development and "psychic freedom" as central premises in feminism, ideas that strongly parallel one of the thematic principles of *The Verge*. In fact, Glaspell's participation in Heterodoxy and the wide-ranging friendships she must have found there probably inspired her to write the play and also provided her with the audience she most wanted to reach.[21]

The Verge anticipates a feminist audience that fully expects to find a character with whom they can sympathize by giving them Claire Archer, a heroine who privileges her right to self-development over maternal and wifely devotion, articulately demands satisfying and egalitarian relationships with men, and is committed to exposing and destroying the conventional social boundaries that crush her individuality. At the same time, Glaspell gives them an unquestionably disturbing character: a mad, inchoate, unsympathetic woman who rejects her daughter, abuses her sister, betrays her husband, and murders one of her lovers because he wants to "save" her from madness. This, too, is Claire Archer.

Through this character Glaspell asks uncomfortable questions about the consequences of a radical individualism that rejects any quality tradition- ally associated with the female sphere. Like Claire, Glaspell performs experiments, although Glaspell's subject is an audience that she intends to "shock to aliveness."

Claire Archer, the central figure of *The Verge,* is, on the surface at least, as radical a departure from the female characters of *Trifles* as one can imagine. She is an upper-class intellectual who has turned to botani- cal experimentation as a way to reject her inherited status as the "flower of those gentlemen of culture" who "made the laws that made New England." Claire attempts to breed plants that resist old forms and pat- terns of existence and can make the leap into a radically new otherness. Her appetite for smashing old forms is not limited, however, to her work in her greenhouse. Claire's drive to escape the "forms moulded [*sic*] for us" becomes one of uncompromising expansion until there is virtually no possibility for human relationship, and here Glaspell perceptively engages one of the central feminist paradoxes of the early twentieth century: how to achieve a healthy sense of individualism without losing some of the more valuable qualities of "womanhood," particularly the sense of com- munity that had informed *Trifles.*

The character of Claire Archer can be read as an extreme composite of the Heterodoxy membership. As Elizabeth Gurley Flynn described her own membership: "It has been a glimpse of the women of the future, big spirited, intellectually alert, devoid of the old 'femininity,' "[22] a descrip- tion that might easily have been written about Claire by a sympathetic drama critic. In addition, the conflicts that define Claire's character bear a striking resemblance to those found in the writings of many Hetero- doxy members. For instance, in 1920 Crystal Eastman, a longtime femi- nist and friend of Glaspell's, wrote an essay on women's freedom for the Village publication *The Liberator* and wondered

> how to arrange the world so that women can be human beings, with a chance to exercise their infinitely varied gifts in infinitely varied ways . . . women will never be great until they achieve a certain emo- tional freedom, a strong, healthy egotism, and some un-personal sources of joy—that is, in this inner sense.[23]

Another Heterodoxy member, Inez Haynes Irwin, publishing eight years earlier, wrote:

> It seems to me that . . . I hang in a void midway between two spheres—the man's sphere and the woman's sphere . . . the duties and conventions of the average woman bore and irritate. The duties and pleasures of the average man interest and allure.[24]

Each of these women expresses clear dissatisfaction with the "old femininity" that defined women as maternal beings whose passionlessness led to the great gift of moral purity. Claire, too, rejects the "duties and conventions" of the cult of domesticity and struggles to find a way to exist outside the "old pattern, done again, again and again. So long done it doesn't even know itself for a pattern—in immensity." This ability to see the cultural patterns that imprison her psyche certainly sets her apart from the characters of *Trifles,* who expressly adopt old patterns uncritically. But as the play progresses, and Claire's patterns appear more self-defeating than liberating, the audience must ask: Is this an advance?

Glaspell's almost nostalgic depiction of female friendship and bonding in *Trifles* is in stark contrast with the absence of such relationships in *The Verge.* Claire's estrangement from both her sister and daughter mark her utter rejection of the female world that had privileged motherhood and sisterhood above all other relationships.[25] The character of Claire's sister, Adelaide, makes it clear that Glaspell was rethinking the simplified female world evident in *Trifles.* Adelaide is a woman who is confident in her "womanliness" and clearly believes in, and flaunts, her moral superiority. In act 2, she confronts her sister in Claire's own separate sphere, a tower room that is "thought to be round but does not complete the circle." Adelaide smugly remarks that "a round tower should go on being round" and opens a confrontation that quickly becomes a metaphorical debate dramatizing the dynamic tensions between an uncritical acceptance of a unified womanhood and an individualism that rejects such uncompromising solidarity. "Be the woman you were meant to be!" demands Adelaide, ". . . just get out of yourself and enter into other people's lives," to which Claire responds: "Then I would become just like you. And we should all be just alike in order to assure one another that we're all just right." Finally,

Adelaide makes the accusation that cuts to the quick of female unity: "A mother who does not love her own child! You are an unnatural woman, Claire." "Well, at least it saves me from being a natural one," Claire snaps, and the lines are drawn. For Adelaide one can either be a "natural" woman or not a woman at all. This kind of dangerous reductionism reminds us that unity, particularly when it associates itself with a perceived moral superiority, can demand rigorous conformity to inflexible ideologies. Adelaide's absolute failure to understand her sister's need to reject conformity to traditional female roles leads Adelaide to announce desperately, and predictably, that "what we need is unity."[26]

Clearly, Glaspell is rethinking the consequences of the moral womanhood that she so easily championed in *Trifles*. But just as Adelaide exemplifies the dangers of moral unity because she is unable to consider the challenges and possibilities that Claire has to offer, so too is Claire incapable of finding value in Adelaide's world. When Adelaide asks Claire, "Why do you want to shut yourself out from us?" Claire easily responds, "Because I don't want to be shut in with you." The empathy and sisterhood of *Trifles* that led Mrs. Hale to say "We all go through the same things—it's all just a different kind of the same thing" has vanished, and the two sisters can no more read the text of each other's lives than Claire could the kitchen of Minnie Wright.

The male characters of *The Verge* have also undergone a significant transformation since the incompetent detectives of *Trifles*. Unlike the men who studiously, and foolishly, avoid prolonged exposure to the female sphere in *Trifles,* the comically named Tom, Dick, and Harry are not only interested in Claire's separate spheres but repeatedly insist on barging in uninvited, marking a completely different relationship between the sexes. This contrast parallels the fact that many feminists had begun to understand same-sex relationships, the cornerstone of the female world of the nineteenth century, as yet another archaic and oppressive Victorian institution. This attitude is nicely summarized in the following quotation by Floyd Dell, a socialist-feminist and old friend of Glaspell's:

> The intensity of friendships between people of the same sex . . . we now regard as an artificial product, the result of the segregation of the sexes and the low social position of women. As women become free

and equal with men such romantic intensity of emotion finds a more biologically appropriate expression.[27]

This new emphasis on heterosexual relationships in the 1920s sprang from writers such as Havelock Ellis, Olive Schreiner, and Ellen Key, who argued that the Victorian ideology of female passionlessness prevented women from experiencing true liberation. Thus, women's sexuality (which was understood only in terms of heterosexuality) became central to feminist thought, and Claire's explicit rejection of motherhood and her embrace of her own sexuality reflects these changes in feminist ideology.[28] This shift away from relationships grounded in the female sphere offered a whole new range of complications that did not elude Glaspell.

Having severed her ties with the female world, Claire pursues the "more biologically appropriate expression" recommended by Dell. But as she moves almost frantically from one unsatisfying relationship to another, she finds that they too require compromises she is unwilling to make. Claire's marriage to Harry, her second, has turned out to be as disappointing as her first. While Claire says that she married Harry because she "thought he would smash something," he has, instead, made a career out of conventionality and wants Claire to do the same. Finding Claire's experiments "unsettling for a woman," he says:

> It would be all right if she'd just do what she did in the beginning— make the flowers as good as possible of their kind. That's an awfully nice thing for a woman to do—raise flowers. But there's something about this—changing things into other things—putting things together and making queer new things—

The two other men of the play, Tom and Dick, are the recipients of Claire's frustrated passion, and, though they say they support her experimentation with "otherness," it becomes more and more evident that they are as threatened by Claire's obsession to find new ways of existing as her husband.

Claire's desire for a man who understands her is one of the defining features of her character, as can be seen in her attempt to convince Tom that he is the "only one—all of me wants":

I want to go it, Tom, I'm lonely up on top here. Is it that I have more faith than you, or is it only that I'm greedier? You see, you don't know . . . what you're missing. You don't know how I could love you.

This is Claire's third try at a satisfying relationship with a like-minded man. Glaspell is obviously trying to make a point about her chances for success and is probably challenging the widespread belief in what was then known as the "companionate marriage."

Many feminists in the 1920s had adopted the behavioral psychologists' interpretation of "adjusted" women. In this view adjustment was linked to strong heterosexual marriages that allowed women to fulfill their "normal" sexuality *and* pursue self-development. For example, Elsie Clews Parson, a well-known cultural anthropologist and Heterodoxy member, wrote that "in the talk of women . . . desire for integral satisfaction in marriage is more consciously or realistically expressed than ever before. Emotional and sexual appeasements are considered as well as social or economic advantage."[29] Yet as Cott points out:

> The companionate marriage model left feminists (as well as any other women) little rationale for avoiding marriage; it removed the ground underneath the objection, made by prior generations, that marriage was a system of domination that imprisoned women's individuality.[30]

Cott also describes a Heterodoxy meeting in which a "perfect" feminist was defined as a woman in a happy marriage.

Not surprisingly, status quo logic of this period supposed that companionate marriages, along with the vote, would put an end to the tumultuous national discussion on the "woman question," since neither posed a serious threat to cultural hegemony and the fictive stable order that all postwar societies crave. *The Verge*, then, breaks stride not only with feminist thought of the period but also with prevailing public sentiment, by insisting that the institution of marriage deserved continued and careful scrutiny. It is not difficult to understand this play as rather courageous in this respect, maybe even as a kind of warning that went largely unheeded. We know now that before long the psychiatric appropriation of "adjustment" went beyond marital models and began undermining many of the central axioms of feminism by insisting that "freedom" could be found through adjustment to and acceptance of existing social norms, not by trying to change or reform those norms. Indeed, this increasing conservatism is already apparent in a review of *The Verge* by Alexander Woollcott, a drama critic for the *New York Times* in the 1920s. Woollcott calls Claire "a neurotic and atypical woman" and goes on to say, "We greatly fear that the average playgoer will be offended by Miss Glaspell's abject worship of the divinity of discontent."[31] Woollcott's choice of terms such as *atypical* and *neurotic,* and his notion that a woman's discontent would prove an unpopular theme among the "average playgoer," not only indicates the extensive influence behavioral psychology (not to mention psychoanalytic theory) exerted on the imaginations of the public but also suggests its essentially antagonistic view of feminism.[32] The fact that Claire's husband and sister send for a psychiatrist who determines within moments that Claire needs "rest" is made more significant in this context.

Tom is the one man in the play who consistently defends Claire's "apartness," calling her a "brave flower of all our knowing." But in the final scene of the play he too betrays her freedom by forcing her into a mold of his own choosing: "I love you, and I will keep you—from fartherness—from harm. You are mine, and you will stay with me! (*roughly*) You hear me? You will stay with me!" As Ruth Hale wrote in her review of the play in 1921, "When finally the man she loved offered no more than his kind of safety and the mere intellectuality of beauty, she saw the jig was up."[33] The play ends with Claire strangling Tom to death and then lapsing into madness. One critic argues that "Claire's madness at the end of the play is a personal triumph, but one to be understood symbolically rather than realistically."[34] This reading is certainly supportable, particularly since Claire consistently expresses a fascination with, and desire for, an insanity that might make it easier to "get out" and beyond imprisoning patterns of being. Yet it is also true that, in spite of her supposed "personal triumph," by the end of the play Claire is left profoundly alienated from both the male and female worlds: "I'm lonely up on top here," she says in her tower room, and in the final scene of the play Claire admits her responsibility for Tom's death with the words: "I did. Lonely." In view of Claire's persistent attempts to forge a mutually freeing alliance with another human being—a companionate marriage, if you will—it is difficult to understand the final scene as anything other than Claire's defeat.

Claire's isolation, along with her desperate act of murder, strongly parallels Minnie Wright and the events that set *Trifles* into motion, with the one salient difference that for Claire there is no jury of her peers to absolve her. The world of *The Verge* contains no Mrs. Hale or Mrs. Peters or their metaphorical equivalent: community. This explicit correlation between the two plays suggests that Glaspell expected her audience to grapple with the consequences of the choices Claire made in her journey to act 3. In addition, the presence of the morally smug Adelaide also indicates that Glaspell meant to deromanticize the utopian quality of the female world of *Trifles*.

The Verge cogently explores the shifting definitions of feminism in the early 1920s, exploiting them to their furthest limit, just as Claire attempts to push her plants (and herself) as far as they can go:

> Plants do it. The big leap—it's called. Explode their species—because something in them knows they've gone as far as they can go. Something in them knows they're shut in to just that. So—go mad—that life may not be prisoned. Break themselves up into crazy things—into lesser things, and from the pieces—may come one sliver of life with vitality to find the future. How beautiful. How brave.

Claire's most cherished experimental plant, Breath of Life, manages to make this leap, bringing with it something that Claire had struggled to integrate into its final form: the gift of reminiscence. "We need," she says, "the haunting beauty from the life we've left." It seems likely that Glaspell wanted her audience, too, to find the ingredients in the feminist project that would best give women the "vitality to find the future." Perhaps Glaspell meant to ask if it was possible to do away with ideologies of unity that create unyielding patterns of existence and at the same time to keep intact the empathy and solidarity that distinguished the female world of the nineteenth century. One critic has noted that the principle theme of *The Verge* is "the necessity for and yet deeper danger of a woman seeking to transcend her social, and indeed, biological role."[35] Yet it is not necessarily transcendence that Claire is after, for her great gift is in knowing how to cross-pollinate the strongest combination of ingredients to produce the strongest possible forms. Glaspell, too, was urging a feminist transplantation that simultaneously rejected the cultural "forms moulded [*sic*] for us" but managed to retain "the haunting beauty from the life we've left." Glaspell asks the question: Just what is it that we must not leave behind?

In her review of *The Verge* for the *New York Times* in 1921, Ruth Hale, drama critic and Heterodoxy member, commented: "Miss Glaspell is the only playwright I ever knew who can tell a story like this. If the surface of life changes by a hair's breadth, she not only knows it, but can convey it in words."[36] For Glaspell the "surface of life" that was most compelling was the psychological landscape of innovative feminist women, and in her characterizations we can develop a better understanding of what it meant to be a woman during one of the most dynamic historical moments of U.S. feminism. Hale concluded her review with a suggestion that is as relevant today as it was when Hale made it: "I do feel very strongly that, if we can not always quite understand [Glaspell], it would be smart of us to try."[37] What we can be sure of is that Glaspell was deliberately attempting to reconstruct the political and personal dilemmas of feminist women who, like Claire, saw their own lives as experiments in womanhood, experiments that continue to rekindle the feminist imaginations of our own times as well.

NOTES

1. See Marcia Noe's biography, *Susan Glaspell: Voice from the Heartland* (Macomb: Western Illinois Monograph Series, 1983), 44. Noe writes that this quote "suggests detachment, or even a polite lack of interest in the specific concerns of the women's movement." Noe, however, does not consider "psychological oppression" to be a specific feminist concern in the early twentieth century, although it was, in fact, one of the prominent themes in the early U.S. feminist movement, particularly among intellectuals.

2. Noe, *Susan Glaspell*, 30.

3. Some of the best sources on these personalities have been: Rosalind Rosenberg, *Beyond Separate Spheres* (New Haven: Yale University Press, 1982); Nancy

Cott, *The Grounding of Modern Feminism* (New Haven: Yale University Press, 1987); Judith Schwarz, *Radical Feminists of Heterodoxy* (Lebanon, N.H.: Victoria Publishers, 1982); and June Sochen's edited collection of essays from the 1910s in *The New Feminism in Twentieth Century America* (Lexington, Mass.: D. C. Heath, 1971).

4. Linda Ben-Zvi, "Susan Glaspell's Contributions to Contemporary Women Playwrights," in *Feminine Focus: The New Women Playwrights,* ed. Enoch Brater (New York: Oxford University Press, 1989), 149.

5. See Cott, *Grounding.* Cott's book provides a sweeping, comprehensive and excellent analysis of the political and philosophical developments in early-twentieth-century feminism. Much of my own analysis is based on Cott's insightful examination of this crucial feminist era.

6. While Elizabeth Cady Stanton had argued for suffrage on the basis of Enlightenment principles (see her 1880s essay "The Solitude of Self"), that argument had been left behind in the suffrage debate at the turn of the century, principally through the influence of Carrie Chapman Catt, who shrewdly recognized the political benefits of adopting, rather than rejecting, public perceptions of female difference.

7. Quoted in June Sochen's *The New Woman: Feminism in Greenwich Village, 1910–1920* (New York: Quadrangle Books, 1972), 47.

8. I am thinking of three works in particular; Carol Gilligan, *In a Different Voice* (Cambridge, Mass.: Harvard University Press, 1982); Mary Belenky, Blythe Clichy, Nancy Goldberger, and Jill Tarule, *Women's Ways of Knowing* (New York: Basic Books, 1987); and Sara Ruddick, *Maternal Thinking: Toward a Politics of Peace* (Boston: Beacon Press, 1989).

9. Beverly Smith, "Women's Work—Trifles? The Skill and Insights of Playwright Susan Glaspell," *International Journal of Women's Studies,* March–April 1982: 173. For another example, see Phyllis Mael's *"Trifles:* The Path to Sisterhood," *Literature/Film Quarterly* 17 (1989): 4. Mael argues that, by using Carol Gilligan's contemporary theory on the differences between male and female moral development, readers can "more fully appreciate [Glaspell's] astute depiction of these two different modes of judging" (283).

10. See Mary Beth Norton, *Major Problems in American Women's History* (Lexington, Mass.: D. C. Heath, 1989), 112.

11. Carroll Smith-Rosenberg, "The Female World of Love and Ritual: Relations between Women in Nineteenth Century America," *Signs* 1 (1975): 2.

12. Susan Glaspell, *Trifles,* in *Plays by Susan Glaspell,* ed. C. W. E. Bigsby (Cambridge: Cambridge University Press, 1987). All subsequent references to Glaspell's plays are to this edition.

13. See Bigsby's introduction to his 1987 edition of Glaspell's plays (11). See also Victoria Aarons's article "A Community of Women: Surviving Marriage in the Wilderness" (*Rendezvous* 21, no. 2 [1986] 3). Aarons writes that "the women's growing awareness of their role in Minnie Wright's exile . . . causes them to create a protective shield around her."

14. See Elaine Showalter's excellent introduction to her collection of autobiographical essays, *These Modern Women: Autobiographical Essays from the Twenties* (New York: The Feminist Press, 1978), 16. Smith-Rosenberg ("Female World") and Cott (*Grounding*) also note the newly developed cultural taboos on homosocial friendships in the late nineteenth century.

15. Judith Stephens, "Gender Ideology and Dramatic Convention in Progressive Era Plays, 1890–1920," in *Performing Feminisms: Feminist Critical Theory and Theater,* ed. Sue-Ellen Case (Baltimore: Johns Hopkins University Press, 1990), 291.

16. Smith-Rosenberg, "Female World," 2.

17. While the end of World War I meant that competing political issues could finally get their public hearing, the enormous fear of the "Reds" forced issues associated with socialism into a highly controversial, if not censored, position. As a result, socialist feminists, such as Glaspell's friend Crystal Eastman, found it increasingly difficult to participate in setting the national feminist agenda. See Cott (*Grounding*) for a more detailed analysis of this backlash.

18. Cott, *Grounding,* 49. A similar description comes from Frieda Kirchwey, the editor of the *Nation* in the 1920s, when she wrote in her introduction to the symposium "Our Changing Morality": "The old rules fail to work; bewildering inconsistencies confront her . . . slowly, clumsily, she is trying to construct a way out to a new sort of certainty in life . . ." (1924).

19. See Schwarz, *Radical Feminists,* for a comprehensive membership list and useful background information on the inner workings of Heterodoxy.

20. Quoted in Cott, *Grounding,* 39.

21. Schwarz (*Radical Feminists*) lists Glaspell as a member based on the "Heterodoxy to Marie" album, a collection of appreciative letters from Heterodoxy members to the founder of the club, Marie Jenny Howe. Glaspell contributed a page to this album.

22. Schwarz, *Radical Feminists,* 1.

23. Eastman's essay "Now We Can Begin" is included in Sochen, *New Feminism,* 23–24.

24. Schwarz, *Radical Feminists,* 44. Irwin published several essays entitled "Confessions of an Alien" for *Harper's Bazaar* in 1912.

25. See Smith-Rosenberg, "Female World," 3.

26. This fragmentation in the female world of the play corresponds to the dissolution of unity in the women's movement after suffrage. As Harriet Stanton Blatch, Elizabeth Cady Stanton's daughter, observed as early as 1918, "Altho all sorts and conditions of women were united for suffrage, that political end has been gained, and they are not at one in their attitude towards life" (Cott, *Grounding*, 66). This lost unity (which in many senses was a constructed unity that could not possibly last) was strongly felt by many political feminists of this period, as this passionate remark by Carrie Chapman Catt in 1920 indicates: "How do I pity those who have felt none of the grip of the oneness of women struggling, serving, sacrificing for the righteousness of woman's emancipation" (85).

27. Quoted in Cott, *Grounding*, 159. This is an excerpt from an essay Dell published in 1924 in the *Nation* entitled "Can Men and Women Be Friends?"

28. See Nancy Cott, "Passionlessness: An Interpretation of Victorian Sexual Ideology," *Signs* 4, no. 2 (1978): 219–36, for an interesting discussion on the roots of passionlessness. It's also important to note that this new emphasis was highly controversial in the feminist movement. For example, Charlotte Perkins Gilman bitterly opposed women's new "licentiousness" as a debased imitation of male immorality, saying that the "New Woman" was behaving "precisely in the manner of that of any servile class suddenly set free" (150.)

29. Quoted in Cott, "Passionlessness," 157.

30. Cott, "Passionlessness," 158. Rosenberg (*Beyond Separate Spheres*) also provides a useful summary of this psychological trend in the 1920s.

31. Alexander Woollcott, *New York Times*, November 20, 1921, 6: 1.

32. John B. Watson was considered one of the most respected leaders of behavioral psychology. In an essay published in the *Nation* in 1924 he discusses his interpretation of women's agitation for freedom: "So many hundreds of women I have talked to have sought freedom. I have tried to find out diplomatically but behavioristically what they mean. Is it to wear trousers? Is it to vote—to hold office—to work at men's trades—to take men's jobs away from them—to get men's salaries? Does their demand for this mystical thing called freedom imply a resentment against child bearing?" (qtd. in Showalter, *These Modern Women*, 142).

33. Ruth Hale, "Concerning 'The Verge,' " *New York Times*, November 20, 1921, 6:1. One can't help but wonder if Hale was punning on Glaspell's relationship with her husband, George "Jig" Cook.

34. Christine Dymkowski, "On the Edge: The Plays of Susan Glaspell," *Modern Drama* 31, no. 1 (March 1988): 101.

35. Bigsby, *Plays*, 22.

36. Hale, "Concerning 'The Verge,' " 6:1.
37. Hale, "Concerning 'The Verge,' " 6:1.

BIBLIOGRAPHY

Aarons, Victoria. "A Community of Women: Surviving Marriage in the Wilderness." *Rendezvous* 21, no. 2 (Spring 1986): 3–11.

Bach, Gerhard. "Susan Glaspell (1876–1948): A Bibliography of Dramatic Criticism." *Great Lakes Review* 3, no. 2 (Winter 1977): 1–34.

Ben-Zvi, Linda. "Susan Glaspell's Contributions to Contemporary Women Playwrights." In *Feminine Focus: The New Women Playwrights*. Ed. Enoch Brater, 147–66. New York: Oxford University Press, 1989.

Bigsby, C. W. E., ed. *Plays by Susan Glaspell*. New York: Cambridge University Press, 1987.

Cott, Nancy. "Passionlessness: An Interpretation of Victorian Sexual Ideology, 1790–1850." *Signs* 4, no. 2 (1978): 219–36.

———. *The Grounding of Modern Feminism*. New Haven, Conn.: Yale University Press, 1987.

Dymkowski, Christine. "On the Edge: The Plays of Susan Glaspell." *Modern Drama* 31, no. 1 (March 1988): 91–105.

Hale, Ruth. "Concerning 'The Verge.' " *New York Times,* November 20, 1921, 6:1.

Kolb, Deborah S. "The Rise and Fall of the New Woman in American Drama." *Educational Theatre Journal* 27, no. 2 (May 1975): 149–60.

Mael, Phyllis. "*Trifles:* The Path to Sisterhood." *Literature/Film Quarterly* 17, no. 4 (1989): 281–84.

Noe, Marcia. *Susan Glaspell: Voice from the Heartland*. Macomb: Western Illinois Monograph Series, 1983.

Norton, Mary Beth, ed. *Major Problems in American Women's History*. Lexington, Mass.: D. C. Heath, 1989.

Rosenberg, Rosalind. *Beyond Separate Spheres: Intellectual Roots of Modern Feminism*. New Haven, Conn.: Yale University Press, 1982.

Schwarz, Judith. *Radical Feminists of Heterodoxy: Greenwich Village, 1912–1940*. Lebanon, N.H.: New Victoria Publishers, 1982.

Showalter, Elaine, ed. *These Modern Women: Autobiographical Essays from the Twenties*. New York: The Feminist Press, 1978.

Smith, Beverly A. "Women's Work—Trifles? The Skill and Insights of Playwright Susan Glaspell." *International Journal of Women's Studies* 5, no. 2 (March–April 1982): 172–84.

Smith-Rosenberg, Carroll. "The Female World of Love and Ritual: Relations between Women in Nineteenth Century America." *Signs* 1, no. 1 (1975): 1–29.
Sochen, June, ed. *The New Feminism in Twentieth Century America*. Lexington, Mass.: D. C. Heath, 1971.
———. *The New Woman: Feminism in Greenwich Village, 1910–1920*. New York: Quadrangle Books, 1972.
Stephens, Judith. "Gender Ideology and Dramatic Convention in Progressive Era Plays, 1890–1920." In *Performing Feminisms: Feminist Critical Theory and Theater*. Ed. Sue-Ellen Case, 283–93. Baltimore: Johns Hopkins University Press, 1990.
Sutherland, Cynthia. "American Women Playwrights as Mediators of the 'Woman Problem.'" *Modern Drama* 21 (1978): 319–36.
Waterman, Arthur. "Susan Glaspell's *The Verge:* An Experiment in Feminism." *Great Lakes Review* 6 (1979): 17–24.
———. *Susan Glaspell*. New York: Twayne Publishers, 1966.
Welter, Barbara. "The Cult of True Womanhood, 1820–1860." In *Major Problems in American Women's History*. Ed. Mary Beth Norton, 122–28. Lexington, Mass.: D. C. Heath, 1989.
Woollcott, Alexander. "Second Thoughts on First Nights." *New York Times*, November 20, 1921, 6:1.

Suppression and Society in Susan Glaspell's Theater

Barbara Ozieblo

The Vienna School, according to an article published by *McClure's Maga-zine* in 1907, had established that "hysteria results principally from sup-pressed affective ideas, and can be cured by awaking anew the restrained thought."[1] Freud's work on the subconscious, Americanized into a "new science of the soul," taught that all repression was pernicious and pre-scribed the freeing of the libido.[2] Susan Glaspell, even in her earliest writ-ing, protested at imposed patterns of behavior that suppressed the real self: "Goodness knows we are cumbered and made uncomfortable enough by conventionality," she wrote in 1897, in a column entrusted to her by the *Davenport Weekly Outlook* when she was just twenty-one.[3] Although she believed that beating up against society's restrictions would allow for greater achievement, she was yet ballasted by the old values that had governed the lives of her forebears; the resulting quandary was to tax her endlessly and dominates her last novel, *Judd Rankin's Daughter* (1945).

The events of her own life pitted her against traditional Davenport society. After reading philosophy at Drake, working on the *Des Moines Daily News,* and studying life in Chicago, the prodigal daughter returned to Davenport to become a full-time writer. The high-hat "literary" circles of the town were now prepared to accept her in spite of her lower-middle-class background and even elected her to the Tuesday Club, presided over by Alice French, the grande dame of Davenport letters, whose short stories extolling a supposedly enlightened capitalism are now happily forgotten.[4] Glaspell worked on her first full-length novel, *The Glory of the Conquered* (1909), and duly gave her lectures at the Tuesday Club, but she did not limit herself to such orthodox pursuits; she openly chal-

lenged her father's authority by "declining to go to church in the morning and ostentatiously setting out for the Monist Society," which met on Sunday afternoons.[5] As if this were not enough to antagonize staid Davenporters, she fell in love with the founder of the society, George Cram Cook, who would father two children and file two divorce suits before he got around to marrying her.

In spite of his much talked of eccentricities, Cook was firmly lodged in that upper crust of society Glaspell had always aspired to. He had thrown up a university lectureship to become a truck farmer on family land and was engrossed in fashioning himself as a gentleman farmer on Tolstoy's model while at the same time impersonating a Nietzschean superman. He had experienced "contact with the conscious soul in the wide-spread world around him" (*RT* 35) and, after an unhappy love affair, suffered "the greatest adventure of his life, the longest and most dangerous swing of the pendulum of his spirit" (160). Susan Glaspell, in the therapeutically hagiographic biography she wrote a few years after his death, compared him to the mystics: "He had done it—what Jesus did, what the great mystics have done, had cast off self utterly and walked with God." All the same, she recognized that "he himself had different names for it—melancholia, intellectual insanity, hyperesthesia of the emotions" (168), and all accounts of Cook coincide in their picture of a genius driven by a terrific energy that lacked direction and bordered on manic psychosis.[6] The Provincetown Players "touched off a fire in him" that flared into an ecstasy of six years, consuming his creative fever and so saving him from the psychoanalyst's couch: today, his novels and poetry forgotten, he is remembered only for his work with the group.[7]

Glaspell and Cook were finally able to marry on April 14, 1913. They took refuge among the most radical and bohemian group of intellectuals of their times, the New York Greenwich Villagers, and with them discovered the joys of summering in Provincetown, a fishing village on the tip of Cape Cod. The villagers were by no means a homogeneous group, for they included "the Anarchists, the I.W.W.'s, the extreme left wing of the Socialists, the females militantly revolutionary about sex-freedom, and the Cubists and Post-Impressionists in art."[8] But Cook and Glaspell soon found a niche for themselves in the "permanent nucleus" of original Provincetowners, writers who, like themselves, had fled small-town values and constrictions but, while rejecting traditional Puritan reticence, were too set in their Victorian ways to create vitally new role models. Their radicalism took them as far as paying lip service to free love but insisted on fidelity within a relationship. Glaspell described their life-style as simple: we "sought to arrange life for the thing we wanted to do, needing each other as protection against complexities, yet living as we did because of an instinct for the old, old things" (*RT* 235). Not all the Provincetowners were content with work and family life, and, as Arnold Goldman distressingly shows in "The Culture of the Provincetown Players," the "morale and integrity" of the original group was threatened by the anarchists and art-for-art's-sakers, who went far beyond the older group's timid rebellions. According to Goldman, Cook, aware of the marital and social conflicts around him, "discovered in himself a natural talent for the psycho-dramatic exercise. Through plays and performance his clan would heal itself."[9]

Yet it is impossible to isolate a discrete event that led Cook to found the Provincetown Players. Glaspell's attempt to explain Jig to the world may help. Recounting his disappointment at a rejection slip attached to a returned short story, she wrote:

> He needed the feeling of a waiting audience, of some one at the other end who would see what he had done and be glad. He felt this was not there for him. More would have come had more been expected. There was the hurt feeling of one who isn't wanted, and the bewilderment of one who knows he has much to give. He began to think about that smaller audience which must be there within the big audience, the creative possibilities in sympathy of writer or artist or actor and audience. As a creator he was social. He talked of older communities. Always he talked of Greece. He talked of that possible American Renaissance. (*RT* 243–44)

Robert Károly Sarlós, in *Jig Cook and the Provincetown Players,* the most exhaustive study to date of the venture, concurs with Goldman in ascribing to Cook a positive desire to use drama therapy as a means of reconciling the different elements of the Cape Cod summer radicals. Looking back over the war years, Hutchins Hapgood could write that: "The

Provincetown Movement was, in part, a social effort to live again—spiritually, to recover from discouragement and disappointment, to be free of the poison of self and the poison of the world."[10] Cook's own words reveal that his aspirations were even higher: he had hoped for "a coral island of our own" in "this alien sea," where he and his friends "could have found the happiness of continuing ourselves toward perfection." Whether his later disillusionment was due to the Provincetowners' desire for Broadway fame or to the failure of his own play *The Spring*, he lamented: "Our individual gifts and talents have sought their private perfection. We have not, as we hoped, created the beloved community of life-givers" (309). Cook's idealism had always been tinged with a longing for the classical perfection, which he eventually found on the Acropolis; and this same idealism had earlier led him to reject Marx's prosaic program of social betterment and, in the 1910s, to doubt Freud's individual-orientated psychoanalysis.

By the same token Cook and Glaspell were appalled by the box office bias of Broadway: they fulminated against plays that followed a set pattern and left nothing whatever to the imagination. Intoxicated by the afflatus of the stage, they had applauded Maurice Brown's Little Theatre in Chicago and exulted at the Irish Players, who had shown the courage to sweep aside conventions that threatened "the humility of true feeling" (*RT* 218). They itched for something similar in New York. They attended the Washington Square Players' performances at the Bandbox but were disappointed by the group's definite preference for European plays: when Cook urged them to produce the work of native writers, he was disconcerted by their inquiries about the precise whereabouts of these American playwrights. A few years later, in the announcement for the first New York season of the Provincetown Players, he promised "ten bills of original plays by American authors." The announcement for the second season categorically stated that the aim of the venture was to give American writers a little theater "to play with," and in the eight seasons given by the Provincetown Players only two foreign plays were staged: Arthur Schnitzler's *Last Masks*, performed during the 1919–20 season, when Cook and Glaspell took a sabbatical winter, and Gustav Wied's *Autumn Fires* during the 1921 "Spring Season" directed by Jasper Deeter. In his farewell address to the Provincetown Players before leaving for Greece,

Cook was forced to admit "a discouraging lack of plays worth doing" and must have remembered that distant embarrassing moment with the Washington Square Players when he confessed that he had not found many Americans "offering a sustained stream of freely experimental work in new dramatic forms."[11]

Rumblings of Freud's theories had reached the United States well before his only visit in 1909. The unconscious had fascinated the nineteenth century, and at the beginning of the twentieth hypnosis and the theory of associations were fast gaining adherents among more adventurous spirits, providing Freud an enthralled audience drawn from both lay people and the medical profession. Clark University, reinforcing its reputation for unorthodoxy, invited Sigmund Freud to lecture at its twentieth-anniversary celebrations. Freud had intended to prepare his lectures on the Atlantic crossing, but by his last afternoon in New York, tired out by sightseeing and suffering from the "rich American food," he had still not decided on the subject matter. Ernest Jones had joined him there and advised him that "a general account of psycho-analysis" would be more suitable to the sanguine pragmatism of the American mind than a discussion of dreams. According to Jones, Freud composed "each lecture in half an hour's walk beforehand" and in his five lectures managed to survey the whole field of psychoanalysis, offering an optimistic and relatively simple version— "condensed almost to the point of caricature"—of the theories he had worked out in *The Interpretation of Dreams, Three Contributions to a Theory of Sex, The Psychology of Everyday Life,* and *Studies in Hysteria.*[12]

Jones admiringly recounts how "Freud delivered his five lectures in German, without any notes, in a serious conversational tone that made a deep impression."[13] Freud set out to convince his audience that hysterical symptoms could be cured without hypnosis once a patient's resistance to remembering past desires was overcome. In order to break down this resistance Freud advocated the use of free associations, interpretation of dreams, and observation of the "small faulty actions" common in everyday life.[14] His insistence on childhood sexuality caused surprise, and he disturbed some—and delighted others—when he stressed the importance of acknowledging sexual impulses, arguing that repressed sexuality was one of the chief factors in emotive disorders. Freud went on to denounce

civilized repressions in favor of the conscious control of wishes and instincts, which could then be sublimated. Reactions to the published lectures were not all favorable: "An ordinary reader would gather that
Freud advocates free love, removal of all restraints, and a relapse into
savagery" was a common objection to his teaching.[15] U.S. proselytizers,
among them Max Eastman, found sufficient evidence in Freud's Clark
lectures to affirm joyously, "We have but to name these nervous diseases
with their true name, it seems, and they dissolve like the charms in a fairy
story."[16] Others were more discerning: Hutchins Hapgood was later to
admit that the 1910s and 1920s had seen a gross "misinterpreting and
misapplying [of] the general ideas underlying analysis," and, as late as
1927, Sandor Ferenczi, who in 1909 had accompanied Freud to the
United States, wrote that psychoanalysis there was still "somewhat superficial and that the deeper side [was] somewhat neglected."[17]

Hapgood was rather older than most of the Greenwich Village set, and
his private struggle against bourgeois values had armed him with a quizzi-
cal detachment that made him a better judge than most. He scorned the
newest fad, believing that "there is something in the human soul which is
beyond analysis, and that is the woe caused by the realization of the
infinite."[18] Others of the group, such as Eastman, however, saw their
salvation in Freud's teaching. He and Floyd Dell, converted at an "evening" devoted to psychoanalysis at Mabel Dodge's salon, were the earliest apostles of Freud in the American intellectual world. Troubled by
writer's block, various symptomatic ailments, and the dilemma of reconciling willful sexual inclinations with their wives' standards of fidelity,
they were dazzled by the promise of psychoanalysis and blinded to its
incompatibilities with the socialist teaching of *The Masses,* which they
edited.[19] They reduced Freudianism to the discovery of the "importance
of sex in human life" and believed that it "suggested an intelligent reap-
praisal of social and moral restrictions"; self-appointed apostles of the
new cure, they wrote for the popular magazines about the unconscious,
dreams, and repressions.[20]

Eastman and Dell carried their enthusiasm into the Liberal Club—a
retreat above Polly's restaurant on MacDougal Street, where "those interested in 'New Ideas' " could meet to talk, drink and dance.[21] Here they
oversaw the anxious and at times cynical Greenwich Villagers' rumina-

tions on the tenets of psychoanalysis and worked hard to convince them to be "psyched" and thereby cured of all writer's blocks, marital infelicities, depressions, and irritabilities. Preferring not to pay out the vast sums that awesome professionals such as A. A. Brill and Smith Ely Jelliffe demanded, the villagers easily shed their inhibitions—those being pre-Prohibition days—and recounted their dreams in the hope of getting to the bottom of their problems. It was a time when intimate thoughts could only be kept secret with great difficulty. Glaspell expostulated, "You could not go out to buy a bun without hearing of some one's complex" (*RT* 250), and Sherwood Anderson (in Chicago) had discovered that "it was a time when it was well for a man to be somewhat guarded in the remarks he made, what he did with his hands."[22] Cook and Glaspell, prompted by Cook's earlier "mystic experiences," were particularly intrigued by the insight into the unconscious that psychoanalysis promised, although they were somewhat dubious about the claims made by popularized accounts. The prevailing belief that insanity could be fended off, or hysterical symptoms cured, by a couple of confessional sessions with a "priestly analyst" struck them as an unwarranted simplification of the problems of humankind.[23] The intellectuals who popularized Freud's teaching sought a scientific justification of the "repeal of reticence" they advocated; they believed that dreams were the manifestations of sexual desires stifled by American puritan society—desires that, if repressed, could lead to unhappiness or even the lunatic asylum.[24] The moral dangers of giving in to all one's wishes were apparent, and Freud's insistence on sublimation in his last Clark lecture was put to good use: a socially undesirable wish could be sublimated into artistic creativity or "any interest, in fact, that serves to work off the vital energies and relieve the nervous system."[25] Floyd Dell was not so optimistic: "There is, very unfortunately, an extent to which the instincts fundamental in mankind seem to be incompatible with civilization as it now exists."[26]

Cook and Glaspell shared Dell's fears and were quite convinced that some desires at least should be held firmly under control. Working out dream analysis scenarios convinced them that this latest nostrum, if taken to extremes, could have disastrous consequences, but it also revealed an inherent histrionicism, which offered enormous promise for the theater—and reminded them of their search for the American playwright. In their apartment on Milligan Place they "tossed the lines back and forth at one another, and wondered if any one else would ever have as much fun with it as we were having" (*RT* 250). Much to their chagrin, the finished play, *Suppressed Desires,* was rejected by the Washington Square Players as "too special"—but, together with Neith Boyce's *Constancy,* it was destined to make up the first bill of the future Provincetown Players.

This sketch gave Glaspell the opportunity to treat ideas less seriously than she was wont to. A few years later, as the acclaimed author of *Inheritors* and *The Verge,* she was described as a dramatist of "thought" and her work compared with that of Eugene O'Neill, which derived purely from "feeling."[27] Here, however, working with Cook, whose mind was "far less scrupulous and more ungirdled" than hers, she indulged in the freedom provided by "comedy (not of character) but of ideas, or, rather, of the confusion or falseness or absurdity of ideas."[28] In later plays and in her novels Glaspell's ambivalence toward the ideas she examines mars any incipient humor.[29] In *Suppressed Desires,* however, Glaspell puts aside all her argumentation and, as she herself wrote, simply has "fun" at the cost of psychoanalysis.

Henrietta Brewster, in *Suppressed Desires,* is addicted to the new fad and worships her analyst, the infallible Dr. Russell; she is preparing a paper on psychoanalysis to give at the Liberal Club, and her husband's worktable is now strewn with the literature, including copies of the *Psycho-Analytic Review* (to which Max Eastman directed those readers of *The Masses* who wished to "understand the daring ideas of Sigmund Freud").[30] Her husband, Stephen, has had more than enough of Henrietta's nonsense: she poisons his life with her search for complexes and, following the example set by physicians at the Phipps Clinic in Baltimore, wakes him every night to discuss and analyze his dreams.[31] Mabel, Henrietta's unsophisticated sister, who believes that psychoanalysis is "something about the war" (306), is visiting from Chicago; Henrietta is convinced that Mabel "needs more from life than she is getting" (311) and pounces on the first "Freudian slip" she makes to carry her off to Dr. Russell's office. Meanwhile, Stephen decides to call on "that priest of this new religion" in the hope that he will be sufficiently honest to "tell Henrietta there's nothing the matter with my unconscious mind" (312) and so free him from his wife's constant nagging about undiscovered complexes.

Dr. Russell, clearly not hampered by the reticence Freud had encountered in his patients, or by any symptoms of transference, arrives at his interpretation in record time. He sees no need to delve too deeply into hidden memories, for the suppressed desires he discovers have nothing to do with childhood traumas. In a mere two weeks he is prepared to affirm that Stephen's dream about the walls of his room "receding and leaving me alone in a forest" (315) has nothing to do with his profession—he is an architect—but is conclusive proof that he wishes to be free of his wife. Mabel's dream that she is a hen told to "step lively!" (305) is slightly more complicated, but is quickly unraveled to show that she wishes she were her sister, *Hen*rietta, because she loves Stephen, *Step/hen* B(e)Rooster. Henrietta is indignant that her mentor should have betrayed her in this way and promises to burn the books on psychoanalysis. Stephen, too, is quite happy to ignore the analyst's dictum and to remain with his wife: Mabel is calmly told to "keep right on suppressing" her desire for Stephen (322), and high-handedly persuaded that "psychoanalysis doesn't say you have to *gratify* every suppressed desire" (320; my emphasis).

The play is a spoof of current unprofessional opinions on psychoanalysis and owes a great deal to a skeptical article by Edwin Tenney Brewster published a few years earlier in the popular *McClure's Magazine*.[32] Brewster (*Suppressed Desires* is of course based on the banal pun in his name) urges the reader to judge Freud's ideas for himself, although he ends up with the suggestion that perhaps "the whole thing is only a crazy dream of Dr. Sigmund Freud." He introduces his topic by comparing the mind to "a tidy little apartment" with unknown "cellars and galleries and caverns" (715), in which the primitive, uncouth impulses are exiled and there range freely. An earlier Greenwich Villager had used similar analogies: we have only to think back to Edgar Allan Poe's "The Fall of the House of Usher" to understand the terrifying implications of Stephen Brewster's exclamation: "I've got the roof in the cellar!" (309).

Brewster gives a number of examples of dream analyses, which he takes from Ernest Jones's accounts of cures effected by psychoanalysis, almost all of them concerned with unhappy marriages and with suppressed desires for another partner. One dream interpretation depends on the pun embedded in the name of a hated doctor who had mistreated the dreamer in childhood and could well have suggested the punning on which *Suppressed Desires* depends. Brewster's article makes one error that Glaspell and Cook perpetuate—he does not distinguish between "suppressed" and "repressed" desires and writes: "Every dream, in the Freudian formula, is the more or less disguised fulfillment of a *suppressed* wish. . . . The worst of it is that these same *repressed* wishes that appear in dreams affect also, most inconveniently, our waking lives" (716–17). According to W. David Sievers, Freud's translator, Dr. A. A. Brill "distinguished between *repression,* which is an unconscious process, and *suppression,* which is a conscious disciplining of one's impulses as required by civilization." Sievers then points out that "Susan Glaspell's satire should rightly have been called *Repressed Desires.*"[33] Strictly speaking, however, it should have been *Repressed and Suppressed Desires:* Mabel is told to suppress, for the good of the Brewsters, desires that are no longer repressed, since the analyst has brought them to the fore in explaining them (Glaspell and Cook do not seem to have been aware of this—they use *suppressed* throughout). The confusion is quite understandable in that, as we have seen, Edwin Tenney Brewster uses the two terms indiscriminately (so does Nathan G. Hale Jr. as late as 1971), while Hugo Munsterberg, the Harvard professor of psychology whose work the Cooks would have known, uses *suppressed* throughout his 1907 article in *McClure's.*[34]

A more serious misinterpretation of Freud lies in Henrietta's selfish dismissal of Mabel's putative suppressed desire for Stephen. Henrietta assures her sister that the lunatic asylum no longer looms, since her desire has been named: "Dr. Russell has brought it into your consciousness—with a vengeance. That's all that's necessary to break up a complex" (320). This facile solution echoes Eastman's optimistic fairy story presentation of psychoanalysis and also Freud's own second lecture at Clark, when, attempting to simplify his already simple examples of psychoanalytic cures achieved by a return to the pathogenic memory, he stated: "We decide to lift the repression, and peace and quiet are restored."[35]

More striking than the easily explained misuse of a scientific term or concept is the preoccupation with the suppression of an individual's right to be her- or him-, self, central to all of Glaspell's plays and novels. The young protagonist of an early story "The Rules of the Institution" questions the validity of insisting on her freedom when this would hurt so many loved ones: "It seemed that affection and obligation were agents holding one to one's place," and yet Judith finally decides that "she owed no allegiance to an order that held life in chains."[36] The novel *Fidelity* (1915), in which Glaspell justifies her own principles of behavior, explores a young girl's "right" to walk off with someone else's husband and the consequences of such an act. In both cases Glaspell recognizes the right of the individual to self-expression but is sorrily aware of the heartache it causes others.

In *The Verge* (1921) Glaspell examines the fate of the woman who does not suppress her desires. The play was acclaimed by members of the Heterodoxy, a radical woman's club, with almost religious respect: here was a playwright who dared to show how society takes its revenge on a woman rebel.[37] Claire Archer, the protagonist, is conscious of humanity's inherent bondage and can no longer believe that humankind at large, let alone a woman, will ever break out of the stifling patterns fixed by society. She realizes that the older order—symbolized by a plant she calls the "Edge Vine," which grows in the shape of a cross—has failed her: she can destroy the signifier but is helpless when faced with its signified. The new dispensation she hopes for cannot, by its very nature, be articulated.

The play opens in a luscious and overheated greenhouse, representative of the socially restricted and shielded space Claire is forced to inhabit; here she experiments with plants. She believes she can exploit a technique of transplanting to create wholly new organisms that are liberated from the previous forms and functions of plant life. Tom, Dick, and Harry (confidant, lover, and husband) violate her sanctum when they flee the symbolically cold house in search of a more gratifying environment. Hoping to end their farcical bickering, Claire attempts to express her Nietzschean desire to overcome established patterns and to break through into whatever lies beyond; of the three men in her life only Tom gropes toward an understanding of her disjointed utterances.

In act 2 Claire's sister Adelaide invades her study, a strangely twisted and uncannily lit tower, which is best interpreted as an outward sign of Claire's isolation and of her rejection of the world, though it is also a symbol of her disturbed mind. Claire is seen througgh "a queer bulging window" (78), about which Christine Dymkowski has perceptively observed: "It is most unusual for a playwright to separate characters from the audience with an actual physical barrier rather than a merely imagined fourth wall."[38] Thus, those entering this enclosed space can be construed not only as invaders of Claire's mind but also as a schizophrenic splitting of her thought. Adelaide's mission is to convince her sister to play the part of the dutiful mother and wife, but Claire is too close to transcendence to take heed; now on the brink of uncovering her latest experiment, the plant she calls "Breath of Life," she is staggered by fear of retaliation from the God whose life-giving powers she has appropriated. Claire seeks a haven in the physical consummation of her relationship with the sympathetic Tom, but in deference to her superior spirit he denies her that ordinary human refuge, whereupon the second act ends with Claire's hysterical plea for "Anything—everything—that will let me be nothing!" (92)

The new plant that signals Claire's success in creating a hitherto unknown life form is unveiled in the greenhouse in act 3. Yet the achievement is clearly ambivalent: any organism is condemned to repetition and stagnation unless it continually overcomes itself. Claire is fully conscious of that baleful dilemma; when Tom finally offers her his love, she is appalled at the prospect of being engulfed by mediocrity and relentlessly chokes him to death. The murder mimics the suffocating norms of society that inevitably silence the creative urge in those who refuse to conform, but the family sees Claire's convulsive action as final proof of her insanity. The play ends on a savagely ironic note as Claire chants the hymn "Nearer, My God, to Thee," which Adelaide, intuiting blasphemy, had previously refused to sing in her presence. Claire, a female Faust, is now her own God and cannot be reached by societal structures and compunctions; she has broken out and is existentially free, alone in the transcendental beyond.

The Verge was Glaspell's most ambitious play and best exemplifies the degree to which the Provincetown Players had assimilated the trends of European theater. As C. W. E. Bigsby points out, "Few writers, before or since, . . . attempted such a radical revisioning of all aspects of theatre."[39] The play's tortured, highly symbolic setting, designed by Cleon Throckmorton, reminded its reviewers of the film *The Cabinet of Dr. Caligari* (1919; released in the USA in the spring of 1921) and was welcomed as the first example of expressionism on the U.S. stage.[40] Glaspell's treatment of her subject also goes beyond the critique of marriage to which Ibsen's *A Doll's House* and innumerable Broadway plays had, by 1921, innured the theatergoing public. Claire does not merely slam the door behind her; she encroaches on forbidden territory in her passion to create new life forms. In a man her Nietzschean overreaching would be considered a normal function of aggression: in a woman it amounts to the arrogation of faculties reserved for God—and for men. Claire has rejected the roles of wife, mother, and mistress that are open to her and rebels against the suppression of self that society would enforce upon a woman, only to discover that the penalty is total alienation. Paradoxically, in an age that considers hysteria to be the result of repression, she is repudiated as a hysteric by her family—and by most audiences, who have tended to see in her "an almost clinical type for the psychoanalytical laboratory."[41] In *Suppressed Desires* the triviality of the argument allowed for lightheartedness, but in *The Verge* Glaspell's relentless investigation of the secrets of our civilization reveals tragedy to be the only possible outcome.

Glaspell welcomed the emancipation heralded by psychoanalysis and by the "repeal of reticence," but her Victorian heritage disposed her to doubt its long-term value; she could not envisage a world devoid of human interdependencies and, to her credit, understood that these implied a sacrifice of so-called freedom. Thus, each time she ventured out to conquer new liberties for her protagonists, she found herself reaching back to the old traditional values, even when these implied the immolation of the self. For Glaspell, Freud and Eastman notwithstanding, the suppression of some of humankind's desires seemed essential to preserve society from its heart of darkness.

NOTES

1. Hugo Munsterberg, "The Third Degree," *McClure's Magazine* 24 (October 1907): 621.

2. Floyd Dell, "The Science of the Soul," *The Masses* 8, no. 9 (July 1916): 30–31.

3. Susan Glaspell, "Social Life," *Weekly Outlook* 2, no. 11 (March 13, 1897): 7. This was an unsigned column that appeared regularly in the *Weekly Outlook:* Glaspell was society editor for the paper from its first issue, July 11, 1896, until she left Davenport for Drake University, in Des Moines, to study for a degree in Philosophy in September 1897. In a monograph, *Susan Glaspell: Voice from the Heartland* (Macomb: Western Illinois University, 1983), Marcia Noe argues convincingly that the "Social Life" columns were written by Glaspell (87).

4. Alice French wrote under the pen name Octave Thanet, and her stories were much admired in the last two decades of the nineteenth century for their positive treatment of traditional values. For a full treatment of her life and work, see George McMichael, *Journey to Obscurity: Biography of Alice French* (Lincoln: University of Nebraska Press, 1965). She undoubtedly influenced Glaspell's early writing and must have been a role model for the younger writer at the beginning of her career: Glaspell's experience as a student and newspaper reporter made her adopt quite different views on society, women's suffrage, capitalism, and socialism.

5. Susan Glaspell, *The Road to the Temple* (New York: Frederick A. Stokes, 1927), 120. Further references to this work will be made in the text, as *RT*. The Monist Society was founded by George Cram Cook and Floyd Dell as a gesture of rebellion against the Davenport Socialist party, which, as Glaspell wrote, "had to be treated a little too respectfully."

6. Ronald R. Fieve, in *Moodswing: The Third Revolution in Psychiatry* (New York: William Morrow, 1975), describes swings between elation and depression and comments that these "have seemed to plague creative people in particular" (48). He acknowledges the help psychoanalysis can give sufferers of this emotional disorder but believes it is best controlled chemically. There is evidence in Cook's fragmented notes and in his letters in the Berg collection, as well as in Glaspell's *The Road to the Temple,* that he did indeed suffer periods of hyperactivity followed by depressions, which he would alleviate by drinking. Hutchins Hapgood described Cook at work: "the extreme passionate concentration and excitation, alternate fear and hope, a suspense, the agony of imagination, final breathless exhausting success . . . so that at moments he was almost unbalanced" (*A Victorian in the Modern World* [1939; reprint, Seattle and London: University of Washington Press, 1972], 374–75). Helen Deutsch and Stella Hanau, in their history of the Provincetown Theatre, say: "Jig Cook was untouched by the modern horror of sounding sincere or idealistic. His subjection to

an idea could almost amount to hysteria" (*The Provincetown: A Story of the Theatre* [New York: Farrar and Rinehart, 1931], 40).

7. Mary Heaton Vorse, *Time and the Town: A Provincetown Chronicle* (New York: Dial Press, 1942), 117. Edna Kenton wrote: "George Cook was not only the founder of the group; he developed and sustained the Provincetown Players through their career as no other single one did or could. His was the single spirit dedicated wholly to the experiment" ("Provincetown and MacDougal Street," in *Greek Coins,* ed. George Cram Cook [New York: George H. Doran, 1925], 22).

8. Hapgood, *A Victorian,* 379.

9. Arnold Goldman, "The Culture of the Provincetown Players," *Journal of American Studies* 12, no. 3 (1978): 295, 230.

10. Hapgood, *A Victorian,* 393.

11. Quotations are from the announcements for the 1916–17, 1917–18, and 1922–23 seasons of the Provincetown Players, now in the Beinecke Library, Yale University. According to Edna Kenton, the Players staged ninety-seven plays by forty-six American authors (Eugene O'Neill and Susan Glaspell were the most prolific contributors). Kenton stated that "the Provincetown Players limited themselves from the beginning to the production of unproduced plays by American playwrights, and this law of theirs is perhaps the only one they have kept in its pristine purity" ("The Provincetown Players and the Playwrights' Theatre, 1915–1922," copy in the Beinecke Library, Yale University, 88). In the 1922–23 interim season announcement Cook states that ninety-three plays by forty-seven American playwrights were staged; Sarlos gives the numbers as ninety-seven plays by forty-seven American playwrights. See note 1 of Linda Ben-Zvi's introduction to this volume.

12. Ernest Jones, *Sigmund Freud: Life and Work,* vol. 2: *Years of Maturity, 1901–1919* (London: The Hogarth Press, 1955), 62–63; Nathan G. Hale, *Freud and the Americans: The Beginnings of Psychoanalysis in the United States, 1876–1917* (New York: Oxford University Press, 1971), 5.

13. Jones, *Sigmund Freud,* 2:63.

14. Sigmund Freud, "Five Lectures on Psycho-Analysis" (1910), in *The Standard Edition of the Complete Psychological Works of Sigmund Freud,* trans. James Strachey (London: The Hogarth Press, 1957), 37.

15. Jones, *Sigmund Freud,* 2:63. Jones eventually convinced Freud to write out the lectures, which were published in English translation in the *American Journal of Psychology* in 1910.

16. Max Eastman, "Exploring the Soul and Healing the Body," *Everybody's Magazine* 32 (June 1915): 750.

17. Hapgood, *A Victorian*, 383; Sandor Ferenczi, *New York Times*, June 5, 1927, 2, 4:3. Quoted in Frederick J. Hoffman, *Freudianism and the Literary Mind* (1945; reprint, Baton Rouge: Louisiana State University Press, 1967), 66.

18. Hapgood, *A Victorian*, 384.

19. For a full discussion of Eastman and Dell's reconciliation of Freud and Marx's teachings, see: Leslie Fishbein, "Freud and the Radicals: The Sexual Revolution Comes to Greenwich Village," *Canadian Review of American Studies* 12, no. 2 (Fall 1981): 173–89.

20. Hoffman, *Freudianism*, 58; William L. O'Neill, in *The Last Romantic: A Life of Max Eastman* (New York: Oxford University Press, 1978), argues that Eastman, needing the money, deliberately simplified psychoanalysis in his articles for the popular *Everybody's Magazine* in order to make the subject accessible to its readers (58).

21. Allen Churchill, *The Improper Bohemians* (New York: E. P. Dutton, 1959), 62.

22. Ray Lewis White, ed., *Sherwood Anderson's Memoirs* (1942; reprint, Chapel Hill: University of North Carolina Press, 1969), 339.

23. Hale, *Freud*, 411.

24. Agnes Repplier, "The Repeal of Reticence," *Atlantic Monthly* 113 (March 1914): 297. Floyd Dell was one of the early believers in the damage done by the repression of sexual desires, even though ultimately he was skeptical of the benefit of unleashing all repressions:

> By means of the technique of dream-analysis, Freud has discovered that the "unconscious," the hidden part of the mind, is full of "complexes," knotted groups of emotions and thoughts, which have been "repressed," thrust back out of consciousness as shameful. He found, moreover, that these repressed complexes were sexual in character. Repression, that is to say, was shown to be one way in which the mind deals with emotional forces—"libido"—which cannot find free play in civilized life. It is, however, a poor way, for the repression may give rise to a symptom called neurosis. ("The Science of the Soul," *The Masses* 8, no. 9 [July 1916]: 30)

25. Peter Clark Macfarlane, "Diagnosis by Dreams," *Good Housekeeping* 60 (March 1915): 286.

26. Floyd Dell, "Speaking of Psychoanalysis: The New Boon for Dinner Table Conversationalists," *Vanity Fair* 5 (December 1915): 53.

27. Isaac Goldberg, *The Drama of Transition: Native and Exotic Playcraft* (Cincinnati: Stewart Kidd, 1922), 472.

28. Ludwig Lewisohn, *The Drama and the Stage* (New York: Harcourt, Brace, 1922), 104.

29. Her last play for the Provincetown Players, *Chains of Dew* (1922), inquires into the consequences of Nora's extension of the birth control campaign into the Midwest; the comedy of fanaticism glimmers in act 1 but is snuffed out almost immediately by Glaspell's indecisive stand on woman's emancipation. Dotty, the provincial heroine whom Nora converts to her struggle, finds herself caught between the temptation of a new way of life and the obligation to continue in the role of sacrifice-exacting idol that is imposed on her by her poet-husband. Eventually, duty wins: Dotty gives up her newly acquired position as president of Bluff City's first Birth Control League in order to devote herself to her husband's needs. Glaspell is too much aware of the necessary destruction involved in breaking out of societal molds to enjoy the intricacies of plot that she creates and so "wabbles dangerously," caught "between the hilarious satire of *Suppressed Desires* and the grim sincerity of *The Verge*." Alison Smith, "The New Play," *New York Evening Globe*, April 28, 1922; quoted in Gerard Bach, "Susan Glaspell (1876–1948): A Bibliography of Dramatic Criticism," *Great Lakes Review* 3, no. 2 (1977): 11.

30. Susan Glaspell and George Cram Cook, *Suppressed Desires*, in *Representative One-Act Plays by American Authors*, ed. Margaret Gardner Mayorga (Boston: Little, Brown, 1922); subsequent references to this work will be made in the text. Max Eastman, "A New Journal," *The Masses* (April 1914): 9.

31. Charles F. Oursler, "Behind the Madman's Dreams," *Technical World* 21 (April 1914): 207; quoted in Hale, *Freud*, 410.

32. Edwin Tenney Brewster, "Dreams and Forgetting: New Discoveries in Dream Psychology," *McClure's Magazine* 29 (October 1912): 719; subsequent references to this work will be made in the text.

33. W. David Sievers, *Freud on Broadway* (New York: Hermitage House, 1955), 27.

34. Hale, *Freud*, 400, 405; Munsterberg, "The Third Degree," 614–22.

35. Freud, "Five Lectures," 27.

36. Susan Glaspell, "The Rules of the Institution," *Harper's Monthly* 128 (January 1914): 208.

37. Susan Glaspell, *The Verge*, in *Plays by Susan Glaspell*, ed. C. W. E. Bigsby (Cambridge: Cambridge University Press, 1987). Subsequent references to this work will be made in the text. Hapgood, *A Victorian*, 377.

38. Christine Dymkowski, "On the Edge: The Plays of Susan Glaspell," *Modern Drama* 31, no. 1 (March 1988): 101.

39. Bigsby, *Plays*, 19.

40. Kenneth Macgowan acknowledged that Throckmorton's set was "expressionistic"; he first used the term with reference to a play apropos Eugene O'Neill's *The Hairy Ape* (1922). See Kenneth Macgowan, "The New Play," *New York Evening Globe*, November 15, 1921; and Mardi Valgemae, *Accelerated Grimace: Expressionism in the American Drama of the 1920s* (Carbondale: Southern Illinois University Press, 1972), 179.

41. Goldberg, *Drama*, 475.

Reflections on *The Verge*

Karen Malpede

Claire, the heroine of Susan Glaspell's *The Verge,* is not a nice woman. She is self-involved. She ignores everyone else's feelings and all her domestic duties, for the sake of her own work. She has several lovers, whom she teases openly, in front of one another and in front of her adoring husband, Harry Archer. She detests her conventional sister, Adelaide, and is openly cruel to her equally conventional daughter, Elizabeth, toward whom she feels not a shred of maternal solicitude or warmth. In a final, brutal moment she kills Tom Edgeworthy, the only person in the play she truly loves.

Hedda Gabler, the most well-known nasty woman in modern drama, has, at least, the decency to kill herself (and to cut off her line by killing her unborn child) after thoroughly disrupting the lives of those around her. She atones for the "sin of being" and rebels against the captivity of the female in one sudden, wordless, masculine act of firing a pistol into her skull. "People don't do such things," the play's last words belong to Judge Brack, one of Hedda's would-be captors.

Claire survives the murder she commits, arguably gone mad but with the lucidity of madness, her verbal capacity all intact. Claire talks us through her dawning understanding of her actions, much as any tragic hero, surrounded by the bodies of his beloved dead, talks us through his final self-revelation.

Hedda Gabler kills herself because she is trapped, not only by the conventions of the nineteenth-century bourgeois housewife but also by the particularly fierce inner contradiction such conventions serve to enforce. Hedda wants to breathe the exalted air of freedom, but she is afraid to leave the house. Gabler, like many of Ibsen's heroines, displays

123

the restless temperament of the creative personality, but she shows neither a shred of artistic talent nor of artistic discipline. Ultimately, she is doomed by what her author, Ibsen, saw as her own infernal emptiness. In plays by men female characters are never artists, are *never* able, therefore, to create and to reflect upon a destiny uniquely theirs. Male playwrights have been too frightened of the female artist ever to reify her form.

Yet Glaspell's Claire is an artist, passionately, obsessively involved. Claire's need to envision and to make gives the play its driving force; there is no other energy equal to hers, no other need as great. Claire stands at the center of this work as a woman character has seldom stood at the center of a drama; she is not the victim but, instead, the executioner of a great and savage plot. Claire's work is breeding plants, and she is on the verge of creating a new species, "Breath of Life." Her struggle is the creator's struggle from first to last. Everything in her upper-class milieu conspires against her. Every move she makes transgresses the proprieties of her sex and station. Yet she makes every move, takes every chance, is active, restless, ceaselessy involved in her creation. The energy of the play revolves around her not because, like Hedda, she is a parasite, sucking other's lives, but because she is the active source, the vibrant center that attracts.

The plant, of course, is a metaphor for self-creation. If Claire could make a new species, she would have made a new woman—one capable of life on life's own terms, a free, unfettered being. It is a life and death struggle, this one for self-creation; at any moment the soul might turn stagnant, and the life force it animates might wither on the vine. The artist, the creatrix, undertakes this struggle, entwines her every reason for living around it. Breath of Life is the creative spirit, the spectacular ability to bring form and essence into being.

Claire is the woman struggling to create herself as artist, struggling to liberate herself from the two thousand years or more of prohibition against the female creative self. Claire is a revolutionary character in a revolutionary play written by a revolutionary woman.

Claire kills her beloved, Tom, in a final lyric passage of an increasingly lyric play, because he represents to her the false ideal of romantic love that has slain women's independent creative selves since romantic love began.

TOM: I love you, and I will keep you—from fartherness—from harm. You are mine, and you will stay with me! (*roughly*) You hear me? You will stay with me!

CLAIRE: (*her head on his breast, in ecstasy of rest. Drowsily*) You can keep me?

TOM: Darling! I can keep you. I will keep you—safe.

CLAIRE: (*troubled by the word, but barely able to raise her head*) Safe?

TOM: (*bringing her to rest again.*) Trust me, Claire.

CLAIRE: (*not lifting her head, but turning so she sees Breath of Life*) Now I can trust—what is? (*suddenly pushing him roughly away*) No! I will beat my life to pieces in the struggle to . . .

TOM: To *what* Claire?

CLAIRE: Not to stop it by seeming to have it. (*with fury*) I will keep my life low—low—that I may never stop myself—or anyone—with the thought it's what *I* have. I'd rather be the steam rising from the manure than be a thing called beautiful! (*with a sight too clear*) Now I know who you are. It is you who puts out the breath of life. Image of beauty— *You fill the place—should be a gate* (*in agony*) Oh, that is it is *you*—fill the place—should be a gate! My darling! . . . Never was loving strong as my loving of you! Do you know that? Oh, know that! Know it now! (*her arms go round his neck*) Hours with you—I'd give my life to have! That it should be you—(*he would loosen her hands, for he cannot breathe. But when she knows she is choking him, that knowledge is fire burning its way into the last passion*) It *is* you. It is you . . .

"No! Your are *too much!* You are *not* enough," Claire screams, as she strangles him. The words in every woman's heart in that most sacred moment, not of death but, rather, of orgasmic union, the knowledge that plunders love in a world in which both partners are not free. "You are *too much!*"—I cannot be myself. "You are *not* enough"—I cannot find myself in you.

Claire could lose herself in love. Claire, the beautiful, vivacious, brilliant, is pursued by love all through the play. Harry, the husband; Tom, the doomed lover, whose love for her was chaste; and Dick, the man with whom she is actually having an affair; the daughter Elizabeth, craving a mother's love—all these people lust after Claire, each would claim her for their own, turn her into an image not herself.

Yet real love is not possible in a world in which the woman is not first of all free to become herself through the act of creation. Human beings make culture in order to know themselves as parts and as reflections of the living world. Insofar as women have been forbidden to make culture, women have also been forbidden knowledge of self in the world. Lacking unique destinies, independently wrought, women have lacked dignity, have ultimately lacked the ability to morally reckon with themselves.

A destiny is found through an act of transgression: one steps outside the accepted norm and suddenly recognizes self as distinct and begins, then, if one is made of heroic mettle, to hold self accountable. All the great tragedies teach us this. Claire is a tragic heroine—one of the first. She is given a transgressive action, and she is given words, by her female author, so that she might reflect on what she's done.

When a whole group of American women began to write plays in the 1920s out of a collective feminist consciousness, they often depicted women killing men. Glaspell's most well-known play, *Trifles,* revolves around this theme, as does Sophie Treadwell's *Machinal,* a Broadway hit in 1928, revived successfully in New York in 1990.

Yet by the 1990s popular culture has bowdlerized any radical metaphoric meaning from women's murderous impulses. Now in commercial films and plays women murder their men, their rapists, or their men's wives, as part of the general violent culture in which we live, in which all conflicts are shown to be satisfactorily dealt with by annihilating one's opponent. Patriarchy justifies the brutality of its rule by spinning tales of the murderous intentions of *the other* (as the Gulf "war," more aptly named "slaughter," gives horrifying proof). That women, if given half the chance, will murder men is a cherished, dirty little patriarchal fantasy, albeit sometimes true.

Glaspell's denouement is no longer a satisfactory model for contemporary women playwrights, who must go beyond the annihilative ending in order to further subvert the plot of a society so bent on violence. But this critique in no way diminishes the power of what Glaspell did or the power of reading, or staging, her play today. *The Verge* remains a great drama, and Claire remains a great and necessary character.

The Verge: L'Écriture Féminine at the Provincetown

Marcia Noe

On November 14, 1921, the Provincetown Players produced Susan Glaspell's *The Verge*. The play features a protagonist, Claire Archer, who subordinates everything in her life to her efforts to create new forms of plant life. As the play progresses, Claire becomes increasingly alienated from anything and everyone except her life work. As the play builds to a third-act climax, in which Claire reaches the outer limits of sanity as the culminating achievement of her life work, the "Breath of Life," bursts into bloom, she cuckolds her husband, rejects her daughter, insults her sister, and attempts to seduce her friend Tom, only to strangle him when she fears their involvement might interfere with her work.

As might be expected in a Broadway season that featured *Peg o' My Heart* and *Blossom Time*, *The Verge* alienated even those critics who had come to expect experimentalism in a Provincetown production. Maida Castellun of the *New York Call* said it was "vague and repetitious in form."[1] J. F. Holmes of the *New Statesman* termed it "a pretentious travesty of emotion and truth."[2] Kenneth Macgowan wrote that "the play is clogged, not only with a figure that affrights so many, but with abstruse phrases and very lengthy talk."[3] Alexander Woollcott called it "miscellaneous, unselective, helplessly loquacious—like a stenographic report of someone thinking aloud."[4] To open *The Verge* at random and glance at the dialogue on almost any page is to understand why these critics said what they did:

CLAIRE: Yes! (*As often, the mocking thing gives true expression to what lies somberly in her*) The war. There was another gorgeous chance.

HARRY: Chance for what? I call you, Claire. I ask you to say what
you mean.

CLAIRE: I don't know—precisely. If I did—there'd be no use saying
it. (*At Harry's impatient exclamation she turns to Tom.*)

TOM: (*Nodding*) The only thing left worth saying is the thing we
can't say.

HARRY: Help![5]

Disliked by most theater critics of the 1920s and largely ignored by
scholars of U.S. drama today, *The Verge* is Susan Glaspell's most misunderstood play. The purpose of this essay is to show how this perplexing play
can be illuminated by contemporary feminist theory, specifically, Elaine
Showalter's feminist poetics and Hélène Cixous's concept of *l'écriture
féminine*. Moreover, this essay will also demonstrate how a close examination of *The Verge* can reveal some limitations of feminist critical theory.

The American feminist critic Elaine Showalter coined the term *gyno-
critics* to describe the feminist critics' attempt to "construct a female framework for the analysis of women's literature, to develop new models based
on the study of female experience, rather than to adapt male models and
theories."[6] In "Toward a Feminist Poetics" she defines women's literary
history by delineating three developmental phases through which women's
writing has passed: the Feminine, Feminist, and Female stages. Showalter
dates the Feminine phase from 1840 to 1880 and describes it as a phase in
which "women wrote in an effort to equal the intellectual achievements of
the male culture and internalized its assumptions about the female nature."[7] During the Feminist phase, from 1880 to 1920, women writers
concentrated on dramatizing the way a patriarchal society has oppressed
women. In the Female phase, which dates from 1920 to the present,
women writers have concerned themselves primarily with representing the
female experience through their art. Showalter cites Dorothy Richardson
and Virginia Woolf as writers who "think in terms of male and female
sentences and divide their work into 'masculine' journalism and 'feminine'
fictions, redefining and sexualizing external and internal experience."[8]

If we look at Susan Glaspell's career from the perspective of Showalter's
developmental stages, we can see that it recapitulates the literary history

of women described above. Glaspell began writing short stories and novels around the turn of the century. Most, in the sentimental tradition of women's fiction that prevailed in the nineteenth and early twentieth centuries, are written according to a formula that reinforces patriarchal values and the feminine ideal. Thus, in her first novel, *The Glory of the Conquered* (1909), Glaspell's heroine is a talented artist who sacrifices her career to help her invalid husband.

In 1916, however, Glaspell became interested in writing plays when the little theater company she and her husband founded became successful. *Trifles,* her first solo dramatic effort, demonstrates that men and women in our culture have different values, different perspectives on life, different modes of thinking, of attacking problems. In this one-act play Glaspell simultaneously valorizes the way women see and deal with the world and illuminates the way men oppress women with their masculine modes of perception and operation. In *Trifles* Glaspell creates two female characters, tangentially attached to a murder investigation, who prevent the sheriff and the county attorney from finding the clues that would convict their neighbor, Minnie Wright, of murdering her husband. Likewise, *Woman's Honor,* another of her early one-act plays, exposes the hypocrisy of the double standard of morality society has established for men and women.

With *The Verge,* however, Glaspell progressed to the Female phase of development, concerned first and foremost with dramatizing the female experience. Claire Archer is portrayed as the antithesis of the feminine ideal in every conceivable way: she is an ungracious hostess, an unfaithful wife, an unloving mother. Much of the critical commentary on this play, both at the time of its production and in recent years, centers on Glaspell's attitude toward her protagonist; the fact that there is no consensus on this point suggests that Claire should be viewed from a new critical perspective.

"If it was Miss Glaspell's intention to satirize the type of erotic, neurotic, ill-tempered, and platitudinous hussy who dramatizes herself into a 'superwoman' and even 'puts it over' on her gentlemen friends . . . she has admirably succeeded. If, however, like the feminine majority of her audiences, she, too, accepts this fraudulent female as an authentic 'superwoman,' we can only express our opinion that Claire is not convincing," wrote Robert A. Parker in the *Independent*.[9] "Reason . . . finds something repellant and dubious about her fanatical feminism, her lack of restraint and repose," wrote the reviewer for the *Liverpool Daily Post and Mercury*.[10]

Contemporary critics have also disagreed about this aspect of the play. C. W. E. Bigsby says that, "Clearly Glaspell is critical of Claire,"[11] and Arthur Waterman writes that "we must realize that Claire has gone too far."[12] By contrast, Christine Dymkowski believes that "Claire's madness at the end of the play is a personal triumph."[13]

If, however, we view *The Verge* as the play that stands at the pinnacle of Susan Glaspell's development as a female writer, as a play written in the female mode, and as an attempt not to celebrate feminism or illustrate male oppression but, rather, to represent, through Claire, the female experience, we have taken an important first step in coming to terms with this play.

In *The Verge* Susan Glaspell is neither idealizing the superwoman nor is she parodying the fanatical feminist; instead, through Claire she is showing us what it feels like to be the Other, the alien, to be Cixous's newly born woman. If we persist, as many critics have, in seeing *The Verge* as a play written in the feminist mode and Claire as a superwoman hell-bent on transcending the boundaries men have set for women in a patriarchal society, we have oversimplified the play. To view it as a "dramatic presentation of the modern feminist's approach to life,"[14] as Waterman does, is to miss the rich complexity of its achievement.

We can understand more fully how *The Verge* celebrates the female experience if we view the play from the perspective of contemporary French feminist critical theory, specifically that of Hélène Cixous. Cixous and her countrywomen Julia Kristeva and Luce Irigaray seek in various ways to establish a uniquely female form of writing, a mode of using language that opposes itself to the kind of discourse that males typically create, with its linear movement, logical pattern of organization, and reasoned arguments supporting a thesis.

Cixous contends that Western culture is built on a number of binary oppositions, such as Culture/Nature, Mind/Body, Reason/Emotion. This process marginalizes and silences women, since the female principle ultimately emerges as the subordinate term in such oppositions. Cixous writes in her essay "Sorties" that "the movement whereby each opposition is set up to make sense is the movement through which the couple is destroyed. A universal battlefield. Each time, a war is let loose. Death is always at work."[15]

To oppose this hierarchical, phallogocentric pattern of oppositions through which masculine privilege emerges victorious and maintains supremacy, Cixous proposes that women develop a discourse of their own that emerges from the female experience. *L'écriture féminine* is fluid, nonlinear prose, characterized by broken syntax, repetition, multiple voices, long, cumulative sentences, embedded clauses, parenthetical assertions and other disruptions of traditional prose style.

Readers who find *The Verge* "miscellaneous, unselective, hopelessly loquacious," as Alexander Woollcott did, or feel that "Claire's verbal attempts become repetitious and awkward,"[16] as Arthur Waterman did, may find the play more understandable if they view it within the context of Cixous's critical theory. Viewed from this perspective, the play can be seen to develop and valorize a uniquely female point of view in three ways. First, Claire's enterprise, the creation of revolutionary plant forms, can be viewed as analogous to the efforts of theorists such as Cixous and Irigaray to create a uniquely female form of language. Second, through setting, lighting, action, and dialogue, Glaspell sets up a number of binary oppositions that emphasize the symbolic system Claire sets out to destroy. Third, the language of the play, which almost all readers find obscure and tedious, can be seen as an attempt to create a form of *l'écriture féminine*, a uniquely female style of writing.

At the heart of *The Verge* lies Claire Archer's life work: creating new forms of plant life. Glaspell clearly distinguishes between Claire's efforts and the kind of horticultural projects that result in beautiful flowers or better species. When Claire's daughter, Elizabeth, describes her mother's goal in life as trying to create "a new and better kind of plant," Claire quickly corrects her: "They may be new. I don't give a damn whether they're better" (49). She goes on to explain her task further: "These plants—(*Beginning flounderingly*) perhaps they are less beautiful—less sound—than the plants from which they diverged, but they have found— otherness" (52).

The term *otherness* is used frequently by Claire to describe what she is trying to achieve. Like Cixous's newly born woman, Claire strives to transcend all limits, all bounds, not only for her plants but also for herself. Claire is trying to oppose the rationality of a patriarchal system by seeking out madness, by embracing "otherness," by breaking through old structures to create new ones. We might see her as a semiotician with plants, deconstructing the old symbolic order of plant species established by men as she develops a new set of symbols: "They have been shocked out of what they were—into something they were not; they've broken from the forms in which they found themselves. They are alien. Outside" (52).

The similarity between Claire's efforts and those of the feminist theorists whose aim is to break out of male patterns of discourse can be more easily seen by comparing the language Claire uses to describe what she is trying to accomplish with the language Cixous uses in her manifesto "The Laugh of the Medusa":

Cixous

A feminine text cannot fail to be more than subversive. It is volcanic; as it is written it brings about an upheaval of the old property crust, carrier of masculine investments; there's no other way. There's no room for her if she's not a he. If she's a her-she, it's in order to smash everything, to shatter the framework of institutions, to blow up the law, to break up the "truth" with laughter.[17]

Glaspell

I want to break it up! I tell you, I want to break it up! If it were all in pieces, we'd be (*A little laugh*) shocked to aliveness—(*To Dick*) wouldn't we? There would be strange new comings together— mad new comings together, and we would know what it is to be born, and then we might know— that we are. Smash it. (*Her hand is near an egg*). As you'd smash an egg. (19)

Cixous

Flying is woman's gesture—flying in language and making it fly. We have all learned the art of flying and its numerous techniques; for centuries we've been able to

Glaspell

But our own spirit is not something on the loose. Mine isn't. It has something to do with what I do. To fly. To be free in air. To look down from above on possess anything only by flying; we've lived in flight, stealing away, finding, when desired, narrow passageways, hidden crossovers. It's no accident that *voler* has a double meaning, that it plays on each of them and thus throws off the agents of sense. It's no accident: women take after birds and robbers just as robbers take after women and birds. They (*illes*) go by, fly the coop, take pleasure in jumbling the order of space, in disorienting it, in changing around the furniture, dislocating things and values, breaking them all up, emptying structures, and turning property upside down.[18]

the world of all my days. Be where man has never been! Yes— wouldn't you think the spirit could get the idea? The earth grows smaller. I am leaving. What are they—running around down there? Why do they run around down there? Houses? Houses are funny lines and down-going slants—houses are vanishing slants. I am alone. Can I breathe this rarer air? Shall I go higher? Shall I go too high? I am loose. I am out. But no; man flew, and returned to earth the man who left it. (31)

Cixous begins "Sorties" by enumerating the oppositions upon which the patriarchy bases and maintains its power:

Activity/passivity,
Sun/Moon,
Culture/Nature,
Day/Night,

Father/Mother,
Head/heart,
Intelligible/sensitive,
Logos/Pathos.

Form, convex, step, advance, seed, progress.
Matter, concave, ground—which supports the step, receptacle.[19]

Cixous's method is to disrupt these structures by creating a new and different language, one that comes from woman's body, destroying the old hierarchical oppositions through its fluid, explosive power. In *The Verge* we see similar sets of binary oppositions: light/dark, in/out, hot/cold. There is a strangely bulging tower that incorporates both curves and straight lines; there is the failed experiment, the Edge Vine, and the successful new species, the Breath of Life.

The setting for act 1 is described as "a place that is dark, save for a shaft of light from below which comes up through an open trap door in the floor" (1). Similarly, Claire is keeping her laboratory extremely warm at the expense of the rest of the house, where the temperature is very cold. Much of her energy in act 1 is expended in trying to keep her family and friends out of the nice, warm laboratory, where they are determined to enter so that they can eat breakfast more comfortably. Thus, the conflict of binary oppositions is dramatized in *The Verge,* as the men in the play try to force their way into a warmer room and Claire, concerned about her plants' environment, tries to keep them out in the cold.

Act 2 finds Claire in her sanctuary, "a tower which is thought to be round but does not complete the circle. The back is curved, then jagged lines break from that, and the front is a queer, bulging window—in a curve that leans" (58). The tower, incorporating both linear and spherical shapes, is a new form, emblematic of Claire's triumph in creating new forms of plants. As in act 1, the action centers on Claire's efforts to keep others out of a place that is special for her.

In act 3 Claire's enterprise comes to fruition: the Breath of Life is seen to have broken through to a new species; she has successfully undermined the masculine structures that threatened to contain her. Indeed, Claire functions in *The Verge* similarly to the way Catherine Clément describes the hysteric in the opening section of *The Newly Born Woman:* "The hysteric unties the familiar bond, introduces disorder into the well-regulated unfolding of everyday life, gives rise to magic in ostensible reason."[20] Surveying the situation at the end of *The Verge,* as Tom lies dying amid broken glass while the Breath of Life flourishes and Claire fires a revolver and sings "Nearer My God to Thee," the reader who can see Claire as Clément's hysteric can achieve a new understanding of this seemingly bizarre and melodramatic ending.

In dialogue, as well as in setting, lighting, and action, Glaspell highlights the structures that undergird masculine dominance by focusing on oppositional images. Perhaps nowhere else in *The Verge* are the comic limitations of masculine investment in these structures more clearly illustrated than when Claire's husband, Harry, says: "What do you think I caught her doing the other day? Reading Latin. Well—a woman that reads Latin needn't worry a husband much" (22–23). He later adds, "I suppose a woman who lives a good deal in her mind never does have much—well, what you might call passion" (23).

Glaspell uses dialogue not only to emphasize binary oppositions but also to violate the audience's expectations, thus creating a new language, a new means of expression for Claire. One technique Glaspell uses is to end a sentence with a noun clause. The audience, which has been led to expect a more concrete direct object, is left puzzling over just what her sentence meant. Early in the play Claire, in describing her work, says: "I want to give fragrance to Breath of Life—(*Faces the room beyond the wall of glass*)—the flower I've created that is outside what flowers have been. What has gone out should bring fragrance from what it has left" (17). Another way Glaspell violates her audience's expectations is to delay closure. Claire characteristically uses fragments and questions as well as short, simple sentences and exclamations, forms of syntax we would not expect in dramatic dialogue:

Not the madness that—breaks through. And it was—a stunning chance! Mankind massed to kill. We have failed. We are through. We will destroy. Break this up—it can't go farther. In the air above—in the sea below—it is to kill! All we had thought we were—we aren't. We were shut in with what wasn't so. Is there one ounce of energy has not gone to this killing? Is there one love not torn in two? Throw it in! Now? Ready? Break up. Push. Harder. Break up. And then—and then—! But we didn't say—"And then—" The spirit didn't take the tip. (34)

Through violating the norms of dramatic discourse, the norms of logic and linear progression, Glaspell creates her own form of *l'écriture féminine*, one that is ideally suited to Claire's rebellious purpose. The most radical example of Glaspell's innovative use of language to emphasize Claire's efforts to break free of the prison of forms into otherness is the blank verse that Claire speaks in at various points in the play:

> Yes; but we are so weak we have to talk;
> To talk—to touch.
> Why can't I rest in knowing I would give my life to reach you?
> That has—all there is.
> But I must—put my timid hands upon you,
> Do something about infinity.
> O, let what will flow into us,
> And fill us full—and leave us still.
> Wring me dry,
> And let me fill again with life more pure.
> To know—to feel,
> And do nothing with what I feel and know—
> That's being good. That's nearer God.

(83)

Though *The Verge* has baffled and irritated many critics, audiences, and readers since it was first produced in 1921, at least one person came away from the play convinced that Susan Glaspell had created a new form of drama. "What Charlotte Brontë did for the novel, Susan Glaspell is doing for the play," read the *Illustrated London News*'s review of the play's 1925 London production: "She is making it effeminate. I do not use the word in any derogatory sense. In a word, she has broken away from the masculine tradition." The reviewer went on to say that Glaspell was an innovator rather than an imitator, imbuing her play with the feminine qualities of passion, instinct, rebellion, intuition, and spirituality. "This is Susan Glaspell's distinction," concluded the writer. "She has carried these feminine distinctions into the drama."[21]

But even as an examination of *The Verge* through the lens of feminist theory can give the reader new insight into this play, an examination of Cixous's concept of *l'écriture féminine* with respect to *The Verge* can highlight some limitations of this theory. Claire's struggle to create a new kind of plant has failed with the Edge Vine, which is seen early in the play to be reverting to type. Her efforts with the Breath of Life, however, are successful. At the climax of the play she discovers it has flowered into a new creation; in the stage directions Glaspell describes it as "a plant like caught motion" (94). This oxymoron heightens the paradoxical nature of Claire's enterprise, which she explains later in the play in blank verse:

> Breath of the uncaptured?
> You are a novelty.
> Out?
> You have been brought in.
> A thousand years from now, when you are but a form too long repeated.
> Perhaps the madness that gave you birth will burst again,
> And from the prison that is you will leap pent queernesses
> To make a form that hasn't been—
> To make a prison new.
> And this we call creation. (105–6)

In this speech Claire begins to realize that her efforts to achieve otherness are doomed to failure. She now knows she is trapped by forms, for, no matter how hard she tries to break outside the old forms, all she gets is another form, one that will seem revolutionary for a time but will ultimately become as confining as the one from which it came. She has discovered that the language of plants works similarly to the language of words. She is trapped by form in the same way that we are trapped by language structures that come before all else and create the way we see the world. She has discovered what Frederic Jameson calls "the prisonhouse of language."

Just as Claire is trapped by form, feminist theorists who urge women to write their bodies, to find in *jouissance* a source of power and inspiration to overthrow masculine forms of discourse and create their own language, are similarly trapped. Hélène Cixous writes

> If woman has always functioned "within" man's discourse, a signifier referring always to the opposing signifier that annihilates its particular energy, puts down or stifles its very different sounds, now it is time for her to displace this "within," explode it, overturn it, grab it, make it hers, take it in, take it into her women's mouth, bite its tongue with her women's teeth, make up her own tongue to get inside of it.[22]

But after she has "made up her own tongue" she is still left with a tongue, a language, a form of discourse. No matter how destructive, rebellious, or innovative she becomes, she is still imprisoned within language. Cixous's ultimate goal is to destroy the power that men have by destroying their language. "The one who is in the master's place, even if not the master of a knowledge, is in a position of power," she says in a dialogue with Catherine Clément. "The only way to bar that is to execute the 'master,' kill him, eliminate him, so that what he has to say can get through, so that he himself is not the obstacle, so it will be *given*." She later describes this kind of giving: "The person who transmits has to be able to function on the level of knowledge without knowing."[23]

Clément, Cixous's colleague, acknowledges how impossible this task is when she replies, "I see no way to conceive of a cultural system in which there would be no transmission of knowledge in the form of a coherent statement."[24] Cixous herself seems to recognize the paradoxical nature of "functioning on the level of knowledge without knowing: when she writes, "At the present time defining a feminine practice of writing is impossible with an impossibility that will continue; for this practice will never be able to be *theorized*, enclosed, coded, which does not mean it does not exist."[25]

The same awareness is articulated by Claire in *The Verge* when her daughter asks her to explain what she's trying to do with her plants. Claire's response is that "one would rather not nail it to a cross of words—with brass tacks." Her husband replies, "But I want to see you put things into words, Claire, and realize just where you are" (51).

Like Claire Archer, the feminist theorist committed to *l'écriture féminine* is caught in a vicious circle; she cannot escape structures except through annihilation. If she tries to explain her enterprise, she must do it with language, within the very structures she is trying to break out of. If she doesn't explain or define it, she has no way of validating its existence.

Near the end of *The Verge* Claire's lover, Dick, looks at the Breath of Life, the "plant like caught motion" and says: "It's quite new in form. It—says something about form" (105). Like the Breath of Life, *The Verge* is both a new form and a commentary on form. Through this remarkable play Susan Glaspell attempts to show us the futility of attempting to transcend form, a lesson that the proponents of *l'écriture féminine* would do well to heed.

NOTES

1. M. Castellun, "*The Verge:* Daring Venture in Drama by Susan Glaspell," *New York Call*, 16 November 1921, 4.

2. J. F. Holmes, "*The Verge,*" *New Statesman*, 4 April 1925, 746.

3. K. Macgowan, "Seen on the Stage," *Vogue* 59 (15 January 1922):48–49.

4. A. Woollcott, "The Play—Provincetown Psychiatry," *New York Times*, November 15, 1923,7:1.

5. S. Glaspell, *The Verge* (Boston: Small, Maynard, 1922), 33. Subsequent references to this play will be made parenthetically in the text.

6. E. Showalter, "Toward a Feminist Poetics," in *The New Feminist Criticism*, ed. E. Showalter (New York: Pantheon Books, 1985), 131.

7. Ibid., 137.

8. Ibid., 139.

9. R. A. Parker, "Drama—Plays Domestic and Imported," *Independent*, December 17, 1921, 296.

10. *Liverpool Daily Post and Mercury*, September 18, 1925.

11. C. W. E. Bigsby, *A Critical Introduction to Twentieth Century American Drama* (New York: Cambridge, 1982), 1:32.

12. A. Waterman, *Susan Glaspell* (New York: Twayne, 1966), 81.

13. C. Dymkowski, "On the Edge: The Plays of Susan Glaspell," *Modern Drama* 31 (March 1988):91–105.

14. A. Waterman, "A Critical Study of Susan Glaspell's Works and Her Contributions to Modern American Drama." Ph.D. diss., University of Wisconsin, 1956, 191.

15. H. Cixous and C. Clément, *The Newly Born Woman* (1975), trans. B. Wing (Minneapolis: University of Minnesota Press, 1986), 64.

16. Waterman, "Critical Study," 197.

17. H. Cixous, "The Laugh of the Medusa," in *New French Feminisms*, ed. E. Marks and I. de Courtivron (New York: Schocken Books, 1981), 258.

18. Ibid.

19. Cixous and Clément, *Newly Born Woman*, 63.

20. Ibid., 5.

21. *The Illustrated London News*, April 11, 1925, 644.
22. Cixous and Clément, *Newly Born Woman*, 95–96.
23. Ibid., 140.
24. Ibid., 141.
25. Ibid., 92.

Part 3
Full-length Female
Figures

Beyond *The Verge:* Absent Heroines in the Plays of Susan Glaspell

Jackie Czerepinski

Susan Glaspell was, for many years, cited principally for her part in the founding of the Provincetown Players, a group remembered mainly for bringing Eugene O'Neill to the stage. In recent years, however, Glaspell has been rediscovered as a feminist playwright whose often experimental scripts deserve both study and production. Critics and historians such as Marcia Noe, Gerhard Bach, Linda Ben-Zvi, and others have contributed to this recovery. A collection of four Glaspell plays, edited by C. W. E. Bigsby in 1987, has made her work again accessible.

The most widely published and best known of her works is her first play, *Trifles*—tightly constructed, naturalistic in its characters and settings, and remarkable for its economy of means. In this 1916 one-act Glaspell used a device to which she would return in later, longer plays: a protagonist who never appears onstage. As Christine Dymkowski remarks, "Although noted by critics, this use of an absent central character has not received much comment" (93). The absent characters in Glaspell's plays *Bernice* and *Alison's House* are the focus of this essay. By examining Glaspell's creation of characters who never appear and their relationship to others of her works, we can begin more fully to understand her skill as a dramatist and to unravel the complexities of her dialogue with her audience and with herself. Glaspell's use of this device foregrounds ways of knowing and knowledge based on gender as it privileges absence and silence.

In *Trifles* the ability of Mrs. Peters and Mrs. Hale to read the story of Minnie Wright's life, written in the everyday objects of her kitchen, creates a system of female signifiers incomprehensible to the men, the trained investigators whose job it is to read signs. The truths discovered by the female characters contradict traditional, male, notions of legality and morality. This gendered system of meaning operates more subtly but still powerfully in *Bernice* (1919) and *Alison's House* (1930). As in *Trifles,* the mystery at the heart of each play is the motive that drove the absent protagonist; the central concern for the audience is the reading of these missing characters. Significantly, the characters who solve the mystery by opening the truth of the protagonist's life for us are inevitably female. These "seers" are also women who live in the margins of conventional patriarchal society. Further, they discover what is right—each of the plays has a strong moral dimension—not through applying "universal" ethical standards but, instead, through empathy, a feeling *into* the lives of the protagonists. Glaspell contrasts these diviners with men, and male-identified women, who are negative or neutral forces—stultifying at worst, spiritually stunted at best—incapable of the vision granted to the women because they are contained in a conventional world constructed and ruled by words.

In *Bernice* Glaspell's first full-length play, produced by the Province-town Players in 1919, the protagonist is dead when the play begins. The characters gather at the news of Bernice's death: her gentle bewildered father; her lifelong servant, Abbie; her unfaithful husband, Craig, who is a hack writer of popular literature; his sister, Laura; and Margaret Pierce, Bernice's perceptive, devoted friend.

When Abbie tells Craig that Bernice committed suicide he, unable to bear the news alone, tells Margaret. She cannot believe that Bernice would take her own life and presses Abbie, who admits that Bernice died a natural death but that her last request was that Craig be told she ended her own life. In torment Margaret struggles with the meaning of the strange deathbed wish, unable to tell Craig the truth and un-willing to believe that "Bernice's life was hate." She sees, finally, that the lie has transformed the shallow widower, as Bernice knew it would, and recognizes that out of Bernice's created fiction great truths may grow.

Bernice first emerges as a palpable and powerful figure through the setting. Bernice's home anticipates the qualities of the woman who will be described by the other characters: "You feel yourself in the house of a woman you would like to know, a woman of sure and beautiful instincts, who lives simply" (159). The first reference to Bernice is in terms of this setting. "Bernice made this house," her Father says; "Everything is Bernice. You can't get Bernice out of this room" (160). The home is isolated, difficult to get to but well worth the trip, just as Bernice was "off by herself"—beyond the understanding of most. Certainly, the men, and the male-defined, cannot fully comprehend her.

Father's Bernice was "without malice," a woman "amused by things she—perhaps couldn't admire in us she loved" (222), and "wistful" because "she wanted to give—what couldn't be given" (223). Although he dearly loved his daughter, admired her, he admits "there were things [about Bernice]—outside what I understood" (163). Like so many other men in Glaspell's plays, he sees the protagonist through a collection of social roles, as "my little girl" and Craig's wife. Father believes, in common with the rest of the masculine world, that husbandly domination of the wife is both natural and necessary: "Craig didn't dominate Bernice. I don't know whose fault it was" (224).

Craig is a writer who squanders his talent by producing popular drivel. His absence at Bernice's death is a consequence of his affair with another woman—the latest in a string of other women—to whom he turned because he "never felt she—couldn't get along without me" (170). In his attempt to justify his absence he says to Margaret, "[A man] has to feel that he moves—completely moves—yes, could destroy—not that he would, but has the power to reshape [his wife]" (174).

Craig's sister, Laura, is the completely conventional, socially successful woman encased in a world of "shoulds." She is the only character who refers to Bernice as "Mrs. Norris" and she says of her: "It isn't as if Bernice were—like most women. There was something—aloof in Bernice" (177). She views Craig's adultery as Bernice's fault: "It's unfortunate Bernice hadn't the power to hold Craig. . . . It's what a wife should want to do" (186).

Laura appears in different guises in virtually all of Glaspell's plays to represent women content with the status quo. They are upright wives and mothers—the pillars of society who mark the line between social acceptability and the territory inhabited by the women Glaspell champions. As Dymkowski notes in her excellent analysis:

Central to Glaspell's plays is a concern with fulfilling life's potential, going beyond the confines of convention, safety, and ease to new and uncharted possibilities, both social and personal. This need to take life to its limits and push beyond them implies a paradoxical view of life's margins as central to human experience—as the cutting edge that marks the difference between mere existence and real living. (91)

In the plays under discussion here it is the diviners who live in the margins; the protagonists have literally and figuratively gone beyond them. Because the absent women transcend the social roles that define the majority, what they realize beyond ordinary limits cannot be understood by those contained within the social world.

Margaret Pierce is the seer in this play, the one who understands the truth and provides it for the audience. She is a woman at the edge of conventional life—unmarried, largely alone, and dedicated to fighting for those imprisoned for voicing unpopular thoughts—"a wreck of free speech," Craig calls her. Glaspell reinforces Margaret's marginality in a confrontation between her and Laura, who describes Margaret as: "You who have not cared what people thought of you—who have not had the sense of fitness—the taste—to hold the place you were born to" (189).

Bernice counted on Margaret's gift for insight. "Margaret sees things," Bernice is reported as saying. Margaret senses that there is something left to do or to see: "I feel something we don't get to. . . . I think she would expect us to—find our way. . . . She had not meant to leave us here" (196). Craig and Abbie's assertion that Bernice died by suicide violates Margaret's knowledge of the woman who "*was* life." In a characteristic Glaspell stage direction we get: "(MARGARET *stands motionless, searching, and as if something is coming to her from the rightness. When she speaks it is a denial from that inner affirmation.*) No! I say—No! . . . I don't believe it. What you told me—*I don't believe it*" (204). Thus, ultimate knowledge comes from feeling, from an understanding based on shared experience and identification, just as it did in *Trifles*.

The "rightness" from which Margaret's certain knowledge comes is closely allied with the life force that Glaspell describes as flowing through Bernice. These deeply felt but vaguely described forces can be apprehended only by those with "the tenderness of insight" (*Bernice* 229), a tenderness belonging to female outsiders. While Glaspell *names* these energies—"the rightness," "all of life," for example—they are beyond articulate explanation, greater than the power of language. Describing Bernice in act 2, Margaret says, "What she was came true and deep from—." The line ends in a dash: Bernice's source is beyond naming. The last words spoken in the play are Margaret's: "No. Not for words." And the play ends with a stage direction: "(*She closes her hand, uncloses it in a slight gesture of freeing what she would not harm*)" (229).

Margaret's benediction for Bernice's life exemplifies Glaspell's ambivalence about language and her concomitant exploitation of the enormous communicative potential of nonverbal signs. Her use of stage settings as descriptors is the most obvious example of the latter. Glaspell's symbolic use of settings is ably discussed elsewhere, but it is worth noting here that in *Bernice,* as in *Alison's House,* changes in the setting mirror the course of the action. The superficial changes that the characters make in Bernice's room in an attempt to distance themselves from their loss are rescinded at the end of the play: the room is given "back to Bernice."

Glaspell's complex and emotionally specific stage directions often carry ultimate meanings as well. In *Trifles,* for example, the women agree to suppress the evidence against Minnie Wright without debate and without saying that they have decided anything. What they cannot express in words is physically expressed. Frequently, Glaspell also invokes images of gesture to delineate absent characters. In both *Alison's House* and *Bernice* the protagonist's open, outstretched hands are cherished memories for the other characters and important signs for the audience. This reliance on the unspoken privileges silence.

The privileging of absence parallels Glaspell's treatment of silence. Death—absence—gives Bernice a power she did not have in life. Margaret says of Bernice and Craig, "There was something in her he might have drawn from and become bigger than he was" (186). In the end Craig does become "bigger than he was." For Margaret as well, Bernice's absence is empowering: "Why does Bernice—her death—make that so simple tonight? Something is *down.* I could see things as I never saw them" (189). Absence has a gravitational force, drawing the other characters to the physical and psychic spaces left by the protagonists.

Ironically, Craig's eventual redemption is based on a lie. Glaspell's questioning of traditional moral and ethical systems is thus as strong here as it was in *Trifles*. What matters is not the reified language—"crime/justice," "lie/truth"—but the enhancing of human potential. Craig is Bernice's gift to the future, remade by his mistaken belief that "he really had Bernice," that his unfaithfulness drove her to suicide. "This," he says, "—has given Bernice to me" (226). The giving of life-sustaining gifts, the capability to shape life anew, as Dymkowski describes it, is the "action" both Bernice and Alison, in *Alison's House*, perform without stepping on the stage.

Reading the protagonist is again the issue in *Alison's House*, for which Glaspell won the Pulitzer Prize in 1931. The absent character at the center of the action is Alison Stanhope, a reclusive poet who has been dead for eighteen years when the play begins. Her family has gathered on the last day of the nineteenth century to dispose of the family home and to bring Agatha, the sister who devoted her life to caring for Alison, to town to live. But Agatha possesses a secret, a packet of Alison's poems never seen by any eyes except the poet's. Agatha's ineffectual attempts to destroy the legacy draw attention to it. The revelation of Alison's thwarted, illicit love forces the family to confront the essential Alison, themselves, and the future. The seeing and saying in this play divides characters along gender lines, although Glaspell grants at least partial insight to some of the male characters. She invokes generational distinctions as well.

In *Alison's House* Glaspell characteristically uses the setting as a symbol of the protagonist. As the plot takes us nearer to the truth about what drove Alison Stanhope, the action moves from the sitting room to Alison's bedroom, from the public to the private. The newspaper reporter who introduces us to Alison as a publicly revered poet begins with the house. Knowles has heard about the sale of the home and wants to see, "most of all, the house . . . especially the room that was used by Miss Alison Stanhope" (4). This public figure is contrasted with the sister-aunt the family remembers.

Stanhope, Alison's brother and the head of the family, remembers and reveres the public Alison: "She was a great soul, and a poet" (13). His memories concern her outward life, her reading aloud from Emerson and Milton, the care she took of her flowers. Much of Alison's value for

Stanhope lies in the sacrifice she made of her love on the altar of convention: "Alison didn't desert her family" (74). Until Alison's poems surface, and he is helped to perceive their worth, Stanhope is unconscious of the enormity of Alison's sacrifice and unwilling to let the deepest truths in her poetry be given to the world he persuaded Alison not to defy. Alison did "the right thing," and he wishes the depth of her love and the anguish of its denial burned with the poetry. Stanhope wants to preserve Alison in her nineteenth-century maiden role.

Louise, the wife of Alison's nephew Eben, is even more rigidly conventional than is Stanhope. She is mildly embarrassed that people say Alison "was different—a rebel" (13). She is fearful of the family's being thought odd and unwilling to have things "stirred up." Glaspell uses Louise, as she used Laura, to furnish the conventional reaction to the outcast diviner, Elsa.

Stanhope's daughter, Elsa, has defied society by running off with a married man. In Glaspell's universe her marginality goes hand in hand with her vision. Elsa says of the recovered poems, "I know their value—as no one else knows" (145). "Because Alison said it for women" (150), Elsa and Ann, who represent their generation as well as their gender, want to see Alison's poems given as a gift to the future. As in *Bernice,* the dead can alter the living; the past can give to the future. As in *Bernice,* the missing protagonist is a matrix through which the other characters relate. Doing things for her, in her memory or as she would have done them, shapes the behavior of the other characters. When Elsa enters the house she says, "But won't you just [let me stay] because Alison would do it?" and the family does.

Like Bernice, Alison had insight: "Alison knows," she is often quoted as saying. What Alison knew came to her, as to the other women, through experience and empathy rather than through inquiry or education. She, who so often "made little presents" for those she loved, who created stories to provide comfort, is still giving presents and offering comfort through the other characters and through the poetry that the family will give to the world. Stanhope says: "She loved to make her little gifts. If she can make one more, from her century to yours, then she isn't gone. Anything else is—too lonely" (154).

None of Alison's poems are, in fact, read in the play; even the poet who "said it for women" speaks on the stage only through the other characters. The initial reason for this particular silence was the refusal by Emily Dickinson's family to allow use of her poems; emptying the play, however, of Alison's own words, except those remembered by other characters, reinforces her absence and her silence. "Issues of expression . . . are the essence of her work," Bigsby says of Glaspell (29). Claire's descent into inarticulate madness in *The Verge* and Allie Mayo's voluntary aphasia in *The Outside* exemplify, as does the silence of the missing protagonists, Glaspell's suspicions about the efficacy of language, particularly for her marginalized women.

The absent heroines are linked by analogy to Glaspell as the biographer of her domineering and charismatic husband, Jig Cook. Like Glaspell in *The Road to the Temple*, Alison and Bernice have a double relationship to the performed text: they are invisible within it at the same time that they determine its course and shape. Of *The Road to the Temple* Ann Larabee says: "Her own body was invisible. . . . Claiming Cook as sole redeemer made him Glaspell's possession, her personal Christ, contained in the Gospel she had written for him. She was priest, controlling his incarnation" (100).

Links of empathy and identification join Glaspell to her characters just as they connect the diviners to the protagonists in *Trifles, Bernice,* and *Alison's House.* There are a number of similarities between the playwright and her protagonists, a creator-created relationship Glaspell explores dramatically in *The Verge,* in which Claire's goal for herself, as for the plants she is creating, is to go beyond what things have been before. All of the heroines have, as a "birthright," a clearly demarcated place in the conventional society in which they cannot be contained. None of Glaspell's insightful women is comfortably married, a shared quality that deserves more attention when Cook is considered in relationship to Glaspell's work. All, with the exception of Claire, are childless. In *Bernice,* in fact, Craig mentions "losing our boy before we had him." Glaspell suffered a miscarriage shortly before writing the play. With the exception of Madeline in *Inheritors,* all of the women are of an age with Glaspell.

Among the characters Glaspell shows onstage, in all of her plays, there is not one for whom she expresses the unalloyed admiration she has for

Bernice and Alison. Bernice seems to be the New Woman Glaspell envisioned and perhaps wanted to become; Alison appears to be the figure she found herself to be later in her career. Surely Glaspell's skills as a dramatist would have allowed her to draw both women. That she chose not to do so is another reflection of her ambivalence toward a language and a stage dominated by the same patriarchal forces that controlled the world beyond the theater.

The similarities between character and author go a long way toward explaining the place of *Alison's House* in Glaspell's body of work. By 1930, when Eva Le Gallienne's Civic Repertory Company produced the play, Glaspell was no longer at the center of theatrical activity; *her* Provincetown Players had ceased to exist in 1922. Equally important were the crucial changes in the social and political climates; women's issues had, in a sense, gone underground. As Sharon Friedman remarks: "Paradoxically, the winning of the vote in 1920 signalled the decline of feminism. The failure to incorporate certain feminist gains into personal life gradually distanced the career woman from the family woman, and the feminist became an object of ridicule, if not pity" (72). What more natural, then, than to go back to the beginning of the struggle to create a heroine acceptable even to the notoriously conservative Pulitzer Prize committee? What heroine more appropriate than one who said it for women? *Alison's House* was Glaspell's last play. Bigsby, among others, blames Cook's death for ending Glaspell's theatrical career. Vital though that may have been, the loss of her theater and the changes in the world seem as strong barriers to continued experimentation.

Neither *Bernice* nor *Alison's House* enjoys the high reputation of *Trifles,* but the thread that connects them—the power arising from absence and silence—is a thread running through all of Glaspell's work. The absent women are much more than the facts of their lives, more than the society at large recognizes them to be. The truths of their existence can only be deciphered for us by female characters at the margins of convention. Morality founded in "universal" principles, knowledge based in propositional logic and warranted by "universal" truths, are inappropriate—insufficient—for comprehending the "rightness." Glaspell's concerns are, consequently, not "merely" feminist but profoundly feminist, even in these seemingly conventional works.

WORKS CITED

Bigsby, C. W. E. Introduction. *Plays by Susan Glaspell.* Cambridge: Cambridge University Press, 1987.

Dymkowski, Christine. "On the Edge: The Plays of Susan Glaspell." *Modern Drama* 31, no. 1 (1988): 91–105.

Friedman, Sharon. "Feminism as Theme in Twentieth-Century American Women's Drama." *American Studies* 25, no. 1 (1984): 69–89.

Glaspell, Susan. *Alison's House.* London: Samuel French, 1930.

———. *Bernice. Plays.* New York: Dodd, Mead, 1927.

Larabee, Ann. "Death in Delphi: Susan Glaspell and the Companionate Marriage." *Mid-American Review* 7 (1987): 93–106.

Bernice's Strange Deceit:
The Avenging Angel in the House

Sharon Friedman

You who have come of a younger and happier generation may not have
heard of her—You may not know what I mean by the Angel in the
House. . . . She was intensely sympathetic. She was immensely charming.
She was utterly unselfish. She excelled in the difficult arts of family life. She
sacrificed herself daily. . . . [S]he was so constituted that she never had a
mind or a wish of her own, but preferred to sympathize always with the
minds and wishes of others. Above all—I need not say it—she was pure.
Her purity was supposed to be her chief beauty—her blushes, her great
grace. In those days—the last of Queen Victoria—every house had its
Angel. And when I came to write I encountered her with the very first
words. The shadow of her wings fell on my page; I heard the rustling of her
skirts in the room. Directly, that is to say, I took my pen in hand to review
that novel by a famous man, she slipped behind me and whispered: "My
dear, you are a young woman. You are writing about a book that has been
written by a man. Be sympathetic; be tender; flatter; deceive; use all the
arts and wiles of sex. Never let anybody guess that you have a mind of your
own. Above all, be pure." . . . I turned upon her and caught her by the
throat. . . . Had I not killed her she would have killed me.
—Virginia Woolf, "Professions for Women"

In the early decades of the twentieth century the insistence upon the
truth—the goal of verisimilitude, the "desire to get closer to the fact"—
was the dominant chord in American drama, and women playwrights did
not hesitate to portray issues that drew upon the "facts" of their lives as
women. Playwrights such as Rachel Crothers, Zoë Akins, Zona Gale,
Clare Kummer, and Lulu Vollmer, who gained access to the theater dur-

ing a time of intense feminist activity, often portrayed women's issues from the point of view of the "New Woman." This prototype, as Deborah Kolb notes, was "unafraid to challenge male decisions and male dominance"[1] as she sought her identity. One manifestation of this quest for identity, often apart from men, was the wife's revolt within marriage, which Arthur Hobson Quinn observed in the plays of the early 1920s and related to the feminist movement.[2]

The protagonist of Susan Glaspell's *Bernice*,[3] her first full-length play, written in 1919, is one such wife whose insurrection points to multiple truths. It is a play built on a wife's deception, and the audience is left to sort out the conflicting meanings that emerge when fantasy is the instrument of revolt. Bernice cannot be defined against any type, not even one as progressive as the New Woman. As Christine Dymkowski argues, Glaspell's characters have a need to take life to its limits, and the "edge is imbued with both possibility and danger."[4]

Susan Glaspell's plays defy easy categories. Her eccentric plots challenge the audience to look at conventions that govern our behavior from alternative perspectives.[5] With *Bernice* Glaspell seems poised between the feminist awakening in *Trifles* (1916) and the modernist revolt in *The Verge* (1921). Irving Howe formulates the modernist view as a turn from "truth to sincerity, from the search for objective law to a desire for authentic response."[6] This movement toward introspection is implicit in Glaspell's preoccupation with consciousness and the power of the imagination to shape the way we think about our lives (to "feel our feelings," in the words of critic Isaac Goldberg). And as an early modernist, Glaspell is also inspired by her Romantic predecessors to value subjectivity and the prerogative of the individual to ignore mundane limits in creating the universe that her mind perceives. In *Bernice* Glaspell allows her protagonist to "reinvent the terms of her reality." Through her own fiction she fulfills her conflicting needs to uphold and undermine, simultaneously, a conventional role for women: the self-sacrificing wife, the inspiring muse, the angel in the house.

As in *Trifles*, Glaspell gradually brings the audience into the mind of a female character who never appears onstage. Bernice has recently died when the drama begins, but the way in which she has orchestrated the events surrounding her death makes her central to the play. Although she died of natural causes, she enjoined her servant to tell her husband Craig that she had taken her own life. Bernice is conscious of her errant husband's need to possess her (he blames his unfaithfulness on her remote nature), and she manages to alter appearances so that she retains her autonomy while providing her husband with the illusion that he has had her.

As Bernice had anticipated, Craig is shocked but stirred as he construes this information as a revelation of Bernice's love for him. Fearing that he had never really possessed Bernice, the despair of her suicide convinces him that she was, indeed, disturbed by his infidelity and, thus, completely his.

Glaspell has expressed a rudimentary feminism in her portrayal of a relationship based upon power. Bernice is a woman who is aware of the social and psychological role that her husband requires her to act out and of the effect of that role for their relationship. She is conscious of Craig's need to possess her as a woman, to seek his image in the reflection of her devotion, and she is conscious of the strength that he derives from this illusion.

Craig has deluded himself in all areas of his life. He is a writer whose insecurities about the depth of his work are camouflaged by glib prose. When Bernice's close friend Margaret accuses him of creating "a well put-up light" that "doesn't penetrate anything," he acknowledges his difficulty "to be real" in writing for the public. His feelings of powerlessness as a man are covered over by affairs with women whom he is able to dominate. Only Bernice, the wished-for keeper of his myths, has remained, until now, aloof and unyielding.

And yet it is not Bernice whom Craig wants but, rather, the acquiescence of her spirit. Craig's almost bizarre acceptance of Bernice's purported suicide might be explained by his view of her as the "unattainable other," mystically tied to eternity. Michele Murray has identified this recurrent image in fiction as "the woman worshipped precisely because her remoteness from common humanity allows her lover to believe in a permanence that can withstand change and death."[7] The other characters in the play bear out Craig's perception of Bernice, as they describe her as "off by herself," at times "detached," but somehow, deeply immersed in the "flow of life," serene and secure in herself. For Craig, Bernice, remote in life, becomes truly unattainable in death and even more desirable. At the same time, Craig's belief that his wife has sacrificed her life for his love insures the myth that he has had this desirable woman. Her death seals this myth, for she can never revoke it. Through Bernice, Craig approaches immortality. In a confessional speech to Margaret he admits his past failure as well as the resolve that Bernice's sacrifice has given him to shed his deceptive self.

> CRAIG: I wonder if I could have got past that failure . . . of never
> having had her. That she had lived and loved me—and died
> without my ever having had her. What would there have
> been to go on living for? Why should such a person go on
> living? Now—of course it is another world. This comes
> crashing through my make-believe—and Bernice's world gets
> to me.
>
> (226–27)

Bernice reflects the distinctive male and female visions of reality that Sandra M. Gilbert and Susan Gubar discern in the texts of early-twentieth-century writers. They argue that these "literary traces" correspond to a "dissonance between male and female responses to crucial historical experiences"—the suffrage movement, World War I, the entry of women in the labor market.[8] Although the play makes no direct reference to feminism, and only marginal references to progressive ideologies of its time (Darwinian theory, free speech, the defense of political prisoners), the modern tenor of the sexual struggle is salient. Craig expresses anxiety in the face of Bernice's autonomy, and Bernice, in her deceit, struggles to maintain an equilibrium between his needs and her desires.

This underlying sexual tension is expressed by the other characters in the play as they reveal their respective attitudes toward Bernice. Her father and sister-in-law, in different ways, defend male dominance. Unaware of the alleged suicide, they articulate the view that Craig has not "had" Bernice. They sympathize with his frustration, although they locate its source according to their own conventional assumptions.

The father believes that Craig did not "dominate" Bernice because, ultimately, he just "didn't have it in him"—"As I haven't had certain things in me" (224). He is here empathizing with his vision of Craig's spiritual impotence. After a youth fighting for Darwinian thought, the father has retreated from the world, and he views any sign of ineffectual behavior as a kind of impotence. The sister-in-law, Laura, locates the source of Craig's frustration in Bernice. Perceiving Bernice's indifference to Craig's infidelity, she surmises that Bernice "hadn't the power to hold Craig" (186).

At the other end of the spectrum, Bernice's best friend, Margaret, closer to the prototypical New Woman, confronts Craig about his need to contain another in order to feel more in control. She recognizes the necessity for Bernice to be separate in order to reciprocate the love of another individual. Margaret pays homage to the supreme freedom of the mind and the spirit to go where it will. In her work she fights for the rights of political prisoners and for free speech, and this carries over into her philosophical debate with Craig about his need to "have" Bernice. Indeed, the unraveling of the plot and the resolution of the play in essence center on Margaret's desire to understand Bernice on Bernice's terms.

When Craig confides the purported suicide to Margaret, she expresses disbelief. Bernice "was life." "She came from the whole of life" and could under no circumstances take that life. Margaret's skepticism does not abate until, finally, at the end of act 2, Abbie reveals to her a second truth: Bernice had really died of natural causes but had implored her to tell Craig that she had taken her own life. This second revelation is an even greater shock for Margaret, because, once again, it does not coincide with what she knew of her friend. Her husband's infidelity would not drive Bernice to such revenge—a deed of unrelenting torment. Act 3 dramatizes the resolution of these conflicting revelations with Margaret seeing the transformation in Craig's character as he grows committed to a more purposeful life. Believing that his wife died for love of him convinces him of his worth, and imbues his life with new meaning. Margaret, in turn, comes to understand Bernice's strange deceit as "a gift to the spirit," "a gift sent back through the dark" (229), from one who had the power to enter into the lives of those around her and to transform them. In the final gesture of the play Margaret closes and then opens her hand to free the spirit she would not harm.

The critics essentially accept Margaret's word for Bernice. Isaac Goldberg, Glaspell's contemporary, writes that she was "largely the playwright of woman's selfhood" and that this "acute consciousness of self . . . begins with a mere sense of sexual differentiation" in *Trifles* and develops into "the highest aspirations of the complete personality, the individual," in *Bernice*.[9] Ludwig Lewisohn draws on Margaret's words in speaking of Bernice's "spiritual radiance" and maintains that she "sought even as she died to lend him [Craig] that power" that he lacked.[10] Christine Dymkowski sees still another dimension to this gift—the power to "break the mould of his life" and "to reach beyond his limits." Although this critic cautions that we "need not take Margaret's assessment [of Bernice] on trust," she maintains that it is necessary to see "Bernice's achievement" in the context of the power relationships between men and women that Margaret identifies in her words with Craig. Without imposing her expectations on Craig ("like man's power over women"), Bernice "allows him free scope" to realize his true self.[11]

The interpretive problem remains, however, in reconciling Bernice's resistant behavior in life and the compliant image of herself that she conjures up just prior to her death. How can Bernice's fiction of self-abnegation, the denial of her life, be an "authentic response" to a male-female conflict that reflects the consciousness of a fully realized individual? Furthermore, can the audience accept without reservation the horrifying scheme of a counterfeit suicide as a gesture symbolic of a "gift to the spirit"?

The attempt to reconcile sacrifice with selfhood, and deceit with a deeper truth, calls forth the modern perspectives that we have said informed Glaspell's work: the Romantic, the Feminist, the Modernist. To the extent that this play can sustain all of these readings is tribute to Glaspell's portrayal of dramatic conflict within an individual whose needs express different truths.

Is Bernice, then, possessed of a nineteenth-century Romantic sensibility, perceiving truths that transcend mundane conflict, even gender-based conflict? After all, Bernice has not capitulated in life. It is only her fictionalized death that inspires her husband. This view seems consistent with the portrait of Bernice drawn by the other characters in the play. She is seen as remote from the ordinary concerns of most people yet able to see into these concerns from a larger perspective, one filled with understanding. In almost Emersonian language Margaret pays tribute to Bernice's spiritual self-reliance:

> Everything about her has always been—herself. That was one of the rare things about her. (183)

> I do things that to me seem important, and yet . . . I don't get to the thing that I'm doing them for—to life itself. . . . Bernice did. (200)

Indeed, Bernice was Margaret's angel as well.

> It's been the beauty in my life. In my busy, practical life. Bernice— what she was—like a breath that blew over my life and—made it something. (183)

This Romantic, transcendental reading, however, ignores the power that Bernice, in creating this deception, sought for herself: the power to create an autonomous existence, which her husband's needs denied her, and the power to undermine the sanctity of her husband's vision now predicated on complete falsehood. Bernice's "transcendent life force," her "joyous sacrifice,"[12] takes on a more sinister design as we see Craig live out a lie reminiscent of his most destructive fantasies. Unlike Margaret, who is content to coexist with her muse, Craig proclaims that a man has to "feel he . . . completely moves—yes, could destroy—not that he would, but has the power to reshape the—" (174). Bernice's fictional response becomes subversive parody as she mocks the suicide attempt, which Gilbert and Gubar have alluded to as "men's ultimate sexual dominance" over women.[13] Craig draws a hollow inspiration from this avenging muse. We cannot ignore the dramatic irony in his resolve to live a truer life. If his old life had been "make-believe," what truth underlies his resurrection?

The real Bernice remains enigmatic, silent, and inaccessible. Her reliance on deceit, subterfuge, and to some extent providential circumstance suggests the "disguised hostility" in Victorian women writers, observed by Gilbert and Gubar, "who could not imagine female characters who might win sexual struggles through their own direct actions." A character's hostility had to be "distanced and disguised so that . . . it stood outside intentionality."[14]

Is Bernice, then, so disguised that she has the New Woman, Margaret, her confidante, speak for her and defend her action? In order to insure Margaret's compliance, has she duped her as well into seeing the nobility of her sacrifice against her initial and perhaps better judgment? The staging of the play bears out Bernice's omniscience as she lies in state in the adjacent room to which the characters keep returning as if seeking their place in the universe she has created. The directions for the first scene describe the house of a woman who is "sure of her instincts." In the final scene Craig, in full control of his newly acquired power, rearranges the house according to Bernice's plan.

Viewed through still a different lens, however, Bernice's reticence to act directly might imply the Modernist's preoccupation with struggle rather than victory, the "devotion to the problematic." Howe writes that the pre-Modernist search for truth involves "an effort to apprehend the nature of the universe, and can lead to metaphysics, suicide, revolution, and God." With the loss of faith the desire for authentic response "involves an effort to discover our demons within, and makes no claim upon the world other than the right to publicize the aggressions of candor." Some comfort is found in the wounds.[15]

Bernice has not committed suicide for love, but, in creating this illusion, she accommodates two desires: to find a transcendent truth that inspires her devotion, even to one who demands her sacrifice, and to release the demons within that are stifled by this particular truth. She simultaneously gives Craig faith and mocks Craig's faith. This angel may remain in the house, but she will undermine its very foundation.

NOTES

1. Deborah S. Kolb, "The Rise and Fall of the New Woman in American Drama," *Educational Theatre Journal* 27 (May 1975):149.

2. Arthur Hobson Quinn, "The Significance of Recent American Drama," in *Contemporary American Plays,* ed. Arthur Hobson Quinn. (New York, 1923), xxi, xxii.

3. Susan Glaspell, *Bernice*, in *Plays* (Boston: Small, Maynard, 1920), 226–27. All further references to this play appear parenthetically in the text.

4. Christine Dymkowski, "On the Edge: The Plays of Susan Glaspell," *Modern Drama*, no. 1 (March 1988):91.

5. See Linda Ben-Zvi's discussion of Glaspell's manipulation of "conventional dramatic form and conventional gender demarcations and values," in *Feminine Focus: The New Women Playwrights,* ed. Enoch Brater. 147–66. New York: Oxford University Press, 1989.

6. Irving Howe, "The Culture of Modernism," in *Decline of the New,* New York: Harcourt Brace, 1970, 9.

7. Michele Murray, *A House of Good Proportion* (New York: Simon and Schuster, 1973), 350.

8. Sandra M. Gilbert and Susan Gubar, "Introduction," *The Female Imagination and the Modernist Aesthetic* (New York: Gordon and Breach Science Publishers, 1986), 2.

9. Isaac Goldberg, *The Drama of Transition* (Cincinnati: Stewart Kidd, 1922), 474.

10. Ludwig Lewisohn, *Drama and the Stage* (Freeport, N.Y.: Books for Libraries Press, 1922), 105.

11. Dymkowski, "On the Edge," 97–98.

12. C. W. E. Bigsby, *A Critical Introduction to Twentieth Century American Drama,* vol. 1: *1900–1940* (Cambridge: Cambridge University Press, 1982), 26. These are Bigsby's descriptive terms for Bernice. He sees in the play a tendency toward "mawkish sentimentality."

13. Sandra M. Gilbert and Susan Gubar, *No Man's Land,* vol. 1 (New Haven: Yale University Press, 1988), 56.

14. Gilbert and Gubar, *No Man's Land,* 66, 72–73.

15. Howe, "Culture of Modernism," 9.

Chains of Dew and the Drama of Birth Control

J. Ellen Gainor

In the early twentieth century in America an organized movement for the legalization of, and dissemination of information about, birth control began to take hold, particularly in urban areas, where rapid population growth strained the limited resources of immigrant and working-class communities. In addition to the work of birth control activists such as Emma Goldman, Mary Ware Dennett, and Margaret Sanger, numerous journalists expressed views on the controversy in such progressive organs as *The Masses* and the *New York Call*. Less well-known is the artistic response to the movement, which saw in the struggles of the poor and the oppressed the dramatic potential of their plight. Ranging from undisguised agitprop to social comedy, the drama of birth control depicted some highly politicized, some seemingly more objective positions, on the movement. Over less than a decade, through the tumultuous 1910s and war years and into the 1920s, these scripts mirrored the growth of the campaign for birth control, reflecting its rapid evolution from its roots in anarchism and socialism to its endorsement by bourgeois America. The title of one history of the birth control movement in the United States, James Reed's *From Private Vice to Public Virtue,* attests to this evolution. This essay will examine four scripts written between 1914 and 1922—Lawrence Langner's *Wedded: A Social Comedy* (1914), Rose Pastor Stokes and Alice Blaché's *Shall the Parents Decide?* (1916), Mary Burrill's *They That Sit in Darkness: A One-Act Play of Negro Life* (1919), and Susan Glaspell's *Chains of Dew* (1922)—to explore their connections to the movement and to analyze the various aspects of this cultural phenomenon they represent.

According to historian Linda Gordon, "The birth control movement of the second decade of the twentieth century expressed the interests of a growing working class, largely immigrants, who recognized the evaporation of America's promise of upward mobility" and thus had to face the reality of their economic and social status and the unlikelihood of their change (xx–xxi). The movement, of course, was predicated "on a morality that separates sex from reproduction" (Gordon xv)—something that was not possible until the twentieth century, when opposition to contraception as tantamount to support of extramarital sex declined (107) and the change in racial and ethnic composition of urban centers began to have impact on groups concerned about the transformed profile of the U.S. population, previously of white Anglo–northern European descent.

Contrary to subsequent popular myths of U.S. culture, the atmosphere of sexual freedom associated with the "flapper" era had actually begun to emerge in the previous decade (Reed 61; Gordon 187). Prior to World War I New York's Greenwich Village was the center of bohemian life and sexual freedom (Gordon 187). In this cultural center of the country (having surpassed Chicago by the 1910s) Greenwich Village artists generated the stories, images, and life-style that defined the period culminating in the "roaring twenties." These same people were often deeply involved with political concerns and saw their art and writing as integrally connected to their social activism. John Reed, Emma Goldman, Mabel Dodge, Theodore Dreiser, Sinclair Lewis, Max Eastman, Edna St. Vincent Millay, Susan Glaspell, George Cram Cook, and numerous others formed the community.[1]

In the 1910s many of these figures were committed to socialism and ameliorating the condition of the working class as well as to a number of specific causes, such as women's suffrage and birth control. Max Eastman's periodical, *The Masses,* publicized the views of the Greenwich Village artist/activists, and was, according to Irving Howe, "for a brief time . . . the rallying center . . . for almost everything that was then alive and irreverent in American culture" (qtd. in O'Neill, *Last Romantic* 40). According to Eastman's biographer, William O'Neill, "The *Masses* aimed to promote both art and revolution, which in those days everyone thought went together" (40). In many ways *The Masses* was a true community publication, produced by, but also for, Greenwich Village and those sympathetic to its identity.[2]

Yet the number of individuals actively engaged in revolutionary causes was relatively small—John Reed and Emma Goldman among them. *The Masses* had a modest subscriber list, and at its height only sold twenty-five thousand copies (O'Neill, *Last Romantic* 41), suggesting that the concerns raised in the journal did not transcend the boundaries of the community or reach the working classes, who were often the focus of the contributors. Hutchins Hapgood, a longtime resident of the Village whom Eastman felt was a "sentimental rebel" and insufficiently radical (46), said years later of the publication, "Some of the artists of *The Masses* revealed in their illustrations the same moral attitude as Max in his writings; not so much impelled by love of the people or the working-class, as by an effective machinery for the demonstration of superiority" (313). Hapgood, who identified himself in his memoirs as "a Victorian in the modern world," often voiced highly opinionated, regressive or offensive views, but in this instance his sense of the journal's—and perhaps by association many members of the community's—real separation from the subjects of their sociopolitical concern may be valid.

All of the authors of these birth control dramas were connected in some way with Greenwich Village, and one of the interesting features of these plays, several of which are also clearly concerned with issues of race and class, is the implicit position of the playwright vis-à-vis his or her characters. These viewpoints, in turn, reveal facets of the movement itself, which initially was composed of many different constituencies that, for varying reasons, found themselves united in support of birth control. The plays also raise provocative questions about the impact of drama for the movement and, by association, for other political causes. As Glaspell's was the only play ever to be produced,[3] and only two were ever published—Langner's and Burrill's, and in publications known to "preach to the converted"—one must ask what motivated these authors to consider the movement in dramatic form and whether it appears that their works met their goals.

Although the birth control movement in the United States is now associated closely with the work of Margaret Sanger, many other individuals were already active in the campaign before Sanger's commitment to the cause. In the late nineteenth century the "voluntary motherhood" movement was already underway, having evolved from the earlier radical utopian movements that fostered notions of perfectionist eugenics.[4] By the early twentieth century the notion of voluntary motherhood had spread enough to cause alarm in the government, and in 1905 President Roosevelt became associated with attacks on women who wanted small families, appropriating the phrase "race suicide" to describe their behavior. Between 1905 and 1910 birth control became "a public national controversy" (Gordon 133–34). As Gordon points out, "the race-suicide alarm did not emerge out of the imagination of Roosevelt . . . but was a backlash, a response to actual changes in the birth rate, family structure, and sexual practice." The true significance of this reaction was related to a number of other issues, including concern over women's rejection of their primary role of motherhood, the sense that the United States needed a growing indigenous population (that is, descendants of original WASP settlers), and the related fear of an immigrant, poor and/or nonwhite takeover of the Yankee race (134).

Around 1910 leading U.S. intellectuals and those favoring voluntary motherhood began to be influenced by European sexual theorists such as Edward Carpenter, who had established a connection between sexual oppression and other forms of economic and imperial oppression (Gordon 183–84), thus helping to form a stronger link between issues facing the working class and population concerns. These new lines of argument influenced many who believed that birth control education for the poor was essential—that prosperous Americans were using it anyway, and thus keeping it from the poor was socially destructive (186).

In this climate Lawrence Langner published the earliest of the birth control dramas, his 1914 one-act, *Wedded: A Social Comedy*. Langner (1890–1962) was by profession a patent attorney but had a lifelong love of the theater, helping to found two of the most influential American theater companies of the early twentieth century, the Washington Square Players—one of the first groups in the Little Theatre movement, and a friendly competitor to the Provincetown Players[5]—and its outgrowth, the Theatre Guild, which was committed to producing work of the highest theatrical standards but not likely to find commercial production on Broadway.

In his memoir, *The Magic Curtain,* Langner recalls the drama as his first dramatic effort:

> I nursed a thoroughgoing contempt for Broadway. I was eager to work for a better theatre, and the success of my patent practice during the first years seemed to assure me of the ultimate leisure for creative writing to which I had looked forward. One evening I sat in my room with a pad of paper before me, and with a pencil I wrote on it the words "Licensed, a Social Comedy, by Lawrence Langner." On second thought, I struck out the name of the author. The play was on the subject of birth control, and showed somewhat melodramatically the sad results of ignoring the teachings of Margaret Sanger. Surely I would be arrested for writing such a play, which, by advocating birth control, was against the law! I thought of the effect on my clients, who would doubtless be horrified to learn that their foreign patent solicitor had been jailed. Changing the name of the author to "Basil Lawrence," I started to write my first serious play. . . . *Licensed* first saw the light of day between the covers of Margaret's [Anderson] magazine [the *Little Review*]. (79–81)

Langner's reminiscences, published in 1951, are of interest both for their sense of the historical climate in which he wrote his play and for the way that the passage of time colored his memory of that moment. In 1914 Sanger had just begun her campaign for birth control, having started publishing her first periodical, the *Woman Rebel,* in March of that year (Kennedy 22). "The *Woman Rebel* discussed and advocated contraception— the June issue for the first time called it 'birth control' " (23). It was not until 1915, however, during her "self-imposed exile" (72) in Europe, following her arrest for violation of the Comstock laws,[6] that Sanger's fame as a birth control reformer began to spread. Thus, Langner's memory already associated the movement in 1914 with Sanger, although he more probably knew of the campaign from other sources among his Greenwich Village compatriots and readings. His story of the pseudonymous publication and the title *Licensed* are also intriguing, for the November 1914 issue of the *Little Review,* in which the play first appeared, entitles it *Wedded: A Social Comedy* and lists Langner as the author.

Nevertheless, Langner's sense of the outspokenness of his work may accurately reflect its reception, although it now appears innocuous and, as he correctly remembers, melodramatic. *Wedded* is not a broadly humorous piece, its subtitle probably referring to the generic categorization of works ending with marriage. The plot is simple, of the social problem play variety. Langner may possibly have taken the tone and structure of his work from the European realist/naturalist theater of Ibsen, Shaw, and others, whose work had recently come to the United States via a number of touring companies from abroad.

Wedded is set in a "cheap district" of Brooklyn, and, although Langner does not specifiy the ethnicity of his characters, his use of dialect in the play suggests some notion of class through poor grammar and quaint pronunciation and idiom. The scene is the " 'best' parlor of the Ransome's house" (8) on Janet Ransome's wedding day. Unfortunately, Janet's fiancé, Bob, has just died, and is to be seen stretched out on the sofa. This situation holds, of course, the potential for grotesque comedy, but the characters appear so realistically distraught that the humor may be unintentional. Janet and her mother now await the arrival of Reverend Tanner, who was to have performed the wedding ceremony. While waiting, Janet reveals that she is pregnant by Bob, and after the minister's arrival the two women try to convince him to claim that the wedding was performed before the death, making the expected child legitimate and saving the Ransome family from disgrace.

In the short space of a one-act drama Langner compresses many of the issues related to the burgeoning birth control movement. The early dialogue of the mother and daughter reflects class (and possibly ethnic) prudery and morality associated with the nineteenth century (and possibly immigrant culture). The mother clearly has never taught her daughter anything about reproduction, asking her: "Are you sure? D'ye know how to tell fer certain [if she is pregnant]?" (9), and later admitting, "I've always brought her up to be innercent about things" (15).

After the minister's arrival Langner's dialogue echoes the class-based arguments that were being used in support of birth control education:

MRS. RANSOME: I can forgive her, sir, but not him. . . . I wanted her to marry a steady young fellow of her own religion, but I might as well have talked to the wall, for all the notice she took of me.

TANNER: It's what we have to expect of the younger generation, Mrs. Ransome. Let me see—how long were they engaged?

MRS. RANSOME: Well, sir, I suppose on and off it's bin about three years. He never could hold a job long, an' me and her father said he couldn't marry her—not with our consent—until he was earnin' at least twenty dollars a week—an' that was only right, considerin' he'd have to support her.

TANNER: I quite agree with you. I'm sorry to see a thing of this sort happen—and right in my own congregation, too. I've expressed my views from the pulpit from time to time very strongly upon the subject, but nevertheless it doesn't seem to make much difference in this neighborhood.

(12)

The minister's intimations concerning "this neighborhood" reflect the reformers' view that the middle and upper classes already had the knowledge to limit their families and that it was the lower classes that sorely needed birth control education. Janet makes this patently clear in a speech to the minister, who does not want to acquiesce to their wishes concerning the marriage register:

D'ye think I wanted a baby? I didn't want one. I didn't know how to stop it. If you don't like it—it's a pity you don't preach sermons on how to stop havin' babies when they're not wanted. There'd be some sense in that. That'd be more sense than talkin' about waitin'—an' waitin'—an' waitin'. There's hundreds of women round here—starvin' and sufferin'—an' havin' one baby after another, and don't know the first thing about how to stop it. (15)

Despite her placement outside the bohemian community, Janet also voices the new notions of free love, the philosophy of sex without marriage that was embraced by many Greenwich Village residents.

JANET: We did wait. Isn't three years long enough? D'ye think we was made of stone? . . . We waited until we couldn't hold out no longer. I only wish to God we hadn't waited at all, instead of wastin' all them years. . . .

TANNER: . . . Ah! Then your idea was to marry *simply* because you were going to have a baby!

JANET: Of course it was. D'ye think we wanted to marry an' live here on the fifteen a week he was getting? . . . But when this happened—we had to get married—starve or not. What else could we do?

(15)

Janet ultimately voices the socialist rhetoric of many birth control advocates in her final condemnation of the financial and social inequalities she has observed:

Bob said the rich people do it. He said they must know how to do it, because they never have more'n two or three children in a family; but you've only got to walk on the next block—where it's all tenements— to see ten and twelve in every family, because the workin' people don't know any better. (16)

The minister is finally willing to compromise his scruples provided Janet express her repentance for her sinful behavior. Realizing the long-term implications for herself and her family if she does not, she grudgingly acquiesces, and the minister signs the wedding documents.

Langner's audience for *Wedded* was the readership of the *Little Review,* which also published the work of James Joyce, T. S. Eliot, and H.D., among other modernist writers. The journal's progressive readership would, most likely, already have been sympathetic to Langner's views on contraceptive education, but the play nevertheless synthesizes the lines of argument circulating in the 1910s. Langner's sympathy for, but clear distinction from, his characters exemplifies the divide between many Greenwich Village habitués and the subjects of their political focus. The bohemian free love proponents and middle-class artists/professionals wrote about and discussed their concern for, and affinity with, the working class but, nevertheless, retained separate lives, rarely touched directly by the problems they explored artistically and intellectually.

Rose Pastor Stokes, however, proved a notable exception to the Village norm. Stokes (1879–1933) was born into the working class, her family Jewish immigrants in cigar manufacturing. Having made an early commitment to socialism and activism, she participated extensively in the famous New York restaurant and hotel workers' strike of 1912 and was a columnist for the *Jewish Daily News*. Under the influence of Emma Goldman she wrote a play, *The Women Who Wouldn't* (1916), about a woman who becomes a labor leader. In that same year she became an activist in the birth control movement (Gordon 238). Stokes simultaneously supported Sanger in her efforts (223) and joined Provincetown Players actor Ida Rauh (who was also Max Eastman's wife) in illegally distributing leaflets on birth control outside Carnegie Hall (229). Typical of official response to the birth control movement, Rauh was arrested for her actions, while Stokes, who was by now married to a wealthy and influential New York businessman with socialist sympathies, and whose trial would therefore have been highly publicized, was not.

Through a mutual acquaintance on the faculty of Columbia University, Stokes met Alice Guy Blaché (1873–1968), a French film director, who was among the founders of Solax, one of the early film production companies in the New York area. Blaché's memoirs, transcribed after her death, detail her meeting with "Mrs. Rose Pastor Stock [*sic*][7] of whom people told scandalous tales" because of her advocacy of birth control (88). Blaché recalls Stokes's impassioned commentary:

"I encourage birth control. I have taken work in a factory in order to mingle with women workers. . . . Have you seen some of the hovels in Brooklyn where many families live in a single room? Where the woman who is always pregnant may lose courage and ask help of an abortionist, who may leave her mutilated for life, if not dying? What I advocate is that a loving couple not fear to unite, taking precautions, so that they may have children when they desire them, and can care for them, and rear them to be healthy." (88)

Blaché, clearly taken with Stokes, decided to collaborate with her on a film about birth control, and the two wrote a full-length screenplay in 1916. Blaché does not chronicle their work together, except to note that she had "suggested to [Lewis J.] Selznick that he make a propaganda film with her [Stokes]," to which, she recalls, "He laughed in my face" (89).[8]

Their unpublished typescript, in Rose Pastor Stokes's papers at New York University, contains a cover sheet, probably from Blaché, proclaiming: "*Mme Alice Blaché presents her crowning cinema achievement 'Sacred Motherhood' with the world's best loved rich woman Rose Pastor Stokes (written by Rose Pastor Stokes and Alice Blaché).*" The script itself, which contains numerous handwritten emendations, carries the typed title "Shall the Mother Decide?"—*Mother* changed in longhand to *Parents,* suggesting the evolution during this period of the "Voluntary Motherhood" movement toward the fight for birth control, which Stokes viewed as an issue for the couple deciding together.

Blaché's remark to Selznick about "a propaganda film" is key here, as the script pushes all the birth control buttons in use at the time. Both propagandistic and melodramatic, the script blatantly depicts the impact of the lack of contraceptive education on the working class and strongly opposes all the current anti–birth control arguments. Framed by a dialogue on the need for birth control between Stokes and Blaché, *Shall the Parents Decide?* tells the story of Helen, a worker for the Patriot Paper Box Company. Helen observes the struggles of working women around her and fears the repercussions of marriage and a life like her mother's, with its attendant large family and poor maternal health. Helen joins a birth control league (probably modeled on Mary Ware Dennett's National Birth Control League, which had been founded in 1915 [Kennedy 76]) and begins to engage in activism on its behalf. Meanwhile, she has become aware of the affair of her employer, Simon Sulphur, and another factory employee, one of her former friends. Sulphur, married with a family of his own, opposes birth control. He has an illegitimate child with his mistress, and the child, born with a birth defect, is given up for adoption. Helen, suspicious of Sulphur's activities, has photographed him surreptitiously with her pocket Kodak. Later, when she is arrested and brought to trial for her activist work,[9] she uses her photographs to have Sulphur exert his influence to have her found not guilty. The script ends with Helen's acquittal.

Stokes and Blaché's work heavy-handedly emphasizes a number of the central elements of the birth control debate in the 1910s. First, it shows the connections between socialism and the movement at the time. The need for contraceptive education was perceived as a working-class—not a feminist—issue, part of, but subordinate to, larger questions of economics. As Stokes says in the frame narrative, "A man burdened with an over-large family cannot afford even to rebel against low wages" (3). Stokes explicity counters the Roosevelt position, remarking "Family limitation does not mean race suicide" (8). She comments on the Neo-Malthusian League, a European group whose views were brought to the United States by Sanger and others, who believed that overpopulation caused poverty and that population control could prevent poverty, ultimately leading to the creation of a perfect society (Gordon 76–77).[10] Stokes points out that in Holland (the source of birth control techniques early in the century), where the work of the league had flourished, there had been a marked improvement not only in the health of the citizens but also an overall increase in population, due to the related decline in infant mortality (8–9).

Linked to Neo-Malthusianism and the quest for a perfect society was the eugenics movement, "expounded by all the American birth control activists" (Gordon 87). Stokes speaks explicitly to this issue: "Wherever a husband or wife is ill, or is discovered to have a transmittable disease or taint, it is of the utmost importance to society and the race that until they are well, they bring no additional children into the world to inherit the defects" (4). In addition to the questionable medical veracity of these arguments—eugenicists also believing for some time in the inheritability of acquired characteristics (Gordon 120)—the eugenics movement also took unscientific moral stands, exemplified by the script's having the illegitimate child born with a birth defect, the "punishment" for a child born out of wedlock. Stokes presents a related argument in the frame narrative: "From the moral standpoint, the fear of being burdened immediately with a rapidly increasing family is the chief bar to early and universal marriage and thus really becomes one of the most vital causes of prostitution and other sexual irregularities" (6–7). Specious as these theories now sound, they illustrate clearly the varied strains employed by supporters of birth control, who developed a range of economic, medical, and social rationales to promote their cause.

In the same year as Stokes and Blaché were writing *Shall the Parents Decide?* Margaret Sanger founded her second periodical, the *Birth Control Review*. By the late 1910s Sanger had become one of the leading voices in the movement; Mary Ware Dennett's group, the National Birth Control League, had disbanded in 1919 (Kennedy 94), and Emma Goldman was focusing more on other political issues. The *Review* published "articles on such subjects as child labor, eugenics, demography, and the legal status of birth control." Although it could not legally print contraceptive information, it provided a forum for ideas relating to the movement, publishing pieces by Havelock Ellis, Olive Schreiner, and Eugene Debs, among others (89). Yet as Linda Gordon notes, the *Review* was moving in an openly racist direction by the end of the decade (278), reflecting the opinions of the branch of eugenics that shared concerns about the contamination of America's Yankee stock and the loss of white dominance with the former "race suicide" camp. Emblematic of this view was the opinion of Guy Irving Burch, who supported Sanger and worked to "prevent the American people from being replaced by alien or Negro stock, whether it be by immigration or by overly high birth rates among others in this country" (qtd. in Gordon 279).

In the September 1919 issue of the *Review* Sanger published a one-act drama by Mary Burrill written especially for the publication (and thus probably not intended for production).[11] *They That Sit in Darkness: A One-Act Play of Negro Life* speaks directly to the racial concerns of Sanger and her readership. Unlike the earlier birth control dramas, with their urban, working-class focus, Burrill's play is set in the rural South, in the "dingy and disorderly" home of the Jasper family (5). The racial identity of the Jaspers is never mentioned explicitly beyond the subtitle; rather, the play uses stereotypical Negro dialect and situations to encourage the racist fears associated with poverty and overpopulation.[12]

Employing melodrama and propaganda of the most blatant variety, *They That Sit in Darkness* chronicles a brief but eventful episode in the

By Cornelia Barns

"Remember, Mrs. Judd, another child will kill you—"
"But, doctor, tell me— —"
"I cannot."

lives of the Jaspers. Malinda Jasper, age thirty-eight, has an eldest daughter, Lindy, age seventeen, and five other children, plus a week-old infant who is crippled with a birth defect to its limbs.[13] Although she has been advised to stay in bed for at least three weeks, Mrs. Jasper is already back at work with her daughter, both of whom take in washing to augment their meager living.

Some of the play's early dialogue reveals the racist stereotyping by the author; Mrs. Jasper has sent her young son Miles to purchase milk for the children, but he has not yet returned:

MRS. JASPER: . . . Ain't Miles come back wid de milk yet? He's been gawn mos' en hour—see ef he's took dat guitar wid 'im.

LINDY: (*Going to the door and looking out.*) I doan see it nowheres so I reckon he's got it.

MRS. JASPER: Den Gawd knows when we'll see 'im! Lak es not he's some'airs by de road thumpin' dem strings—dat boy 'ud play ef me or you wuz dying'! Ah doan know whut's goin' come o' 'im—he's just so lazy en shif'lis!
(5)

We soon learn that Malinda Jasper has had an even harder time than we imagine; she has had three other children, two of whom died, and a third daughter who got pregnant and left home at an early age (7). When a visiting nurse comes by to see how the family is getting along, Burrill makes a strong appeal for the repeal of the Comstock laws, one of Sanger's ongoing battles.

MISS SHAW: Well, Malinda, you have certainly your share of trouble!

MRS. JASPER: (*Shaking her head wearily.*) Ah wonder whus sin we done that Gawd punish me an' Jim [her husband] lak dis!

MISS SHAW: (*Gently.*) God is not punishing you, Malinda, you are punishing yourselves by having children every year. Take this last baby—you knew that with your weak heart that you should never have had it and yet—

MRS. JASPER: But whut kin Ah do—de chillern *come*!

MISS SHAW: You must be careful!

MRS. JASPER: *Be careful!* Dat's all you nu'ses say! You an' de one what come when Tom wuz bawn, an' Selma! Ah been keerful all Ah knows how but whut's it got me—ten

> chillern, eight livin' an' two daid! You got'a be tellin'
> me sumpin' better'n dat, Mis' Liz'beth!

MISS SHAW: (*Fervently.*) I wish to God it were lawful for me to do
so! My heart goes out to you poor people that sit in
darkness, having, year after year, children that you are
physically too weak to bring into the world—children
that you are unable not only to educate but even to
clothe and feed. Malinda, when I took my oath as a
nurse, I swore to abide by the laws of the State, and the
law forbids my telling you what you have a right to
know!

(7)

Although the Jasper family has dreams of a better life—education in
Tuskegee for Lindy, surgery for another of the crippled children, and an
improved quality of life for the rest—it is not to be. Malinda's weakened
heart soon gives out, and, after her death, Lindy realizes she must abandon her ambitions and stay at home to care for the children, most likely
to perpetuate the cycle of poverty and ignorance with her own family to
come. Burrill's drama is an undisguised plea for changes in the legal
status of contraceptive education, created with a clear sense of how her
story will play on fears of Negro overpopulation among her audience.[14]

Written immediately following World War I, Burrill's drama also typi-
fies several key shifts with the birth control movement. First, in setting
her drama in the rural South, Burrill demonstrates the spread of the
movement away from the urban centers of the Northeast. Second, as an
individual writing solely for the movement through the *Birth Control
Review*, Burrill herself represents the postwar splitting off of the campaign from the platforms of other organizations or political groups, such
as the Socialist party, which were relegating birth control to a position of
less importance or were conflicted about supporting the cause.

After the war Sanger intentionally guided the birth control movement
in an antipolitical direction, which allowed it to become a free-standing
issue that could be embraced by many individuals or groups whose other
positions potentially were in conflict. She also made the strategic shift
away from the working class and toward the growing middle and upper

classes as the objects of her campaign, particulary with respect to her expanding need for fund-raising. She began to attract "professionals" to her cause, not only those in medicine but also in other occupations who could prove influential within their communities or on a national scale. According to Linda Gordon, this transition radically altered the entire structure of the movement. The professionals' influence "transformed birth-control leagues from participatory membership associations into staff organizations" (249), with the predominantly male professionals in advisory capacities and their wives and other women maintaining "amateur" status in the organization, primarily in staff positions (251).

Sanger's American Birth Control League, founded in November 1921 (Kennedy 94), "organized its local affiliates through upper-class women's clubs, even high-society charity groups" (Gordon 290) and was "an organization of predominantly WASP middle-class people, a high proportion from small towns" (293). This change in socioeconomic and demographic focus exemplifies the rapid and marked evolution of the movement, from its early concern with the plight of the working class and its politically radical roots to a more conservative, strategically savvy organization that understood the real power base in postwar America.

Susan Glaspell had an excellent opportunity to observe the development of the birth control movement from her position amid Greenwich Village bohemia. In the 1910s, Sanger and her first husband, the artist William Sanger, were part of the same circle as Glaspell and her husband, George Cram Cook. Hutchins Hapgood, at whose home the first (then unnamed) Provincetown Players dramas were staged in 1915, notes that the Sangers started summering with their circle on Cape Cod in 1912 (170); Cook and Glaspell started coming the next year (Sarlós 44). The Sangers frequented Mabel Dodge's salons in New York (Gray 57–58), as did many of the Provincetown group, and, as an early devotee of Emma Goldman, Margaret Sanger would have had even more opportunity to cross paths with the artistic community that included Goldman and Glaspell. With the advent of *The Masses* and the *Woman Rebel* everyone in the Village knew of the birth control movement, and many supported (and practiced) contraception as part of the free love philosophy.[15]

In the summer of 1916 the Provincetown Players focused on some of the hypocrisies of that philosophy in their production of Wilbur Daniel Steele's *Not Smart*. The farce, although not explicitly about birth control, concerns the repercussions of extramarital affairs and the moral contradictions that complicate the discovery of pregnancy—particularly when the couple crosses class lines and the woman is unmarried. During the 1918–19 season the Provincetown group again considered some of the issues related tangentially to the birth control movement in their production of Bosworth Crocker's (Mrs. Ludwig Lewisohn) *The Baby Carriage*, a drama showing the effects of poverty and overpopulation on the working-class, immigrant neighborhoods of New York. These dramas reflect the Village's interest in some of the issues central to the campaign for birth control, and, as part of the Provincetown Players, Glaspell would have been closely concerned with these productions.

Glaspell had even more direct access to the movement and those intimately connected with it through her membership in the Heterodoxy Club, a woman's group that met every other week from 1912 through the early years of World War II for luncheon, a guest speaker, and conversation (Schwarz 1). Glaspell was an early member (14), as were Mary Ware Dennett, who became Sanger's chief antagonist in the cause of birth control, and Rose Pastor Stokes (22). According to Heterodoxy historian Judith Schwarz: "Sanger was angry at Heterodoxy members for not becoming more involved with *her* birth control. . . . Sanger spoke at a Heterodoxy meeting in 1914 and reported that she 'struck no responsive chord' " (81; my emphasis).

Schwarz's sense of the Heterodoxy membership is key here, for she identifies a tension among the various activisms of the individuals in the club, although she believes they supported larger social reforms perceived to be linked to feminist issues, their one point of commonality (25, 31–32). Thus, it is not surprising that the membership would not back Sanger in her single-issue campaign. The fact that Dennett, soon Sanger's adversary, was also of their number may additionally have deterred some of them from seeming to side with the latter too overtly.

It is difficult to say if Glaspell also knew the other plays about birth control, but it would not be unreasonable to assume that she might have. She knew Langner through her connections with the Washington Square Players, and the Provincetown Players produced plays of his in the 1919–

20 and 1920–21 seasons. As already noted, she and Stokes were members of Heterodoxy, a group that was small and close enough for its members to know of one another's work. And through knowledge of the involvement of fellow Provincetown member Ida Rauh, Glaspell may have paid special attention to the *Birth Control Review*.

By 1921 Dennett and Sanger were employing extremely different strategies to reform the Comstock laws and promote contraceptive education. Sanger no longer worked with radicals, rather "those eager for reform but not desperately in need of fundamental social change" (Gordon 246), as was the activist Left. While Dennett worked to "repeal the obscenity statutes as they applied to contraception," Sanger favored a more narrow change that would only allow doctors to use their discretion concerning patient information connected with "the cure or prevention of disease" (Kennedy 219–20). For whatever reason(s), it appears that Glaspell found the general structure of the Sanger campaign more dramatically compelling, for it clearly serves as the backdrop to her 1922 play, *Chains of Dew*.[16]

The play opens in Nora Powers's office at the Birth Control League in New York City (1.1) The office, cluttered with pamphlets and papers, closely resembles the depiction of Sanger's office near Union Square in the Village (Gray 142–43), although Glaspell carefully avoids naming the group either the *National* Birth Control League (Dennett) or the *American* Birth Control League (Sanger). The " 'excess family' exhibit" and posters of undesirably large and desirably small families that hang on the set's walls duplicate the photographic spreads in the April 1919 issue of the *Birth Control Review*, which featured images of large, poor families with headlines proclaiming, "Shall Women Have Families like These—Or Shall We Let Them Control Births?" (10–11). Even Nora's staff, the "office girls" who happen to be off for "a Jewish holiday" (1.3), parallel Sanger's, whose assistant, Anna Lifshiz, helped spread Sanger's campaign by having her mother translate Sanger's pamphlets into Yiddish (Gray 144).

In the opening scene Nora is trying unsuccessfully to reproduce a letter on the office mimeograph machine when her friend Leon Whittaker, the associate editor of the *New Nation*, appears. Leon is awaiting the arrival of Seymore Standish, a poet whose work he champions and publishes in the *New Nation*. Just from these few details, it would seem Glaspell is

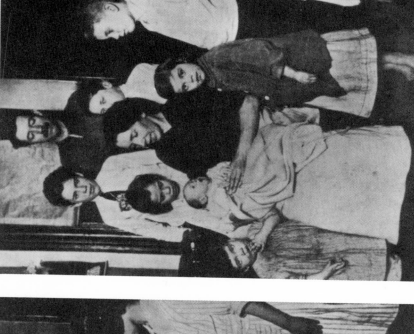

Mr. P——, the father of this family is in the hospital suffering from chronic illness. All the children are anemic and the mother is in a very poor state. The children are under-fed and under-sized. The skin and bone frame of the boy is an example of what malnutrition does to children in the families of the poor. The little girl in the back of the picture is several years older than the girl in the foreground, but is under-developed because of the hardships and want she has endured. There was another child which succumbed at once to the Spanish influenza.

Mr. and Mrs. S——, are 31 and 29 years old respectively. During sixteen years of their marriage ten children have been born. Seven, the baby three weeks old, are living. One child is tubercular and three others anemic. The father is a longshoreman. For the past three weeks he has been battling beside his fellows for higher pay and better conditions. And as he fights he must be weakened by the knowledge that his family is in greater want than ever. The mother is a janitress and in return for caring for the house, the family receives free rent. Mrs. S—— said that last winter she has shoveled one hundred and twenty tons of coal.

creating a story based on individuals and organizations she knew well. By introducing Leon and his work, contrasted with Nora and her work, Glaspell sets out the aesthetic/activist dichotomy that served as a point of conflict for the Village at that time. The *New Nation*, with its commitment to political radicals and social causes[17] as well as to poetry, closely resembles both *The Masses* and Eastman's subsequent periodical, *The Liberator*, started in 1918 (O'Neill, *Last Romantic* 68). Leon appears loosely modeled after *The Masses'* managing and literary editor and *Liberator* contributor, Floyd Dell (38–39).[18]

In the very funny opening moments of the play Leon tries to read one of Seymore's latest poems to Nora, while she desperately attempts to make the mimeograph machine work amid bell-ringing and mechanical squeaks. Exasperated by Nora's divided focus, Leon exclaims, "Since you care more about birth control than you do about poetry—," breaking off in disgust. Nora apologetically replies, "I thought I could do both" (1.3), encapsulating the pull between aestheticism and activism synecdochically represented here by poetry and birth control.

Glaspell soon complicates the debate by introducing two additional characters, Seymore Standish, who "does not 'look like a poet'" but, rather, "a prosperous American of the sophisticated sort" (1.7), and James O'Brien, who is visiting the United States from Ireland. Standish—who, we learn, is a bank head from the Midwest in addition to being a poet (1.22)[19]—is bemused by but a bit patronizing about Nora's commitment, which her friends seem to have heard about ad nauseam. O'Brien, however, is a newcomer, and Glaspell uses this for its dramatic potential to create dialogue about Nora's cause:

O'BRIEN: (*Brightly*) Tell me, what is birth control? (*As they look at him, he grows confused.*) Oh, yes—yes, in a way, I know, to be sure. But why—(*looking around the room*)—all this demonstration about so personal a matter?

NORA: (*Now on her job*) I'll tell you why the demonstration. Because our laws are so benighted and vulgar that they do not permit a personal matter to be carried on in a personal way. The demonstration is to demonstrate the stupidity of the law. The cruelty. The vulgarity. The brainlessness.

> (*With growing excitement, personally directed against the young man*) Do you wish to give birth to seven children you cannot feed? Have you no respect for children? A child has a right to be wanted. You bring into this world an impoverished, defective, degenerate—But here. I will give you our literature.
>
> LEON: (*With relief*) Yes, that will be better.

$$(9–10)$$

With deft comic balance Glaspell avoids letting the early moments of *Chains of Dew* degenerate into agitprop drama by maintaining a humorous distance from all the characters. Nora's zealousness is as gently satirized as the artistic narrowness of Leon, who believes that "every time we get down to essentials . . . we're choked off by birth control" (1.13). But the seriousness of the birth control campaign nevertheless surrounds the first act through the scenic dominance of its images. Glaspell also makes it clear that birth control is perceived as primarily a women's issue, one that makes the men uncomfortable and that they prefer be "spoken of—somewhat sparingly" (1.11).

Although Nora's public work parallels that of the Sanger campaign in the early period of the American Birth Control League, Nora's private life resembles another facet of the movement more germane to Village life. Near the close of act 1, we learn that Seymore and Nora are romantically involved, playing out the conventional scenario of a married man and a progressive single woman. Historian Caroline Ware remarks on the perpetuation of the double standard under the free love philosophy in her study of Greenwich Village (258), and, as Linda Gordon observes: "Sexual freedom made birth control important for women. The possible impermanence of love made birth control an absolute necessity" (193).

Seymore, who is about to return to his midwestern home, family, and society, bemoans the stifling atmosphere there that he feels hinders him as a poet. He resents that Nora, who to him represents uninhibited life, should be more concerned about her work than their relationship, remarking ironically: "It's awfully unselfish of you to care so much, Nora. It isn't as if it were a thing you'd ever have any personal use for. (*They look at one another a moment.*)" (1.34). But Nora, thrilled at a telephone call concerning a woman's recent donation to the cause of a thousand dollars, clearly has her priorities set. After Seymore's departure, however, she realizes that she can address both the professional and the personal by going "into the field" with her work (1.35), specifically to Seymore's hometown in the midwest, to organize the community on behalf of birth control, at the same time placating the men by perhaps convincing Seymore to change his life for the sake of his art. Thus, Glaspell sets the stage for the ensuing action, which shifts to "Bluff City" (2.1.1) for the remainder of the play.

From the complex network of characters and plot in act 1 alone, it is obvious that Glaspell's *Chains of Dew* is different from the other dramas of birth control. Although the movement is certainly important to the play, it is not exclusively a politically or socially motivated work, as are Stokes and Blaché's or Burrill's, for example. Glaspell is clearly concerned with providing a good play, balancing humor with social and love interests. As we see in her other works like *Inheritors,* she is committed to demonstrating the realities of certain contemporary social issues, and she takes pains to incorporate accurate historical details into the fabric of the overall piece.

One of the fascinating aspects of *Chains of Dew* from this historical perspective is how up to the minute Glaspell is in her depiction of the birth control movement. She recognizes the recent shifts in both target and technique within Sanger's campaign and uses these as nuances to give her drama a feel of immediacy. Two moments from the first act exemplify this sensitivity: the relatively minor plot detail of the telephone call concerning the donation and the more central plot element of Nora's fieldwork. As noted, Margaret Sanger had recently begun to focus on the middle and upper classes and to rely on these groups to support her efforts financially. When Nora receives the call near the end of act 1, she exclaims triumphantly, "Another thousand for birth control!" (1.34). The adjective *another* lets us realize that, as pleased as Nora is, this success is not unique; other thousands have preceded this one. And the fact that this donation comes from a single individual demonstrates clearly the socioeconomic class that is bolstering the cause. The plot device of "fieldwork" even more directly parallels recent developments in Sanger's campaign, as does the play's move to a Midwest setting.

Act 2 opens in the living room of the Standish home in Bluff City. We already have a strong image of Seymore's life there from his comments in the first act, and these are initially confirmed by the visual impact of the setting: a comfortable space with a copy of the Sistine Madonna hung on the wall up center and his wife Dotty in "a low seat by his chair" (2.1.1). Seymore has just returned from his trip east, and to his wife's claim that she has been busy during his absence he condescendingly replies:

Busy? Oh, yes, without a doubt. The Monday luncheon club, the Thursday bridge; also the Wednesday, Friday and Saturday bridge; dinner at Elmhurst, Edith's dinner—you haven't told me who was there, either. Then—oh yes, the Verder's tea. Poor Dot. It's a hard life. (2.1.1).

Dotty surprises us and Seymore by explaining that she has actually been busy "studying 'How to Understand Poetry' " (2.1.6–7). Glaspell also humorously begins to disrupt our expectation of Dotty and their midwestern life by having the picture of the Sistine Madonna suddenly come loose, swinging wildly at angles on one screw. Dotty, in Seymore's absence, has begun to take the painting down but "didn't know what else to put up" (2.1.3) in its place. Glaspell uses this none-too-subtle image to alert us to the changes to come—changes not only in Dotty's character but affecting the entire structure of their lives.

Seymore connects the painting to the birth control images he has just seen:

SEYMORE: . . . I was laughing to think of certain other pictures of mother and child I saw in New York. In New York they have some amazing new pictures. One—a mother with nine children. The other—a mother with two children.

DOTTY: Well I wish you'd brought them home. I'd like some new pictures.

SEYMORE: They're not at all suited to the town.

DOTTY: But I think it would be nice to have some things not suited to the town.

SEYMORE: . . . Dotty, tell me, did you ever hear of birth control?

> . . . I mean a group of women banded together to keep
> other women from having children. Going to men and
> trying to change the laws so women can be told how not
> to have children. Isn't it dreadful, Dotty?
>
> DOTTY: Why, I don't know. I suppose the reason is—
> SEYMORE: Oh let's not consider reasons. . . .
>
> (2.1.4)

As we begin to realize that Seymore's self-presentation of himself and
his wife in act 1 (he progressive, she conservative) may need inverting, we
also see that Dotty has a much more thoughtful nature than we had been
led to believe. In a conversation with her mother-in-law, Dotty voices
what might now be considered a sense of the social construction of
gender identity:

> DOTTY: Do you think, mother, that it's hard to be any other way
>   than the way you are?
> MOTHER: Well, I suppose that depends on just how you are.
> DOTTY: Don't you think sometimes you are as you are—because
>   you've *been* that way. . . . And you've been that way—well
>   because you are supposed to be that way. When you do
>   certain things—bridge and dancing—then you're the kind
>   of person who plays bridge and dances. But what sort of
>   person would you be—if you did something else?
> MOTHER: I've sometimes wondered myself.
>
> (2.1.13)

Increasingly, we see that Dotty may be out of place in her environment.
She is not only more thoughtful but more socially conscious as well, a fact
that separates her from the women in her social circle, one of whom, Mrs.
MacIntyre, voices the snobbery that we see also in Seymore:

> I wish something could be done about laundresses having children. I
> had such a good laundress—and now she's going to have another.
> But—one doesn't like to talk to those people about—things. (2.1.20)

Through this conversation Glaspell sets the stage for Nora's arrival and, with her, the arrival of the birth control campaign to Bluff City. Again, in this speech Glaspell demonstrates a keen perception of the current state of the movement, for it was exactly the Mrs. MacIntyre types that were being targeted for conversion to the belief in the larger social good of the campaign. Increasingly moving away from direct involvement with the immigrant or working classes (as depicted by Stokes and Blaché, for example), the movement now focused on those with money and power to enact reform that could then potentially help the poor. Soon after her entrance Nora is asking Mrs. MacIntyre and Dotty if they can "talk a little about birth control" (2.1.26):

NORA: . . . You'll let me show you some of our literature
                   I know. Of course, you get the idea, you're really
                   with it, aren't you?
MRS. MACINTYRE: I cannot say that I am. It may be true that—
                   people of one's own sort are doing this in New
                   York—I should have to verify the facts. . . . I have
                   been married for twenty-two years and—
NORA: (*Ingenuously*) And how many children have you?
                   . . . I wish you would take a walk with me
                   through the East Side. . . . Do you believe that
                   women have any rights over their own lives?
                                                    (2.1.26–27)

Nora quickly makes a convert of Dotty, naming her "first president of the first birth control league of the Mississippi Valley" (2.1.29), while Seymore's mother, who has born seven children, volunteers to "make some dolls for birth control" (2.2.9). Dotty decides to replace the picture of the Sistine Madonna with the pictures from the "excess family" exhibit that Nora has brought with her (2.2.20), and the second act comically closes on Seymore's distress at the disruption of his home and the dissolution of his image of the wifely Dotty.

Act 3 opens with Dotty's inspired announcement that Seymore has been selected by her "to introduce Bluff City to birth control" and "to make the opening speech" during the "first general meeting" that is to take place in their home (3.2). This plot development exactly parallels the strategy employed by the American Birth Control League: the deployment of small-town women's or charity groups, which often called upon male professionals as their spokesperson. Linda Gordon details, for example, one "Mrs. C. C. Edmonds, of 1414 Wealthy St., S.E., Grand Rapids, Michigan," who "was collecting 'influential people' for a local group" (290).

Employing dramatic irony, Glaspell has Dotty exclaim, "I'm so glad for you too, Seymore, that you have this chance to let them know—what you really are!" (3.3). The denouement of the drama revolves around the women's discovery of what, indeed, Seymore is: a narrow-minded, self-centered, and class-conscious individual who exploits a martyr complex to mask his own selfish wish for others to cater to his needs and bolster his ego. Although Nora tries to convince Dotty to leave him and return with her to New York (3.34), Dotty realizes her part in Seymore's self-delusion is too great. She believes in his talent as a poet and feels she must support him despite the understanding of his character she finally has. Seymore perceives Dotty's distress as stemming from the harsh realities of birth control and, to "protect" her, asks Nora and his other New York friends to leave. Promising to make everything as it was before—a prospect that, much to Seymore's confusion, does not seem to appease Dotty—Seymore returns to the sanctity of his role as beleaguered husband-poet, the role he has constructed for himself and without which he clearly could not function.

Just as Seymore depicts himself as "chained" by his family, career, and social circle (3.10), chains that Glaspell's title implies are as ephemeral as dewdrops, so birth control also becomes a metaphor in the play. The movement comes to stand for Dotty and her mother-in-law's potential for independence from domestic conventions and social roles that have been imposed upon them but which, like the "chains of affection" binding Seymore (3.24), they ultimately cannot break. Ironically, although women of their class may have learned how to control their fertility, they have yet to gain real control over the trajectory of their lives. Grounded in the realities of the campaign for birth control in the early postwar years, *Chains of Dew* expands beyond docudrama to provide an image of women's struggles among their commitments to their families, other women, and themselves. With gentle humor Glaspell demonstrates that, for women with families, the quest for independence and meaningful roles in society will not be easy, particularly in America's heartland.

NOTES

1. For a detailed discussion of literary figures in Greenwich Village at this time, see Edmiston and Cirino.

2. For a sense of the array of contributors, including Glaspell, see O'Neill, *Last Romantic* 33n.

3. The Provincetown Players produced *Chains of Dew* at the end of the 1921–22 season, after Glaspell and Cook had already departed for Greece. Significantly, the *New York Times* review of April 28, 1922 (20:2), makes no mention of the birth control content. There were clearly many problems with the production, which are chronicled in the Harvard Theater Collection's unpublished correspondence with Edna Kenton, a Provincetown Players member and their close friend.

4. For a fuller discussion of these facets of the history of the birth control movement in the United States, see Gordon 84–93.

5. The Washington Square Players produced the premiere of Glaspell and Cook's first collaboration, the Freudian spoof *Suppressed Desires,* in 1914 (Langner 90–92).

6. Sanger's arrest stemmed from violation of section 211 of the Criminal Code of the United States, which "was part of the so-called Comstock law" that prohibited the mailing, transporting or importing of "obscene, lewd, or lascivious" material (Kennedy 23–24). For a detailed discussion of the laws relating to birth control and their implications at the time, see Dennett.

7. I believe this to be a transcription error on the part of the editors, rather than Blaché's mistake. As the women worked together for some time on their script, it seems logical that Blaché would know Stokes's name.

8. Ironically, Margaret Sanger used a propaganda film as early as 1917 in support of her work. The film, which contrasted working-class to upper-class families, seems to have much in common with the Stokes and Blaché script. See Kennedy 88.

9. Stokes and Blaché presciently anticipate here the events of November 1920, when Monsignor Joseph Dineen of New York had the police captain of the Forty-Seventh Street precinct shut down a birth control meeting at Town Hall and arrest Margaret Sanger (Kennedy 95–96).

10. For a detailed discussion of the league, see Ledbetter.

11. Burrill remains a mystery; I have been able to locate no details about her other than her writing for the *Review*.

12. It should also be noted, however, that racial sensitivity was not a strong suit of *The Masses* either. For a discussion of this issue, see O'Neill, *Echoes* and *Last Romantic*.

13. Note the similarity to Stokes and Blaché's scenario here, with the moral overlapping the medical rationale for the plot detail.

14. For an informative discussion of the early reception of birth control tactics in the black community, see Gordon.

15. In a somewhat oblique passage in Glaspell's biography of Cook, she discusses her health problems and her doctor's admonition not to have children (*Temple* 239). It seems likely, therefore, that she and her husband practiced birth control, as she gives no subsequent indications that they had a celibate marriage.

16. *Chains of Dew* has never been published. A typescript was deposited for copyright purposes at the Library of Congress; to the best of my knowledge this is the only extant version. Page references will be to this text.

17. Leon is working on a petition to free "John Maxwell," "a man in prison because he writes what he sees as the truth about things" (1.4).

18. Dell was an early close friend of Jig Cook and also a member of the Provincetown Players.

19. Glaspell may have modelled Standish loosely on Wallace Stevens, whose work the Provincetown produced in the 1919–20 season. Stevens, clearly a better poet than Standish, was a lawyer for a Hartford, Connecticut, insurance company, writing poetry in his spare time, yet remaining active in Hartford social circles. For information on Stevens, see Richardson.

WORKS CITED

Blaché, Alice Guy. *The Memoirs of Alice Guy Blaché.* Ed. Anthony Slide. Trans. Roberta and Simone Blaché. Metuchen, N.J.: Scarecrow Press, 1986.

Burrill, Mary. *They That Sit in Darkness: A One-Act Play of Negro Life. Birth Control Review* (Sept. 1919): 5–8.

Crocker, Bosworth. *The Baby Carriage.* In *Fifty Contemporary One-Act Plays,* ed. Frank Shay, 119–31. New York: D. Appleton, 1925.

Dennett, Mary Ware. *Birth Control Laws: Shall We Keep Them, Change Them or Abolish Them?* New York: Frederick H. Hitchcock, 1926.

Edmiston, Susan, and Linda D. Cirino. *Literary New York: A History and Guide.* Boston: Houghton Mifflin, 1976.

Glaspell, Susan. *Chains of Dew*. Library of Congress, Washington, D.C.

———. *The Road to the Temple*. New York: Frederick A. Stokes, 1927.

Gordon, Linda. *Woman's Body, Woman's Right: Birth Control in America*. Rev. ed. New York: Penguin, 1990.

Gray, Madeline. *Margaret Sanger: A Biography of the Champion of Birth Control*. New York: Richard Marek, 1979.

Hapgood, Hutchins. *A Victorian in the Modern World*. New York: Harcourt, Brace, 1939.

Kennedy, David M. *Birth Control in America: The Career of Margaret Sanger*. New Haven, Conn.: Yale University Press, 1970.

Kenton, Edna. Letter to Susan Glaspell, May 5, 1922. Harvard Theatre Collection, Cambridge, Mass.

Langner, Lawrence. *The Magic Curtain: The Story of a Life in Two Fields, Theatre and Invention, by the Founder of the Theatre Guild*. New York: E. P. Dutton, 1951.

———. *Wedded: A Social Comedy*. *Little Review* 1, no. 8 (Nov. 1914): 8–18.

Ledbetter, Rosanna. *A History of the Malthusian League, 1877–1927*. Columbus: Ohio State University Press, 1976.

O'Neill, William L., ed. *Echoes of Revolt: "The Masses," 1911–1917*. Chicago: Quadrangle Books, 1966.

———. *The Last Romantic: A Life of Max Eastman*. New York: Oxford University Press, 1978.

Reed, James. *From Private Vice to Public Virtue: The Birth Control Movement and American Society since 1830*. New York: Basic Books, 1978.

Richardson, Joan. *Wallace Stevens: The Early Years, 1879–1923*. New York: Beech Tree Books, 1986.

Sarlós, Robert Károly. *Jig Cook and the Provincetown Players: Theatre in Ferment*. Amherst: University of Massachusetts Press, 1982.

Schwarz, Judith. *Radical Feminists of Heterodoxy: Greenwich Village, 1912–1940*. Rev. ed. Norwich, Vt.: New Victoria, 1986.

Steele, Wilbur Daniel. "*Not Smart:*" *A Farce*. In *The Provincetown Plays,* ed. George Cram Cook and Frank Shay, 241–72. Cincinnati: Stuart Kidd, 1921.

Stokes, Rose Pastor, and Alice Guy Blaché. *Shall the Parent Decide?* Tamiment Library, New York University.

Ware, Caroline F. *Greenwich Village, 1920–1930: A Comment on American Civilization in the Post-War Years*. Boston: Houghton Mifflin, 1935.

Woollcott, Alexander. Rev. of *Chains of Dew*, by Susan Glaspell. *New York Times*, April 28, 1922, 20:2.

Glaspell and Dickinson: Surveying the Premises of *Alison's House*

Katharine Rodier

> The Props assist the House
> Until the House is built
> And then the Props withdraw
> And adequate, erect,
> The House support itself
> And cease to recollect
> The Scaffold, and the Carpenter—
> Just such a retrospect
> Hath the Perfected Life—
> A past of Plank and Nail
> And slowness—then the Stagings drop
> Affirming it a Soul.
>
> > —Emily Dickinson, variant reading of no. 1142

Divergent renderings of a human life may each contain its own truth. The truth they contain, however, like that of gossip, belongs partly to the creating sensibility.

> —Patricia Meyer Spacks, *Gossip*

Nine days before the centenary of Emily Dickinson's birth, on December 1, 1930, Eva Le Gallienne's Civic Repertory Theatre opened its production of Susan Glaspell's *Alison's House,* a play inspired by Glaspell's reading of Dickinson's life and the posthumous revelation of her work.[1] Although the play won the 1931 Pulitzer Prize for drama, recent critics reappraising Glaspell's significance largely ignore or dismiss *Alison's House.* Most often remarked as Glaspell's last play, as her final experiment with an absent focal character whose influence impels the play's conflicts and resolution, *Alison's House* does have its admirers. Citing its juxtaposition of Glaspell's hallmark technique with more traditional virtues, such as its sustained dramatic line and its adherence to "the unities of setting and time," Arthur E. Waterman claims "the play is one of Miss Glaspell's finest" (*Glaspell* 88). But more recently, C. W. E. Bigsby condemns *Alison's House* as a shaky construct. In excluding it from his 1987 edition of *Plays by Susan Glaspell,* he explains:

> *Alison's House* is not a good play. In attacking social conventions it remains in thrall to theatrical convention. The adventurousness of her earlier work, her concern to press character to the point of disintegration, her sense of language as itself limiting access to feeling gives way here to a conventional three-act play whose contrivances are painfully obvious. (27)

For readers like Bigsby, Glaspell's most overt contrivance may be that she fashions her absent character, a reclusive poet named Alison Stanhope, so patently after the legendary persona of Emily Dickinson. Some reviewers imply that Glaspell merely animates a popular icon—or that, in transplanting a hardy literary myth to her native Iowa, she perpetuates the innuendo that marked Dickinson studies at the time. Prior to 1938 the poet's few biographers insisted that heartbreak engendered her eccentric reclusion, along with her astounding poetry, as seems the case with Glaspell's Alison. But the year 1930 peaked the "confused decades" of Dickinson scholarship (Lubbers 198). Then, even less than now, there was no definitive Dickinson—only a handful of books about the poet and some volumes of heavily edited poems and letters. To create her own poet Glaspell culls details from sometimes conflicting sources, devising a tale both derivative and new, by coordinating anecdotes from published and personal sources with her own experience. As Bigsby intimates, the Stanhope family's debate over Alison's legacy figures, in part, the playwright's "debate with her own past" (28), a life allegedly "radical, wild . . . Bohemian" (Glaspell, *Temple* 235) but which Glaspell—whom a friend once dubbed "truly sentimental" (qtd. in Garrison, *Vorse* 82)—calls simply "an instinct for the old, old things" (*Temple* 236). Yet more significant, the play's distinctive adaptation of Dickinson rumor and fact demonstrates the investigative and synthetic scope of its creator's mind. In constructing *Alison's House,* Glaspell showcases both contemporary angles and Victorian gingerbread, not merely to edify a designer's whim but also to justify qualities that inhere in her considerable resources. If we assess those materials, the "Plank and Nail" of the play, we can comprehend more clearly the ways Glaspell joins them. In other words, exposing the foundation of *Alison's House* helps account for the apparent quirks of the play's structure, which framed for Glaspell both an interpretation of current quarrels over Emily Dickinson and an instance of self-definition.

Christine Dymkowski defines the dramatic movement in *Alison's House,* a progression many critics describe as Chekhovian—literally, as a chronicle of changing times:

> Focusing on the way old-fashioned, conventional morality hinders self-fulfillment, the play is appropriately set on December 31, 1899—the edge between one century and another—and ends at midnight, with "distant bells ring[ing] in the century" and new values (pp. 154–55). The battle between the old and the new in the Stanhope family takes place through the agency of their aunt/sister Alison, a famous poet, who has been dead for eighteen years and in whose house the action is set. (105)[2]

As the Stanhopes convene to dismantle Alison's home, inhabited since the poet's death by Agatha, her spinster sister, they squabble over their various urges to revere Alison and to exploit her legacy, for her art has become well-known, if not something of a commodity. The house beckons into its atmosphere of melodrama and humor a parade of insiders and outsiders. Among them we find John Stanhope, Alison's surviving brother; his secretary, Ann, the daughter of a woman linked to him in local gossip; Louise, a righteous in-law, who is "the only person in this family who has any sense of family . . . and she's another family" (71); her husband, Eben, whose own writing began to fail when he married her; another would-be poet, reporter Richard Knowles, who takes a shine to Ann; Ted, dredging tabloid-grade dirt about his famous aunt, desperate to pass his Harvard English class; and two prospective buyers who wish to convert the homestead for "summer boarders" (62). In act 1 the aging Agatha nearly burns down the house, seeking to protect a secret concerning her dead sister. When Agatha dies, onstage, to climax act 2, she entrusts a portfolio of Alison's previously unknown poems to their niece, Elsa, a returned prodigal daughter who would not renounce her love for a married man. Act 3 confirms that during her lifetime Alison had forsworn a romance similar to the passion Elsa has embraced, choosing instead a sequestered life of writing, reading, walking alone by the Mississippi River, and playing confidante to the family children. Notably, Glaspell assigns to Elsa, the vital "New Woman," the role of preserving Alison's newly discovered poems. In the course of insuring the survival of Alison's art, Elsa and Stanhope, her estranged father, reach a tearful reconciliation, and the play ends in the name of love.

Although *Alison's House* premiered to mixed theatrical reviews, its critics almost unanimously recognized Glaspell's borrowings from the life and lore of Emily Dickinson, who by 1929 had become "a literary phenomenon" (Hays 107)[3]—and, by the time of the play's debut, the subject of four popular biographical works. Calling *Alison's House* "the Emily Dickinson story" became a critical cliché. *Outlook*'s reviewer notes as well Eva Le Gallienne's careful promotion of the Glaspell-Dickinson connection:

> *Alison's House* . . . purports to deal, rumors assiduously circulated by Miss Le Gallienne's press department and others have it, with the effects on Emily Dickinson's family, years after her death, of some of her poems previously unknown. Although the locale of *Alison's House* is Iowa, the allusions to Emily Dickinson and her family are sufficiently direct to be obvious to one who knows as little about the poetess' circumstances as I do. . . . [Glaspell's] characters . . . are all . . . living under the spell of the retiring yet strangely powerful personality of the dead woman—call her Alison or Emily. (711)

In *The Commonweal* Richard Dana Skinner concurs that *Alison's House* is "based, so rumor has it, on certain incidents suggested by the life of Emily Dickinson" (187). And in the *New York Times* on December 2, 1930,

Brooks Atkinson bluntly declares, "For Alison of *Alison's House* . . . read Emily Dickinson" ("Discussion" 1:31).

Neither Atkinson nor the *Nation*'s critic, Mark Van Doren, applauded when Glaspell's play won the Pulitzer Prize. Atkinson subtitles his response, "*Alison's House* as the Most Unsatisfactory Dramatic Award Made during the Past Few Years" ("Laurels" 8:1), although he admits he respects Glaspell's other work. Van Doren—who in 1929 writes of Dickinson, "What we know of her belongs to the universe of poetry; what she was is perfectly hidden away" ("Nerves" 348–49)—finds the 1931 prize-winner to possess "mighty few" merits:

> Emily Dickinson has suffered many indignities from her biographers, but none so heavy-handed as this. The falseness of this play consists in its saying so simply that a great poet—whether it is Emily or Alison does not matter—is personal in this fashion. No known poet has ever been dissected by a surgeon so skilful that he could say: "This part, gentlemen, is the person and this part the poet." Artists do not reveal themselves, or use themselves, or perhaps know themselves that well; and usually we shall find that they have had other things to bother about in their art than their strictly private affairs. So in special degree with Emily Dickinson, who to be sure gave up a lover and left her manuscript to be burned by an unmarried sister, but whose recently published "love poems" are more of a mystery than biography will ever solve. The more we know about her, the less we know about the significance of her poems to herself—except that we do know their immense significance to her as poetry. ("Pulitzer" 590–91)

Although he overlooks the more original elements of Glaspell's play, reading it as flat exploitation, Van Doren rightly wishes to exonerate the visionary Dickinson from misrepresentation as what we might now term a confessional poet. But his critique betrays his own acceptance of one of the unverified "personal" Dickinson myths he professes to deplore. As Mabel Loomis Todd, who coedited Dickinson's poems, asserts over eight months earlier in the *Saturday Review,* Dickinson "lived in seclusion from no love disappointment" (99), a reiteration of Todd's previous contention in the preface to the 1891 series of Dickinson's poetry.

Not unlike Glaspell, Van Doren constructs here his own Emily Dickinson: the "great poet." Writing well before any scholarly study of Dickinson's life—and certainly before the advent of modern contextual criticism—he may simply intend to spare a "highbrow" poet "lowbrow" treatment, to counteract the raging speculation that Dickinson's mythicized biography invites, but, in doing so, he overstates the case against an artist's conceivable self-exploitation in her work. To be sure, Dickinson's poems warrant close formal consideration, but acknowledging the range of the poet's "private affairs" may help elucidate such a textual focus. In her case that range includes more than the fact that she did not marry: Dickinson refused to count herself among Amherst's "saved"; had witnessed the deaths of beloved friends and relatives; feared blindness from a recurring eye ailment; formed passionate attachments to both men and women; possessed a wicked wit; and came from a well-to-do family, affording her the privilege to read widely, to study Latin as well as chemistry, physiology, and botany, to cultivate amazing flowers year round, and to entertain the neighborhood children as well as to write—rich experiences for an artist to manipulate, as her 1,775 poems attest.

A century after the poet's death this more concrete picture of Emily Dickinson emerges, but what images could Susan Glaspell have received prior to staging *Alison's House* in December 1930? Publishing little during her life, Dickinson died in 1886. Her sister, Lavinia, burned her letters as Dickinson had directed but commissioned Mabel Loomis Todd and Thomas Wentworth Higginson to edit the neatly stitched bundles of poems she found tucked away in the poet's room. After painstakingly trying to regulate Dickinson's unique creations into forms they hoped the public would approve, in 1890 the editors produced a selection entitled *Poems,* which became a rampant success, selling well enough to prompt immediate reprintings, followed by new selections in 1891 and 1896 and an edition of letters, which Todd published in 1894. Initially under family management, a private trust had become a public property.

But when Lavinia Dickinson and Todd disputed the ownership of a plot of land that Austin Dickinson, the poet's brother, had left Todd—who had been his lover for twelve years—upon his death in 1895, Dickinson's literary estate suffered a parallel schism, with Dickinsoniana divided between, bickered over, and marketed by both Dickinson and Todd heirs into the twentieth century. After the Dickinson-Todd feud—which went to court and was the talk of Amherst, with locals siding over both the litigation and the liaison—Emily Dickinson's early renown declined into "a subterranean taste from about 1897 to 1924" (Benfey 80), despite a new edition of poems entitled *The Single Hound,* brought out in 1914 by Martha Dickinson Bianchi, daughter of the poet's brother and his wife, Susan. Both mother and daughter deeply resented Todd, further complicating the promotion of Dickinson's work.

In 1924, responding to a selection of Dickinson's poems edited by Conrad Aiken, modernist writers began to claim her poetry as prototypical, catapulting her work into the midst of "poet-critics who were at war with one another," where "each review changed . . . to an open attack and a concealed 'apologia pro specie sua' " (Lubbers 110). In the same year Bianchi published *The Life and Letters of Emily Dickinson,* a popular favorite, which, according to Christopher Benfey, "preserve[d] the sentimental image of Dickinson as an eccentric spinster who was disappointed in love and wrote charming poems about birds and flowers" (81), an image that contributes to Glaspell's conception of Alison. This offering ran through six editions by November 1929 "at the same time that Gatsby only went to a second printing . . . and Faulkner had sold a total of 4,000 copies of his first two novels in four years" (Hays 106–7). Also in 1924—the year Susan Glaspell's husband, George Cram Cook, died in Greece, and she returned to the United States after an expatriation of nearly two years—Bianchi coedited *The Complete Poems of Emily Dickinson. The Complete Poems* were by no means complete; Bianchi introduced *Further Poems of Emily Dickinson* in 1929. Not until 1955 would Dickinson's complete works be consolidated and restored to their intended difficulty, idiosyncrasy, and brilliance in Thomas H. Johnson's variorum edition.

The poet's centennial year, 1930, welcomed—in addition to Glaspell's play—Dickinson commemorations, compilations, bibliographies, and other tributes, including a novel.[4] Also during this year, Bianchi edited another partial volume, *The Collected Poems.* As Klaus Lubbers points out, 1929 and 1930 "form a unity in the intensification of critical attention to, and public interest in, Emily Dickinson. In 1929 attention was chiefly devoted to the poet's work, while it centered on the person in the centenary year" (140). Perhaps wishing to ascribe the unforgettable, and salable, work to an unforgettable woman, in 1930 three writers introduced book-length studies of Dickinson. All in part pursue Bianchi's 1924 *Life,* in which she embroiders, among other anecdotes, an account of one of Dickinson's rare trips, her 1855 journey to Washington, Baltimore, and Philadelphia:

> Certainly in that first witchery of an undreamed Southern springtime Emily was overtaken—doomed once and forever by her own heart. It was instantaneous, overwhelming, impossible. There is no doubt that two predestined souls were kept apart only by her high sense of duty, and the necessity for preserving love untarnished by the inevitable destruction of another's life. (47)

Of these three biographical works MacGregor Jenkins's *Emily Dickinson: Friend and Neighbor* is a personal reminiscence intended to negate Dickinson's reputation as "morbid recluse" (21). According to Lubbers, Jenkins's " 'Miss Emily' almost exactly resemble[s] Madame Bianchi's 'Aunt Emily' " (151). The other books each identify "a lover of Emily by name; they far exceed *Life and Letters* in their scope and thoroughness, although . . . written without the cooperation of . . . Bianchi" (149). While Josephine Pollitt, in *Emily Dickinson: The Human Background of Her Poetry,* and Genevieve Taggard, in *The Life and Mind of Emily Dickinson,* target different suspects as Dickinson's married lover, both follow Bianchi's titillating lead, even as they disparage her inaccuracies. Of these three works Glaspell definitely knew Taggard's: a character in her 1931 novel *Ambrose Holt and Family* gives to the protagonist copies of "Virginia Woolf's *A Room of One's Own* and Genevieve Taggard's *Emily Dickinson*" (262). But all were widely available, affording a reader like Glaspell a range of detail and speculation.[5] As Waterman describes the inception of *Alison's House,* the playwright uses the biographical matter to base an artistic exploration as well as something of an artist's exposé:

> Inspired by reading Genevieve Taggard's *The Life and Mind of Emily Dickinson* and still intrigued by the dramatic potential of a play treating the conflict between the artist and the world . . . Glaspell wrote her

version of Emily Dickinson's "quarrel with the world." Because she was not permitted to use Miss Dickinson's name nor any of her poetry, Susan Glaspell named her heroine Alison, set the play in the Midwest, and used Emerson's poems. Nevertheless, Alison Stanhope is a thinly disguised Emily Dickinson. (*Glaspell* 86–87)[6]

Although suggesting the play's broader artistic purpose, Waterman stops short of elaborating the connection he notes, instead reiterating the critical commonplace.

To be sure, the explicit parallels between Alison Stanhope and Emily Dickinson are undeniable, particularly in light of the image these sources purvey. Even during the poet's lifetime she was a notorious figure—given her irreverent humor, perhaps intentionally so. New to Amherst in 1881, Mabel Loomis Todd writes to her parents about a fascinating apparition whom she would soon meet:

I must tell you about the *character* of Amherst. It is a lady whom the people call the *Myth*. She . . . seems to be the climax of all the family oddity. She has not been outside of her own house in fifteen years. . . . No one who calls upon her mother & sister ever see her, but she allows little children once in a great while, & one at a time, to come in, when she gives them cake or candy, or some nicety. . . . But more often she lets down the sweetmeat by a string, out of a window, to them. She dresses wholly in white, & her mind is said to be perfectly wonderful. She writes finely, but no one *ever* sees her. . . . Isn't that like a book? So interesting.

No one knows the cause of her isolation, but of course there are dozens of reasons assigned. (Qtd. in Leyda 357)

Recalling Alison, her niece and nephew, now grown, conjure up a character much like Todd's:

EBEN: . . . She is sitting here with her papers—with her thoughts, and the words for her thoughts. She is wearing a white dress . . . and her small hands hover over what she has. Her eyes—Heavens! Have I forgotten them?

ELSA: They are clear—like golden wine.

EBEN: Her brown hair is parted in the middle, and held loosely at the neck. She is looking straight ahead, as if into something. But she is waiting for the right word to come. . . . There is a knock at the door. It's me. I am crying. She makes a funny little face. She says—Tell Alison. . . . She tells me the story of the bumblebee that got drunk on larkspur and set out to see how drunk you could get in heaven . . .

ELSA: Then another knock. No, a pounding. . . . Alison—Alison. . . . Aunt Agatha won't give me a cookie, because I pulled the cat's tail. She tells me Aunt Agatha can't help being like that, and that the cat would agree with her . . . and we laugh; and she writes me a little poem about a cookie that had no tail. She gives me candy, and stands at the door so Aunt Agatha can't get in, but God, she says, could come down the chimney.

(124–25)

Glaspell's poet, who renounced adultery as did the Dickinson of Bianchi, Pollitt, and Taggard, resembles as well Jenkins's friend and neighbor and Bianchi's beloved aunt, who scribbled to Bianchi and her siblings about flowers, pies, "The Bumble Bee's Religion," and Aunt Lavinia's kitties. Obviously, Susan Glaspell confects Alison in part from this tradition. Furthermore, Alison, like Dickinson, is survived by a brother and sister; preferred to write in an upstairs room; marked her copies of Emerson's writings; and tended a conservatory adjacent to her home.

Alison's House also reflects Glaspell's acquaintance with Dickinson's own published writing. Alison's eyes are "like golden wine," a description that barely revises the self-portrait Dickinson sent to Higginson: "I . . . am small, like the wren; and my hair is bold, like the chestnut burr; and my eyes like the sherry in the glass that the guest leaves" (qtd. in Bianchi 241). Glaspell's line, ". . . and see how drunk you could get in heaven," recalls the sentiment of poem no. 214, "I taste a liquor never brewed." A line she gives Ted Stanhope in act 1—"He never got me full but once"—recalls the rhythm of poem no. 49's first line, "I never lost as much but twice." And Dickinson's God, the "Burglar! Banker—Father!" of the same poem, the "Papa above!" (no. 61), the force of "Heavenly

Hurt" (no. 258), which she challenged until she died, could certainly come down the chimney.

Remarkably, Glaspell's play appears to amend some of Bianchi's distortions. Bianchi's subtitle to *Further Poems of Emily Dickinson—Withheld by Her Sister Lavinia*—smugly implies a willful suppression of the poet's art by her surviving sister, which Bianchi recovers for her 1929 readers. (Lavinia Dickinson had died thirty years earlier.) But in *Alison's House* the poet's sister becomes a heroine for her dying act of committing Alison's remaining poems to Elsa. Moreover, Eben's vision of Alison corresponds to Dickinson's appearance in the austere 1848 daguerreotype, the poet's only known likeness, not to the retouched version published in the 1924 *Life and Letters*—with a grand ruche at her neck and a bouncy coif, "as if she had just stepped from a Boston beauty parlor" (Rich 179). And curiously, when the Stanhopes repeat that Alison "was everywhere" (114), or "was at home in the universe" (24), they sound less like Martha Dickinson Bianchi than like Mark Van Doren in the 1929 *Nation* review of *Further Poems,* which Glaspell, ironically enough, might well have read.

Van Doren, who would publish works on Dryden, Shakespeare, Thoreau, and Hawthorne, is but one twentieth-century critic concerned with refining for modern tastes the images of authors from the past, which Dickinson's biographers seem bound to do. But a poet never actually appears in *Alison's House*. What Glaspell stages, instead, is a family in conflict, another image drawn from Dickinson's history—and a truly public image, though one less publicized than the Myth of Amherst. In fact, Lubbers lists a number of Glaspell's contemporaries who went on record as "well aware of the history of the publication and the feud between the Todds and the Dickinsons" (123), among them Genevieve Taggard.[7] Yet in her 1930 biography Taggard mentions the lawsuit only in a brief chronological note (351). Pollitt makes no comment on the lawsuit, whereas Jenkins, and his sister's dear friend, Martha Dickinson Bianchi, scorn any reference to Mabel Loomis Todd, the detested rival of Bianchi's mother. In effect, Glaspell's play develops a less overt but equally significant aspect of Dickinson publicity, one she may have worked harder to find. But considering Dickinson's popularity before 1897, coverage of the extended litigation, beginning in 1896, could have spread far beyond central Massachusetts:

If Mabel and Austin's affair was long a hushed, unmentionable matter that Amherst people only whispered of, the lawsuit opened the floodgates. Newspapers in the region ran articles about the litigation between the two prominent families and local gossip flourished. . . . Amherst . . . awaited the clash of hostilities. (Longsworth 410–11)

Regardless of her possible access to printed accounts of the Dickinson feud, Glaspell knew at least one personal source of Amherst information—and innuendo: the playwright's friend, Mary Heaton Vorse, a former Amherst resident, best known now as a labor journalist and fiction writer. Glaspell first met Vorse during their Greenwich Village days and at Provincetown grew to be one of her closest friends. Vorse owned the fishing wharf that became the Provincetown Players' stage and participated in their productions and other escapades. After Jig Cook's death Vorse introduced Glaspell to the next important man in her life, Norman Matson, a journalist and novelist, with whom the playwright was involved until the relationship shattered in 1932.

Born in New York in 1874, Vorse essentially grew up in Amherst, although her family traveled frequently, spending winters in New York or Europe. Mabel Loomis Todd mentions Vorse's mother, Ellen Heaton, both in her diary and in her letters (Leyda 393; Longsworth 162). An adolescent at the time Emily Dickinson died, Vorse may have been among the Amherst children charmed by the poet's legend. Recalling her childhood, Vorse writes:

In the summers we lived in Amherst. . . . There were such men . . . as Austin Dickinson, with his red wig and his mole. Austin Dickinson was individual, and pithy of speech, as were his sisters, Emily and Lavinia. Amherst bred people of personality and character. (*Footnote* 23, 25)

As Dee Garrison points out, Amherst also bred people of the "Dimity Convictions" that Dickinson mocks in poem no. 401 (*Vorse* 4). Later the town's repressive atmosphere would drive Vorse to a Paris art school and then to New York, but she would return intermittently, sometimes for months, until Ellen Heaton's death in 1910.

Most likely, Vorse, the youngest child of a prominent family, could have known the 1891 gossip about the newly published, best-selling, five-years-buried Dickinson:

> To no purpose did Mrs. Todd try to refute spreading rumors by supplying information in letters and lectures. On all sides distant relations and good old acquaintances felt called upon to publish their reminiscences in the daily press, and some reviews readily snatched them up. Besides, there circulated among old Amherst people a rumor brought forward as evidence against Mrs. Todd's protestations—an unconfirmed story of Emily's betrothal to a promising youth who had come to nought because her father had interposed his veto. Once the secret of the secluded life had been touched, the legend of the broken heart kept preying on curious minds. (Lubbers 35)

Taggard's *Life and Mind* develops this notion of paternal intervention in Dickinson's affairs. But in Vorse's own recollection the mythic Dickinson appears unlike Bianchi's good Aunt Emily, or the noble side of Glaspell's Alison, who, while at one point is rumored a "rebel" (13), is more emphatically declared "timid of the world" (148). She is ironic, "a quiet firebrand" (qtd. in Garrison, *Vorse* 11), as was said of Vorse herself:

> Why Miss Emily retired from the world, as I heard it from intimates of the Dickinson family: Emily was escorted home from some evening gathering by, I assume, a college student—and she paused at the doorway to chat, and apparently at some length. When she came in, her father took her to task for her lack of decorum in staying out in the dark, talking to a young man at that hour. This produced a quarrel—not the first one between father and daughter—but Emily ended this one by saying, "Very well, if I can't be trusted, I will never go out of the house again." I also heard this quoted as, "I will never go out with anyone again." (qtd. in Leyda 478–79)

Basically, Vorse could have supplied her playwright friend with any number of alternative speculations on Dickinson's withdrawal—based on the same minimal evidence as the early biographies. As Hutchins Hapgood reminisces, "Mary's tongue didn't ever need to be loosened; drinking or not she went on like a perpetual brook" (qtd. in Garrison, *Vorse* 83).

Vorse, in the 1890s a budding "New Woman" (Garrison, *Vorse* 15–16), may also have perceived the adulterous undercurrent of the Dickinson-Todd lawsuit, initiated while she contemplated her art career and her own wedding. Not publicly verified until 1968 with the donation of the Austin Dickinson–Mabel Todd correspondence to Yale, the affair had been widely assumed in Amherst since its beginnings in 1882. In 1945 Millicent Todd Bingham suggests, but cannot admit, "what she considered her mother's terrible sin" (Longsworth 6), which the townspeople, and undoubtedly the Heatons, sensed:

> If the report of the lawsuit is to be complete, one further aspect of the situation must be reckoned with. For by [September 1897] the area of the feud had spread. . . . Though under cover, a state of discord—mixed with anticipation—was sweeping Amherst. Certain persons contended in whispers that there was more to it than met the eye. They had in mind personal relationships. Partisans took their stand; on one side, those who held that the elderly Squire Dickinson had been too fond of Mrs. Todd—for had they not been seen more than once buggy-riding through the autumn woods together?—and, on the other side, those who maintained with equal vehemence that the close relations known to exist had been purely platonic. . . . Nearly everyone in town was caught in the cross fire. (352)

In a telling correspondence, in Glaspell's version of the saga, Alison's brother finds a "receipt for a carriage, twenty-eight years old," (53) in which he had ridden with the woman he loved outside his own unhappy marriage. Encoded in the same scene are references to "deeds" and to a dispute over a stolen horse that "was in the courts a long time" (54–55)—perhaps oblique representations of the Dickinson-Todd intrigue, which the Dickinson housekeeper affirmed in an 1897 deposition that was never entered in court and did not appear in the trial records (Longsworth 412–14).

In short, Mary Heaton Vorse's colorful recollections of Amherst fact and legend could easily have fed Susan Glaspell's imagination as the playwright plotted *Alison's House*. Vorse records her perception of her friend's devotion to a challenging project:

> Not enough has been said about Susan Glaspell and her quality of enthusiasm when a new idea absorbed her. Long after the Province-town Players I remember when the idea of *Alison's House,* a story based on Emily Dickinson's life, first possessed her. Seeing Susan in those days when she was first plunging her mind into Emily Dickin-son's story was seeing a creative force at work. (*Time* 124)

As Vorse confirms, a playwright as scrupulous and inventive as Susan Glaspell would be unlikely to dedicate herself to a conventional interpre-tation of a best-selling tale, a connect-the-dots portrait of the Poet of Amherst. Glaspell's intensity may have derived from the demands of sorting a wealth of dramatic material then assimilating and personalizing her own preferred texts, both written and oral, to forge an authentic identity for her poet.

In her study of gossip, its social and literary functions, Patricia Meyer Spacks asserts that:

> [Gossip] . . . calls attention to ambiguities of facticity and interpreta-tion . . . and to the crucial importance and complexity of context. When information comes by means of gossip, one can hardly avoid noting that it has been filtered through multiple consciousnesses. The problem of assessing its values inheres in the act of receiving it. (8–9)

Receiving the nebulous truths about Dickinson and her family through perhaps several variants, Glaspell may have recognized the fundamental unreliability of any single account of a human life, particularly one the public seems eager to own. She may also have concluded that conjecture is itself the central fact of any thorough study of identity. Accordingly, in creating her fictive poet, Glaspell dramatizes biographical *method* as well as her own inventions and familiar Dickinson details, approximating Alison through conjecture rather than characterization, calling on an entire cast to constitute for an audience an indefinite but nonetheless "real" poet. As Spacks explains, biography and gossip both explore actual experience, differing in that biography claims authority over its subject, a claim that Glaspell's polyphonic method exempts her from making, contrary to critics' claims *for* her authorial intentions. In developing Alison through the memory of others, Glaspell may "tell all the Truth" she knows about the Dickinsons by "tell[ing] it slant," as Dickinson herself might urge (no. 1129), using the "shadow discourse" of gossip (Spacks 206) to encompass a number of provocative speculations without asserting any to be fact.

Besides the dramatic possibilities of reproducing the kaleidoscopic images of the Dickinsons' story, what other factors could determine Glaspell's staging of *Alison's House?* Ultimately, her handling of the Dickinson myths may reflect her recent concern to capture the Olympian persona of her husband, George Cram Cook, in her memoir of their life together, *The Road to the Temple,* first published in England in 1926. As she describes it, *Temple* tells "the story of an extraordinary American romance . . . [a]nd a weight, an influence impossible to calculate," which she hints she has already treated in another guide, doing "it wrong the first time" (qtd. in Noe 153). In truth, making a myth is a collective venture, although transcribing one may not be; while Glaspell embeds Cook's own language into her text, she evokes his memory essentially from a single perspective, her own—an inevitable limitation she seems driven to compensate for. To compose a "spiritual biography of a man who had dreamed much and achieved relatively little" (Noe 153), Glaspell must reconcile her intimate knowledge of a fully human being, foibles and all, with the loss of her sometime mentor and muse, submerging references to "melancholia, and drinking and irregular affairs" (qtd. in Noe 164) beneath idealized recollections of his irrepressible vision and impact on her own art. Recreating Jig Cook was a task of immense importance to Susan Glaspell, one she felt bound to do well, worrying over the scope of its contents and over its reception.[8]

It was Cook—who styled himself a poet—who first compelled Glaspell to move from the prose writing that had supported them to try her hand at writing plays. After spoofing the psychoanalytic craze with Cook in *Suppressed Desires* and helping him realize his dream of a theater troupe in the Provincetown Players, she wrote *Trifles,* her best-known work, at his behest, wryly recalling that he had "forced" her into the new pursuit (qtd. in Noe 86) by announcing a play of hers "for the next bill" (Glaspell, *Temple* 255), when no play in fact existed. For Cook drama was a community enterprise infused with a spirit of fun, an obsession that truly captivated his more disciplined, more productive wife. His death created a void for her, which *Temple* partially labors to restore. In 1925 she edited her first posthumous tribute to him, a collection of his poems, *Greek Coins*, but, even though her involvement with Matson helped her again "see . . . life . . . from life" (qtd. in Noe 184), after Cook died Glaspell would write only *Alison's House* as an attempt at the medium he loved. She would, however, collaborate with Matson on *The Comic Artist* (1928), an endeavor that may have reminded her of earlier collaborations. Under these circumstances working on a play about the Dickinson ghost may have called up Cook's as well.

Notably, many of the details Glaspell records about her mythic husband can be charted against the parallel Dickinson/Stanhope myths, suggesting several paradigmatic identities: all poets; all visionary; all "alive" for their survivors, who produce their works posthumously, with some conflict; all eccentric, although in Cook's case given to flamboyance rather than reclusion. All descend patrilineally from elected political officials—congressmen, governors—and from lawyers. Although Dickinson's male relatives attended Dartmouth, Yale, and Amherst, both Alison and Cook have Harvard connections, Cook graduating in 1893. All share an affinity for trademark garb: the women's white dresses, Cook's "black hat" and "flowing cape" (Garrison, *Vorse* 82), which he exchanged for a traditional Greek tunic when, disillusioned with the theater, he and Glaspell expatriated in 1922. All three poets could make anything grow; in fact, Cook's "marriage-song" metaphor for his love for Glaspell was "The Greenhouse" (Glaspell, *Temple* 201–2). All inspire speculation, if not gossip. Cook's humor may also inform the play, not through the specter of Alison but, rather, in the wisecracking exchanges between Ted, Eben, and John Stanhope over Louise's rigidity, and through Ted's relentless demand for Alison trivia. Considering that Glaspell's next novel, *Ambrose Holt and Family*, depicts a male poet and his wife's struggle to define herself against him, the playwright's ongoing study of the artist certainly crosses genders. Perhaps in *Alison's House* Glaspell transmutes the image of her poet-husband—who "had a rare gift for romantic, intense love" (*Temple* 389) and who renounced the theater community he founded—into a passionate female figure who renounces the world and transforms her passion into poetry.

In another regard Bigsby casts *Alison's House* as a postscript to Glaspell's relationship with Cook. As he reads it, Glaspell's intent in the play is to provide "yet another justification for herself and her actions" (27). He submits that "the moral complexities of her originally adulterous affair with Jig Cook never really seem to have ceased fascinating her" (26). What Bigsby overlooks is the fact that Glaspell and Cook's adulterous courtship was by no means the playwright's only exposure to infidelity during the nearly twenty-five years that intervened for her between meeting Cook and writing this play. Advocates of sexual "varietism" (Watson 144, 157) while touting the finally problematic virtues of "companionate marriage" (Garrison, *Vorse* 82–83),[9] Cook and his circle enthusiastically tested the bonds of matrimony in sometimes painful service to love and art. In criticizing the uneasy marriage of convention and unconventionality in Glaspell's play, Bigsby objects to its "reiterated pattern of would-be and actual adulterous affairs [that] begin to seem like a pathological inherited condition rather than the focus for a debate about morality and passion" (27–28). But seen in the fuller context of the playwright's life, her effort to reconcile a conservative Iowa upbringing with the demands of twentieth-century female freedom, the patterns of pain and desire in *Alison's House* begin to seem realistic rather than pathological; a virtual fact of life, which Glaspell's investigations into the Dickinsons' nineteenth-century passions may have intensified for her. Perhaps, then, Glaspell is not simply playing in her own adulterous shadow, as Bigsby implies, nor in the vast one that Cook throws over her even in his absence. Perhaps her last play reflects a condition she has come to accept as reality: the interplay of human desires bound within a frame of convention, or three-act play as metaphor for marriage.[10]

Of Glaspell's early fiction, one critic notes, "the heroine invariably resemble[s] the author" (Watson 19). Bigsby's equation of Glaspell with her character, Elsa, seems apt, considering Elsa's resignation to the consequences of fulfillment with a man who left a wife and two children for her. "Happy, and unhappy" (103), she calls this love "a miracle you have to pay for, sometimes" (116) and "a flame—burning fiercely—in sorrow" (118).

Elsa's attitude may indeed mirror her creator's, evolving from what Cook calls her youthful and "overpowering ideal of life-long constancy to an early and vanished love" (qtd. in Noe 38) through years with a "man . . . driven by a daemon" (94) and other difficult relationships. But the unconventional yet self-possessed Elsa is not the playwright's only self-image in *Alison's House*. Other characters in the play enact roles that Cook or his death helped script for Glaspell, including the posthumous guardian and initial publicist of the poet's works, Agatha;[11] Ted, the biographer tempted toward exploitation; protective John Stanhope; Louise, the wife of a lapsed poet; and the reporter with a poem in his pocket, Knowles, who suggests the playwright herself, who remembers: "After less than two years of newspaper reporting I boldly gave up my job and went home to Davenport to give all my time to my own writing. I say boldly because I had to earn my living" (qtd. in Kunitz and Haycraft 541). Such a writer would probably long for Virginia Woolf's *A Room of One's Own,* with its financial security, which Glaspell juxtaposes with the life of Dickinson in *Ambrose Holt and Family;* like Dickinson/Alison, she liked "to work in an upstairs room, feeling safe there, shut away from the world" (*Temple* 231), later seeking solitude in a shack in the Truro woods. Like Cook, Glaspell may have conceived of herself as a poet, having eulogized Joe O'Brien, Vorse's second husband, in *The Masses* (Garrison, *Vorse* 100–101) and her own husband in the lyrical language of *Temple.* Among the play's other characters Ann, who loves the journalist-poet, may characterize Glaspell's love for Matson. But in any case, each member of the cast is a poet's survivor—as was Glaspell, who writes, "When Jig died . . . I thought of myself as the observer" (qtd. in Noe 183)—questioning how a poet should be read, whether promotion of art is its preservation, whether individual identity can truly be immortalized.

Many critics contend that when Jig Cook died Susan Glaspell lost her fire for the theater, her will to "bring . . . down fire from heaven to the stage," as Cook describes it (qtd. in *Temple* 264). Although imagining a Delphic theater, Cook had in effect given up on American drama by the time of his death, a loss that his wife may have shared. He asserts: "One man cannot produce drama. The drama is born of one feeling animating all the members of a clan—a spirit shared by all and expressed by the few for all" (252). At Provincetown, for Glaspell, "Life was all of a piece, work not separated from play, and we did together what none of us could have done alone" (qtd. in Sheaffer 355–56). In *Alison's House* she literally sets a fire onstage—and sets fire as the drama's dominant image. But she also frets about the play's presentation, writing: "*Alison's House* opens December first. Don't believe it will get over—fear it won't be well played" (qtd. in Noe 176). Her last venture into transmitting her work through a dramatic community may have underscored for her that a playwright, like a poet, works essentially alone, in some measure like an absent force: the figure who never appears onstage, whose vision and intention define a play's action and resolution, but—as the model of Dickinson and Cook may have reminded her—may not oversee the work's eventual production. Possibly moved by the challenge of such production as it charged her own life, Glaspell collapses several stories and identities into *Alison's House*, fixating upon the drama of the survivor as the most resonant way to evoke an artist, centering her play around a cipher in order to affirm a historical, artistic, and personal community of souls.[12]

NOTES

Epigraph from Emily Dickinson, variant reading of no. 1142. In her handwritten texts Emily Dickinson typically offers possible substitutes for designated words in a poem. In this variant, based on my reading of R. W. Franklin's facsimile edition, I use Thomas H. Johnson's capitalization and punctuation (Dickinson mostly uses what appear to be dashes) but adhere to the main text as Dickinson presents it. Her alternate words include *conscious and* for *adequate* in line 4; *sustain* for *support* in line 5; *time* and *state* for *past* in line 10; *Scaffolds* for *Stagings* in line 11; and *Pronouncing* for *Affirming* in line 12. In his 1960 edition of Dickinson's poems Johnson reprints *Scaffold* (line 7) as its alternate, *Auger,* which Dickinson appears to spell *Augur,* perhaps knowingly, considering her predilection for puns and the scope of the poem.

    1. A newspaper clipping in the Susan Glaspell file of the Berg Collection of the New York Public Library documents a preliminary run for the play in Liverpool, November 1930.

    2. All references to the play are from *Alison's House* (New York: Samuel A. French, 1930).

3. See Peter L. Hays, "Who Is Faulkner's Emily?" for a discussion of a darker regional interpretation of the Dickinson myth as it appears in William Faulkner's "A Rose for Emily." I am indebted to Susan Baker for bringing this note to my attention.

4. The novel *Emily* is by MacGregor Jenkins, author of *Emily Dickinson: Friend and Neighbor*. In 1876 Dickinson's Amherst acquaintance Helen Hunt Jackson published a novel whose protagonist has Dickinson affinities, *Mercy Philbrick's Choice*.

5. Pollitt's book was published in January of 1930, those of Taggard and Jenkins in May of that year.

6. Neither Waterman in *Susan Glaspell* nor Marcia Noe in her dissertation study includes the source for this interesting detail regarding Glaspell's possible request to use Dickinson's name and poems in the play. If she did indeed apply for and was denied permission, her attitude toward her material, as well as her intended treatment of the subject, may well have changed.

7. Other such critics Lubbers lists are Herbert Gorman, Rolfe Humphries, Edward Sapir, George Whicher, and Newton Arvin.

8. See Marcia Noe, "A Critical Biography of Susan Glaspell," 150–54 and 163–64.

9. See Dee Garrison, *Mary Heaton Vorse: The Life of an American Insurgent,* 81–83, for a discussion of the "entrapping" (82) aspects of this dynamic for Glaspell, Vorse, and Neith Boyce, in particular.

10. Never legally wed to Matson, Glaspell "let it be known around Davenport" (Noe 170) that they were married, a widely publicized fiction that became so much a fact that in 1932 they wondered if their union required legal dissolution, not knowing whether Massachusetts recognized common law marriage.

11. The death of Glaspell's mother in February 1929 in Davenport may further inform the playwright's characterization of the physically frail, mentally disoriented Agatha. See Noe 163–64, 170–71.

12. For their assistance with this essay, I am grateful to Linda Ben-Zvi, Margaret Higonnet, Krysia Jopek, Karen Laughlin, Richard V. McLamore, Vicki Moeser, Brenda Murphy, Nevil Parker, Andrea Rossi-Reder, Marianne Sadowski, Patricia R. Schroeder, Craig D. Smith, and Milton R. Stern.

WORKS CONSULTED

Rev. of *Alison's House,* by Susan Glaspell. Civic Repertory Company, New York. *Outlook* (12 Dec. 1930): 711.

————. *Theatre Arts Monthly* (Feb. 1931): 96–102.

————. *Theatre Magazine* (Feb. 1931): 25–26.

Atkinson, Brooks. "Discussion of an Artist." *New York Times*, December 2, 1930, 31.

————. "Pulitzer Laurels: *Alison's House* as the Most Unsatisfactory Dramatic Award Made during the Past Few Years." *New York Times*, May 5, 1931, 8:1.

Barlow, Judith E. Introduction. *Plays by American Women: 1900–1930*. New York: Applause, 1985.

Ben-Zvi, Linda. "Susan Glaspell's Contributions to Contemporary Women Playwrights." In *Feminine Focus: The New Women Playwrights*, ed. Enoch Brater, 147–66. Oxford: Oxford University Press, 1989.

Benfey, Christopher. *Emily Dickinson: Lives of a Poet*. New York: Braziller, 1986.

Bianchi, Martha Dickinson. *The Life and Letters of Emily Dickinson*. New York: Biblo and Tannen, 1971.

Bigsby, C. W. E., ed. *Plays by Susan Glaspell*. New York: Cambridge University Press, 1987.

Bingham, Millicent Todd. *Ancestors' Brocades*. New York: Harper and Brothers, 1945.

Buckingham, Willis J. *Emily Dickinson's Reception in the 1890s*. Pittsburgh: University of Pittsburgh Press, 1989.

Chinoy, Helen Krich, and Linda Walsh Jenkins, eds. *Women in American Theatre*. New York: Crown, 1987.

Dickinson, Emily. *The Complete Poems of Emily Dickinson*. Ed. Thomas H. Johnson. Boston: Little, Brown, 1960.

Dymkowski, Christine. "On the Edge: The Plays of Susan Glaspell." *Modern Drama* 31 (1988): 91–105.

Fergusson, Francis. Rev. of *Alison's House*, by Susan Glaspell. Civic Repertory Company, New York. *Bookman* (Jan. 1931): 513–14.

Ferlazzo, Paul J., ed. *Critical Essays on Emily Dickinson*. Boston: G. K. Hall, 1984.

Franklin, R. W. *The Editing of Emily Dickinson*. Madison: University of Wisconsin Press, 1967.

————. *The Manuscript Books of Emily Dickinson*. 2 vols. Cambridge: Belknap Press of Harvard University Press, 1981.

Friedman, Sharon. "Feminism as Theme in Twentieth Century American Women's Drama." *American Studies* 25 (1984): 69–89.

Garrison, Dee. *Mary Heaton Vorse: The Life of an American Insurgent*. Philadelphia: Temple University Press, 1989.

————, ed. *Rebel Pen: The Writings of Mary Heaton Vorse*. New York: Monthly Review Press, 1985.

Gelb, Arthur, and Barbara Gelb. *O'Neill.* New York: Harper and Row, 1973.

Glaspell, Susan. *Alison's House.* New York: Samuel French, 1930.

———. *Ambrose Holt and Family.* New York: Frederick A. Stokes, 1931.

———. *The Road to the Temple.* New York: Frederick A. Stokes, 1927.

Hays, Peter L. "Who Is Faulkner's Emily?" *Studies in American Fiction* 16 (1988): 105–10.

Jenkins, MacGregor. *Emily Dickinson: Friend and Neighbor.* Boston: Little, Brown, 1930.

Kunitz, Stanley J., and Howard Haycraft, eds. *Twentieth Century Authors.* New York: H. W. Wilson, 1942.

Langner, Lawrence. *The Magic Curtain.* New York: E. P. Dutton, 1951.

Le Gallienne, Eva. *With a Quiet Heart.* New York: Viking, 1953.

Lewisohn, Ludwig. *Expression in America.* New York: Harper and Brothers, 1932.

Leyda, Jay. *The Years and Hours of Emily Dickinson.* Vol. 2. New Haven: Yale University Press, 1960.

Longsworth, Polly. *Austin and Mabel.* New York: Farrar, Straus and Giroux, 1984.

Lubbers, Klaus. *Emily Dickinson: The Critical Revolution.* Ann Arbor: University of Michigan Press, 1968.

Noe, Marcia. "A Critical Biography of Susan Glaspell." Ph.D. diss., University of Iowa, 1976.

Phillips, Elizabeth. *Emily Dickinson: Personae and Performance.* University Park: Pennsylvania State University Press, 1988.

Pollitt, Josephine. *Emily Dickinson: The Human Background of Her Poetry.* New York: Harper and Brothers, 1930.

Rich, Adrienne. "Vesuvius at Home: The Power of Emily Dickinson." In Ferlazzo, 175–95.

Sarlós, Robert. *Jig Cook and the Provincetown Players.* Amherst: University of Massachusetts Press, 1982.

Sayler, Oscar. *Our American Theatre.* Westport, Conn.: Greenwood, 1970.

Sewall, Richard B. "Emily Dickinson." In *Voices and Visions,* ed. Helen Vendler. New York: Random House, 1987.

———. *The Life of Emily Dickinson,* vol. 2 New York: Farrar, Straus and Giroux, 1974.

Sheaffer, Louis. *O'Neill: Son and Playwright.* Boston: Little, Brown, 1968.

Skinner, Richard Dana. Rev. of *Alison's House,* by Susan Glaspell. Civic Repertory Company, New York. *Commonweal,* December 17, 1930, 187–88.

Smith, Beverly A. "Women's Work—*Trifles?* The Skill and Insight of Playwright Susan Glaspell." *International Journal of Women's Studies* 5 (1982): 172–84.

Spacks, Patricia Meyer. *Gossip.* New York: Knopf, 1985.

Stein, Karen F. "The Women's World of Glaspell's *Trifles*." In Chinoy and Jenkins, 253–56.

Stephens, Judith Louise. "Women in Pulitzer Prize Plays." In Chinoy and Jenkins, 245–53.

Taggard, Genevieve. *The Life and Mind of Emily Dickinson*. New York: Knopf, 1930.

Todd, Mabel Loomis. Rev. of *The Life and Mind of Emily Dickinson*, by Genevieve Taggard. *Saturday Review*, September 6, 1930, 99.

Van Doren, Mark. "Nerves like Tombs." *Nation*, March 20, 1929, 348–49.

———. "The Pulitzer Prize Play." *Nation*, May 27, 1931, 591–92.

Vorse, Mary Heaton. *A Footnote to Folly*. New York: Farrar and Rinehart, 1935.

———. *Time and the Town*. New York: Dial, 1942.

Waterman, Arthur E. *Susan Glaspell*. New York: Twayne, 1966.

———. "Susan Glaspell (1882?–1948)." *American Literary Realism* 4, no. 2 (Spring 1971): 183–91.

Watson, Steven. *Strange Bedfellows: The First American Avant-Garde*. New York: Abbeville, 1991.

Wolff, Cynthia Griffin. *Emily Dickinson*. New York: Knopf, 1986.

Conflict of Interest: The Ideology of Authorship in *Alison's House*

Karen Laughlin

One of the acknowledged hallmarks of Susan Glaspell's dramatic writing is the device of the "absent center, " the structuring of the play around a female character who never appears but whose impact on the present characters and action is powerfully felt.[1] In *Alison's House,* Glaspell's last play and the one that brought her the 1931 Pulitzer Prize, the absent character is Alison Stanhope, a thinly veiled likeness of Emily Dickinson, whose house is being prepared for sale eighteen years after her death. While her presence is evoked in the play's earliest scenes, Alison's influence becomes pervasive upon the discovery of an unpublished packet of poems expressing her unfulfilled love for a married man.

As if anticipating recent critical theory's pronouncements of the "death of the author,"[2] this final absent heroine in Glaspell's theater is a *writer,* and one about whom, even by 1930, a considerable legend had been built up. *Alison's House* opened at Eva Le Gallienne's Civic Repertory Theatre on December 1, 1930, just nine days before the centenary of Emily Dickinson's birth, and it appears that Le Gallienne carefully promoted the play on the basis of the Alison-Dickinson link.[3]

Contemporary reviews of the play were, at best, mixed, and the subsequent awarding of the Pulitzer Prize was generally seen as either an outright error or a misguided attempt to reward Glaspell and Le Gallienne for their "artistic integrity and high purpose" (Toohey 92). In 1944 one of the Pulitzer jurors justified the award in terms that hint at the play's conventional outlook:

The choice, really, was between a play [*Elizabeth the Queen*] acted with great acclaim . . . in the older fashion of romantic verse drama,

and a play acted down on 14th Street by Miss Le Gallienne's struggling Civic Repertory Company which *plumbed the deep American
love of home and family* still existing outside the confines of New York
cubby hole apartments, and which also brought the strange story of
Emily Dickinson to dramatic life. (Toohey 93; my emphasis)

More recently, critics have also been somewhat dismissive of the play,
noting its "capitulation to commercialism and conventionality" (Adler
134). Even C. W. E. Bigsby, whose recent edition of four of Glaspell's
earlier plays has done much to enhance the current revival of interest in
Glaspell's drama, describes *Alison's House* as "perhaps, a rather slight
affair." While noting the connection with Dickinson, Bigsby's critique
emphasizes a different biographical connection, that between Alison's
story and that of Glaspell herself, describing the play as "a piece of self-
justification by a woman who had, in effect, run off with a married man
and who in this play offers a justification of her violation of social taboo"
(*Drama* 33).

Certainly *Alison's House* is not Glaspell's most experimental play. Its
style is realistic, and its family-oriented three-act structure concludes with
the expected reconciliation of Alison's brother, the current Stanhope patriarch, and his wayward daughter, Elsa. But whatever its literary or theatrical merits, Glaspell's dramatization of the absent poet offers a fascinating
look at the construction of the female author and the ideological tensions
at work in this construction. Far from being a straightforward "piece of
self-justification," the shaping of Alison by both Glaspell and the play's
characters reveals a number of ideological contradictions. As Bigsby's
remarks suggest, a basic tension in the play exists between what women,
in Glaspell's view and experience, *are*—that is to say, sexual beings,
desiring subjects, as well as creative artists—and what they *ought to be,*
as implied in Bigsby's reference to "social taboo." In Alison and her more
modern counterpart, Elsa, Glaspell adds to her dramatic repertoire two
assertive and expressive female characters who challenge patriarchal con-
straints on female behavior through their frank acknowledgment and
expression of their own desire.[4] Yet Glaspell's supposed defense of this
rebellion not only acknowledges the power of the social ideals and institutions that limit and mediate their self-expression but also reinforces this

power even as it purports to challenge it. "The women have their way with this drama," as one early reviewer puts it (Hutchens 100), but "their way" is itself contradictory, as the play explores the competing interests of propriety and property, or class and gender, as well as of different models of female sexuality.

In *The Proper Lady and the Woman Writer* Mary Poovey offers a broad definition of ideology as both "virtually inescapable"—since it governs not just political and economic relations but also social relations and even psychological stresses—and as "always developing. As ideology evolves, its internal dynamics may change, its implications for a particular group may alter, or its inherent tensions may be exposed in what is generally perceived as a crisis of values" (xiv).[5] Glaspell seems to be invoking just such a "crisis of values" when she sets her play on the last day of the nineteenth century, in the "old Stanhope homestead in Iowa" (3).[6] Setting the play eighteen years after Alison Stanhope's death (twenty years after that of Dickinson) enables Glaspell to establish the conflicting values at work in the Alison-Dickinson story in terms of a conflict of generations, essentially opposing the traditional, Victorian values of Alison's brother and her sister, Agatha, to the modern outlook of Father Stanhope's children, Eben, Ted, and Elsa, as well as his young secretary, Ann. Poised uncertainly between these two positions stands the figure of Alison, the poet.

The play's opening immediately gives prominence to the act of writing as the curtain rises on Ann sitting at a typewriter in the library, sorting papers she retrieves from a horsehair trunk. Glaspell quickly dispels the possibility that Ann might be the anticipated Dickinson figure with the entrance of an outsider, a reporter named Knowles, who shares the audience's curiosity about the papers on which Ann is at work and asks to see "the room that was used by Miss Alison Stanhope" (4). Knowles's interest in Alison's house—he has been assigned to write a newspaper story about its closing—immediately foreground's Alison's position as *author*, about whom he wishes to collect relevant data. It appears, however, that at this point in the story there is a significant gap between Alison's person (or persona) and her poetry. The family, notes Ann, has "published her poems," but, according to Knowles, Alison herself "isn't dead. Anything about her is alive. She belongs to the world. But the family doesn't seem to know that" (5). In a striking parallel to the workings of Foucault's author-function, we see that Knowles isn't satisfied with the mere existence of Alison's published work, though this provides him with a starting point. A published poet himself, he has come to retrieve the author he admires: "where—how—[the poems] were written. The desk she sat at. The window she looked from" (6). For Knowles, at least, glimpsing the traces of Alison's life provides a way of "explaining events" or images in her work and of pinning down their meaning (see Foucault 984, 988).

Glaspell brings Alison's authorial persona into focus by relying, at least partly, on allusions to the Dickinson biography and legend.[7] Knowles's sensitive search for information about Alison finds a crude parallel in the questions posed by Ted, a crass and rather dull-witted college student, who was only two when his Aunt Alison died. In a sharp jab at academia's involvement in authorial construction, Glaspell portrays Ted gathering information for his Harvard English professor, who is eager to hear about everything from Alison's eating habits to that central facet of the Dickinson legend, her unfulfilled (?) "love affair" (36). What he can't supply by copying down his family's reminiscences, Ted makes up, in a desperate attempt to salvage a failing grade.[8]

The fond reminiscences of Alison's nephew, Eben, capture Dickinson's legendary love for nature and kindness to children, linking them explicitly to Alison's poetry:

> The fun we used to have down here as kids—Elsa and I. Especially when Alison was here. Remember how she was always making us presents? . . . An apple—pebbles from the river—little cakes she'd baked. And always her jolly little verses with them. (36)

Eben's wife, Louise, on the other hand, is made uncomfortable by Knowles's probing, afraid that it will "revive the stories about Alison," stories that "she was different—a rebel" (12–13). And while Stanhope accepts the fact that "you can't have a distinguished person in the family without running into a little public interest" (12), he is visibly upset by Louise's suggestion that Alison's oddness might be somehow related to Elsa's more recent, and ongoing, affair with a married man (13). As the play progresses, both Stanhope and, more pointedly, Alison's sister,

Agatha, increasingly take on the role of protectors of Alison's privacy, seeking to shield her personal life from the probing of either Knowles or Ted. "Why can't they let her rest in peace?" Agatha asks in exasperation when she first hears of the reporter's presence (22), and her desire to protect Alison from public scrutiny climaxes in her unsuccessful attempt to burn the mysterious envelope later revealed to contain Alison's unknown love poems. Act 2 ends with the rather melodramatic death of Agatha, who, unable to burn the envelope, entrusts it to Elsa. The play's final act, then, develops the consequences of this gesture, with the family arguing over whether these, Alison's most personal poems, should be burned as she, or at least Agatha, apparently wished, or else released to Elsa and, eventually to Alison's reading public.

The play's developing construction of the figure of Alison thus comes to revolve around the issue of privacy, as it relates to Alison's personal life and that of the Stanhope family in general. The legend of Emily Dickinson's reclusiveness, of course, makes this an apparently natural focal point for Glaspell. Dickinson scholars have long discussed privacy as a factor in both Dickinson's personal life and her poetic language.[9] Christopher Benfey's *Emily Dickinson and the Problem of Others* takes the privacy question a step further than most, however, when he links it with an increasingly acute concern for privacy in late-nineteenth-century society in general. Benfey cites three major sources to explain this renewed interest in privacy: (1) Hannah Arendt's contention that during this period "the older distinction between public and private, a distinction heavily dependent upon notions of private property, yields to the modern opposition of the social and the intimate"; (2) Roland Barthes's tracing of the role of photography in creating "a new social value, which is the publicity of the private"; and (3) an 1890 *Harvard Law Review* article by Louis Brandeis and Samuel Warren that responded to the invasion of private life threatened by both photography and newspaper reporting by establishing the first legal definition of privacy in the United States (Benfey 56).

As Benfey notes, Brandeis and Warren are "at pains to indicate the extent to which privacy is constitutive of the person." Linking privacy explicitly with the issue of publication, they write, "The principle which protects personal writings and all other personal productions, not against theft and physical appropriation, but against publication in any form, is in reality not the principle of private property, but that of an inviolate personality" (qtd. in Benfey 57). Now legally defined as the "[license] to be still," privacy, according to this argument, separates from the question of private property and becomes linked, instead, with a concern for "the social and the intimate" (in Arendt's formulation) or with a notion of personal integrity and the right to refrain from sharing the secrets of one's inner life.

In Glaspell's exploration of privacy in *Alison's House* we see this restructuring at work. Knowles's characterization as a reporter indicates journalism's role in breaking down the barriers between private and public life.[10] And the very fact that act 3 centers on the *debate* over whether the family should make the newly discovered (and highly revealing) love poems available for publication, on the one hand, demonstrates Glaspell's acceptance of the family's right to privacy.[11] On the other hand, in the passionate arguments of Eben, Elsa, Ann, and Knowles in favor of publication, Glaspell suggests that it is the family's social responsibility to relinquish that right. Echoing Knowles's initial insistence that Alison "belongs to the world" (5), Eben applies this argument to the newly discovered poems late in the third act: "No question about it," he concludes. "They were too big for just us. They are for the world" (148).

In his critique of the play Thomas Adler describes the resolution of this debate as a foregone conclusion. Identifying the outsider/journalist Knowles as the play's *raisonneur,* Adler argues that Glaspell answers the question of whether Alison and her poems "belong to the family or to the world . . . at the onset [of the play], so even though the exact content of the poems remains hidden, the dramatist's stance is immediately clear, diluting audience interest" (133). I do not think Glaspell's answer to this question is quite so simple. And I would argue that it is the fact of asking this question, or, more precisely, the *process* of answering it, that gives this play its interest. As the play's third act unfolds, the debate about privacy or publication suggests that the transition from a concern for private property to a link between privacy and identity (or between "the social and the intimate") may not be a smooth one, especially when that which is to be kept private involves a woman's sexuality and creative expression.

To begin with, Adler's formulation of the play's central question immediately invokes the question of property. To whom does Alison, and especially her poetry, *belong?* The answer to this question apparently was not difficult so long as Alison was seen as the author of "jolly little poems" about bees, flowers, and cookies (Adler 125). But now the poems also reveal Alison's explicitly sexual desire, which is all the more threatening to the social order Stanhope represents because the apparent object of her affection was a married man. Eben, Elsa, their father, and, eventually, Ted read the poems in the privacy of Alison's room, which, significantly, serves as the setting for the play's final act. Even before knowing the contents of the portfolio, Stanhope lays claim to it as family (i.e., *his*) property, suggesting that "Agatha didn't know what she was doing" when she gave it to Elsa (128). Once aware of its contents Stanhope again invokes his patriarchal privilege, announcing his plan to "burn them in [Alison's] own fireplace—before her century goes" (142).

In explaining his motives, Glaspell's patriarch also makes clear the link between the poems, as family property, and the nineteenth-century ideal of feminine propriety. Chivalrously, he plans to "protect" his sister, arguing that she *chose* privacy by not publishing her poems, since "she was of an age when people did not tell their love" (148–50). In planning, in effect, to censor the love poems,[12] Stanhope seemingly frames his actions in terms of Arendt's distinction between the social and the intimate. The poems, since they tell of a forbidden love Alison voluntarily renounced, are too personal for public circulation and should be destroyed, as Alison apparently wished. Already implicit in this argument, of course, is the role of chastity as a key ingredient in the nineteenth-century view of correct feminine behavior. Alison's dual renunciation (of her married lover and of making her love for him public by publishing her poetry) indicates the extent to which she apparently internalized this ideal, even at the cost of self-denial.[13] In appealing to the principle of intimacy (as well as that of individual autonomy), Stanhope seeks to replicate Alison's renunciation, thereby maintaining the public image of Alison as the sexless, nineteenth-century "Angel of the House."[14]

In contrast with Stanhope's chivalry, the opportunistic Ted apparently could care less about his aunt's intimate feelings or "inviolate personality." Also appealing to his family privilege and his desire to "protect"

Alison, he argues in favor of the poems' publication because he sees them as a marketable commodity (143–45). While Glaspell leads us to sympathize with Ted's desire to see the poems published, she also appears to dismiss Ted's modern form of chivalry as simply masking another attempt to salvage his failing grade, or as another of his get-rich quick schemes (143, 145). The contrast between Stanhope's appeal to the apparently modern conception of privacy and Ted's proprietary concerns is summed up in Stanhope's line, "I promise you my sister's intimate papers are not going into your vulgar world" (145).

Between Stanhope's attempt to maintain Alison's "inviolate personality" and Ted's crass view of the author as producer of marketable goods stands the romantic or expressive view of authorship advanced by both Elsa and Ann. Breaking up the fight between Ted and his father and brother, Elsa claims to know the value of Alison's poetry "as no one else knows" (145). Like Stanhope himself, Elsa recognizes the poems as expressive of Alison's passion, of a "love that never died—the loneliness that never died" (139). But whereas Stanhope wants to keep that expression private and personal, Ann urges Stanhope to leave the matter of the poems' fate to Elsa:

STANHOPE: Elsa! Why should I leave it to Elsa?
ANN: To a woman. Because Alison said it—for women.
STANHOPE: Alison was not like Elsa. Alison stayed.
ANN: Then let her speak for Elsa, and Mother, and me. Let her
           have *that* from it. [For her own sake—let her have that
           from it!]

(150)[15]

For Ann, at least, Alison's self-expression is explicitly gendered, an overt acknowledgment of female sexuality and the desires that the nineteenth-century code or propriety either controlled or denied. Though she may have written without personally seeking notice, as a *writer* Alison broke the code of female modesty to take on the position of speaking (or authorial) subject.[16] In love themselves, Ann and Elsa insist that Alison's writing should not remain a self-enclosed act of personal expression. Rather, they argue, the poems are inherently "social" (to return to Arendt's formulation). Alison spoke "for women," and it is through publication of her poems that Alison's love will, albeit indirectly, be fulfilled.[17]

For Stanhope, Ann's argument is compelling, especially when she evokes the now virtually complete convergence of Alison and her poetry by referring to Stanhope's plan to burn the manuscripts as tantamount to taking life (150). But Glaspell does not resolve the debate until there is one final exchange between Stanhope and Elsa, now left alone in Alison's room. Resorting to his final, most telling argument, Stanhope himself lays claim to direct affinity with Alison's self-expression, by affirming that he, too, renounced an illicit love, staying in an unhappy marriage with Elsa's mother for the sake of the children, and especially for Elsa. What comes into focus here is what Bigsby calls the "reiterated pattern of would-be and adulterous affairs" ("Intro." 27), which Stanhope invokes as he attempts to lay the blame for the poems' destruction on Elsa. While, for the moment, only Elsa's ongoing affair with a married man is a matter of public record, publishing the passionate love poems would allow people to see *all* of the Stanhopes as potential adulterers.

With this argument we glimpse, with Glaspell, a further function of the ideal of feminine propriety and a basic conflict of interest at work in the play. What Stanhope seeks to protect is not Alison's personal privacy or even her choice to avoid public recognition of her poetic gift but, rather, the family name—in other words, the family's social standing and, by implication, the property to which that social standing is attached. Though much of Glaspell's dialogue (as spoken by characters on all sides of the debate) invokes the "modern" reformulation of privacy as intimacy and personal identity, these closing arguments suggest that even this reworked definition ultimately functions to protect "men's property and their peace of mind."[18]

On the surface of things Glaspell appears to reject this view in the play's conclusion. As the village bells ring in the new century, Stanhope hands the poems over to Elsa, recalling Alison's love for making "little gifts" (154), and embraces his wayward daughter, apparently convinced that he no longer needs to repudiate her for her violation of the social code. In a scene eerily reminiscent of the closing of Strindberg's *The Father,* Elsa and Stanhope mutually acknowledge each other: "Father! My Father!" Elsa cries, and Stanhope replies lovingly, "Little Elsa" (155).[19]

Within the context of the play there is something very satisfying both in Stanhope's act of handing over poems to their "rightful owner," Elsa, and in the reconciliation of father and daughter as the curtain falls. The powerful love poems are, we assume, to be published, as a "gift" from Alison's century to Elsa's (154), and Elsa's sins against the old social code are forgiven.[20] But in this link between the poem's potential publication and the renewed bond between Stanhope and his daughter we can see further complexities of Glaspell's construction of authorship and of Glaspell's own position within ideology.

First, the presentation of the poems themselves as another of Alison's "little gifts' recalls Hélène Cixous's discussion, in "The Laugh of the Medusa," of "the whole deceptive problematic of the gift." Responding to Derrida's discussion of Nietzsche, Cixous writes: "Woman is obviously not that woman Nietzsche dreamed of who gives only in order to. Who could ever think of the gift as gift-that-takes? Who else but man, precisely the one who would like to take everything?" (259). Alison's poems, in the play, are in some senses a gift from one woman to another: in Alison's experience of love they speak to Elsa's, and, at the close of act 2, they were explicitly handed to Elsa by Alison's sister, Agatha. But now, as the play closes, they are given to Elsa by Stanhope, and his very act of giving them in Alison's name can be construed not as a "woman's gift" but, rather, as a "gift-that-takes." In effect, Alison's poems, like her house (which Stanhope sells to another couple in the play's second act), are still Stanhope's to dispose of. And this gesture also suggests the extent to which the publication of Alison's writing, and hence the expression of her desire, is mediated by her socially powerful brother, much as its subsequent interpretation may be mediated by the likes of Ted and his Harvard professor.[21]

Glaspell herself further mediates Alison's sexuality by accepting the heterosexual myth that based Emily Dickinson's withdrawal from the world on her renunciation of a male lover. In contrast with Adrienne Rich's call for a lesbian feminist reading of Dickinson and her work, Glaspell's focus on the love poems in constructing her Dickinson figure does appear to assume "heterosexual romance as the key to a woman artist's life and work" (Rich 158). This is hardly surprising given the biographies available to Glaspell at the time she wrote the play and the critical fashion for tracing the masculine references in Dickinson's poems to a mysterious male lover.[22] But in working out Alison's influence on her other female characters, Glaspell maintains a connection between the persistent myth of heterosexual romance and the Victorian code of propriety these women supposedly reject. Alison's love, we are repeatedly told, was both heterosexual and chaste, sublimated in her writing. While female sexual desire occasionally bubbles up (like the disruptions of language from Kristeva's semiotic) in the play's dialogue, as in Elsa's admission to Ann that "when you love you want to give your man—everything in the world" (118), in general it is "love," not desire, that drives and wounds the characters in the play. Though Elsa has broken with propriety in her choice of a lover, she repeatedly idealizes her passion, internalizing her father's emphasis on propriety and redefining it in terms of romantic love, which, for Glaspell, has now become the "proper" way to contain female desire.[23]

The reconciliation of Stanhope and Elsa, in all of its conventionality, is equally complex. While we can infer that, in forgiving Elsa, Stanhope may jeopardize his standing in his narrow-minded community, the father-daughter embrace visibly acknowledges Stanhope's standing within the family. This gesture suggests that Elsa, like Strindberg's little Bertha, has now acknowledged Stanhope as her true parent.[24] While Elsa, now infantilized as "Little Elsa," may still be involved with her married lover, the image with which Glaspell leaves us is that of Elsa now assuming her "proper place" as her father's daughter.[25] Like that of other women whose lives were ruled by the Victorian social code, Elsa's power, though not entirely negligible, is largely restricted to the power to influence her father. And while the balance of power does seem to be tipping in favor of the younger generation as the play closes, Glaspell cannot envision "a revision of the family unit so complete that patriarchy would be unacceptable."[26] Nor can she completely dismantle the class privilege that Stanhope's patriarchal control continues to uphold.

This is hardly surprising given Glaspell's own position as a woman author whose literary career began at about the time she portrays Elsa as receiving the poems from her father. Perhaps we see in these ideological conflicts the struggles of Glaspell herself to reconcile a middle-class family background and her own efforts to maintain a semblance of family life with the social and aesthetic rebellions in which she also played an active part. But rather than resorting to biographical detail to justify Glaspell's conventionality, by way of conclusion I want to return to Bigsby's criticism of *Alison's House* to consider how the ideology of authorship I have been exploring in the play functions in Bigsby's construction of Glaspell as author of *Alison's House*. After dismissing the play as exposing "the extent to which Glaspell still felt it necessary to engage in a debate with her own past and with a morality which, if scarcely irrelevant, had lost a great deal of its immediacy," Bigsby goes on in the introduction to his edition of Glaspell's plays to praise Glaspell for "having written some of the most original plays ever to have come out of America" (28, 30). These highly original plays, we assume, are the ones Bigsby has chosen to anthologize, and, not surprisingly, *Alison's House* is omitted. The latter play, Bigsby implies, is not forward looking enough, since its concerns about "morality" were not especially pressing in the 1930s and, by implication, are even less so today.

In this argument Bigsby is assuming a progress in social attitudes, presumably toward adultery and the "New Woman," which Glaspell questions in her play (and which we in turn might question given the decline suffered by feminism after women won the vote in 1920).[27] In playing off against each other changing definitions of privacy and feminine propriety, *Alison's House* seems to suggest that the myth of progress may be a way of mystifying the relations, particularly relations of ownership, that are still being used to keep women from controlling their own property—be it personal or literary.[28] Even if Glaspell has, to some extent, "sold out" to commercialism and convention in *Alison's House* (as critics like Bigsby contend), Glaspell and her own work may be subject to an expropriation similar to that experienced by Alison and Elsa, as they and their work end up, literally, in patriarchal hands. This expropriation occurs not only in the initial lack of recognition of Glaspell's contributions to American theater but also in a "recovery" of her work by critics whose appreciation of her contribution seems grudging at best and whose readings tend to overlook the ideological conflicts of interest that give a play like *Alison's House* its resonance and relevance even today.

NOTES

1. For discussions of this technique see, for example, Dymkowski, who sees it as a way of making what is apparently marginal central; Noe, who comments

on "the unseen woman around whom [*Alison's House*] is built (60); and Waterman, who argues that "*Alison's House* demonstrates conclusively that Susan Glaspell's most effective and most characteristic dramatic technique was her centering a play around an off-stage character" (88). Early reviews of the play also commented on the power of the absent Alison. See, for example, Hutchens 101–2. Also see Czerepinski in this volume.

2. It is perhaps worth noting that at the time Glaspell was writing *Alison's House* New Criticism, with its emphasis on the autonomous literary text, was just beginning to take root in the United States, under the influence of critics such as F. R. Leavis, who had been a part of the analogous Scrutiny movement in England in the 1920s. For an illuminating discussion of the establishment of New Criticism as the dominant approach to literary studies, see Eagleton's chapter on "The Rise of English."

3. The review of the play published in *Outlook,* for example, notes "rumors assiduously circulated by Miss Le Gallienne's press department" of the link between Alison and Dickinson. An excellent discussion of the links between Dickinson and Glaspell, and possible sources for Glaspell's reconstruction, can be found in Rodier. I am indebted to Rodier's work for several ideas that helped to shape the present essay.

4. In her discussion of rebellious heroines in several of Glaspell's plays (including brief references to *Alison's House*), Ozieblo argues that this threat to male authority may be a major factor in Glaspell's exclusion from the dramatic canon.

5. I wish to thank my colleague Laura Rosenthal for bringing Poovey's work to my attention.

6. Waterman suggests that Glaspell transposes Dickinson's story from Massachusetts to Glaspell's own home state of Iowa at least partly because she was unable to secure from the Dickinson family the rights to use Emily Dickinson's name or her poetry (Waterman 86, cited in Rodier 7).

7. For a useful discussion of distinctions between the "authorial persona" (defined as "an ensemble of instituted virtues, rights, liabilities, capacities"), the "individual who writes," and the historically constituted "authorial subject," see Saunders and Hunter, esp. 482–83.

8. Ted's inventions perhaps suggest Glaspell's own awareness of the fictive nature of much of the information about Dickinson's life that she read in preparation for writing the play.

9. For feminist analyses of Dickinson's reticence and refusal to publish, see, for example, Pollock (esp. chap. 8, " 'Some—Work for Immortality—': The Female Artist as Private Poet") and Dobson.

10. In the play's third act Knowles's request for a photograph of the now dead

Agatha also brings into play the role of photography in making the private public. Elsa, who hesitates to relinquish the photograph without her father's permission, muses, "Aunt Agatha, who lived always in this house, now wanted, for a moment, by the world" (119). Photography is also given prominence as Agatha and Elsa, moments earlier, study the photograph of Alison's rejected suitor, which hangs on the wall of her room (114). It is tempting ro relate the Knowles character to Glaspell's own stint as a reporter for the *Des Moines Daily News*.

11. In writing her play, Glaspell was apparently obliged to respect the Dickinson family's right to privacy. See note 6.

12. Formulating Stanhope's planned action in terms of ownership and Alison's transgression of the social order recalls Foucault's argument concerning the close links between the emergence of the author-function, with its attendant system of ownership of texts, and the potentially transgressive quality of those texts. See "What Is an Author?" (esp. 982).

13. In her chapter of Dickinson as "The Reticent Volcano" Dobson notes the personal costs of internalizing this ideal, commenting, "The 'divine reticence' affirmed by Dickinson's friend, the Rev. John Dudley, reflects conventional thinking, and requires much from the 'exalted' state of femininity, particularly the erasure of self and a radically reserved demeanor" (99). See also Poovey's discussion of "the paradoxes of propriety" as it developed in the seventeenth and eighteenth centuries. Particularly relevant here is her discussion of the "paradox of modesty," which "necessarily established the terms in which real women both consciously conceptualized and evaluated their own behavior and even unconsciously experienced their own gender" (23).

14. When gendered in this way, Brandeis and Warren's concept of the "inviolate personality" also takes on new meaning. While it may be acceptable, in Stanhope's view, for Alison to write, publication would reveal Alison's own violation of her society's social norms.

15. In the Samuel French edition of the play the final line of this passage is incorrectly attributed to Elsa.

16. In a similar vein Poovey argues, citing Hannah More, that "writing for publication . . . jeopardizes modesty, that critical keystone of feminine propriety; for it not only 'hazard[s] . . . disgrace' but cultivates and calls attention to the woman as subject, as initiator of direct action" (36).

17. As footnote to Ann's argument, Knowles quotes Emerson's "The House" in an appeal to Stanhope based on the principle of the timelessness of art (151). His argument, echoed by both Elsa and Eben, that Alison's poems immortalize the past and should therefore be permitted to speak for all time provides another link between the expressive view of authorship and the argument for

publication. As Saunders and Hunter note, "It is not discourse but print that allows the writer to take on the ethical attributes of an author who speaks for all men for all time" (507).

18. This phrase from Poovey, who applies it to eighteenth-century warnings against female self-indulgence.

19. In "Glaspell and Contemporary Women Playwrights" Linda Ben-Zvi comments on Glaspell's knowledge of Strindberg's work and suggests that Glaspell's *Trifles* may be an answer to the Swedish playwright's *Miss Julie* (Ben-Zvi 153, 163–64). Similarly, *Alison's House* serves, in some ways, as answer to *The Father,* though I am more inclined to see the play as a tribute to a number of Glaspell's modern precursors. Others have commented, for example, on how the sale of the house in act 2 recalls Chekhov's *Cherry Orchard* (see Bigsby, "Intro." 27; and Adler 132). In spite of its derogatory tone, Bigsby's observation that the play's "reiterated pattern of would-be and actual adulterous affairs begins to seem more like a pathological inherited condition than the focus for a debate about morality and passion" (27–28) also suggests a parallel with Ibsen's *Ghosts*. For an excellent discussion of the complexities of Strindberg's misogyny in *The Father,* see Finney.

20. This conclusion suggests, then, that Elsa is still a Stanhope after all. It is interesting to note that her illicit love affair in fact still allowed her to keep the family name, however "besmirched."

21. My argument here is rooted in Poovey's contention that under the code of propriety "it was crucial that women act upon, and even experience their sexuality only in mediate terms" (6).

22. An excellent discussion of these sources and critical trends can be found in Rodier.

23. See, for example, Elsa's description of her love as providing companionship, keeping her from being alone (147), as well as her earlier remark to Eben that, casting aside your painfully constructed self for your lover, "it all means something" (122).

24. It is tempting to see both the gesture of handing over the poems and the father-daughter embrace in terms of Elin Diamond's remarks on the Brechtian gest as it can be appropriated by feminism to make visible "social attitudes about gender" (91). The latter gest also raises the question of the place of Elsa's mother. It would seem that she, too is an "absent center" but one presented by Glaspell only as the woman who made Stanhope's life unhappy.

25. This image accords, indirectly, with Taggard's biography, which presents Dickinson's father as a dominant and controlling figure in the poet's life. Whereas Taggard suggests that Edward Dickinson was largely responsible for Emily's

reclusiveness, Glaspell in a sense collapses the roles of Emily's father and brother, indicating that it was Stanhope who asked Alison to stay when her married suitor came for her (Glaspell 140–41).

26. I have borrowed this phrase from Poovey's discussion of Letitia Hawkins's *Letters on the Female Mind* (32).

27. On this decline, see O'Neill.

28. In making this argument, I am adapting the argument of Susan Staves that the apparent changes in married women's ownership of property did not in fact empower them. Rather, Staves argues, adjustments in the law, while superficially reflecting significant change, tended to share an underlying patriarchal structure. I wish to thank my colleague Helen Burke for drawing this argument to my attention.

WORKS CITED

Adler, Thomas. *Mirror on the Stage: The Pulitzer Plays as an Approach to American Drama*. West Lafayette, Ind.: Purdue University Press, 1987.

Benfey, Christopher. *Emily Dickinson and the Problem of Others*. Amherst: University of Massachusetts Press, 1984.

Ben-Zvi, Linda. "Susan Glaspell's Contributions to Contemporary Women Playwrights." In *Feminine Focus: The New Women Playwrights,* ed. Enoch Brater, 147–66. New York: Oxford University Press, 1989.

Bigsby, C. W. E. *A Critical Introduction to Twentieth-Century American Drama*. Vol. 1. Cambridge: Cambridge University Press, 1982.

———. "Introduction." *Plays by Susan Glaspell*. Cambridge: Cambridge University Press, 1987.

Chatfield-Taylor, Otis. Rev. of *Alison's House*, by Susan Glaspell. Civic Repertory Theatre, New York. *Outlook* 156 (Dec. 12, 1930): 711.

Cixous, Hélène. "The Laugh of the Medusa." Trans. Keith Cohen and Paula Cohen. In *New French Feminisms,* ed. Elaine Marks and Isabelle de Courtivron, 245–64. New York: Schocken, 1981.

Diamond, Elin. "Brechtian Theory / Feminist Theory: Toward a Gestic Feminist Criticism." *TDR* 32 (Spring 1988): 82–94.

Dobson, Joanne. *Dickinson and the Strategies of Reticence: The Woman Writer in Nineteenth-Century America*. Bloomington: Indiana University Press, 1989.

Dymkowski, Christine. "On the Edge: The Plays of Susan Glaspell." *Modern Drama* 31 (March 1988): 91–105.

Eagleton, Terry. *Literary Theory: An Introduction*. Minneapolis: University of Minnesota Press, 1983.

Finney, Gail. *Women in Modern Drama*. Ithaca: Cornell University Press, 1989.

Foucault, Michel. "What Is an Author?" Trans. Josué Harari. In *Textual Strategies: Perspectives in Post-Structuralist Criticism,* ed. Josué Harari. Ithaca: Cornell University Press, 1979. Rpt. in *The Critical Tradition: Classic Texts and Contemporary Trends,* ed. David H. Richter, New York: St. Martins, 1989.

Glaspell, Susan. *Alison's House.* New York: Samuel French, 1930.

Hutchens, John. "Comedy in the Saddle." Rev. of *Alison's House,* by Susan Glaspell. Civic Repertory Theatre, New York. *Theatre Arts Monthly* 15 (1931): 95–106.

Noe, Marcia. *Susan Glaspell: Voice from the Heartland.* Macomb: Western Illinois University Press, 1983.

O'Neill, William L. *Everyone Was Brave: The Rise and Fall of Feminism in America.* Chicago: Quadrangle Books, 1969.

Ozieblo, Barbara. "Rebellion and Rejection: The Plays of Susan Glaspell." *Modern American Drama: The Female Canon,* 66–85. Rutherford: Farleigh Dickinson University Press, 1990.

Pollock, Vivian R. *Dickinson: The Anxiety of Gender.* Ithaca: Cornell University Press, 1984.

Poovey, Mary. *The Proper Lady and the Woman Writer: Ideology as Style in the Works of Mary Wollestonecraft, Mary Shelley, and Jane Austin.* Chicago: University of Chicago Press, 1984.

Rich, Adrienne. "Vesuvius at Home: The Power of Emily Dickinson." *Parnassus: Poetry in Review* (Fall–Winter 1976). Rpt. in *On Lies, Secrets, and Silence: Selected Prose, 1966–1978.* New York: Norton, 1979.

Rodier, Katharine. "Glaspell and Dickinson: The Premises of *Alison's House.*" MS, 1991.

Saunders, David, and Ian Hunter. "Lessons from the 'Literrary': How to Historicise Authorship." *Critical Inquiry* 17 (Spring 1991): 479–509.

Staves, Susan. *Married Women's Separate Property in England, 1660–1833.* Cambridge, Mass.: Harvard University Press, 1990.

Taggard, Genevieve. *The Life and Mind of Emily Dickinson.* New York: Knopf, 1930.

Toohey, John. *A History of the Pulitzer Prize Plays.* New York: Citadel, 1967.

Waterman, Arthur E. *Susan Glaspell.* New York: Twayne, 1966.

Part 4
Re-Visioning the
Dramatic Canon

Susan Glaspell: Mapping the Domains of Critical Revision

Gerhard Bach

The rediscovery in the 1980s of Susan Glaspell for the dramatic canon of American literature has not come unchallenged. "Inclusionist" and "exclusionist" critics have engaged in rhetorical bouts over this writer's stature in and for American drama, and their positions are easily summarized. What is there to rediscover in a writer who, by all outward signs, has secured her place in the literary canon? the inclusionist critic will ask. After all, *Trifles* (1916) has been anthologized more consistently than any other one-act play of the early-twentieth-century American theater. The exclusionist critic, on the other hand, will ask: Why try to claim for Glaspell a fame she so obviously does not deserve? After all, the fiction she wrote (nine novels and about fifty short stories) mostly testifies that she is better dead than read. A similar, less blatant exclusionist position will address her play writing career: Why set her up as a dramatist seminal to the early modern American theater? There were other women in the theater before her time, and there were other men in the theater at her time who lived up to their promises; Glaspell's dramatic career, after all, was short-lived and could not sustain itself without the male support of such luminaries as Eugene O'Neill and George Cram Cook.

Are the Glaspell revivalists, like Jay Gatsby, digging for the big treasure among the debris of cultural unretrievables? Or are they, instead—in the wake, for example, of Sacvan Bercovitch and new historicism or Annette Kolodny and feminist re-visionings—contextualizing, and substantiating, their own aesthetic experience with Glaspell's texts as cultural signatures? To rediscover Glaspell in such a context, Bercovitch would argue, connotes meaning making by restructuring the historical dimension of this writer and contextualizing her contemporaries in our own terms. Bercovitch claims

> that race, class and gender are formal principles of art, and therefore integral to textual analysis; that language has the capacity to break free of social restrictions and through its own dynamics to undermine the power structures it seems to reflect; that political norms are inscribed in aesthetic judgment and therefore inherent in the process of interpretation; that aesthetic structures shape the way we understand history. (viii)

In Glaspell's case the inclusion into textual analysis of, specifically, class and gender components enforces a completely new reading of this dramatist's signature on that chapter of literary history vaguely summarized as "The Rise of Modern American Drama." We realize that our conceptions about the emergence of the modern American drama and theater may have been misguided and are in dire need of correction. Besides discovering an actual dramatic oeuvre by Glaspell, we discover another, possibly more important detail, namely that Susan Glaspell's dramatic opus reflects, more so than the combined plays of any other American playwright of the early twentieth century, the development of modern American drama as an indigenous art. A study of her plays, therefore, opens the way to a complete revision of theories of what constitutes American drama, challenging several positions long cherished by cultural history, drama criticism, and critical theory.

To begin such a study of her work there are three general areas that must be covered. Each deserves fuller treatment, now that Glaspell criticism has entered the phase in which such investigations are about to begin.[1]

The first such area is concerned with the formulation of a more definite cultural history of the pre-Provincetown and Provincetown years. The specific question here is to what extent the cultural environment within which Susan Glaspell grew up was a nurturing or stifling one for a writer. As more fully developed investigations in related eras (Lears 1981) and in related critical fields (Kolodny 1975) have shown, explorations of this kind tend to destabilize conventionally accepted American cultural myths.

The second area to deserve critical attention concerns the simplification process of literary history. Its effect has been the consistent neglect of the so-called secondary dramatists of the burgeoning American theater and the role they played, through experimentation, in defining the new drama. Susan Glaspell again is a prominent case in point. Our knowledge of her progression from local color journalist to dramatist is sketchy; even less do we know how the dictates of drama criticism at her time influenced Glaspell's artistic orientation.

While these two areas of investigation relate to unresolved issues in literary and cultural history, the third area concerns the larger issues of contemporary critical theory and canonical formation. The challenges of theory, which require us to define our bases of critical and aesthetic judgment as well as to address the reformation and restructuring of the literary canon, have considerable impact on Glaspell scholarship. Critical reactions to her dramatic writings have increased noticeably in the 1980s, and, perhaps as a response, *The Verge* (1921) has found its way onto the stage again after a seventy-year silence.[2] Also different critical approaches are being employed to contextualize the play for our time (Ben-Zvi 1989; Dymkowski 1988; Friedman 1984; Ozieblo 1990). And finally, claims are being made for the inclusion of Glaspell works, beyond *Trifles*, particularly *The Verge* and *Inheritors* (1921) in order to insure a more balanced representation of Glaspell's contribution to American drama. Susan Glaspell does, as Bigsby demands, deserve "more than a footnote in the history of drama" (1987, 30).

The first issue in need of critical reconsideration, the cultural backdrop of Glaspell's artistic development, reveals an interesting chain of historical links: (1) Susan Glaspell the writer is part and parcel of the Provincetown Players, that experimental theater group working on Cape Cod and in New York from 1915 to 1923; (2) the Provincetown Players are a significant part of the little theater movement in the United States; (3) the roots of the little theater movement are found in the Chicago Renaissance, an awakening and concentration of artistic forces at the turn of the century; (4) some of the intellectual roots of the Chicago Renaissance can be traced to Davenport, Iowa, as represented in such individuals as George Cram Cook, Floyd Dell, and Arthur Davison Ficke; (5) Davenport has more to claim for itself in the latter half of the nineteenth century than as an economically sound location on the Mississippi, its largely German immigrant population giving it one of the first municipal opera houses in the Midwest as well as socialism—thus, it is a city characterized by a somewhat liberal but primarily provincial and bourgeois culture of elegance; (6) Davenport is also the birthplace of Susan Glaspell; and (7) steeped in fin de siècle midwestern sentiment to the point of ultimate dissent, Glaspell joins other midwesterners in their move to the east coast and becomes one of the founders of the Provincetown Players.

These are the links in the chain that forms the cultural context from which the Provincetown Players emerge. An elaborate chain of relations and relationships exists, few of which have been critically explored to show that a considerable number of cofounders of the Provincetown Players on the shores of Cape Cod have a provincial midwestern background and have been nurtured on "the culture of elegance" against which they now rebel. Their age no longer fulfilled Van Wyck Brooks's demand to provide "a culture adequate to [their] needs" (qtd. in Matthiessen xvii). Susan Glaspell, experiencing this inadequacy in her own midwestern background, is one of those participating in the definition and artistic expression of a culture that would be more adequately suited to such needs. She does this in the plays she begins to write for the theater that she helps to establish.

Such an unassuming provincial beginning had little chance with the literary historians. They have preferred to render the excitement of a cultural awakening in more highly dramatic terms—*upheaval, explosion, revolution*. Oliver Sayler crystallizes the explosion theory in his influential study of the artistic beginnings of the modern American theater, *Our American Theater* (1923). The chroniclers of the early twentieth century, especially those who are part of the movement itself, embellish this view in their sentimental accounts. In her autobiography, *Time and the Town: A Provincetown Chronicle* (1942), Mary Heaton Vorse summarizes this attitude: "The success of the Provincetown Players was . . . one of those explosions of talent which from time to time transforms art and science" (116). It is a sensibility shared by those who were part of a short-lived movement in need of embellishment, appropriate perhaps in the realm of autobiography but no longer so in literary history. But historians have yet to reconsider their acceptance of the "theory of explosion." The rather simple fact that in 1915 a group of artists and writers gathered in Provincetown, Massachusetts, to act plays they themselves had written still represents, in the minds of cultural historians, a "profound cultural upheaval" and even a "spiritual revolution" (Sarlós 2–3).

What we witness here is a reversal of cause and effect. This becomes obvious when we relate the Provincetown experiment to the cultural and social context from which it emerges. The artistic outpouring of the Provincetown Players' experiments is not the cause of America's cultural upheaval but, rather, its effect, its artistically expressed result. The Provincetown plays reflect, on a larger scale, the culmination of a cultural value formation process, breaking with the notions of the genteel tradition and espousing modernism. Thus, it is not surprising that, on closer scrutiny, the artistic forms of these plays may often be radical, while the themes projected in them are traditional. Susan Glaspell sums up this point in her recollection of the conflict between surface images and underlying realities: "We were supposed to be a sort of 'special' group— radical, wild. Bohemians, we have even been called. But it seems to me we were a particularly simple people, who sought to arrange life for the thing we wanted to do, needing each other as protection against complexities, yet living as we did because of an instinct for the old, old things" (*Road to the Temple,* 235–36).

Despite such immediate evidence, theater history has continued to romanticize its own cherished "theory of explosion": before 1915 there was Broadway; after 1915 there was art. This overlaps neatly with a second theory prevalent among the historians of the theater, the "theory of singularity," as embodied by Eugene O'Neill. Although the beginnings of modern American drama were diversified and represented by more than just a handful of promising playwrights, historians of the theater still prefer the version that it was O'Neill who single-handedly "battled to lift American drama to the level of art and keep it there" (Gelb 5).

Both these concepts are so convincingly self-congratulatory that they have gone basically unchallenged, and thus the underlying questions remain unanswered. Who, besides O'Neill, are the forty-some writers contributing to the transformation of American theater? What and where are their cultural roots? How do their one hundred and some plays reflect the development of American drama at this time? Which male and female traditions and innovations are represented? How does O'Neill fit into this emerging pattern? What interdependent artistic relationships exist among the more prolific Provincetown writers? How does Glaspell's continuous flow of new productions for the Provincetown reflect this development? Where does expressionism in American drama originate? Is it a singular achievement (O'Neill and/or Glaspell), or is it a collective achievement (the realization of George Cram Cook's idea of the theater as collective artistic expression)?

Literary history and criticism have been satisfied to assimilate the inadequate particularizations of cultural history. While the history of the theater of the Provincetown Players has been recorded in several accounts (Kenton 1925; Deutsch and Hanau 1931; Sarlós 1982), the dramas themselves have not been made available, nor has the reception of the Provincetown plays by the New York school of theater reviewers been investigated in greater detail.[3] A wealth of material that would be able to tell the story of the beginnings of modern American drama from the perspective of the plays produced has remained untouched. The reason for this is the combination of the two "theories" of explosion and singularity: "O'Neill and the Provincetown"—the Eastern version of the Western myth of single-handed achievements.

Criticism has been content with this intensely misleading simplification of literary history. Very few critics have noticed the imbalances and contradictions in the continued portrayal of O'Neill as the representative Provincetown playwright. Elsewhere I have argued that the one writer representing the Players' achievement *as well as* their loss is Susan Glaspell and that, for various reasons historical and critical, O'Neill is actually the least representative of their aims (Bach 1990). Another aspect slighted by literary history concerns the interrelations of the diverse Provincetown writers and the cross-fertilization of their ideas. The relationship between Eugene O'Neill and Susan Glaspell illustrates this well. Quite contrary to some myth-inflating imaginations of O'Neill as the loner in the theater, we find that a close professional alliance existed between these two writers during that crucial phase around 1920, when the Provincetowners were beginning to experiment with expressionism. In this phase each was closely watching the other, and O'Neill was in fact ready to work some of Glaspell's experiments into his own work (Ben-Zvi 1982, 1986; Larabee 1990). Thus, in the seminal 1921–22 phase of the Provincetown experiment, formal and thematic parallels can be found to exist between *The Emperor Jones* (1921) and *The Outside* (1917) as well as between *The Hairy Ape* (1921) and *The Verge* (1921), constellations that have not yet been fully researched.

Another untouched issue is audience response and critical reception. And it is precisely this issue in which discoveries could be made that would reposition the imbalanced history of the evolution of drama in the United States. Again, Susan Glaspell's work lends itself to such investigation exceptionally well. No other Provincetown playwright worked so consistently within the theater's self-defined artistic boundaries and for its stated artistic aim. Therefore, the critical response to the productions of her plays, from the scant early reviews of *Suppressed Desires* (1915) and *Trifles* to the immense diversity of voices responding to *The Verge*, would add greatly to our understanding of this writer's short-lived career as a dramatist. What do we know about Glaspell's reactions to such responses? Does she accommodate her writing to the critics' reactions, and, if so, how? To what extent is the fact of male domination in the theater and in theater criticism an influential, possibly inhibiting factor in Glaspell's career?

These questions, and here especially the last one, are central when we consider the fact that all of her plays written for the Provincetown stage are dominated by female protagonists. Two randomly chosen examples illustrate the wealth of issues and materials waiting to be addressed. These examples reflect the responses of male critics to essentially feminine/feminist issues. In his review entitled "Mr. Hornblow Goes to the Play" Arthur Hornblow comments on the two women in *Trifles* with these assumedly deliberate words: "[*Trifles* is] an ingenious study in feminine ability at inductive and deductive analysis" (21). Which subliminal gender concepts are encrypted in such a statement? Why does the reviewer feel it necessary to stress these abilities rather than comment on the difficulties the two women in the play experience in establishing a female bond of solidarity against the "law"? Similarly, a reviewer of *The Verge* exposes his substantial gender bias when he suggests his version of the play's significance: "If it was Miss Glaspell's intention to satirize the type of erotic, neurotic, ill-tempered, and platitudinous hussy who dramatizes herself into a 'super-woman' and even 'puts it over' on her gentlemen friends . . . she has admirably succeeded. If, however, like the feminine majority of her audiences, she, too, accepts this fraudulent female as an authentic 'superwoman,' we can only express our opinion that Claire is not convincing." The reviewer concludes, just a trifle condescendingly: "Perhaps the play was ripped untimely from the author's brain" (Parker 296).

Perhaps it was. It is a statement richly promising for contemporary critical reconsideration, especially, as I have previously suggested, in the area of critical theory and canon formation. Perhaps *The Verge* was ripped untimely from Glaspell's imagination, as were, arguably, *Inheritors* for its critique of American jingoism, *The Outside* for its statement on female imprisonment, and *Trifles* for its ironic-radical incrimination of man-made law and woman-made justice. But how much patina of irony time has added in each case to Parker's verdict. Obviously, the critical observer today would point to the fact that the times were not ripe for these plays, that the theater critics at Glaspell's time were enculturated in a mold of complacency too slick to allow for the crevices of dissent, doubt, and difference.[4] In the first "wave" of Glaspell research (Waterman 1966; Bach 1977, 1978) such critical biases were not yet considered ample evidence of an era rich in culturally gendered concepts and dogmas; today it is impossible to disregard these telling details of stereotypification. The critical tools to put them into perspective are there, in reader response criticism, in the new historicism, or in feminist critical theory, ready to reassess the significance of Glaspell's dramatic works for contemporary readers and audiences.

Feminist readings of Glaspell ushered in this re-visioning process in the mid-1980s, with contextualizations varying from the sociocultural (Dymkowski 1988) to the psychological (Larabee 1987). For obvious reasons, such criticism has concentrated on *The Verge*, while *The Outside* and *Inheritors*, arguably no less expressive of the author's position and no less influential in the Provincetown's development, come in as a distant second. This progress in critical revaluation is an ambiguous achievement. On the one hand, it has bolstered the claim for inclusion of *The Verge* in the canon, the main argument being that this play culminates Glaspell's achievement and thus more fully represents the author's art than her showpiece, *Trifles*. On the other hand, while this discovery of the "other" Glaspell has been long overdue, there is a danger of it becoming just as exclusionary as the previous selectivist criticism. To fully credit the achievements of the first woman writer on the American art theater scene, the reasons for Glaspell's success must be accounted for as stringently as those responsible for the author's eventual failure and retreat. Thus, although they are needed to complete the pattern, Glaspell's post-Provincetown plays have been ignored almost totally: *The Comic Artist* (1927); *Alison's House* (1930), the Pulitzer winner in drama for the 1930–31 season; and *Springs Eternal* (1945, unpub.).

Alison's House, especially, deserves critical revision, since it expresses Glaspell's cultural and artistic dilemma most immediately. Beyond its inherent flaws and merits this play is the summary statement of the author's affinity and anguish as a female artist in America with the fate of the female artist in the modern age. As a reflection of the artist's individuality, *Alison's House* focalizes Glaspell's overarching theme of woman's self-defined space between heritage and legacy. As a summary account, the play possibly generalizes these issues to its own detriment; they have been presented more directly, and dramatically, with greater diversity and impact, in her previous plays. But the basic motif—the desire, often the demand, of the female self to define an inviolable physical or spiritual realm—remains alive to the very end of Glaspell's career as a dramatist, attesting to her undiminished dedication to a cause. Such continuity is apparent in a number of parallels, not just in theme but in structure and context as well.

Alison's House, for instance, shares such an affinity with *Trifles*. In both plays Glaspell investigates the impact of an offstage character on those who, physically and spiritually, invade her formerly (self-)protected space. In both, the search onstage for clues that might fill the void left by death and/or abandonment brings to life the offstage character—in a sequence of self-revealing reenactments of memories, doubts, and fears, in a struggle to make sense. The remarkable contradiction is that the absent "voice" has shifted center, from enforced seclusion (the rural homemaker) in *Trifles* to self-willed seclusion (the suburban artist) in *Alison's House*.

In a similar parallel, namely woman's defense of place and space as inviolable or sacred, *Alison's House* reenacts the theme of *The Outside*. Again, memory plays a decisive role in the revelation of woman's place as defined by the outside world (imprisonment through invasion) and the inside world (self-imprisonment through protection, conservation).

In a further parallel *Alison's House* reverberates Glaspell's inveterate concern with traditional American values and the threat of their indiscriminate exploitation in the twentieth century, as expressed most forcefully in *Inheritors*. While in the later play Glaspell chooses symbolic representations (Alison's poems as a legacy of a passing "dark" age to a more promising age of enlightened sensibilities), *Inheritors* addresses with forceful realism the changing interpretations of historical and historic events across the three generations of pioneer, settler, and entrepreneur. There are vanishing frontiers in both plays, with impacts decidedly more drastic for the uncompromising women than for the mostly "agreeable" men.

The most obvious recourse, in *Alison's House,* however, is to *Bernice* (1919), Glaspell's first long play, whose importance in the author's development has been consistently overlooked. There are affinities between these two plays that suggest that, with *Alison's House,* Glaspell was redrafting an earlier notion and pattern. The one affinity is structural. In *Bernice* Glaspell first uses the cyclical pattern upon which all later plays (and many of her novels) are grafted: in this cyclical pattern Glaspell portrays characters who realize how unresolved issues of the past impinge upon the present and, unless answered, threaten to infect the future. It is a pattern that seems to become formulaic the more Glaspell loses touch with theater in action.[5] A second, more important affinity is Glaspell's choice of the artist as the dramatis persona to represent the struggle of the liminal female self against fixity, convention, or tradition. The issue yet to be addressed by critics is Glaspell's gendered bias: while in *Bernice, The Verge,* and *Alison's House* the creator-artists are tragic heroines, their male counterparts in *Chains of Dew* (Standish Seymore), *Inheritors* (Professor Holden), and *The Comic Artist* (the Rolf brothers) are either caricatures of the "artist" or tragicomic failures (not unlike Glaspell's husband, George Cram Cook). None of these men occupy center stage.

All of Glaspell's plays, then, are radical statements in a double way.

Within their own context they address women's need for self-defined space and the many-faceted denials with which the dominant culture responds. In a wider context that would reflect these issues upon the author herself, they address the artist's struggle to appropriate for herself the givens of male-dominated culture in the United States, that is, to have an audience. In other words, as long as Glaspell works within the Provincetown Players community—the writers, actors, stage designers, and the audiences—there is a discourse community within which her art can function and develop.[6] Outside of such a community, which is Glaspell's condition after 1925, the dramatic contexts she creates and the characters that move within them become increasingly arbitrary. The limitations of this condition, and Glaspell's awareness of them, are only fully understood if we accept the notion that the denial of self-created space is common to all Glaspell heroines, active and alive as well as passive and silenced. Barbara Ozieblo observes that the liminality of Glaspell's heroines is defined by this homelessness: "[Her] women seek self-definition as women at home and beyond; that is, they enter the male sphere, thus being both inside and outside society" (74). Breaking and entering the protective shell of conventionally defined "male spheres" may characterize the "activists" Madeline (*Inheritors*) and Claire (*The Verge*); it only partially explains Bernice and Alison, whose legacy is not in their actions but, rather, in what they chose not to do when they were alive. What binds these different plays together is the radicalness Glaspell conveys in either stance of opposition—the impulse to act or the decision to retroact. Her plays belonging to the post-Provincetown phase are characterized by such retroaction.

   The Verge is the play at once indicative of this oppositional stance and moving beyond it. Read as a feminist statement surpassing the limits of its historicity, *The Verge* appears in the vicinity of other, similar historic rediscoveries, such as Kate Chopin's *The Awakening* (1899) and Charlotte Perkins Gilman's "The Yellow Wallpaper" (1892) (see Fetterley 1986). Parallels in these works abound—as, for instance, inside-outside metaphors, which occur in all three works, or male antagonist grouping, with Tom (platonic companion), Dick (erotic suitor), and Harry (dried-up husband) in *The Verge* resembling Robert, Arobin, and Mr. Pontellier in Chopin's novel. But the major statement combining these three is the portrayal of the "mad" woman in her (self-) appointed place: the closet or attic, the "pigeon house," or the twisted tower. These are the accepted and prominent contemporary readings identifying patterns of similarity or cohesion. While these works speak to us about their time with equal intensity, *The Verge,* being less definite in historical setting and time, speaks more intensely so to us about our time than the fictions by Chopin and Gilman. This is the quality that also makes *The Verge* stand out from the other Glaspell plays. To clarify this, I suggest a rereading of *The Verge* from a reader/audience response position.

When in 1921, after the premiere performance on the Provincetown stage, Percy Hammond vents his exasperation in a review entitled "What *The Verge* Is About, Who Can Tell" (10), he expresses his defeat in *making sense* of this challenging text. He also refuses, like so many of his male colleagues, to complete the text in reviewing his own response to it or, in reader response terms, to fill in the gaps as Wolfgang Iser describes the process. *The Verge,* in acting upon its audience, becomes what *Hamlet* is for Stephen Booth: the tragic story of "an audience that cannot make up its mind" (137). The fact that in the 1920s the enigma presented by *The Verge* is rejected should not simply be accepted as evidence of the play's faultiness. The causes for this rejection must be investigated and related to a contemporary response: What does Glaspell's text "do"? What response does it incite from a modern audience?

In such a context Lewisohn's critique of the critics sounds rather prophetic, when he says of *Inheritors:* "If the history of literature, dramatic or non-dramatic, teaches us anything, it is that Broadway and its reviewers will someday be judged by their attitude to this work" (515). Similarly, in response to the original performance of *The Verge,* Stark Young, writing for the *New Republic,* says: "No play of Susan Glaspell's can be passed over quite so snippishly as most of the reviewers have done with *The Verge*" (41). What in these plays is it that would cause their rejection? Why specifically would *The Verge* cause New York art critics to question one another about their critical premises in a press battle lasting for almost two months?

The "public" reaction to *The Verge,* if we accept the press reviews as reflecting the public's view correctly, is so divided that it leaves no middle ground. The play is endorsed by the "art critic" minority of New York's theater reviewers. It is also supported quite noisily by the "people's voice" of the New York avant-garde, the *Greenwich Villager*. Two weeks following the premiere performance this paper's reviewer sounds the public dispute in a front-page article entitled "Claire—Superwoman or Plain Egomaniac? A Non-Verdict Disputation" (1). Then there is the urban American suffrage movement strongly promoting the play as a cause célèbre. The majority of New York's theater reviewers, however, condemn the play, even though they do wait until their authority, Alexander Woollcott, has presented his verdict in the *New York Times*. "The Play—Provincetown Psychiatry" (Woollcott) and "*The Verge*—Bad Insanity Clinic" (Dickinson), are rather moderate headlines to utterly condemning reviews. What a "queer study of eroticism" *The Verge* is, sniffs John Ranken Towse, and concludes, "If a moral must be deduced, it must be that only the neurotic or insane have the right idea of life" (9). Arthur Pollock responds to this and other derisive critiques, sensing a dissatisfaction among his colleagues about the lack of entertainment the play provides. Even the critics, he says, "want entertainment first and fast. They want the glad play or the novel, that by surprises or sweet sentiment they may have no trouble keeping awake. And so whatever robs them of the amusement they're seeking they call dull, unintelligible, neurotic, melodramatic" (7).

In retrospect, the failure of *The Verge* to come across has several reasons. One is the culturally determined assumption of the purpose of theater, a mold into which this play does not fit. It does not entertain social conventions; it attacks them. Another reason, more threatening in Glaspell's time, but one that readers and audiences today possibly find to be the electrifying one, is that the play deconstructs its own premises of communication. Neither language nor visual impression function in the "normal" patterns, facts to which the critics of the time could only respond in self-defense with such "rationalizing" terms as *perverse, insane,* and *queer*. These terms reflect an attitude of helplessness; critics fail to understand and describe this new mode of stage enactment and representation, since it has not been encountered on American stages before. Only later will it be referred to as "expressionism."

As is typical of expressionist drama, meaning is conveyed through channels supplementing the spoken word. The setting "speaks" to the audience; the atmosphere enveloping the action expresses the unseen inner life of the protagonists. Much of what is intended is not expressed verbally but visually. In *The Verge* Glaspell, like O'Neill in his expressionistic plays, gives elaborate and detailed directions about setting, action, and individual characters' motions and emotions. Here Glaspell's choice of images is as suggestive as the dialogue itself. At the outset of the play the "verge"-context is introduced imagistically before action and dialogue unfold. First, it is a dividing line between two realms of existence indicating contrasting elements, opposing forces, polarities—outside and inside, darkness and light, heat and cold, the object and its shadow. Further details of the greenhouse, in which the action is about to unfold, culminate in the following direction:

> *At the back grows a strange vine. It is arresting rather than beautiful. It creeps along the low wall, and one branch gets a little way up the glass. You might see the form of a cross in it, if you happen to think it that way. The leaves of this vine are not the form that leaves have been. They are at once repellent and significant. (58)*

Here Glaspell presents the second visual definition of what the verge signifies. The initial polarities amalgamate; they are shown to be complementary rather than contrasting. The leaves of the strange plant are repellent and significant "at once." In fusing the initial polarities, this plant represents the verge not as a line separating realms of existence but, rather, as a junction of promise, creation. "The leaves . . . are not the form that leaves have been." That the polarities embodied by the plant take the form of a cross foreshadow the events to follow. The plants that Claire, the protagonist, creates become the cross on which she will find herself nailed in the end.

Consistently throughout the play, then, the parameters of meaning are presented in visual form, allegorically, before any verbal exchanges or (self-)explanations occur. In each act the allegorical setting provides for the expression of an idea that apparently cannot or should not be approached primarily or initially through language.

The Verge, as is quickly established when the characters appear onstage and do start talking, is a play about the loss of language, the loss of the ability to communicate and relate, and, consequently, the loss of self. Progressively, as we witness the characters expressing themselves in so many words about Claire's state of mind and Claire trying to express herself to them in words that are lost on them, the rift between Claire and the collective of antagonists widens. As dialogues unravel, colloquial language (Dick, Tom, Harry, Adelaide, Elizabeth) and stylized language (Claire) engage in battles of "speaking past the other." Increasingly in acts 2 and 3, communication breaks down and ends in imprisoning speechlessness. Claire is the only one to realize in the others this emerging pattern of words imprisoning their speakers. Worse than that, she recognizes in her own language the tendency of speech patternization. As she attempts to describe what she is doing with her plants, words are shaping themselves into patterns, lifeless molds. It is a forceful irony, reminiscent of Shakespeare's *Tempest,* that Glaspell would choose poetry to reveal such imprisoning patternization.

There are three men in Claire's life who combine their efforts to "save" her from creating new life. Within their frame of reference her actions and intentions border on the insane. They are united in the motivation to save her from this madness. But their motives are selfish; only the degrees of selfishness or male egotism is what distinguishes them from one another. Their varying degrees of selfishness also define their varying degrees of masculinity. In turn, their degree of masculinity defines their state of patternization, or their ability to communicate themselves to Claire. Tom, the least selfish, and consequently also the least masculine one, comes closest to breaking through to Claire in an intense struggle to "save" her for his world. But the inner logic of communication through words turns against itself:

TOM: Your country is the inside, Claire. The innermost. You are disturbed because you lie too close upon the heart of life.

CLAIRE: (*restlessly*) I don't know; you can think it one way—or another. No way says it, and that's good—at least it's not shut up in saying. (*She is looking at her enclosing hand, as if something is shut up there*)

TOM: But also, you know, things may be freed by expression. Come from the unrealized into the fabric of life.

CLAIRE: Yes, but why does the fabric of life have to—freeze into its pattern? It should (*doing it with her hands*) flow. (*Then turning like an unsatisfied child to him*) But I wanted to talk to you.

TOM: You are talking to me.

(85–86)

Plainly, in talking to each other, they fail to communicate. Talk is a deceptive lure, and for a brief moment Claire tends to believe that she is capable of getting through to Tom. Actually, however, talk divides them further and imprisons each in monadic cells of incommunicability. Tom's attempt to pull her back into an existence that, for Claire, is not life is more endangering than physical imprisonment, and in a heightened state of clarity—"*with sight too clear*" (99)—Claire takes action to free herself from this last deceptive bond. In murdering Tom, her companion in adversity and still her adversary, "*she has taken a step forward, past them all*" (100). While this step beyond the bounds of sanity frees her, it is a freedom that for her can only be found in the solitary icy regions of speechlessness, the silence of madness.

Once there, in that silent prison created by the "madness" that, earlier in the play, Claire had declared to be "the only chance for sanity" (82), Claire/Glaspell releases the audience to pursue meaning outside the play in their own boundaries of reality. This is compelling in a twofold way. The expressionistic setting of the play quite physically distances the spectator from the action. The greenhouse as well as the tower both are self-enclosed structures, and the spectator looks into the action without being part of it. Glaspell's choice of highly abstract language for her dialogues intensifies this distance. The audience observes Claire's gradual progression into the inner world with interest but without compassion. As within the course of action Claire alienates herself from her circle of family and friends, Glaspell, by means of such aesthetic devices as expressionistic settings and abstract language, alienates the audience from Claire's immediate conflict, leaves the question of the verge as boundary between sanity and insanity unresolved, and thus confronts us with a truly contemporary issue. Who defines the border, its lines of demarcation as well as its range, and who decides on which side of this border resides "insanity"?

This is the question that, directly or indirectly, arises from all of Glaspell's plays. Initially, Glaspell "toys" with the issue. In *Suppressed Desires* its mode of presentation is comedy and satire; in *Trifles,* stark realism; in *Woman's Honor,* social protest; in *The Outside,* symbolism. Experimentation with dramatic styles does not hide the fact that Glaspell very early on finds her theme in the variety of boundaries existent in her culture. While the earlier protagonists, after experiencing life on the verge, are still given options to choose which side to turn to, the women in her plays after *Bernice* are left with only a margin of choice. In adjusting to that fact, they also realize that, notwithstanding their own definitions of sanity and insanity, they end up on the side marked "wrong."

Despite the progress in literary history and criticism, despite renewed efforts in lifting Susan Glaspell out of the obscure realm of second-ratedness, Glaspell's dramatic works are still waiting to be fully discovered, for their individual merit, as a unit, as cultural manifestations of modernism in American drama, and as a culturally overarching art addressing issues of contemporary concern. Consequently, rediscovering Glaspell beyond the level of individual literary merit means clearing away several highly cherished cultural American myths and much of the debris in their wake. Depending on where we decide to trim and prune these myths do we determine the applicability of Claire's words in *The Verge,* that we "need not be held in forms moulded [*sic*] for us" (64).

NOTES

1. Mary Papke has published *Susan Glaspell: A Research and Production Sourcebook* on Glaspell's plays and fiction; Veronica Makowsky has published *Susan Glaspell's Century of American Women,* a critical study of her work; and a Glaspell biography, by Linda Ben-Zvi, is being completed. Together with the existing research tools (Waterman; Bach; Noe) and the host of essays and articles from the 1980s, these authoritative materials will provide new incentives for scholarly investigation.

2. The play was produced in the Nelke Experimental Theatre at Brigham Young University (BYU) on March 16, 1991. The production was part of a one-day conference on "Susan Glaspell—Rediscovering an American Playwright,"

hosted by the BYU English Department. A conference report and play review appeared in *Theatre Journal* (March 1992).

3. The only extensive study of the Provincetown plays is in German (Bach 1979). For a partial summary in English, see Bach 1978.

4. Supporting reviews from the male majority of theater critics were few and far between and came primarily from the seasoned Glaspell supporters, such as Ludwig Lewisohn, Stark Young, and Kenneth Macgowan.

5. Edmund Wilson considers this Glaspell's major weakness as a playwright: "Dramatist friend who had a formula: three points—condition at the beginning of the play 'which grows'—obstacle at end of second act, which is removed by surprise—ditto at end of third act" (385).

6. In *The Road to the Temple* Glaspell attests to the importance of an actual stage in the process of her playwriting activities (255). Mary Heaton Vorse confirms this influence: "Susan Glaspell was a natural. . . . She had attended no course in playwriting but she had what was better, a stage at hand on which she could see how a play worked out" (124).

WORKS CITED

Bach, Gerhard. "O'Neill's Provincetown Connection: Anmerkungen zum Mythos einer zur Legende stilisierten Beziehung." In *Eugene O'Neill 1988: Deutsche Beiträge zum 100. Geburtstag des amerikanischen Dramatikers*, ed. U. Halfmann, 34–47. Tübingen: Narr, 1990. ("O'Neill's Provincetown Connection: Deconstructing an American Cultural Myth." An English version is forthcoming.)

———. "Susan Glaspell (1876–1948): A Bibliography of Dramatic Criticism." *Great Lakes Review* 3, no. 1 (1977): 1–34.

———. "Susan Glaspell—Provincetown Playwright." *Great Lakes Review* 4, no. 2 (1978): 31–43.

———. "Susan Glaspell—Rediscovering an American Playwright." *Theatre Journal* 44, no. 1 (1992): 94–96.

———. *Susan Glaspell und die Provincetown Players: Die Anfänge des modernen amerikanischen Dramas und Theaters*. Frankfurt: Peter Lang, 1979.

Ben-Zvi, Linda. "Susan Glaspell and Eugene O'Neill." *Eugene O'Neill Newsletter* 6, no. 2 (1982): 21–29.

———. "Susan Glaspell and Eugene O'Neill: The Imagery of Gender." *Eugene O'Neill Newsletter* 10, no. 1 (1986): 22–27.

———. "Susan Glaspell's Contribution to Contemporary Women Playwrights." In *Feminine Focus: The New Women Playwrights*, ed. Enoch Brater, 147–66. Oxford: Oxford University Press, 1989.

Bercovitch, Sacvan. *Reconstructing American Literary History*. Cambridge, Mass.: Harvard University Press, 1986.

Bigsby, C. W. E. "Introduction." *Plays by Susan Glaspell*, 1–31. Cambridge: Cambridge University Press, 1987.

Booth, Stephen. *An Essay on Shakespeare's Sonnets*. New Haven: Yale University Press, 1969.

"Claire—Superwoman or Plain Egomaniac? A Non-Verdict Disputation." *Greenwich Villager* (Nov. 30, 1921): 1.

Deutsch, Helen, and Stella Hanau. *The Provincetown: A Story of the Theatre*. New York: Farrar and Rinehart, 1931.

Dickinson, Weed. "*The Verge*—Bad Insanity Clinic." *New York Evening Telegraph*, November 15, 1921. Qtd. in Bach 1977, 19.

Dymkowski, Christine. "On the Edge: The Plays of Susan Glaspell." *Modern Drama* 31, no. 1 (1988): 91–105.

Fetterley, Judith. "Reading about Reading: 'A Jury of Her Peers,' 'The Murders in the Rue Morgue,' and 'The Yellow Wallpaper.' " In *Gender and Reading: Essays on Readers, Texts, and Contexts*, ed. Elizabeth A. Flynn and Patrocinio P. Schweickart, 147–64. Baltimore: Johns Hopkins University Press, 1986.

Friedman, Sharon. "Feminism as Theme in Twentieth Century American Women's Drama." *American Studies* 25, no. 1 (1984): 69–89.

Gelb, Arthur, and Barbara Gelb. *O'Neill*. New York: Harper and Row, 1962.

Glaspell, Susan. *The Road to the Temple*. New York: Stokes, 1927.

———. *The Verge*. In *Plays by Susan Glaspell*. Ed. C. W. E. Bigsby, 57–101. Cambridge: Cambridge University Press, 1987.

Hammond, Percy. "What *The Verge* Is About, Who Can Tell." *New York Herald*, November 15, 1921, 10.

Hornblow, Arthur. "Mr. Hornblow Goes to the Play." *Theatre Magazine* 25 (Jan. 1917): 21–24.

Kenton, Edna. "Provincetown and Macdougal Street." In *Greek Coins*, ed. George Cram Cook, 17–30. New York: Doran, 1925.

Kolodny, Annette. *The Lay of the Land: Metaphor as Experience and History in American Life and Letters*. Chapel Hill: University of North Carolina Press, 1975.

Larabee, Ann E. "Death in Delphi: Susan Glaspell and the Companionate Marriage." *Mid-American Review* 7, no. 2 (1987): 93–106.

———. " 'Meeting the Outside Face to Face': Susan Glaspell, Djuna Barnes, and O'Neill's *The Emperor Jones*." In *Modern American Drama: The Female Canon*, ed. June Schlueter, 77–85. Rutherford: Fairleigh Dickinson University Press, 1990.

Lears, T. J. Jackson. *No Place of Grace: Antimodernism and the Transformation of American Culture, 1880–1920*. New York: Pantheon, 1981.

Lewisohn, Ludwig. "*Inheritors*." *Nation* 112 (Apr. 6, 1921): 515.

Matthiessen, F. O. *American Renaissance: Art and Expression in the Age of Emerson and Whitman.* New York: Oxford University Press, 1941.

Noe, Marcia. *Susan Glaspell: Voice from the Heartland.* Western Illinois Monograph Series, no. 1. Macomb: Western Illinois University, 1983.

Ozieblo, Barbara. "Rebellion and Rejection: The Plays of Susan Glaspell." In *Modern American Drama: The Female Canon,* ed. June Schlueter, 66–76. Rutherford: Fairleigh Dickinson University Press, 1990.

Parker, Robert A. "Drama—Plays Domestic and Imported." *Independent,* Dec. 17, 1921, 296.

Pollock, Arthur. "The New Play—*The Verge.*" *Brooklyn Daily Eagle,* Nov. 17, 1921, 7.

Sarlós, Robert K. *Jig Cook and the Provincetown Players: Theatre in Ferment.* Amherst: University of Massachusetts Press, 1982.

Sayler, Oliver. *Our American Theater, 1908–1923.* New York: Dover, 1923.

Towse, John Ranken. "The Play." *New York Evening Post,* November 15, 1921, 9.

Vorse, Mary Heaton. *Time and the Town: A Provincetown Chronicle.* New York: Stokes, 1942.

Waterman, Arthur E. *Susan Glaspell.* New York: Twayne, 1966.

Wilson, Edmund. *The Twenties,* ed. Leon Edel. New York: Farrar, Straus and Giroux, 1975.

Woollcott, Alexander. "The Play—Provincetown Psychiatry." *New York Times,* November 15, 1921, 23.

Young, Stark. "After the Play." *New Republic,* December 7, 1921, 41.

Susan's Sisters: The "Other" Women Writers of the Provincetown Players

Judith E. Barlow

As Helen Chinoy points out in her introduction to *Women in American Theatre,* there has been in this country a striking "association of women with regional, institutional, little, art, and alternative theatres."[1] The association goes back at least as far as the second decade of this century, when the so-called Little Theatre movement, partly inspired by such innovative European companies as the Moscow Art Theatre and Dublin's Abbey Theatre, spawned hundreds of amateur, semiprofessional, and professional troupes across the United States. Discussing American influences, Robert Károly Sarlós suggests that "the impact of outstanding women was perhaps greater" than that of men in creating the "cultural awakening" of which this theatrical revolution was a part.[2] Activists and artists such as Emma Goldman, Margaret Sanger, Isadora Duncan, and Gertrude Stein challenged traditional notions about society and the arts, including women's roles in both.

The most important of the Little Theatres that emerged just before the United States entered World War I was the Provincetown Players, which began on Cape Cod in 1915 and—in its first incarnation—closed its doors in New York City in 1922.[3] While many of the other Little Theatres produced works by such recent European and British playwrights as Ibsen, Strindberg, Chekhov, and Shaw, the Provincetown was dedicated to supporting plays by American dramatists and involving them in the productions. During its seven-year run the group produced roughly one hundred plays by some fifty dramatists;[4] it broke its commitment to native drama only once, to perform Arthur Schnitzler's *Last Masks.*[5]

The role of women in the Provincetown Players cannot be overestimated. In 1916, when the group formally established itself and made plans to find a New York theater, thirteen of the twenty-nine individuals listed in the incorporation papers were women.[6] Mary Heaton Vorse, a fiction writer, political activist, and feminist journalist who covered the 1915 International Congress of Women in Amsterdam, owned the Provincetown wharf on which the first two seasons of plays were performed.[7] Louise Bryant was a journalist and activist (her relationship with radical John Reed would be romanticized in the film *Reds* more than half a century later), while Ida Rauh was a feminist and socialist who held a law degree, worked for the Women's Trade Union League and supported birth control, and had visited Russia. Rauh not only acted in and directed individual plays for the Provincetown but was, for a time, one of the chief administrators of the group.[8] When she directed the original production of Eugene O'Neill's *The Dreamy Kid* she took the unprecedented step of going to Harlem to recruit a black cast[9] instead of following the custom of the time by putting white actors in blackface.

A slightly later addition to the Provincetown was Nina Moise, who worked with the group in 1917 and 1918. According to Robert Sarlós, "Moise could not singlehandedly turn the performances professional even had she wished, yet her expert control made an impression on the Players, and they were never the same thereafter."[10] M. Eleanor Fitzgerald came on board in October of 1918 and served as the group's secretary-treasurer for several years, although keeping the books seems an unlikely job for an anarchist friend of Emma Goldman. In a more traditional role Christine Ell ran the Greenwich Village restaurant that served as the group's main gathering and eating spot.[11]

More than a third of the plays performed by the Provincetown were written or coauthored by women, an astonishingly high percentage considering the scarcity of works by women on the commercial stage, then and now. The most important female dramatist in the group was unquestionably Susan Glaspell, who saw eleven of her plays on the Provincetown boards. (Only Eugene O'Neill's fifteen productions surpassed this number.) Still, Glaspell had plenty of female company: Neith Boyce and Rita Wellman had four plays each performed; Djuna Barnes and Edna St. Vincent Millay contributed three apiece; and works by Edna Ferber, Alice Rostetter, Evelyn Scott, Mary Caroline Davies, Florence Kiper Frank,

Louise Bryant, Grace Potter, Mary Foster Barber, Bosworth Crocker, Rita Creighton Smith, and Alice Woods filled out the bills.

Some of the performed works were written by women not actively involved with the Provincetown or, like O'Neill's early plays, were written before the authors joined the theater group. Novelist Edna Ferber, whose greatest theatrical successes would be her collaborations with George S. Kaufman, apparently adapted *The Eldest* from her own short story after she heard that the Provincetown was planning to perform an unauthorized stage adaptation of it.[12] Two of the three Edna St. Vincent Millay plays performed by the group—*Two Slatterns and a King* and *The Princess Marries the Page*—were written while Millay was at Vassar and, indeed, read like the work of a particularly clever college student. Rita Creighton Smith's Freudian melodrama *The Rescue,* which anticipates both O'Neill's *Strange Interlude* and his *Mourning Becomes Electra,* was developed for the famous Harvard '47 play writing workshop.[13] Conversely, some plays written by women members of the Provincetown during this period were not, for various reasons, performed on their stage. Presumably, writers were aware that certain kinds of dramas were not likely to find favor with the Provincetowners. When Millay wrote the medieval melodrama *The Lamp and the Bell* for a Vassar anniversary, she admonished her sister Norma: "Don't let any of the *Provincetown Players* get hold of it to read. I mean this most seriously. They would hate it, & make fun of it, & old Djuna Barnes would rag you about it, hoping it would get to me."[14]

The Provincetowners were an often contentious lot, and Millay's comment suggests that there were animosities among the women as well as the men. (Edmund Wilson believed that Barnes was jealous of Millay's success,[15] much as George Cram Cook would grow envious of O'Neill's theatrical triumphs.) Regardless of personal friendships and enmities, it is probably erroneous to suggest that the women—actresses, playwrights, directors, staff—had a clear sense of themselves as a group separate from the men. More likely, as Anne Corey argues, they viewed themselves and the male members of the group as radicals whose feminism was part and parcel of their rejection of bourgeois codes.[16] Through an examination of the plays by women performed at the Provincetown, however, we can begin to get a picture of the interests and perspectives of a collection of talented female writers early in this century. While few of their short dramas would fit anyone's definition of "great art"—an accolade rarely accorded the one-act play, in any case—many are important literary, cultural, and social documents that reflect sincere attempts to fuse theatrical originality with social concerns. Moreover, the group did spawn one major woman playwright whose importance is only now being fully recognized: Susan Glaspell. By looking closely at the work of her female colleagues, we can gain both a deeper understanding of the context of Glaspell's work and a sense of the cross-fertilization that undoubtedly took place among people committed to the idea of theater as a communal enterprise.

Gerhard Bach rightly observes that "Glaspell's preference for female characters is established at the very beginning of her playwriting career."[17] Not surprisingly, most of the plays by her sister writers of the Provincetown also place women at the center of the action. The women of the Provincetown were particularly concerned with the problems inherent in male-female relationships, both inside and outside of marriage, and this became the subject of numerous tragic and comic plays. Their male colleagues, of course, were turning their attention to similar issues in works such as Alfred Kreymborg's satirical *Lima Beans* and O'Neill's Strindbergian *Before Breakfast*. But while Kreymborg found a comic resolution to marital problems in the wife's capitulation to her husband's taste in vegetables and O'Neill depicted a man driven to suicide by the harridan he was forced to marry, the women offered a particularly female (if not always feminist) perspective on the state to which every woman supposedly aspired.

Neith Boyce's *Winter's Night*[18] shared the opening bill of the 1916 Provincetown summer season with John Reed's *Freedom* and a revival of Glaspell and her husband George Cram Cook's *Suppressed Desires*. Powerful in its own right, *Winter's Night* may also have been one inspiration for Glaspell's most famous play, *Trifles*, the story of a farm woman who apparently strangles the taciturn husband who has denied her any joy in life. Glaspell claimed that she wrote *Trifles* in ten days after Cook announced a play of hers for the third bill of 1916, and she drew the plot from an experience she had had as a newspaper woman years before.[19]

Still, Glaspell was surely familiar with *Winter's Night,* which likely had already been performed when she conceived *Trifles* and which, according to Floyd Dell, was itself based on a family story related by Cook.[20]

Born in 1872, Neith Boyce was slightly older than most of the other Provincetowners, already in her early forties when the theater was founded. Like Glaspell, she was a midwesterner and, also like Glaspell, she worked as a reporter early in her career. An acquaintance of such feminist activists as Henrietta Rodman, Crystal Eastman, and Emma Goldman,[21] Boyce was an established fiction writer when she began offering plays to the Provincetown, and she continued writing fiction during her association with the group. According to historian June Sochen, Boyce and her husband, Hutchins Hapgood, summered in Provincetown but spent the rest of the year in the New York suburb of Dobbs Ferry, where she raised their four children and wrote.[22] While she created four plays for the Provincetown and worked on another dozen that were never produced—as late as 1938 she completed a patriotic radio drama[23]—Boyce was primarily known as a writer of short stories and novels.

Winter's Night is set in a farmhouse at the coldest time of the year, a location and season Glaspell also used in *Trifles.* Rachel Westcott and her brother-in-law Jacob have just returned from the funeral of Daniel, Rachel's husband and Jacob's brother. Rachel shares with Glaspell's Minnie Foster the situation of being a childless middle-aged woman, and she too has found expression for her feelings in her needlework. But where Minnie's quilting is apparently restrained within conventional patterns such as the log cabin quilt on which she is working—the true aesthetic pleasure in her life came from her singing and the songbird her husband killed—Rachel is in love with bright colors and fabric and style. She has decorated the farmhouse with her handiwork, and she dreams of going to the city to start her own shop. Rachel has been a good wife in society's terms—"I always did my duty by my husband" (81)—and she vows to wear the prescribed mourning black for a year. Despite the long illness that turned him bitter, Daniel Westcott was not quite the kind of dour, stifling husband to whom Minnie Foster was married. Still, it is clear that Rachel found the marriage unfulfilling and that Daniel's death has relieved rather than devastated her: "I'm free now. . . . I can have what I've always wanted—more life, something going on, and a business of my own" (83). What Linda Ben-Zvi writes of Glaspell's characters applies equally to Rachel: she breaks "the stereotype of women desiring stability and the comfort of place."[24] Rachel has had more than enough of this home and wants change and movement. The fight between the life and death instincts that C. W. E. Bigsby sees as a central theme in Glaspell's work is clearly at the heart of Boyce's play as well.[25]

As in O'Neill's *Beyond the Horizon*—another drama that may have been influenced by *Winter's Night*[26]—part of the tension in this play arises from the fact that both brothers were in love with the same woman. Jacob has bided his time and now assumes that it is his chance to wed Rachel (a belief that has precedent in the several ancient, and modern, societies in which it is customary for widows to be "given" to their husband's brother). In Jacob's eyes the only life for a woman is love; because Rachel "never rightly loved Daniel" (83), she has been cheated of her life. Rachel is appalled by Jacob's unexpected declaration of passion as well as his complete failure to understand both her past life and her present desire for independence and a career. Jacob shares with the male characters in *Trifles* an inability to comprehend a female perspective that envisions a world beyond the domestic one. He tries to prevent Rachel from leaving by physically blocking her way and attempting emotional blackmail, claiming she owes him a debt of gratitude.

Winter's Night, again like *Trifles,* is a naturalistic play with symbolic overtones. One layer of irony is provided by the biblical allusions in the names: the biblical Jacob was the husband of Rachel, and Boyce's Jacob wants to claim his namesake's privilege. Moreover, Daniel was imprisoned in the lion's den, but Boyce inverts both the biblical story and conventional lore about which sex is "trapped" in marrriage; in a line added during revision of the play Rachel sums up her situation: "I'm in prison here. I have been for years!" (84). Boyce's equivalent of Glaspell's caged bird in *Trifles* are the potted plants Rachel grows—begonias she tries to protect from the withering cold, as she herself tries to survive in the aesthetic and emotional deprivation of the farm. Jacob does not deliberately destroy the plants the way John Wright strangled the bird, but he does inadvertently knock one over and break it, just as he would, with the best of intentions, prevent Rachel's "flowering." Indeed, one crucial difference between *Trifles* and *Winter's Night* lies in the balance between the protagonists and the antagonists: Daniel seems to have been somewhat kinder and more tolerant than John Wright—one cannot imagine Wright allowing his wife to paint the woodwork white and put red and blue rugs on the floor—and, so too, Jacob is a well-meaning if potentially dangerous man who serves Rachel tea and begs her to take him with her wherever she might go. Appropriately, neither of these two men is murdered by his wife, as John Wright apparently is; Daniel dies of natural causes, and Jacob kills himself when Rachel rejects him. In an ironic twist on cultural gender expectations Boyce presents us with a *man* driven to suicide by his failure in love.

Rachel is less a victim of the two men than of the assumption that marriage is the ideal situation for all women. In this way Boyce's play is more radical than many of the feminist novels from the period that June Sochen cites, novels in which "the personal, emotional satisfaction of true love was the object of the feminist quest."[27] More assertive and articulate than Minnie Wright (who, of course, never actually appears in *Trifles*), Rachel orders Jacob: "Move out of my way" (84). When he insists that she stay because she is obligated to him for his years of devotion, she cruelly calls him "crazy" and predicts that he'll end in the asylum. Boyce evokes audience sympathy for the desperate Jacob at the same time she makes clear that Rachel needs and wants to live her own life, to create her own story, outside the rural domestic sphere.

Moreover, Rachel never receives the same kind of female sympathy that Minnie—whether she knows it or not—gains in *Trifles*. While Glaspell gives us Mrs. Peters and Mrs. Hale, who unravel Minnie's story and come to see the similarities in their own lives, Boyce provides only a brief glimpse of Rachel's neighbor Sarah. According to three scripts in Yale's Beinecke Library, Sarah had a few more lines in the original Provincetown version of the play than in the later published edition and expresses more sympathy for the "trials" Rachel has borne. Still, her condolences are clichéd and formulaic. Sarah's hope that Rachel will "have a good rest, and a little peace and quiet" is deeply ironic: her words are punctuated by the sound of Jacob's suicide shot (85). "Peace and quiet" are what Rachel seems to have had most of her life, and what Daniel and Jacob will find in the grave; she craves the color and bustle of the city. In the melodramatic conclusion to the drama, it is Sarah who collapses in the conventional womanly faint, grabbing Rachel *"round the knees"* as she falls. Rachel *"pulls away from her, clapping her hands to her ears"* (85); she does not want to be dragged down by Sarah or the world she represents.

Whereas *Trifles* and *Winter's Night* are tragedies about rural marriage, Alice Rostetter's *The Widow's Veil* is a satirical look at its urban counterpart. Rostetter wrote only one play for the Provincetown, and, judging by the histories of the group, her participation was limited to that comedy, in which she appeared in the role of Mrs. Phelan. *Veil* was a popular success: it premiered in January 1919, was chosen for the Review Bill in April (regular Review Bills featured the best plays of the season), and, along with two other short works, was subsequently presented for a six-day run at the Recital Hall in Newark.[28] George Cram Cook and Frank Shay included it in the collection of Provincetown plays they published in 1921.[29]

Veil's location is: "The meeting place of tender-hearted women. The floor's the fifth" (182). The actual set of the play is "a dumb-waiter shaft" that opens onto the kitchens of young Katy MacManus and her apparently widowed neighbor, Mrs. Phelan. This ingenious setting—exactly how the Provincetown executed it is not clear[30]—allows us to hear noises from apartments throughout the building; in fact, the program lists "Lewis B. Ell and Others" as the providers of "Voices and Other Sounds" (182). The dumbwaiter serves as a kind of architectural alimentary canal: milk and bread are hoisted to the apartments; garbage is sent down. Drab brick walls reinforce the notion of women on the periphery: these two neighbors are free to hold their conversation only in the relatively safe space that is neither in the public arena nor in their private living units, for Mrs. MacManus dreads being overheard in her own apartment.[31] Even in this marginal territory, however, the power resides with the male janitor, who summons the residents with shrill whistles but ignores their demands for heat.

By keeping the men offstage, Rostetter invites us to see the world from the women's perspective. Mrs. MacManus is a ten-day bride who fears that her husband is dying. The most obvious humor arises from Mrs. Phelan's inept attempts to comfort the young woman, for her cheerful conversation is dominated by references to death rattles, corpses, graves, wakes, departing souls, and black-bordered handkerchiefs. Mrs. Mac-

Manus seems genuinely distraught at the thought of losing her husband, a lusty young man who selflessly encouraged her to remarry if he didn't survive his illness, until she tries on a widow's veil lent her by Mrs. Phelan and is assured: "Ye were born for the style! Ye should never wear anything else" (197). Mrs. MacManus checks in a mirror to confirm the attractiveness of the veil. By the next morning her husband has recovered and is bellowing loudly for newspapers, water, and meat. Mrs. Mac-Manus returns the veil and her own hat to Mrs. Phelan and admonishes her to give them back to her mourning cousin: "The hat's hers and I'm thankin' her for the loan and sorry I can't be usin' it" (204).

How sincerely Mrs. MacManus regrets her husband's recovery is part of the joke of the play, and surely one strand of the humor is to mock her vanity: her looks matter more to her than her husband. Mrs. Phelan, too, is a stock comic character—the well-meaning friend who can't seem to keep away from a sore subject, the nosy neighbor who thrives on gossip and others' misfortune (she repeatedly sends her son to check for black crepe on the neighbor's door). *Veil* is also, however, a mordantly anti-romantic view of love among the masses. Mrs. Phelan's last comment on Mr. MacManus's recovery is an exclamation of pity for his "poor, pretty young" wife (205), an odd expression of sympathy that suggests a great deal about the older woman's own marriage. When Mr. MacManus is ill, his wife remembers his amorousness and kindness; as soon as he's well, she resents his imperious demands.

The almost surrealistic background "music" of *Widow's Veil*, in addition to the movement of the dumbwaiter, consists of fragmentary conversations from various apartments and the howls of a baby on the sixth floor—suffering, according to his mother, from "his father's bad temper."[32] Another "choral" accompaniment to the action is provided by a single woman in an upstairs apartment who insists that old maids are "the lucky ones . . . believe me!" (185). Mrs. McManus does not kill her husband, as Minnie Foster in *Trifles* apparently did, nor does she view with relief his actual death, as Rachel does in *Winter's Night*. Still, the appeal of widowhood in this dark comedy suggests that even for a ten-day bride the honeymoon is over.

At first glance Mary Caroline Davies's *The Slave with Two Faces* seems to have little to do, stylistically or thematically, with either *Win-*

ter's Night or *Widow's Veil*. This was Davies's only play for the Provincetown—she was primarily a poet, the author of seven volumes of verse[33]—and she was evidently not an active participant with the group. Robert Sarlós calls *Slave* a "comparatively successful poetic allegory" and reports that "Alfred Kreymborg composed and played a musical accompaniment" to the work. The setting was "a series of stylized cut-outs representing a grove of birches and bushes."[34] On the surface *Slave* is precisely the kind of allegory to appeal to a group whose god was Dionysus and whose savior was Nietzsche.

As two young girls wait for Life, the First Girl explains to her friend that Life will give you everything you want as long as you show no fear: "What you see you must take."[35] The slightest cowardice, she warns, will turn Life into a brutal master who will destroy you. Eventually, Life approaches the Second Girl and tries to entice her with flattery. She muses: "I think he wants me to be afraid, so I will say it. I have heard that men are like that. I am not afraid, but I will say it to please him." Life then exclaims that "there is nothing so beautiful as a woman's hair flying in the wind"—a successful attempt to get the Second Girl to remove her royal crown. Promising to be a "kind master," Life instead proceeds to whip and kill her (334).

As an allegory about life—"Be strong, or you will be destroyed"—the play is scarcely subtle. It dramatizes the contest between the forces of life and those of death, a competition presented even more explicitly in Louise Bryant's *The Game* (in which Life and Death play dice for human souls) and with more subtlety and complexity in Glaspell's *The Verge* and *The Outside*. As an allegory about gender relations, however, it is far more powerful. Although Life destroys characters of both sexes, the focus in *Slave* is on the destruction of a woman. Obviously, the Second Girl is not using the term *men* generically when she pretends to be fearful because that's what "men" like, and Life's compliments, followed by demands that she "obey" him, are a clichéd courtship ritual followed by a deadly marriage. *Slave* can be seen as a parable about the dangers of a woman being seduced into playing the traditional subservient role: once she feigns weakness and gives a man the title of master, he takes advantage of his position and destroys her. The First Girl—a kind of "New

Woman"—survives precisely because she retains her power (symbolized by her crown) and her autonomy.

While the gender implications of *Slave* are clearly present, we can only speculate to what extent they were acknowledged by most of the Province-towners. One odd fact is that, when the work premiered, the role of Life was played by Ida Rauh rather than by a male. Was the casting of Rauh as Life an attempt to mute the gender implications of this bitter allegory about relations between the sexes? Or did Rauh, a committed feminist, relish playing the male role and slyly revealing the gender dimension? (Although Rauh was one of the group's best actresses, the role of Life is not particularly demanding and presumably could have been played by any number of men in the company.) Whatever the case, in their book on the Provincetown, Helen Deutsch and Stella Hanau report that Rauh "rolled out the lines with an appalling zest."[36]

Perhaps the most original spin on courtship and marriage was offered by Djuna Barnes, who contributed three plays to the 1919–20 Province-town season: *Three from the Earth, An Irish Triangle,* and *Kurzy of the Sea.* Like several other Provincetown women, Barnes had begun her writing career as a journalist, and she had already published *The Book of Repulsive Women,* a brief collection of poems and drawings, when she joined the group.[37] Barnes was an active presence at the theater during this period and, according to *New York Times* critic Alexander Woollcott, was frequently seen at performances.[38] A modern novelist, poet, playwright, and painter whose books would later gain her not only fame but notoriety, Barnes wrote a number of short plays during the 1910s and 1920s and a longer drama, *Antiphon,* three decades later; she also spent several years writing for *Theatre Guild Magazine.* Her works for the Provincetown are among the group's most daring in both style and subject matter but still tame when compared to much else in her canon. Near the end of her short play *The Dove,* for example, a young girl slowly bares her older friend Amelia's *"left shoulder and breast, and leaning down, sets her teeth in."*[39] However brave these women writers were about challenging conventional values and exposing the shaky relationships between men and women, lesbian sexuality—violent or loving—was a subject they either chose not to explore or were not welcome to explore on the Provincetown stage.

Barnes's first and most enigmatic play for the Provincetown was *Three from the Earth*. According to Woollcott's review: "[Earth] is enormously interesting, and the greatest indoor sport this week is guessing what it means. We hasten to enroll in the large group that has not the faintest idea—a group which includes such pundits as Burns Mantle, Clayton Hamilton, and, we suspect, the cryptic author herself." He concedes, however, that the play is both "absorbing and essentially dramatic."[40] In fact, the very set itself foreshadows the work's elusiveness, for the curtain rises on a boudoir *"with a great many lacquer screens in various shades of blue, a tastefully decorated room though rather extreme."*[41] This arrangement is both a parody of a realistic stage set (as the plot will parody a polite social visit) and a visual cue that many things are, and will remain, hidden from view. *Earth* concerns Kate Morley, a "handsome" woman around forty years old, *"an adventurist—a lady of leisure"* (62). Kate is an enigmatic figure, who boasts of having "no virtues," and is so concerned with aesthetics that, when told her lover has cut his throat, asks, "How did he look?" (66).

In a witty twist on the usual question of paternity, the "three from the earth"—a trio of rather cloddish peasant men—all know who their father is but are not entirely certain who their mother (or mothers) might be. When Kate talks about "their" mother as a dancer, prostitute, and artist, she may be discussing either herself or her similarities to another woman. When they leave, the youngest man kisses her on the lips—a suggestively incestuous kiss, since he, at least, is apparently her son. For Kate, to be a woman is to play roles: she has had, she says, experience in "an amateur theatrical." Lover, mother, prospective wife (she claims she is about to be married to a Supreme Court judge), artist, actress, and perhaps dancer and prostitute as well, Kate is all things to all men. What is significant, however, is that *she* chooses which roles she wishes to play. As Ann Larabee observes, Barnes's "characters resist violation and control by others."[42] Larabee also notes that, "unlike other Provincetown playwrights, Barnes does not make her odd characters tragic."[43] Kate avoids the grim fate of Emma Crosby in O'Neill's *Diff'rent*, for example, or Claire Archer in Glaspell's *The Verge*, two women whose "difference" leads to madness and to death for themselves and/or someone they love.[44]

One of Kate's observations is that "every woman" has "posed for the madonna" (65). The idea that men create impossible roles for women, then challenge them to fulfill those roles, underlies *Kurzy of the Sea*.[45] Barnes sets *Kurzy* in Ireland at least in part to poke fun at the Irish Catholic tendency to idealize women as virginal mothers. Twenty-three-year-old Rory McRace[46] masks his fear and dislike of the female sex by making ridiculous demands for a prospective wife: she must be "a Queen or a Saint or a Venus, or whatever it is comes in with the tide" (3). Rory is a very picky young man, despite the fact that even his mother concedes he's "a drab thing and a slow" (5). Rory's father, as dim as his son, actually goes fishing for an aquatic daughter-in-law and catches Kurzy in his net. Using a test more common for witches than wives, Rory throws her back in the sea to ascertain whether she's a genuine "saint," where-upon she reveals herself as a barmaid at the White Duck, his father's favorite tavern, and swims away from the chagrined young man.

Kurzy is, as Larabee argues, "a trickster," who is both articulate and powerful.[47] Like the Second Girl in *The Slave with Two Faces*, Kurzy pretends to be mute and weak when in the men's presence, and she gets thrown into the sea for her pains. But the real Kurzy is a survivor, who tauntingly suggests that Rory learn how to swim. "But it will do you little good," she adds, "For by the time you can hold your own, I shall be half way to Cork with a lover on my arm" (12). Rory apparently repents throwing Kurzy away—he tells his mother that he needs a boat—but there's little chance that he can catch her. His last act in the play is to toss down a shot of whiskey.

Kurzy will not be caught for long in the "net" of the men's fantasies, however much she may fuel them with the alcohol she serves. While the men are metaphorically drowning in drink, she is learning to swim, liter-ally and otherwise. Like Susan Glaspell, Barnes is fascinated, amused, and appalled by the romanticized images men impose on women then ask women to live up to. In Glaspell's *Woman's Honor*, for example, "the Scornful One" points out that *woman's honor* is a meaningless term devised by men for their own benefit and glorification, and in *Chains of Dew* Seymore Standish's success as a poet depends on his belief that his wife Dotty is a meek, maternal creature. Dotty's last act in *Chains of Dew* is to allow her husband to return the picture of the "Sistine Madonna" to its accustomed place on the wall, in deference to his cherished image of her. Kurzy, however, turns the tables on the men and their "glorification" of women by showing that Rory and his father can't tell a mermaid from a barmaid. Interestingly, in her final taunt Kurzy speaks of escaping with a "lover"—not a husband—on her arm. The last Rory sees of her as she swims away is his mother's red shawl, a gift that Kurzy apparently holds aloft. She has inherited the maternal mantle but uses it as a banner of freedom rather than a cloak of protection.

Fidelity is the subject of Barnes's third work for the Provincetown, *An Irish Triangle,* dramatically the least interesting of her contributions and more a brief conversation (in sometimes strained dialect) than a fully developed comedy. Barnes was a great admirer of John Millington Synge,[48] and *An Irish Triangle* is a play that, had it been performed in Ireland, would likely have infuriated the Irish even more than Synge's *Playboy of the Western World.* Sexual and emotional loyalty is a major issue in several Provincetown plays by women—not surprisingly, given the group members' concern with evaluating old standards of morality and perhaps forging new ones. Fidelity was, of course, a feminist issue, particularly in the case of the double standard. But whereas many feminists and other women writers of the day sought to erase the double standard by imposing on men the same strict codes of behavior to which women were held[49]—one thinks, for example, of Rachel Crothers's 1909 drama *A Man's World*—the women of the Provincetown came up with a surprising range of views on the subject.

So brief as to be little more than a skit, *An Irish Triangle* is a discussion between young Kathleen O'Rune and her "middle aged" single friend Shiela O'Hare.[50] Kathleen is pleased that her husband John has "gone up on the hill and found her ladyship beautiful"—in other words, that John is having an affair with the mistress of the manor. He closely observes the lady's fashions and manners and reports back to Kathleen, who learns to act and dress like the gentry so she can better her station in life. Kathleen is certain that the other husbands in the area are unfaithful as well, but all their wives have to show for the men's philandering is "a long hair with a bit of a curl to the end that does be matching nothing in the house at all" (4). At first Kathleen's explanation seems like an ingenious defense of male adultery, but in an O'Henryish twist she tells her shocked friend that the "triangle" is about to shift, for, she says, "I've nothing more to learn, but John is rare ignorant." Kathleen is preparing to go up the hill for "close contact" with the master of the manor, "who is soft of tongue and charming, and John says there's a way he's dying to know, the master has of wrapping his puttees" (5).

A direct attack on the virtue of fidelity and a celebration of adultery, *Triangle* is an amusing look at the double standard of marital infidelity and class consciousness. Kathleen claims for herself the same sexual freedom that John, and apparently all other husbands, enjoys. And rather than feeling ashamed about her plans, she defines herself as "a good woman . . . but no fool." While the lord and lady imagine that they are exercising their class privilege by commanding the sexual services of the peasants, the peasants are, in fact, using the gentry for their own advantage. Marriage is an economic stepping stone, and one's spouse is a valuable ally in the class war. There is at least a hint of homosexuality in the play—Kathleen declares, "Where my man can go in body [to the lady] there I go in spirit" (4), while John is so observant of the master that he notices how he wraps his puttees—yet hints of *this* kind of infidelity are kept carefully submerged.

June Sochen asserts that the Provincetowners depict "the problem of woman in the *modern* world,"[51] and, as we shall see, the so-called New Woman does figure in several plays submitted by female dramatists to the company. But the predominant image of the New Woman was, according to Elizabeth Ammons, a "middle-class white ideal,"[52] and many of the protagonists in works by Provincetown women are excluded by class, if not by race, from this popular conception. A significant number of the plays—including Mary Foster Barber's *The Squealer,* Bosworth Crocker's *The Baby Carriage,* Rostetter's *The Widow's Veil,* Glaspell's *Trifles,* Boyce's *Winter's Night,* and Barnes's *An Irish Triangle* and *Kurzy of the Sea*—center around peasants, working-class, or lower-middle-class women who seem in many ways untouched by the contemporary world. The lives of these characters, in farmhouses or huts or tenements, are scarcely different from those that women of previous generations would have led and are generally very distant from the lives enjoyed by their sophisticated, educated creators. Rather, the writers' *approach* to these characters suggests a modern perspective on age-old situations.

Robert Sarlós credits the success of O'Neill's *The Moon of the Carib-*

bees in 1918 with spawning what he calls a wave of "ethnic vignettes, redolent of mood but often short on overt action or apparent structure."[53] The line of influence seems more complicated, however: *Trifles* and *Winter's Night* preceded *Caribbees,* and lack of physical action is characteristic of both the one-act form and much drama by women. Perhaps some of these women writers were, like O'Neill himself, heeding the modernist call to explore the lives of those whom traditionally elitist drama had ignored, as Ibsen had done with his focus on the bourgeoisie, Synge in his peasant plays. Perhaps, too, the women writers of Provincetown recognized that the "problems" identified by feminists were in fact not particularly modern but were, rather, problems faced by women at all times and in all places. Rachel may be an unsophisticated farm woman, but that does not preclude her determination to seek a career. It is also possible that at least some of the Provincetown women felt more comfortable criticizing marriage at a distance—in plays with protagonists clearly separated in time, place, and/or class (although never, apparently, race) from their creators. Neith Boyce is an interesting case in point, for her *Winter's Night* was preceded by two explorations of heterosexual relationships in general and fidelity in particular that lack the trenchancy of her rural tragedy, with its uncompromising look at marriage's disadvantages for women. Moreover, in the first of her earlier works, *Constancy,* Boyce attempted to soften her initially harsh portrayal of relations between the sexes by resetting the action in an exotic locale and period.

Writing about the beginnings of the Provincetown troupe, Robert Sarlós observes that "the plays were first thought of as a profoundly therapeutic party-game for a small, close-knit group."[54] Along with Susan Glaspell and George Cram Cook's *Suppressed Desires,* Neith Boyce's *Constancy* was part of the first bill presented by what would become the Provincetown Players. Originally staged in the home of Boyce and her husband for a group of friends in July of 1915, the two works were revived for a larger audience later that summer.[55] Like *Suppressed Desires*—a spoof on the Freudian fad that was rampant among the bohemian intelligentsia—*Constancy* started out as an in-joke, a play about the stormy relationship between radical Jack Reed (a member of the group) and Mabel Dodge, a well-known Provincetown resident.[56] Further, Ellen Kay Trimberger argues persuasively that there is a strong autobiographical element in *Constancy:* "The play's focus on the issue of fidelity and infidelity," she notes, "was also a central conflict in Neith's marriage."[57] Boyce took the female role in her work, while Glaspell and Cook performed theirs.

Constancy, in its first incarnation, is a dialogue between Rex and Moira, quite obviously Reed and Mabel.[58] Rex cannot understand why his former lover Mabel is so cool to him, despite the fact that he abandoned her then wrote to say that he "never had loved" her and was "in love with another woman, younger, more beautiful" (276). Rex has returned to Moira primarily because his new beloved wants to consign him to a bourgeois hell: she expects him "to live with her in a little suburban house, and come back every night to dinner, and have a yard with vegetables, and a sleeping porch facing the east" (277). Refusing to take Rex back, Moira explains that their love affair made her unhappy: "Don't you remember how I absorbed myself in you, gave up all my other interests, gave up my friends, could see nothing and nobody but you. . . ?" (279). While she concedes that Rex didn't necessarily demand this kind of devotion, she sees an inherent conflict between love and her desire to be independent. Men see no such conflict, however, for Rex's conception of "fidelity" involves plenty of freedom. In what may be a classic male definition of loyalty, Rex argues: "I was always faithful to you, really. I always shall be. I should always come back." Ultimately, the two realize that Rex is "a perfect man" and Moira "a complete woman," hence there is no possibility of reconciliation: "We have annihilated one another" (278–80).

On one level the play offers the traditional split between men's and women's definitions of "constancy": for Rex it is enduring if erratic affection, for Moira it is emotional *and* physical fidelity. Unlike Barnes's Kathleen, Boyce's Moira will not join her partner in sexual adventuring, and once Rex has found another woman, however temporarily, the bonds of love are broken for her.[59] Rather than suggesting that one adopt the other's definition—monogamy or freedom—Boyce postulates that the two genders' views are irreconcilable. On another level *Constancy* also raises the question of how love as women experience it can ever coexist with freedom, since Moira claims that her unhappiness in the relationship preceded Rex's defection. For women love is so all-consuming, demands such sacrifice of self, that it becomes, by definition, destructive.[60] Glaspell explored this latter issue more fully in a number of plays, perhaps in part inspired by *Constancy*. Not surprisingly, *The Verge's* Claire Archer, who seems to embody all of modern women's dilemmas, is the most troubled of all by the dangerous seductiveness of affection. She ultimately murders the man she loves because she fears that her attraction to him will distract her from her horticultural experiments.

Static, talky, and didactic, *Constancy* was not Boyce's best play, but her revisions on it unfortunately diminished the little charm it had.[61] As she revised it into the later version entitled *The Faithful Lover*, she changed the undefined setting to Moorish Venice, the characters' names to Marco and Silvia, and burdened the brief sketch with a Duenna, four Moorish boys, and a Fool with an annoying habit of echoing the main characters' lines. The subtitle was progressively altered from "A Play in One Act" to "A Dialogue" to "A Comedy" to "A Fantasy," as she wrestled with both substance and form, and Rex's biting satire on bourgeois marriage disappeared. Perhaps Boyce was influenced by the poetic fantasies of such colleagues as Edna St. Vincent Millay and Mary Caroline Davies (it's unclear precisely when the last revisions on *Constancy*/*The Faithful Lover* were made), or perhaps she added the fanciful trappings to try to disguise the play's biographical origins: it was one thing to stage a drama about their friends for an intimate audience, something else to present it to the community at large. There is also the possibility that the gender war over fidelity and freedom was so volatile a subject that Boyce felt compelled to distance and dilute her argument by recasting the characters and locale.

Faithfulness is again the subject of Boyce's next play, *Enemies*, but this one was coauthored with her husband. According to Jig Cook, "The authors had written the two-character piece to 'get it off their chests,' "[62] suggesting that work on the play was a kind of therapy. Boyce composed the lines for the character called She while Hapgood created those for He. The couple acted the roles in the initial production, although Hapgood kept forgetting the lines he'd written himself and had to refer to the script. When it was revived later in New York, Justus Sheffield and Ida Rauh took the parts.[63]

Enemies, like *Constancy*, is a debate between the sexes. The issue this time is She's supposed "spiritual infidelity,"[64] her apparently nonsexual relationship with another man. Trimberger relates that Boyce herself had "a serious relationship (although probably not a physical affair)" with an old friend of Hapgood's in 1908–9, and this may well have been one source for the play; Hapgood was apparently very jealous of Boyce's platonic attachment to the other man, despite his own numerous sexual affairs and his professed belief that his wife was as entitled to her freedom as he was to his.[65] This notion of the "soul's infidelities" (128) or of being "spiritually inconstant" was apparently a popular one with the Province-towners, for the latter phrase appears in Mary Vorse's account of the John Reed–Mable Dodge relationship that inspired *Constancy*. Reed, Vorse states, was "casually inconstant in a physical way . . . while Mabel was spiritually inconstant."[66] The same contrast appears in *Enemies*, in which, although He claims he's never been "essentially" unfaithful, he acknowledges "physical intimacies" with other women (127–28). Once again the tension between a woman's desire for love and her fear of losing autonomy arises, for the She of the couple accuses her husband: "You have wanted to treat our relation, and me, as clay, and model it into the form you saw in your imagination" (135). Unwilling to be Galatea to her husband's Pygmalion, She rebels. In sum, She concludes, "men and women are natural enemies, like cat and dog—only more so. They are forced to live together for a time, or this wonderful race couldn't go on" (130). The couple finally reconcile on the grounds that men and women together, however flawed the relationship, is still the best alternative, and at least the two haven't bored each other. The play ends with an embrace and a punning declaration of "an armed truce" (136). This pragmatic conclusion was apparently popular with audiences: *Enemies* was revived at least once,[67] and Hapgood states that it "was one of the first plays to be broadcast on the radio." It is, however, scarcely the "tragic classic in the manner of the Greek drama" that Hapgood claims critic William Bullitt once called it.[68]

Despite being a jointly authored play, or rather a work in which each character's lines were written by a different author, *Enemies* retains a good deal of stylistic consistency throughout, even as it, like *Constancy*, lacks either the theatrical structure or the Shavian wit necessary to bring the debate to life. Nor does it have the dramatic (albeit at times melodramatic) force and uncompromising vision of *Winter's Night*. Interestingly, when she wrote a solo play about fidelity Boyce did not envision a reconciliation between the two sexes, but the jointly composed work offered a truce if not a resolution. The more conciliatory stance of the second play was apparently less threatening to Boyce or her colleagues (or both), for *Enemies* was never recast into a fantasy. In *A Victorian in the Modern World* Hapgood offers this assessment of *Enemies:*

> This play had a significance leading into the lives of many of my acquaintances and still further into a general situation between men and women. Neith and I, like many another couple who on the whole were good fathers and mothers, were conscious of the latent feminism urging men to give up the ascendancy which women thought they had, and women to demand from men that which they didn't really want, namely so-called freedom from the ideal of monogamy.[69]

Hapgood's characterization of feminism here is more than a little disingenuous. Boyce does, in both *Constancy* and *Enemies,* suggest that women still cherish "the ideal of monogamy," but this view is challenged in other plays by Provincetown women, including Rita Wellman's *The Rib-Person,* Susan Glaspell's *The Verge,* and all three works contributed by Djuna Barnes. The debate about monogamy and the double standard that raged within the feminist community was echoed in the Provincetown plays, and the female dramatists' views were by no means as uniformly conservative as Hapgood suggests. Moreover, Hapgood pointedly says nothing about *men's* attitude toward monogamy since he—like Rex in *Constancy* and the autobiographical He in *Enemies*—retains the traditional attitude that sexual freedom is a male prerogative, regardless of what women want.

Even more telling, Hapgood's claim that women only "thought" men had "ascendancy" over women reveals his failure to acknowledge the legal, financial, and societal power men held; it appears that to him feminism was a sham.[70] Yet Hapgood, like such fellow Provincetowners as Harry Kemp, Max Eastman, and Floyd Dell, apparently saw themselves as feminists. In 1913 Dell published a book entitled *Women as World Builders: Studies in Modern Feminism,* in which he discusses, among others, Charlotte Perkins Gilman, Emmeline Pankhurst, Jane Addams, and Emma Goldman. Sounding a good deal like Hapgood, Dell in the introduction to his book denies that men have power over women. Dell employs a clever bit of sophistry to argue that men feign hostility to the women's movement because they want women to learn how to act on their own. Men support feminism because they

> are tired of subservient women; or, to speak more exactly, of the seemingly subservient woman who effects her will by stealth—the pretty slave with all the slave's subtlety and cleverness. So long as it was possible for men to imagine themselves masters, they were satisfied. But when they found out that they were dupes, they wanted a change.[71]

According to Dell's skewed reasoning, the real power has always been held by woman, just as the plantations were actually run by the enslaved. The women's movement, he concludes, is *men's* attempt to gain back their rightful power: men "are responsible for the movement . . . whose demands it must ultimately fulfill."[72] Granted that feminism shortly after the turn of the century was quite a different species than it would be fifty or sixty years later, the comments by Hapgood and Dell suggest just how chilling an environment even the supposedly liberal and bohemian Provincetown Players could be for women who seriously challenged paternal attitudes and patriarchal traditions.[73] It is not surprising that Boyce's most potent dramatic critique of the power men have over women, *Winter's Night,* is also her most coded work, set at a comfortable distance from both the bohemian world of Greenwich Village and Provincetown and the suburban home that she shared with Hapgood.

Still another of the patriarchal traditions examined by the Provincetown's women writers is the notion that motherhood is the most important role, indeed the natural destiny, of all women. According to Lois Banner, author of *Women in Modern America,* "Feminists of all persuasions [in the years before 1920] . . . agreed that the chief fulfillment of a woman's life was motherhood,"[74] and Sochen takes a very questionable essentialist position when she argues that "like all women, the feminists [of the period] had maternal needs. They too wanted to be wives and mothers, *but* they wanted other roles as well."[75] While it is true that mothering is an issue in a number of plays by Provincetown women, motherhood, like marriage, is rarely portrayed as either the end of a quest or the kind of biological mandate Sochen postulates. The women writers of Provincetown were no more likely to idealize motherhood than they were to romanticize marriage.

A number of plays treat motherhood as one among many concerns, or as merely one part of a nexus of social issues. In Bosworth Crocker's *The Baby Carriage,* her only contribution to the Provincetown repertoire, the focus is not the maternal role so much as an age-old economic problem: how a poor family provides for its children. The white carriage Mrs. Lezinsky covets for her expected infant is a symbol of all the middle-class trappings she and her husband, who run a tailor shop, have not been able to give their young sons. Mrs. Lezinsky seems to have little trouble balancing her work in the shop with caring for the children, although she blames her husband's impracticality—he prefers reading the Talmud to mending pants—for their financial straits. The conflict between Karl and his brother, Paul, in Neith Boyce's *The Two Sons,* is created and exacerbated by their mother's unequal treatment of her offspring, but the focus is on the relationship between the two young men and their attitudes toward women. Molly McRace's dilemma in Barnes's *Kurzy of the Sea* is how to get her lazy adult son married and out of her hair (a perhaps timeless dilemma), while Sarah Levy's inability to control her adolescent children in Florence Kiper Frank's *Gee-Rusalem* is a source of comedy.

When the Provincetown women address motherhood as a major concern rather than a secondary issue, they are more likely to present children as a burden than to depict what Sochen refers to as "maternal needs." This is perhaps clearer in two Glaspell plays, *Chains of Dew* and *The Verge,* than in the works of most of her colleagues. In the comic *Chains of Dew,* for example, Seymore Standish's mother declares that the seven children she raised were "too many"[76] and donates $700 to the cause of birth control. The greatest danger a woman faces is not of being deprived of children but, rather, of bearing too many. On a far more ominous note, in *The Verge* Claire Archer totally rejects, even tries to assault, the teenage daughter she believes is interfering with her work. None of the other Provincetown writers offers as graphic and powerful a renunciation of the maternal role as Glaspell does in *The Verge,* but Rita

Wellman also limns the conflict between career and motherhood in *Funiculi-Funicula*,[77] one of the most disturbing if not best written plays of the group. In this work, which preceded *The Verge* by several years, Wellman explores the situation of the mother with no maternal desires.

Rita Wellman had four of her plays performed by the Provincetown between February 1917 and January 1919: *Barbarians*, an antiwar drama that has apparently been lost; *Funiculi-Funicula; The Rib-Person;* and *The String of the Samisen*, based on a Bushido legend about a woman who sacrifices her life rather than betray her family honor.[78] During this period Wellman was also represented on Broadway by *The Gentile Wife*, her first full-length play, which opened in late 1918. Critic John Corbin thought highly enough of it to cite the author as "a new playwright of undeniable attainments and still greater promise,"[79] but *The Gentile Wife* is in actuality a rather muddled melodrama about a Jewish biologist married to an aspiring opera singer. The young wife, Naida, vows to pursue her career and argues that "there are women who are successful both as artists and as wives and mothers,"[80] but the play's attention veers sharply away from Naida herself so that the question of whether she could succeed in balancing these roles is never directly confronted, as it is in *Funiculi-Funicula*.

Funiculi-Funicula presents Alma with a dilemma: how to care for a child and still enjoy the bohemian life-style she craves. Alma is a beautiful artist living in a Washington Square apartment (surely much like those inhabited by members of the Provincetown) that is full of books and "*New Art paintings*" but is "*shabby and neglected.*"[81] She and her lover, Taddema, thought it would be fun to have a baby, but she discovers that she "was never intended to be a mother" (143) and admits she is a bad one. In a speech that even sophisticated Village audiences must have found shocking, Alma says of the child:

> She's always been in our way ever since she was born. Ever since she became a reality she's annoyed us. She's cost us money. She's kept us home when we wanted to go out. She's cried when we wanted to work. She's made our love ridiculous. She's made a family out of us— something we can't stand. We've never forgiven her for making us feel that all our passion was for her sake. (152)

Ida Rauh, the so-called Duse of Macdougal Street,[82] played Alma and very likely evoked sympathy from the audience. Nevertheless, the text provides a markedly negative portrayal of the bohemian pair who once vowed to devote their lives to poetry and passion but have failed as artists and as parents. There is also little to indicate that parenthood is to blame for Taddema's inability to sell poems or Alma's lack of success in drawing. Shallow and self-centered, Taddema complains when the baby is given the one quiet bedroom; Alma forgets to get the child's latest prescription filled, and the couple are setting off for a costume party when Alma discovers that the ailing little girl has died. As the device of the costume party suggests, Alma and Taddema prefer to try on new roles, to keep moving and changing—an apt metaphor for the lives of many of the Provincetowners. (According to Floyd Dell, masquerade balls given by the Liberal Club were a popular Village entertainment.)[83] Parenthood, they discover to their dismay, is a role they cannot shed when they find it irksome.

Funiculi-Funicula is both an apt and an ironic title, and the play itself seems to have been shaped around the words to the song of that name, the melody of which is heard throughout the concluding moments of the drama. A ditty that quickly became a part of popular culture, "Funiculi, Funicula" is subtitled "A Merry Life" and was written "in 1880 to commemorate the opening of the funicular railway to the top of Mt. Vesuvius."[84] The first line states the premise: "Some think the world is made for fun and frolic, / And so do I! / And so do I!" "With laugh, and dance, and song, the day soon passes," the second stanza continues, and indeed singing and dancing are among Alma and Taddema's passions. The chorus—"Hearken! Hearken! Hearken! Music Sounds afar! . . . Joy is ev'rywhere"—forms a bitterly sardonic counterpoint to the stage action. As the play draws to a close, the couple cannot resist the call of the music from a party upstairs, but their joy is abruptly ended when they realize that their daughter is dead. Alma and Taddema's selfish blindness is both underlined and set in a larger context by the song, which callously celebrates a tourist ride to the top of a volcano whose eruptions caused the death of thousands of people.

The most problematic character in *Funiculi-Funicula* is the doctor, a smug, judgmental man who blames Alma for the child's illness. Reminiscent of the reactionary Dr. Remington in Rachel Crothers's *He and She,* Wellman's physician claims that mothers must sacrifice "everything" for their children and that little Bambi has been denied the "quiet and regularity" all children require (146, 144). Finally, the doctor asserts that the baby's illness also stems from the fact that her parents are not married— as if wedding vows would somehow turn Alma into a doting mother. Unfortunately, the only reason Wellman gives the couple for refusing to marry is that they're "afraid to do the things every one approves of" (144). Whether or not Wellman intends the doctor to function as the play's *raisonneur*—the physician as *raisonneur* was already a stock stage figure by 1917[85]—his argument goes essentially unrefuted. And when the baby dies, the doctor's diagnosis, ridiculous as it is in moral and even medical terms, seems to be borne out. Finally, despite the fact that we neither see nor hear little Bambi, hence she scarcely becomes real to the audience, our sympathies are necessarily directed toward this helpless being who has apparently died of parental neglect. Wellman's portrait of a bohemian family, and especially of the female artist, is overwhelmingly negative.

In both *The Verge* and *Funiculi-Funicula* the playwrights present us not with female characters distanced from themselves and their colleagues in terms of economics and locale but, instead, with the educated, urban woman who had, since before the turn of the century, been dubbed the New Woman. Sochen offers a very general but useful definition: "It was a broad term, encompassing many different kinds of women—the essential point in the definition being the changed life style of the American woman, especially the younger middle-class woman. She had more schooling, was economically and socially independent, was more aware of the world's opportunities and problems, and, if she was single, was living in the growing apartment houses of the big cities."[86] Rita Wellman's Alma, like Glaspell's Claire, is a new woman facing the old demands of motherhood.

Like most women of their generation, including many who considered themselves feminists, the Provincetown's female playwrights seemed unable to envision a woman who could balance a family and a successful career.[87] In her 1914 essay "Some American Plays from the Feminist Viewpoint" Florence Kiper (Frank) called for "the drama of the married woman with a vocation,"[88] but very few Provincetowners heeded her call, and those who did paraded an ominous if brief array of neglected and resented children (*The Verge* and *Funiculi-Funicula*) and alienated spouses (Glaspell's *Bernice*). The conflicts these writers depicted on the stage in Greenwich Village echoed those dramatized by Broadway's most successful woman playwright of the period, Rachel Crothers. In *He and She,* for one, Ann Herford decides she must give up the sculpting commission she has won in order to tend to her teenage daughter, who has (apparently because of maternal neglect) taken up with an "inappropriate" young man. The ironic twist is that, while Crothers remained single throughout her life, several of the Provincetowners were themselves married women—some with children—who enjoyed significant literary, theatrical, and/or journalistic careers. In this important instance they did not hold the mirror up to themselves when they created their characters.

In fact, when Kiper Frank herself came to write for the Provincetown, even she declined to explore "the drama of the married woman with a vocation" and turned, instead, to the *un*married new woman. Kiper Frank, a graduate of the University of Chicago, was already an established poet when she wrote her only play for the group.[89] *Gee-Rusalem* is a comedy that tries to poke fun simultaneously at the single new woman, Freudian psychology, and the eugenics movement—and perhaps Zionism and communism as well.[90] The heroine, Sylvia Levy, is a thoroughly modern young person who refuses to be "one of those clinging, parasite, female women! I should say not. I have much too much self-respect. I prefer economic independence."[91] "Independence," however, consists of a job working for her doctor father, for which she earns $18 a week. She spends $15 of that on lunches and transportation; needless to say, Sylvia still lives at home with her family. A woman who enjoys exercising her options, she tells one suitor to make up his mind quickly: "I like to get things settled. Either I'll get married and start a family, or I'll register at the Burton School of Philanthropy and Civics" (17). Sylvia has no intention of being "a regular old maid" but, rather, "one of the New York kind. A mental debutante. Very eager and spontaneous" (57). Kiper Frank understands her New York New Woman well, and she has a good deal of knowing fun at her expense.

Unfortunately, *Gee-Rusalem* rapidly deteriorates into confusion surrounding Sylvia's younger brother's plan to become a Zionist leader, her mother's desire to join an anti-Semitic club, her father's revelation that he has only been pretending to be Jewish, and Sylvia's own determination to marry a man of a different religion because she believes that intermarriage produces stronger children. Kiper Frank was not an accomplished playwright, and *Gee-Rusalem,* which opened in November of 1918, is in many ways derivative of such earlier Glaspell satires as *Suppressed Desires* and *Close the Book*—spoofs of the willfully unconventional. A more detailed look at the New Woman and perhaps itself an influence on *Gee-Rusalem* is Rita Wellman's "farce-satire" *The Rib-Person,* which also preceded Kiper Frank's play on the Provincetown stage by several months.[92]

The "rib-person" of the title is Zelma, another "modern" woman (according to her friend Lucille) who has traveled all over the world and lives with her lover, the thoroughly dependent and comically inept Pumpkin. Zelma fits the description of the "young woman of the leisure class" Floyd Dell praises, one who has achieved "emancipation from middle-class standards of taste, morality, and intellect," as well as his definition of another type of woman—married or single—who uses her "special qualities of sympathy, stimulus, and charm"[93] to attract men. Zelma sleeps until noon and scorns all conventions; when Pumpkin asks her to help him pack his bags because he's going home to his mother, Zelma complains, "This is as bad as being married" (8). Zelma's scorn of marriage, however, does not alter the fact (evident in the title) that she defines herself solely in terms of men and is happy to be dependent on them: as soon as Pumpkin leaves, Zelma calls the young poet Stan to entertain and feed her. Still, her "rib" status does not extend to romanticism, for, as Stan talks of love and ruminates about the cosmos, Zelma contemplates dinner. The playlet ends with Zelma, who freely agrees that she is a "bad woman," preparing to go to India (where she apparently believes the pyramids are) in the company of both Stan and Pumpkin.

Zelma is not the prostitute that Robert Sarlós seems to think she is, not quite the New Woman in the oldest profession.[94] But Wellman is suggesting that one can escape from the conventions of marriage and monogamy, cooking and housekeeping, without being independent. Smoking, traveling, and pleasing men are Zelma's only occupations. To be sure, Zelma's thoroughly modern male companions are no better. Pumpkin is an incompetent escapee from *The American Dream* who can't even find his own suitcase. He has no will or even an identity separate from Zelma, who has given him the nickname Pumpkin, which he understandably loathes. (The audience never learns what his "real" name might be.) He is a rib-person, too, totally dependent on Zelma and his mother. Stan is Wellman's jab at the modern poet: neither his versifying nor his wooing technique can keep his beloved from thinking about her next meal.

Wellman in *The Rib-Person* offers two other versions of the New Woman that are at least a little more promising than the protagonist. Doris is a journalist, who believes that "every woman can do anything" (17) although some, like Zelma, obviously choose to do very little. The apostle of woman's freedom, the forty-five-year-old Doris claims that she has never found any force in her life "strong enough to keep me from doing anything I really wanted to do" (28). Unfortunately, Doris verges on caricature: the tough career woman who, instead of leaning on men, imitates them. She is dressed "in a very masculine style" (17) and leaves her friend Zelma at the end with a warm handshake. Perhaps Wellman is spoofing women who reject the "womanly" ways of a Zelma by aping the other sex, or perhaps she is showing the absurdity of gender roles, for Doris is far more conventionally "masculine" than the helpless Pumpkin or the ethereal Stan. In either case (and the playwright may well have harbored both intentions) Wellman was surely aware that many of the women of the Provincetown—including Susan Glaspell, Djuna Barnes, and Mary Heaton Vorse—entered the traditionally male working world as journalists, and she knew how difficult it was for female reporters of the day to get assignments more substantial than county fairs and society teas. Doris must be stalwart, indeed, to have gained her extraordinary experience covering the Boxer Rebellion in China and the Russo-Japanese conflict.

In some ways closest to the popular idea of the New Woman is Lucille, a young, college-educated artist who can't manage to earn a living. She admires the free-spirited Zelma and has left the security of her parent's home but is unable to support herself. Lucille chooses to go to France to nurse the troops, a relatively conventional choice, since nursing was considered a "woman's job." But unlike Zelma, she is going on her own to do work that she has chosen. As the play ends, the three New Women are heading off to see a world that most of their sisters could only dream about. Zelma, who turns down the canteen job the others have lined up for her, elects to remain a rib-person, while Doris takes the traditionally "masculine" route and Lucille a kind of middle road. Although scarcely a profound work, Wellman's brief comedy offers a glimpse of some of the alternatives to marriage from among which the New Woman could choose. And her view of the new single woman here is far more sanguine than the devastating vision of the New Woman as mother she presents in *Funiculi-Funicula.*

Two other topics seem to have engaged women writing for the Provincetown: war and honor. Edna St. Vincent Millay's *Aria da Capo,* for example, merits more attention than it has received. A powerful antiwar drama that cleverly embeds a tragedy in a seemingly lighthearted harlequinade, *Aria da Capo* is an indictment of the "passive evil" of those who blithely ignore the violence transpiring around them—as timely seventy years later as it was when she wrote it immediately after World War I. Nor was Millay alone in her concern: Glaspell's *Inheritors,* in part a plea for the rights of pacifists, places her also in what Mary Heaton Vorse identified as a "rising tide of protest against the war" by women throughout the world,[95] a protest that began around 1915 and continued into the postwar period. Two plays that pit women's affections against their sense of honor—Mary Foster Barber's *The Squealer* and Rita Wellman's *The String of the Samisen*—offer dramatic disproof of the cliché that nothing is more important to a woman than love. Barber's Margaret is a miner's wife, who "thought the Angel Gabriel and all the saints wasn't near as fine as" her husband,[96] but she refuses to run away with him when she learns he has "squealed" on his radical friends in order to buy his own freedom. Wellman's Tama decides she cannot help her lover kill her husband, despite her antipathy to him, and substitutes herself as a sacrificial victim.

Interestingly, there is a distinct chronological pattern in women's contributions to the Provincetown. Following the lead of Glaspell and Boyce, women writers became progressively more involved in the group over its first few years, and during the two seasons from November 1917 to May 1919 thirteen plays by women other than Glaspell were staged. In 1920–21, by contrast, only Evelyn Scott's *Love* joined Glaspell's works, and by the final season, 1921–22, Glaspell was the sole female dramatist whose plays were being produced by the Provincetown.[97] One reason for this decline is simply the group's shift in emphasis from one-acts to longer forms: fewer plays were presented during the last years. Some fourteen works premiered in 1918–19; only eight new plays appeared in each of the following seasons. One might also speculate that the women, who in some cases had to fit their play writing into time shared with household and family obligations, found the one-act form more congenial and hence were reluctant to follow the trend to longer dramas. Except for Glaspell, only Scott and Florence Kiper Frank had full-length works performed by the Provincetown.[98]

Women may well have been attracted to the Provincetown by what today would be called its feminist structure: emphasis on community, commitment to decision making by consensus, absence of a rigid power hierarchy, and disdain for commercial success. In actual practice, however, this devotion to egalitarian process was never entirely practicable, and it waned as the group evolved from a community of dedicated experimenters toward a more conventional producing organization. Individual personalities were likely also a factor in women writers' departure from the theater. Jig Cook, in many ways the group's guiding force, had difficulties abiding by communal decisions and saw himself as the first among equals, a kind of spiritual leader and prime mover. Norma Millay, Edna's sister and a veteran Provincetown actress, was one person who believed that Cook's increasingly dictatorial attitude led to the dissolution of the theater.[99] Helen Deutsch and Stella Hanau also record that some members of the company had trouble with Cook's "paternalism."[100]

Another attraction of the Provincetown—something virtually unavailable on Broadway—was the chance to have plays directed by empathetic women. Once the original scheme that required authors to stage their own dramas proved unworkable, directors were assigned to most productions. Nina Moise directed Wellman's *Barbarians,* Davies's *The Slave with Two Faces,* and Grace Potter's *"About Six,"* as well as at least two Glaspell offerings, while Helen Westley staged Barnes's *Irish Triangle* and

Kurzy of the Sea. Moise left the Provincetown in the spring of 1918, and Westley directed nothing after *Kurzy* in March of 1920.[101] The connections, if any, between the departures of these directors and the women dramatists might be an interesting subject for study.

What is clear is that when the Provincetown Players disbanded, none of the women playwrights went on to a successful career as a dramatist, as Eugene O'Neill did.[102] Some, like Barnes, Millay, and Glaspell, continued to make their marks on literature through fiction or poetry, but with an occasional exception (Glaspell's *Alison's House,* Barnes's *Antiphon*) their few dramatic works went largely unnoticed. The Provincetown obviously provided these writers with a community of like-minded dramatists, actors, and directors as well as a stage and a receptive audience, which they needed as an alternative to Broadway. Rita Wellman, for one, wryly dedicated the published version of *The Gentile Wife* "to the managers who rejected my plays."

Surely the Provincetown Players' offerings were nothing if not eclectic. What else can one make of the opening bill of the 1918–19 season, which included Edna St. Vincent Millay's verse fairy tale *The Princess Marries the Page,* O'Neill's grim exercise in collective madness *Where the Cross Is Made,* and Kiper Frank's *Gee-Rusalem,* a satire of nearly every contemporary *ism?* It is, therefore, dangerous to make sweeping generalizations about the group's work or about the work of one segment of it, in this case the women: Djuna Barnes, Neith Boyce, Rita Wellman, Alice Rostetter, and the others were individuals with distinct talents and concerns. Still, some patterns emerge from this tentative overview of their dramatic contributions to America's most important early-twentieth-century Little Theatre.

Gerhard Bach divides the plays of the Provincetown into three periods and argues that "an American dramatic literature expressing a sociohistorical awareness was realized in the first two years by a large number of plays reflecting social realism and naturalism." In fact, as far as the women writers are concerned, "social realism" remained popular in such diverse plays as *Winter's Night* (1916), *Funiculi-Funicula* (1917), *The Baby Carriage* (1919), *The Squealer* (1919), *The Eldest* (1920), and Glaspell's *Trifles* (1916) and *Inheritors* (1921). A second, later group Bach identifies as those "favoring an idealism completely devoid of contemporary concerns and tending to symbolic representations of more timeless concerns such as 'love and despair,' 'beauty,' 'death' etc."[103] Stylistically, if not chronologically, Bach's distinction makes sense: allegories such as *The Game* (1916) and *The Slave with Two Faces* (1918) or verse fantasies such as *Two Slatterns and a King* (1918) and *The Princess Marries the Page* (1918) are a far cry theatrically from such realistic tragedies as *Funiculi-Funicula*. In terms of theme, however, the distinction is difficult to sustain. Surely war was a very "contemporary concern" when Millay wrote *Aria da Capo* in 1919, while *Two Slatterns and a King* and *The Slave with Two Faces* have (like *Trifles* and *Winter's Night*) a good deal to say about courtship and marriage, other particular concerns of women in the 1910s and 1920s.

The plays of Glaspell's female colleagues, like those of Glaspell herself, range from serious dramas to satirical comedies (with a few poetic and allegorical fantasies mixed in); if Glaspell seems to have a somewhat greater penchant for light works, this may be because her collaborations with Cook are in a humorous vein. Floyd Dell insisted that "The Village . . . wanted its most serious beliefs mocked at; it enjoyed laughing at its own convictions."[104] Wellman's *The Rib-Person* and Kiper Frank's *Gee-Rusalem*, as well as Glaspell's *Suppressed Desires, Tickless Time, Close the Book,* and *Woman's Honor* (the first two collaborations with Cook), bear out his claim. It may also be, as suggested earlier, that the women writers sensed a covert strain of antifeminism among certain male colleagues at the Provincetown Players and therefore found it difficult to present a serious, positive portrayal of the New Woman. Humor was safer. Such comedies as *The Rib-Person, An Irish Triangle,* and *Kurzy of the Sea* also foregrounded female characters who expressed and fulfilled sexual desires, distinguishing them from the Victorian "angel in the house" who had dominated popular ideology just a few years earlier. When a serious approach to the New Woman was essayed, the playwrights often painted a bleak picture of disaster: *Funiculi-Funicula* ends with Alma mourning her dead child; *The Verge* concludes on a mad Claire's murder of Tom. While they did not put on the stage a female character who successfully balances career and family obligations, they were sensitive to many women's desire to do so—and to the social, economic, and personal forces that made such balance so difficult.

A perhaps surprising number of plays by the Provincetown's female writers, including some of the very best, address the plight of rural women or those in the urban working class. This may well reflect a social concern on the part of these writers, whose generally liberal political sympathies and egalitarian ethos would have led them to emphasize with such entrapped farm wives as Boyce's Rachel Westcott and Glaspell's Minnie Wright or urban wives such as Crocker's Mrs. Lezinsky and Rostetter's Katy MacManus. Ann Larabee is not entirely correct when she argues that "the tensions between progressive middle-class men and women, who were struggling with the boundaries which defined their separate spheres, surfaced everywhere in the writing of both sexes at the Provincetown, becoming the central conflict in their plays."[105] Certainly, middle-class gender conflicts are at the heart of works such as Boyce's *Constancy* and Boyce and Hapgood's *Enemies* as well as the majority of Glaspell's plays.

The progressive middle class is notably absent, however, from a significant percentage of the women's contributions to the Provincetown—from Mary Foster Barber's tragic *The Squealer* to Djuna Barnes's comic *Kurzy of the Sea*—at the same time that tensions between men and women remain center stage. It is likely that some of the female dramatists again felt safer writing about such volatile issues as the dual standards of morality, the silencing of wives, and the oppressiveness of sexual stereotyping in the oblique guise of plays about people "other" than themselves. Equally likely—and surely no two writers' motives were identical—these playwrights understood that many problems identified by middle-class feminists existed for all women in all classes in all places. Rachel Westcott and Minnie Wright, in their grim farmhouses, were as hungry for aesthetic beauty and artistic freedom as was the sophisticated Alma in her Greenwich Village flat. What virtually all these plays share, regardless of the class and locale of their characters, is an honest look at the lives of women, particularly in their relationships to men, and a refusal to idealize or sentimentalize such traditional social icons as courtship, marriage, and motherhood.

As he and Glaspell prepared to leave for Greece, a disappointed Jig Cook addressed a valedictory "To Our Playwrights":

We have given two playwrights to America, Eugene O'Neill and Susan Glaspell: we could have given a dozen by now if the other ten had

appeared. We have looked for them eagerly and we have not found those among you offering us a sustained stream of freely experimental work in new dramatic forms. We do not want plays cut to old theatric patterns but we have produced many mediocre plays because we had nothing better to offer.[106]

Harsh as Cook's judgment may be (and evasive as he is about acknowledging his own failed attempts at play writing), he is right that none of the other dramatists, male or female, created a "sustained stream" of work of consistently high quality for the Provincetown. But his blanket condemnation overlooks the existence of minor dramatic gems such as Barnes's *Three from the Earth,* Boyce's *Winter's Night,* and Millay's *Aria da Capo,* and witty comedies such as Rostetter's *The Widow's Veil* and Wellman's *The Rib-Person.* And surely not all of O'Neill's work would qualify as "new dramatic forms": if *Winter's Night* is cut to the "theatric pattern" of naturalistic melodrama that was already becoming commonplace by 1916, the same is true of O'Neill's *Before Breakfast* and *Diff'rent,* both of which premiered later. Moreover, there is always a danger in equating innovation with quality, as Cook was wont to do. While some of Djuna Barnes's plays, for example, imaginatively fuse new theatrical forms with provocative ideas, an allegorical fantasy such as Louise Bryant's *The Game* provides the opportunity for imaginative staging but is scarcely effective drama.

The "other" women writers of the Provincetown, the "lesser talents" that Mary Heaton Vorse saw revolving around O'Neill and Glaspell,[107] were important in their own right as well as in the influence they surely had on their more accomplished colleagues. While they may not be "the *first* significant women playwrights in the American theater"[108]—Rachel Crothers, for one, preceded them—they hold an important place in the history of this country's drama and theater. A year before the Province-towners began putting on plays in Neith Boyce's living room, Florence Kiper Frank called for a drama that would "set forth sincerely and honestly, yet with vital passion, those problems in the development and freedom of women that the modern age has termed the problems of feminism."[109] The women writers of the Provincetown Players heeded that call.

NOTES

1. Helen Krich Chinoy, "Introduction, Art versus Business: The Role of Women in American Theatre," in *Women in American Theatre,* ed. Chinoy and Linda Walsh Jenkins, rev. and exp. ed. (New York: TCG, 1987), 4.

2. Robert Károly Sarlós, *Jig Cook and the Provincetown Players* (Amherst: University of Massachusetts Press, 1982), 3.

3. Sarlós, (*Jig Cook,* 138–52) makes the convincing argument that the later group calling itself the "Provincetown Playhouse" was essentially a separate organization from the original Provincetown Players. The departure of Susan Glaspell and George Cram Cook effectively ended the Provincetown Players in early 1922.

4. See note 1 of Linda Ben-Zvi's introduction to this volume.

5. Sarlós, *Jig Cook,* 116.

6. Helen Deutsch and Stella Hanau, *The Provincetown: A Story of the Theatre* (1931; reprint, New York: Russell and Russell, 1972), 16–17.

7. See Vorse, *A Footnote to Folly* (New York: Farrar and Rinehart, 1935); and *Time and the Town: A Provincetown Chronicle* (New York: Dial, 1942).

8. June Sochen, *The New Woman: Feminism in Greenwich Village, 1910–1920* (New York: Quadrangle, 1972), 16–18; Sarlós, *Jig Cook,* 194.

9. Deutsch and Hanau, *The Provincetown,* 53; Sarlós, *Jig Cook,* 110.

10. Sarlós, *Jig Cook,* 72.

11. Sarlós, *Jig Cook,* 93 and 146–47, 64–65.

12. See Rachel France, ed., *A Century of Plays by American Women* (New York: Richards Rosen, 1979), 68.

13. The theme of waiting for inherited madness to surface appears in both *The Rescue* and *Strange Interlude,* and both plays make reference to a mad aunt who lives or lived in the house. (Sarlós [*Jig Cook,* 100] also notes the parallels to *Strange Interlude.*) *Rescue*'s set features forbidding portraits of past governors and judges, foreshadowing the decor of the Mannons' home in *Mourning Becomes Electra.*

14. *The Letters of Edna St. Vincent Millay,* ed. Allan Ross Macdougall (New York: Harper, 1952), 116. According to Andrew Field, when *The Lamp and the Bell* was published, "Barnes did damn it with faint praise in a review." See Field's *Djuna: The Life and Times of Djuna Barnes* (New York: Putnam's, 1983), 87. He is justifiably skeptical of Norma Millay's claim that the letter did not suggest tension between Barnes and the Millays.

15. Field, *Djuna,* 84.

16. Anne Corey, "Women in the Provincetown Players." East Central Theatre Conference, Albany, N.Y., February 9, 1991.

17. Gerhard Bach, "Susan Glaspell—Provincetown Playwright," *Great Lakes Review* 4 (1978): 39.

18. Unless otherwise indicated, references are to the revised edition of *Winter's Night,* published in 1928 and reprinted in Rachel France's *A Century of Plays by American Women.* The Hapgood Family Papers Collection at the Beinecke Library contains one holograph manuscript and two typescripts of *Winter's Night,* which, as I discuss, differ in generally minor ways from the later version. The most extensive revisions were made in the latter half of the play. In addition to cutting and slightly changing Sarah's lines, Boyce also removed a melodramatic speech in which Jacob threatens, "I could kill you, and there'd be no help," then rhapsodizes about the "black-haired girl" (Rachel) that he has always loved. None of the three Beinecke scripts bears a date, but it is likely that they contain the version presented by the Provincetown.

19. Susan Glaspell, *The Road to the Temple* (New York: Frederick A. Stokes, 1927), 255–56. *Trifles* appeared on the third bill of the summer, premiering on August 8, 1916. According to Sarlós (*Jig Cook,* 170), *Winter's Night* was first performed on July 13.

20. Sarlós, *Jig Cook,* 21.

21. June Sochen, *Movers and Shakers: American Women Thinkers and Activists, 1900–1970* (New York: Quadrangle, 1973), 75.

22. Sochen, *New Woman,* 19–21. For additional biographical information about Boyce, see Ellen Kay Trimberger, "The New Woman and the New Sexuality: Conflict and Contradiction in the Writings and Lives of Mabel Dodge and Neith Boyce," in *1915, The Cultural Moment: The New Politics, the New Woman, the New Psychology, the New Art, and the New Theatre in America,* ed. Adele Heller and Lois Rudnick, 98–115. (New Brunswick: Rutgers University Press, 1991).

23. The Hapgood Family Paper Collection at the Beinecke Library, Yale University, includes a handwritten list of works and characters that seems to suggest Boyce wrote or coauthored some twenty plays. There are two boxes of fragments, notes, manuscripts, and typescripts of Boyce's plays—both long and short—but it's possible that some of the works on the list never got beyond the scenario stage. Most of the scripts, with the exception of that for the 1938 radio drama *Hurricane,* are undated.

24. Ben-Zvi, "Susan Glaspell's Contributions," 150.

25. C. W. E. Bigsby, "Introduction," *Plays by Susan Glaspell* (Cambridge: Cambridge University Press, 1987), 11.

26. Sarlós (*Jig Cook,* 21) also notes this similarity.

27. Sochen, *New Woman,* 38.

28. Sarlós, *Jig Cook*, 175–76.

29. George Cram Cook and Frank Shay, eds., *The Provincetown Plays* (Cincinnati: Stewart Kidd, 1921).

30. Rostetter even specifies the "smell" coming from Mrs. Phelan's kitchen, but there is no evidence that the Provincetown tried to recreate it.

31. Presumably, we are meant to believe that the women are whispering, since the dumbwaiter shaft obviously is a good conductor of sound.

32. Another connection between men and children is established when we learn that Mr. MacManus was suffering from tonsillitis, an ailment usually associated with childhood.

33. Sarlós, *Jig Cook*, 184. Presumably, she is the same Mary Davies who, according to Andrew Field, "gained fleeting fame as a rhyme-a-dance girl because she wrote some words for a poem on a partner's cuff as they tangoed" (*Letters*, 84).

34. Sarlós, *Jig Cook*, 163, 86.

35. Mary Caroline-Davies, *The Slave with Two Faces,* in *Fifty Contemporary One-Act Plays,* ed. Frank Shay and Pierre Loving (New York: Appleton, 1920).

36. Deutsch and Hanau, *The Provincetown*, 33.

37. Field, *Djuna*, 13–14.

38. An unabashed sexist, Woollcott wrote that "the refreshing sight of Miss Djuna Barnes, bounding up and down the centre aisle like an artless antelope [was] a compensating privilege accorded to the Provincetown Playwrights on first nights, presumably in lieu of royalties" (*New York Times,* April 4, 1920, 6:6:1). Field (*Djuna,* 87) does not mention the "bounding" but does say that Barnes served as an usher.

39. Barnes, *The Dove, A Book* (New York: Boni and Liveright, 1923), 163. It is not clear whether *The Dove* was written during or immediately after Barnes's association with the Provincetown. *A Book* includes *Three from the Earth.* According to Field (*Djuna,* 92), *The Dove* was first "produced by the Studio Theatre at Smith College in 1925"—surely an unusually daring college production for the time. Field adds that it was "then played (unsuccessfully) in The Little Theatre Tournament in New York in May 1926."

40. Alexander Woollcott, "Second Thoughts on First Nights: The Provincetown Plays," *New York Times,* November 9, 1919, 8:2:1. Field (*Djuna,* 90) says that Woollcott penned a parody entitled *Free from the Birth: A Malthusian Sardonicism in One Act.*

41. Barnes, *Three from the Earth,* in France, *Century,* 62.

42. Ann E. Larabee, "The Early Attic Stage of Djuna Barnes," in *Silence and Power: A Reevaluation of Djuna Barnes,* ed. Mary Lynn Broe (Carbondale: Southern Illinois University Press, 1991), 39.

43. Larabee, "Early Attic Stage," 38.

44. *Diff'rent* was performed by the Provincetown on the second bill of the 1920–21 season, roughly a year after *Three from the Earth; The Verge* premiered in November of 1921.

45. Although it's not clear in exactly what order they were written, *An Irish Triangle* preceded *Kurzy of the Sea* onto the Provincetown stage by two months. I discuss *Kurzy* first because it forms a thematic bridge between *Three from the Earth* and *Triangle.*

46. One wonders whether it is accidental that Rory—Irish, "medium height, dark and possessed of a spirited melancholy"—so closely resembles the Provincetown Player's most famous member, Eugene O'Neill. See Djuna Barnes, *Kurzy of the Sea*, MS, Library of Congress, 1920.

47. Ann E. Larabee, " 'Meeting the Outside Face to Face': Susan Glaspell, Djuna Barnes, and O'Neill's *The Emperor Jones,"* in *Modern American Drama: The Female Canon,* ed. June Schlueter (Rutherford, N.J.: Fairleigh Dickinson University Press, 1990), 84.

48. Field, *Djuna,* 28. Field adds that Barnes's enthusiasm for Synge and James Joyce led her to claim Irish ancestry, which "may well be the case through her grandmother Zadel's family" (29). On a negative note, Joan Retallack (who seems to miss the humor in these plays) considers *Kurzy of the Sea* and *An Irish Triangle* "quaint dramas . . . embarrassing imitations" of Synge's work ("One Acts: Early Plays of Djuna Barnes," in Broe, *Silence and Power,* 49).

49. Judith L. Stephens finds the same pattern in Progressive era plays (including *A Man's World*) ("Gender Ideology and Dramatic Convention in Progressive Era Plays, 1890–1929," in *Performing Feminisms: Feminist Critical Theory and Theatre,* ed. Sue-Ellen Case, 283–93 [Baltimore: Johns Hopkins University Press, 1990]).

50. *An Irish Triangle,* in *Playboy* 7, 1921, 3–5. Barnes uses the spelling "Shiela" rather than the more conventional "Sheila."

51. Sochen, *New Woman,* 4; my emphasis.

52. Elizabeth Ammons, "The New Woman as Cultural Symbol and Social Reality: Six Women Writers' Perspectives," in Heller and Rudnick, *1915,* 95.

53. Sarlós, *Jig Cook,* 100–101.

54. Sarlós, *Jig Cook,* 14.

55. Sarlós offers a tentative date of July 15 for the premier (*Jig Cook,* 14–16, 169).

56. Sarlós (*Jig Cook,* 14–15) discusses the source of the play.

57. Ellen Kay Trimberger, "The New Woman and the New Sexuality: Con-

flict and Contradiction in the Writings and Lives of Mabel Dodge and Neith Boyce," in Heller and Rudnick, *1915,* 100.

58. The Beinecke Library, Yale University, has four undated typescripts for *Constancy,* which was later renamed *The Faithful Lover.* What appears to be the first is a heavily hand-corrected incomplete script. The second—titled "Constancy," with "The Faithful Lover" written in a corner—is the one on which my discussion is based. This version is reprinted in Heller and Rudnick, *1915,* 274– 80; all subsequent page references are to the Heller and Rudnick text. What appears to be the third script is entitled *The Faithful Lover,* hence is unlikely to be the script from which the actors worked in the first production; it, too, is incomplete. A fourth typescript—one that includes additional characters and sets the action in Venice—is presumably the last because of its title (*The Faithful Lover*) and because it differs most from the other versions.

59. Unlike Mabel Dodge and the fictional Moira, Boyce did not leave her partner because of his affairs, but Trimberger observes that she was deeply disturbed by Hapgood's infidelities. In a letter to Hapgood, Boyce revealed the split between her personal feelings and her liberal ideas: "I assure you that I can never think of your physical passion for other women without pain—even though my reason doesn't find fault with you" (qtd. in Trimberger, "New Woman," 110).

60. According to Trimberger ("New Woman," 99), the loss of female autonomy in heterosexual relationships is also a central issue in Boyce's novel *The Bond,* "a fictionalized account of the conflicts in Neith's own marriage."

61. There is no clear evidence in either book on the Provincetown—Sarlós's and Deutsch and Hanau's volumes—that *The Faithful Lover* in its final (Venetian) incarnation was ever produced by the Provincetown.

62. Reported in Deutsch and Hanau, *The Provincetown,* 26.

63. Hutchins Hapgood, *A Victorian in the Modern World* (New York: Harcourt, Brace, 1939), 395.

64. *Enemies,* in Cook and Shay, *Provincetown Plays,* 126.

65. Trimberger, "New Woman," 111.

66. Letter from Mary Heaton Vorse to Catherine S. Huntington, January 23, 1962; quoted in Sarlós, *Jig Cook,* 15.

67. Sarlós assigns the play to a "Date Undetermined" in the summer of 1916; according to him, it was revived in November of that year with Boyce and Hapgood reprising their roles (*Jig Cook,* 170–71 and 69–70). In the appendix to their book Deutsch and Hanau fail to mention the first production but concur with Hapgood that Justus Sheffield and Ida Rauh assumed the roles in the November production in New York (*The Provincetown,* 203; and Hapgood, *A Victo-*

rian, 395). It seems likely that the play was first performed that summer in Provincetown then recast for New York if indeed Hapgood was unable to remember his lines.

68. Hapgood, *A Victorian,* 396.

69. Hapgood, *A Victorian,* 395.

70. Sochen (*Movers and Shakers,* 79) says that, in a debate with Lincoln Steffens, "Hapgood playfully presented the anti-feminist point of view," but one must wonder whether the argument was entirely "playful."

71. Floyd Dell, *Women as World Builders: Studies in Modern Feminism* (Chicago: Forbes, 1913), 19.

72. Dell, *Women as World Builders,* 21.

73. Dell, it is true, was given to irony and mockery, and there are elements of these in the introduction to *Women in Modern America.* Still, there is nothing to indicate that his argument at this point—the conclusion to the introduction—is tongue in cheek. Sochen (*New Woman,* 127–35) discusses some of the differences between female and male "feminists" in Greenwich Village, but her conclusions about the desires of the women are suspect.

74. Lois W. Banner, *Women in Modern America: A Brief History* (New York: Harcourt, 1974), 119.

75. Sochen, *New Woman,* 131.

76. Susan Glaspell, *Chains of Dew,* MS, Library of Congress, 1920, act 3, 17. I am grateful to Anne Corey for providing me a copy of this script.

77. I am following the precedent of Deutsch and Hanau, as well as Sarlós, in hyphenating *Funiculi-Funicula.* The published version, which appears in *Representative One-Act Plays by American Authors,* ed. Margaret Gardner Mayorga (Boston: Little, Brown, 1919), omits the hyphen.

78. Sarlós (*Jig Cook,* 72) mentions a "lost" play by Wellman that was a "protest against the war"—presumably *Barbarians. The String of the Samisen* is reprinted in Cook and Shay, *Provincetown Plays,* 207–39. Wellman has other short plays from this period, including *For All Time,* that did not find their way to the Provincetown stage.

79. Review in the *New York Times,* December 25, 1918, 13:2.

80. *The Gentile Wife* (New York: Moffat Yard, 1919), 73.

81. *Funiculi-Funicula,* in Mayorga, *Representative One-Act Plays,* 140.

82. Sarlós, *Jig Cook,* 194. It's hard to imagine that a dedicated feminist like Rauh would have undertaken the role had she not seen opportunities for an at least partly sympathetic portrayal of Alma and her plight.

83. Floyd Dell, *Homecoming: An Autobiography* (New York: Farrar and Rinehart, 1933), 258. Dell recalls working on a masquerade ball dubbed "Pagan

Rout"; Alma and Taddema's neighbors called their party "The Rebellious Rabe-laisian Revel."

84. Margaret Boni, ed., *Fireside Book of Folk Songs* (New York: Simon and Schuster, 1947), 43. Boni uses a comma between the two words of the title.

85. For a discussion of the doctor-raissoneur figure in late-nineteenth-and early-twentieth-century drama, see Maurice Valency, *The Flower and the Castle: An Introduction to Modern Drama* (New York: Grosset and Dunlap, 1963), 79.

86. Sochen, *Movers and Shakers*, 11.

87. I make these generalizations with the caveat that there are at least four plays by women performed at the Provincetown—Grace Potter's *"About Six"*; Evelyn Scott's *Love;* Rita Wellman's *Barbarians;* and Alice Wood's *The Devil Glow*—which have either not survived or which I was unable to obtain. Ironically, about the closest the plays come to portraying a working mother is Mrs. Lezinsky in Crocker's *The Baby Carriage*. She works in the family shop—a very traditional role—and it is clear that her husband is the tailor, while she is his assistant.

88. Kiper, "Some American Plays from the Feminist Viewpoint," *Forum* 51, no. 6 (June 1914): 927. I am indebted to Sharon Friedman for this reference. In 1914 Kiper married Jerome N. Frank and took the name Florence Kiper Frank, hence my subsequent references to her as "Kiper Frank" (Sarlós, *Jig Cook*, 187).

89. Sarlós, *Jig Cook*, 187. In later years Kiper Frank wrote more plays, including some in verse, a few of which were published.

90. The Balfour Declaration, pledging British support for a Jewish homeland in Palestine, was issued in 1917.

91. Florence Kiper Frank, *Gee-Rusalem*, MS, Library of Congress, 1919, 13.

92. *The Rib-Person*, MS, Library of Congress, 1918. Wellman is inconsistent in her use of a hyphen in *rib-person*. For the sake of consistency, I have included the hyphen even where Wellman omits it. According to Sarlós (*Jig Cook*, 174–75), *The Rib-Person* premiered on March 29, 1918, while *Gee-Rusalem* was first performed on November 22 of that year.

93. Dell, *Women as World Builders*, 13, 10–12. Although Dell uses the term *courtesan* for this latter "type," he insists that such women may be faithful wives or those who transgress "certain moral customs."

94. According to Sarlós (*Jig Cook*, 90), the play "concerns a prostitute, upset by the general involvement with the war: even some of her colleagues have volunteered for nursing": "The halting dialogue leaves in doubt whether she has been turned down for service, or just fears rejection." In fact, Zelma calls herself Pumpkin's "mistress"; she is not a prostitute, nor is the inept and infatuated

Pumpkin her pimp. As I discuss, Zelma rejects the canteen job she is offered, while her friends (not "colleagues") join the war effort.

95. Vorse, *Footnote to Folly*, 79.

96. Barber, *The Squealer*, MS, Library of Congress, 1919, 10.

97. Not included in this count are revivals of *The Widow's Veil* and *Aria da Capo* during what Sarlós calls the "unofficial" spring season of 1921 (*Jig Cook*, 161 and 179).

98. Although Kiper Frank's *Gee-Rusalem* is three acts long, it was evidently not a full evening's entertainment. *Gee-Rusalem* was performed with Millay's *The Princess Marries the Page* and O'Neill's *Where the Cross Is Made*, which must have added up to a lengthy program (Sarlós, *Jig Cook*, 174–75).

99. Sarlós gives a largely sympathetic portrait of Cook in *Jig Cook and the Provincetown Players*, but the very title of his volume suggests that the Provincetown was never the community of equals it purported to be. In an interview I did with Norma Millay in 1983, a few years before her death, she expressed her view that it was Cook's authoritarianism that eventually undermined the group.

100. Deutsch and Hanau, *The Provincetown*, 55.

101. My source for information about directors is Deutsch and Hanau, *The Provincetown*, 199–257. Only two productions are listed as having been directed by women during the Provincetown's last two seasons: Florence Enright staged Lawrence Vail's *What D'You Want*, and Margaret Wycherly staged Norman C. Lindau's *A Little Act of Justice*.

102. One exception is Edna Ferber, who enjoyed successful collaborations with George S. Kaufman. But Ferber's fame as a solo writer came in fiction rather than drama, and her only connection with the Provincetown seemed to have been the somewhat reluctant contribution of a state adaptation of her short story "The Eldest."

103. Bach, "Susan Glaspell," 35.

104. Dell, *Homecoming*, 261.

105. Larabee, "Early Attic Stage," 37.

106. Sarlós, *Jig Cook*, 143.

107. Vorse, *Time and the Town*, 123.

108. Larabee, "Meeting the Outside Face to Face," 84; my emphasis.

109. Florence Kiper, "Some American Plays," 931.

Part 5
Novel Women

Lifting the Masks of Male-Female Discourse: The Rhetorical Strategies of Susan Glaspell

Colette Lindroth

While critics have recognized the feminist conviction in Susan Glaspell's dramas, that aspect in her fiction, especially in the short stories, has gone largely unregarded. And yet the stories of *Lifted Masks,* her collection of 1912, are clearly feminist in nature. They are not confrontational; Glaspell seems to take her cue from Emily Dickinson's advice to "tell all the Truth but tell it slant." She clearly recognizes that if she intends to entertain a wide audience she cannot afford to attack popular sentiments directly. Instead, she uses the circuitous tactics of subversion. She does not directly challenge male power or dominance; rather, she sidesteps or ignores it, rendering it either comic or irrelevant. For Glaspell as for Dickinson, "success in circuit lies."

One might easily miss the subversive subtext of these stories. On the surface all is sunny acceptance, genial humor, an apparently straightforward approval of Fourth of July American values of family solidarity, duty, hard work, the goodness of rural values, distrust of foreigners and "city slickers," and a general endorsement of the patriarchal ideals of nineteenth-century America, tempered only by a touch of irony and dry humor. In technique and attitude, however, Glaspell subverts the placid expectations of popular fiction, filling her stories with hints at their subversive subtexts. The title itself directs the perceptive reader to look below the surface, to lift the masks of stereotype and assumption. Significantly, the volume does not take its title from any story within the collection: "Lifted Masks" refers to nothing specific. It can thus be taken as a directive to the reader to lift the masks on all the material in the volume.

Taking the title as directive, one finds in the first story indicators of what these masks might hide. That story, "One of Those Impossible Americans," is a classic of comic subversiveness. Apparently a sweet tale of a sophisticated girl's discovery that "you never can tell" (25) about the suffering hidden behind a successful exterior, the story is, in fact, a humorous dismissal of traditional nineteenth-century sex-role expectations. It presents a reversal of traditional male-female discourse, a reversal of traditional male-female balance of power, and an example of risqué wit by a female author that predates Dorothy Parker's shocking sketches by nearly twenty years.

From the outset Glaspell reverses traditional notions of male competency and power and female timidity and weakness. Significantly, the story is set not in America but, instead, in France, where both its American protagonists are on unfamiliar ground. Virginia, however, has lived in France for some time; consequently, she proceeds with more confidence and experience than William, who has just arrived. Her first act in the story is to take charge of William, shielding him from the sneering condescension of French salesgirls and the soaring upper reaches of French prices. Virginia is kindly and tactful, but Glaspell makes it clear to the reader, though Virginia does not to William, that he is ludicrously helpless and out of his depth here, speaking no French and understanding no bargaining strategies. Traditional sex roles are reversed. Virginia is the experienced guide, interpreter, and protector, and William follows her instructions as meekly as a child.

Glaspell takes care to present this subversion indirectly, however, masking Virginia's independence and self-sufficiency, and William's weakness and naïveté, with enough conventional details to distract the reader from the story's dangerous subtext. Conventional expectations are met by having William's story provide new wisdom for Virginia, for example. Her initial scorn for his clumsiness turns to pitying admiration when she discovers that his extravagance is a pathetic attempt to provide therapy for his mentally ill wife. In conventional terms, then, the young woman learns from the experience of an older, wiser man. Important conventional ideas of male strength and competence, however, are never met. William understands his wife's problems but can do nothing to relieve them; it is quite clear that she is incurable. He is powerless to help any of the females he meets; his good-hearted offer to help Virginia "or any of [her] gang" (25) should they fall on hard times is endearing but ineffectual, since the reader knows that the self-sufficient Virginia is unlikely to need any help. The wealthy businessman, the well-traveled "man of affairs," the embodiment of turn-of-the-century success, is as helpless in this story as the child to which he is more than once compared.

Further removing the story from the conventional expectations of early-twentieth-century popular fiction is the distinctly risqué tone of its beginning. Virginia encounters William in the lingerie section of a French store, "standing there helplessly dangling two flaming red silk stockings which a copiously coiffured young woman assured him were *bien chic*" (1). As if their encounter over the "flaming hose" were not titillating enough, William loudly insists, when they have compromised on a more discreet gray pair, to make a gift of a second pair to Virginia or, when she refuses, "her face the colour of the condemned stockings," to Virginia's mother. Glaspell's awareness of the titillating aspects of the encounter is seen in Virginia's imaginary presentation of the scene to her mother: " 'Mother dear,' she would write, 'as I stood at the counter buying myself some stockings to-day along came a nice man—a stranger to me but very kind and jolly—and gave me—' " whereupon she dissolves in laughter at the thought of her mother's horror at such a message (4). Here the woman is in control of the risqué situation; the naive male has no idea of the impropriety he suggests. As she so often does, Glaspell defuses the dangerous situation with her humor, but its potential to shock even as it amuses is as powerful as Dorothy Parker's wryly cynical tales.

At the outset of her collection, then, Glaspell invites her reader to lift the masks of traditional male-female discourse and power relationships to examine what lies underneath conventional assumptions. What she presents there, always with disarming humor and geniality, is a persistent questioning of authority, a questioning of the rightness of things as they are, above all a comic puncturing of smugness or pomposity, always male.

Glaspell's confidence in both her craft and her message can be seen in her refusal to confine herself to female protagonists. One of her most effective tools in combating pomposity is the impertinent boy, a figure who permits her to subvert traditional ideas of male competency and power in arenas other than male-female encounters. Like a woman, a prepubescent boy is barred from the world of male authority; in Glaspell's hands the boy, like the woman, reveals that much conventional male authoritarianism is really empty bluster.

In "Freckles M'Grath," for example, Glaspell, in the person of Freckles the elevator boy, invades the staunchest strongholds of male power and power brokering—the governor's mansion and the Capitol building—to puncture male pomposity. Her subversive intent is apparent from the start, as she introduces the elevator boy as "by all odds the most important person" in the Capitol (57). The seriousness behind her humor is apparent when she reveals that an important reform bill is to be decided and that the vote of the weak and undependable Senator Stacy is crucial. The representative of masculine control in the story is Henry Ludlow, a lobbyist whose "iron-grey moustache," "sneering look," and condescending attitude toward those fools who think they "could beat" him mark him as a symbol of all that is wrong with male power brokering (61).

Indeed, none of the politicians, up to and including the governor, can stand up to Ludlow. Only Freckles the elevator boy can control him. And it is significant that he defeats Ludlow with weapons that the powerless, whether children or women, have always used—a bland exterior, a willingness to deceive, an unshakable apparent desire to do as commanded, along with a cunning ability to accomplish just the opposite of the command.

Glaspell completely inverts traditional expectations in the confrontation between Freckles and Ludlow, giving the boy all the weapons of control and leaving the lobbyist at his mercy. Anxious to keep Ludlow away from the voting senators, Freckles feigns mechanical problems with his elevator. First the car plunges, then it shoots to the top of the elevator shaft, where Freckles deposits the terrified and enraged Ludlow on the platform, locked away from the stairwell and unable to summon Freckles again. Freckles in his elevator is as powerful as Hippolytus in his chariot, rushing it "past the first and second floors like a thing let loose . . . past floors used for store-rooms, past floors used for nothing at all," until, "within a foot of the top floor of the building," it comes to "a rickety stop." The terrible Ludlow, maker and breaker of lives and reputations, is reduced to sputtering impotence. He is Freckles's "prisoner," rattling "the grating of the elevator shaft" and uttering "strange, loud noises, knowing all the while he could not make himself heard." Finally, he gives up, and, "alone in the State-house attic, Henry Ludlow, eminent lobbyist, sat down on a box and nursed his fury" (62–63).

Even when Freckles, having "won a great victory for reform" and "assured the Governor's future" by keeping Ludlow out of action until the reform bill is passed, finally deigns to rescue his captive, he insists on unconditional surrender. Not surprisingly, Ludlow is in a towering rage when Freckles goes to retrieve him. Here again the expected roles are reversed, with the boy "calmly gazing at the infuriated lobbyist," and the man of power, out of conrol, howling, "I'll beat your head open, you little brat!" But Freckles will have none of this. Ludlow is rescued only when, threatened with the possibility of being permanently stranded at the top of the elevator shaft, he grudgingly withdraws his threats and is permitted to descend by Freckles, who, gracious in victory, generously apologizes "on behalf of the elevator" to his humiliated, impotent prisoner (70). The powerless power broker has been defeated by the cunning boy, and none of the men of government is the wiser.

The naive protagonist's misunderstanding of politics is also used to deflate political pretension in "The Anarchist: His Dog." Here Stubby, like Freckles, a boy who must use his wits to survive in a hostile world, is faced with the loss of his beloved dog, Hero. Stubby, whose hard-earned money goes to help his family, cannot afford the two dollars he must pay for his dog's license. Through his comic but desperate struggle to keep his dog, Glaspell poses serious questions about the possibilities of justice for the powerless. Glaspell uses Stubby the way Mark Twain uses Huck Finn: the child understands none of the significance of what he says and does, but the reader does. None of the authority figures in the story shows any sympathy for Stubby and his problems at first. His father scoffs at the idea that justice might prevail among the poor: "Doing the best you could made no difference to the government; hard luck stories [don't] *go* when it comes to the laws of the land" (233). And the laws of survival are harsh too; when asked if Stubby could keep some of the money he earns for himself and his dog, his father responds savagely: "Look a-here. Just I'me tell you something. You're lucky if you git enough to *eat* this winter. Do you know there's talk of the factory shuttin' down? *Dog* tax! Why you're lucky if you git *shoes*" (233).

As he reflects on the callous indifference of what Pap Finn would call "the guvment," Stubby hears his father talking about anarchists, who are said to be "getting commoner" where he works. When asked what an anarchist is, his father defines it as "one that's against the government. He don't believe in the law and order. The real bad anarchists shoot them that tries to enforce the laws of the land" (234). The literal-minded Stubby, himself rankling under the injustice of a dog tax he cannot afford, declares himself an anarchist and resolves to shoot the policeman who will come to take Hero away from him. Always the American good sport, however, he thinks it only fair to warn his potential victim, writing a letter and sending it to the police department (he's afraid to go there himself):

This is to tell you I am an anarchist and do not believe in the law and the order and will shoot you when you come. I wouldn't a been an anarchist if I could a got the money and I tried to get it but I couldn't get it—not enough. I don't think the government had ought to take things you like like I like Hero so I am against the government. Thought I would tell you first. (237)

Of course, the story ends happily: the press hears of Stubby's predicament and the resulting coverage inspires "citizens with no sense of the dramatic" to send Stubby "enough money to [license] Hero through life" (239). The happy ending, however, does not vitiate the puncturing effect that Glaspell's comic technique, and Stubby's literal-minded innocence, have on paternal and governmental authority. (It is worth noting that the "good" authority figures at the end—the policeman who comes to get Hero and the two newspaper employees—are either very young or female, decidedly untraditional representatives of authority.) The domineering father is wrong; the callous government is powerless; a political movement as dangerous as anarchism is rendered sweetly comic.

Glaspell also uses another device to redefine male-female discourse: she creates unconventional heroes whose apparent weakness, judged by traditional standards of masculinity, would make them failures. Glaspell, however, presents such qualities as sensitivity, uncertainty, and introspection as admirable, creating men much closer to modern standards than they are to turn-of-the-century ideals of masculine omnipotence. In so doing, she enters the male-female discourse herself. As author, she has the power to select the qualities to be admired, and she exercises this power to create male characters who redefine ideas of masculine strength. These male politicians subvert traditional ideas of sex-role differences even more powerfully than the presentation of confrontational women would, since Glaspell uses them to attack male power from within the very stronghold of that power.

In "The Man of Flesh and Blood," for example, Philip Grayson subverts his own political ambitions in order to tell an audience of boys at a reform school that he, too, is imperfect, that he would be in their place except for good luck. Here Glaspell directly challenges the idea that heroism always resides in strength and control. Grayson admits weakness and wrongdoing; he admits he had lost control over his own life until a lucky break enabled him to seize it again. And it is in his admission of weakness, not his successful career, that his heroism is established.

A similar weakness and sensitivity to failure rather than success can be seen in "The Plea." Again Glaspell uses a man of political power to make her point, and again the hero defines himself in a public confession of weakness, not in words this time but in deed. Senator Harrison must vote on the fate of a boy sentenced to death for killing his father and stepmother. First, he votes against clemency, knowing that his political constituency is overwhelmingly opposed to lenience in this case. Upon reflection, however, he changes his mind in public and changes his vote. In conventional terms this might be seen as a cliché of moral victory, with Harrison gaining satisfaction from doing the right thing. Glaspell insists on the real risk of the gesture, however, subverting the idea that power and victory are always masculine prizes. Harrison knows that he has been "humiliated" before his constituents: "They would say he had not the courage of his convictions, that he was afraid" (39). It is clear that he will, in fact, be defeated in politics, that doing the right thing will have no public reward. It is equally clear that he is a hero, and Glaspell ends the story with an identification of Harrison with the natural world around him: "After all, it was not he alone who leaned to the softer side. There were the trees—they were permitted another chance to bud; there were the birds—they were allowed another chance to sing; there was the earth—to it was given another chance to yield" (40). Success for Harrison lies in softness and yielding, not in strength and control.

Even in a love story, the most conventional of forms, Glaspell does the unexpected. In "From A to Z," one of the most complex stories in the collection, Glaspell presents an unconventional couple and an unconventional ending. As she so often does, she disguises the subversive with much that is traditional. Her protagonist, Edna Willard, is a naive young woman fresh out of college and working at her first job, charming in her enthusiasm and youthful energy. To some extent Clifford, the man she falls in love with, also fulfills traditional expectations: older, sadder, and wiser than she, he serves as her guide and educator.

This, however, is as far as conventional expectations go in the story. Edna, like Virginia in "One of Those Impossible Americans," is characterized by an aggressive independence, and Clifford is an entirely unromantic subject. He is "far from young," with "more white than black in his hair," and "lines around his mouth" that reveal that "time, as well as forces more aging than time, had laid heavy hand on him" (78). Far from being a wise protector, he is a failure, one of the "men who, for one reason or other—age, dissipation, antiquated methods—had been pitched over" in his career (80). Not only is he a failure, he is also ill, with a persistent cough that is a mark of emotional as well as physical weakness. He is an alcoholic who can "no more stop himself," as an unsympathetic colleague puts it, than "an ant could stop a prairie fire" (85). Like so many of Glaspell's male figures, however, his appeal comes from his weakness. The strength in the story belongs to Edna, not Clifford.

Edna, despite a naïveté appropriate to a girl of 1912, is a startlingly modern figure. It is she who takes the initiative in the romantic encounter, not once but twice issuing invitations to Clifford and persisting despite his tactful refusals. What little physical contact there is between these ill-matched lovers is initiated by her. When they accidentally meet in a cloakroom and she is frightened by his apparent illness, she touches his arm, precipitating their one embrace: "All resistance gone, he swept her into his arms; he held her fiercely, and between sobs kissed her again and again" (92). Significantly, it is the male who sobs here, the male whose lips are "white," who can only "murmur words too inarticulate to hear." It is Clifford, not Edna, who flees from the encounter, ending the romance, which she has aggressively pursued. Again the subversive aspects of the story are masked; he leaves because he feels unworthy of her, too old and too ill to be her lover. This cannot hide the fact, however, that in this story the strong, aggressive woman pursues a man whose appeal is in his fragility and hesitation, his lack of the public trappings of success.

The essentially unconventional nature of the story is emphasized in its ending. As Edna unsuccessfully tries to find Clifford, she is rescued from exhaustion by Harold, a young man who works with her and is an altogether more appropriate mate than Clifford could ever be. The conventional happy ending of the two young people realizing they are made for each other, however, is rejected by Glaspell. Instead, the story ends with Edna wondering what happens to other people whose love is unsuccessful: "Did things like rain and street-cars and wet feet and a sore throat determine life? Was it that way with other people too? . . . And then did the Harolds come and take them where they said they belonged? Were there not *some* people strong enough to go where they wanted to go?" (100)

Clearly, it is Glaspell's suggestion that Edna is one of those people who will not always let things like "wet feet and a sore throat" determine her life. She rejects the idea that a Harold will come and take her where she is told she belongs. Edna will find her own place; she will be strong enough to go where she wants to go and to get there by herself. Strength, decisiveness, the determination to take control of her own life—these qualities so long admired in men are equally admirable in women like Edna, young though she is.

If Glaspell's feminism is clear, however, her awareness of the taste of a large popular audience is equally evident. She wrote not for a specialized or intellectual market but, rather, for the general public. Her stories originally appeared in mass-appeal publications such as *Harper's Monthly Magazine, American Mercury,* and *Ladies' Home Journal;* and the collection in *Lifted Masks* was critically praised for making a "serious suggestion toward good citizenship and square dealing" as well as for being "heartily funny" (*Outlook, 505*). In order to maintain this mass audience without compromising her feminist convictions, Glaspell relies on several consistent themes and devices: an appeal to popular American virtues like individualism and a sense of honor, an identification of her most likable characters with the natural world, and a skillful use of sentiment tightly controlled by her pervasive humor. All of these devices create the masks behind which her subversive feminism can flourish.

Glaspell's respect for individualism and her sense of the sacredness of the public trust can be seen with particular clarity in "The Preposterous Motive," another story in which her protagonist is a male politician with a serious decision to make. Governor John Berriman faces a choice between ethics and convenience, between conscience and power. Part of a behind-the-scenes political deal, he has tacitly agreed to make an appointment of questionable ethics for great personal gain. He has heretofore given his political decisions little thought, functioning as a cog in a machine rather than as an individual: "He had been put in by the machine, and it had always been assumed that he was machine property. . . . He had an idea that it was proper for him to vote with his friends, and he always did it" (180). By chance, however, he discusses his forthcoming decision with his brother Hiram, an unsophisticated farmer who "knew but little of political methods and had primitive ideas about honesty." Hiram is the first person to ask the governor if his decision is not expedient but right; when John responds that he has no choice, Hiram is contemptuous: "I don't see how you figure that out. You're Governor of the State, and your own boss, ain't you?" (181)

Faced with this straightforward challenge to both his sense of independence and his conscience, John is dumbfounded: "It was the first time in all his life that anyone had squarely confronted John Berriman with the question whether or not he was his own boss, and for some reason it went deep into his soul, and rankled there" (181). He blusters and argues with his brother, but Hiram insists on calling a spade a spade: "What do you mean by saying you're going to put a dishonest man in there to make laws for the people, to watch over them and protect them? If you don't think he's the best man the State has . . . in God's name, *why do you appoint him?*" (183).

As he continues to challenge John's decision, and to scoff at arguments of policy, political obligation, and expedience, Hiram is clearly the voice of conscience: "You're in a position now, John, to be a friend to the people. It ain't many of us ever get the chance of doin' a great thing. . . . Don't you stick to any foolish notions about bein' faithful to the party; it ain't the party that needs helpin'. Your first duty is to the people of this State" (185). Guided by this unarguable wisdom, John Berriman makes the right, not the convenient, appointment, for the first time in his political life satisfying the demands of conscience instead of comfort.

Glaspell, however, does not sacrifice artistic principle in catering to popular taste. While the story has a comfortable happy ending, it is far from naive. Like Philip Grayson in "The Man of Flesh and Blood," John Berriman finds that his act of courage and honesty is fated to be misunderstood by fellow politicians, if not by old-fashioned farmers. His opponent's supporters see it as "a simple matter of selling out; they knew, of course, that it could be nothing else. . . . [T]hey wondered, sneeringly, why he did not 'fix up a better story.' Did he think people were fools? And even the men who profited by the situation puzzled their brains for weeks trying to understand it. There was something behind it, of course" (189).

Glaspell is also aware of the powerful faith in the natural world to be found in the reading public of turn-of-the-century America. It is no accident, for example, that Hiram's moral wisdom in "The Preposterous Motive" is shaped by rural, not urban, life. A similar faith in the power of nature to shape human behavior is found in "His America," one of Glaspell's most serious and emotionally charged stories. In "His America" Herman Beckman, a self-educated, hard-working farmer who has based his life on the principles of Marcus Aurelius, is faced with the condescension of his son Fritz, a brand-new college graduate who means to substitute the standard of a new generation of Americans—material success—for the idealism of his father's contemporaries. Faced with his son's contempt for his own rigorous moral standards, Herman is hurt and appalled. After thoughtful communion with the natural world, however, he rejects Fritz's accusation that idealism is old-fashioned and impractical. As he gazes out over his moonlit acres, he reaffirms his faith in his old-fashioned standards. He sees "an America of realities, and yet an America of dreams," an America of "strength and the dignity and harmony of unity." American idealism is not dead, Glaspell suggests, as long as men of the soil like Herman Beckman still come to this country with dreams "inside [their] hearts" (214).

"His America" is also an excellent example of Glaspell's ability to use popular sentiment without indulging in it. The story is a powerful statement of faith in American idealism, but it is neither weak nor oversimplified. Herman maintains his faith in his dreams, his hard work, and his own integrity, but this is hardly a conventional happy ending. Even the moonlit landscape, which provides him consolation, is a reminder of material failure; those very acres are the ones that must be sold to pay pressing debts. And his pride in his son's success has turned into disillusionment in the face of Fritz's condescension and materialism. Herman's faith in America comes at the expense of faith in the son he can no longer respect, and his story gives voice to popular sentiments without ever becoming sentimental.

Perhaps the most effective device with which Glaspell manages to disguise her subversive subtext, win a popular turn-of-the-century audience, and still speak to modern readers is her pervasive humor. In her best work Glaspell uses humor both to defuse potentially threatening aspects of her feminism and to control potentially sentimental material.

In "One of Those Impossible Americans," for example, sentimental subject matter is controlled by an underlying comic structure. Virginia's encounter with the awkward William in the lingerie section of the French department store is comic from the beginning, since Virginia is so aware of titillating overtones that never occur to William. This situation admits Virginia to a position of power while at the same time preventing the more pathetic material—William's description of his wife's emotional problems—from becoming dominant.

Glaspell's emphasis on comic visual effects controls the potentially pathetic material throughout the story. At the outset the reader's attention is focused on the scarlet stockings, comically grotesque in their inappropriateness as a subject of conversation between William and Virginia. A later visual focus is equally vivid, equally comic, and equally distracting from the pathetic subject matter. Just as William begins to describe his wife's condition to Virginia, he is interrupted by his discovery, in another shop window, of a showy opera cloak: "It was yellow; it was long; it was billowy; it was insistently and recklessly regal." The violet velvet dress he selects to accompany the gaudy cloak is equally excessive, and his choice in hats includes "a rainbow done into flowers, and . . . the kind of black hat to outdo any rainbow" (13).

This comic excess is intensified when, in a markedly proper and dainty little tea shop, William astounds the patrons by "dropping the yellow opera cloak. While he was stooping to pick it up the violet velvet gown slid backward and Virginia had to steady it until he could regain position." His comic awkwardness becomes even more pronounced: "The legs of Virginia's friend and the legs of the tea-table did not seem well adapted to each other. He towered like a human mountain over the dainty thing. . . . It seemed Providence—or at least so much of it as was represented by the management of that shop—had never meant fat people to drink tea. . . . Expansively, and not softly, he discoursed of these things. What did they think a fellow was to do with his *knees?* Didn't they sell tea enough to afford any decent chairs?" (19).

It is only after this comic display that William makes his pathetic revelations—that his wife, her health broken by her harsh existence in former years, has no awareness of their present wealth and that he has made his gorgeous purchases hoping to distract her from her obsession with poverty. Earlier in the story these revelations might have been only sentimental, yet, controlled by Glaspell's use of comedy, they are forceful and surprising. Like Virginia, the reader has made the mistake of seeing William as a kindly buffoon; with Virginia the reader discovers the mistake and judges him with different standards.

In *Lifted Masks*, then, Susan Glaspell speaks with the voice of feminist conviction. Avoiding confrontation or polemic, she still suggests some of the severe limitations of conventional male-female discourse in turn-of-the-century America. She also reveals that much female potential for strength and independence and male potential for gentleness and sensitivity still lies untapped. In encouraging her popular reading public to laugh at attitudes conventionally taken with the utmost seriousness, she manages to exploit the very popular sentiments whose shortcomings she develops with such telling wit.

WORKS CITED

Glaspell, Susan. *Lifted Masks*. New York: Frederick A. Stokes, 1912. Reprinted in *Lifted Masks and Other Works*. Ann Arbor: University of Michigan Press, 1993.
"Lifted Masks." *Outlook*, 2 November 1912: 505.

Forging a Woman's Identity in Susan Glaspell's Fiction

Veronica Makowsky

Although Susan Glaspell is best known today for her plays, she was also the successful author of nine novels from 1909 to 1945 as well as many short stories. Unlike her plays, her fiction is readily accessible to the reader, with its use of an omniscient narrator or a reliable central consciousness, easily comprehensible time schemes, and characters who serve as clarifying foils. Nevertheless, many of her novels do break away from the conventionally structured plot, which Elizabeth Ammons describes as "linear (starts at one point and moves forward to another point)" and "pinnacle-oriented (moves by stages or steps, often clearly identifiable, to a climactic high point)" (51). In contrast to the "well-made play," Glaspell's novels often begin in the middle, with her heroine trapped in an untenable situation from which she needs to think backward and forward in order to extricate herself. Her plots cannot be visualized as arrows slanted upward but, rather, as spirals in which her heroine returns in thought or actuality to a significant part of her past, which she can now understand on a higher level; this comprehension enables yet another turn upward, and so on. In this way Glaspell's work resembles that of many early-twentieth-century women writers in its tendency to invent new forms more expressive of a woman's experience (Ammons 5).

As a highly skilled writer, Glaspell had a command of the strengths and weaknesses of both genres, drama and fiction, and knew how to exploit them. Unlike her plays' reliance on dialogue and action, her fiction often presents the meditative, subtly nuanced, and somewhat abstract reflections of a central consciousness. Although her novels do exhibit more dialogue and less reflection after her years with the Provincetown Players, her fiction remains much more evocative of Henry James than Eugene O'Neill.

Glaspell's fiction does, however, resemble her plays in two significant ways. First, she often constructs scenes around a dramatic confrontation in which gestures as well as words convey meaning. For example, in her short story "Contrary to Precedent" (1904), two women on a porch acknowledge the love of the younger woman for the husband of the older one. In a telling gesture, the married woman repeatedly twists the leaves of the growing plants as she undoubtedly wishes to strangle her young rival.

The second similarity of Glaspell's fiction to her plays is the one I wish to discuss in this essay. Her fiction may be traditional in form, but her themes are quite unconventional. In a sense she is the heiress of the women authors of nineteenth-century domestic fiction, but she takes their conclusions to their logical extreme. In *Woman's Fiction: A Guide to Novels by and about Women in America* Nina Baym sketches the typical plot of such a novel: "It is the story of a young girl who is deprived of the supports she has rightly or wrongly depended on to sustain her throughout life and is faced with the necessity of winning her own way in the world" (11). Glaspell's heroines face similar reversals, although theirs may be the loss of cherished beliefs as well as familial and economic deprivations. Glaspell's heroines also demonstrate the self-reliance that Baym notes in their precursors: they find solutions for their problems, "all [of which] involve the heroine's accepting of herself as female while rejecting the equation of female with child. Thus, while commiserating with their heroine in difficulties not of her own making, the stories hold her entirely responsible for overcoming them" (17). Finally, in many of Glaspell's novels, as in those Baym describes, "the men . . . are less important to the heroine's emotional life than the women" (38), or, for Glaspell, the heroine's exploration of herself.

Glaspell's fiction does however exhibit three important differences from that of her nineteenth-century predecessors. First, her heroines are not usually unmarried young girls seeking a happy ending in marriage but, rather, mature women, ranging in age from their mid-twenties to their sixties, who generally are or have been married. Second, for Glaspell "And they lived happily ever after" is the beginning, not the end, of her heroine's life, and, significantly, she questions the happiness of those endings. Susan K. Harris states that "the middle portions" of nineteenth-century women's novels "establish an area of female independence, competence, and emotional complexity" (21), which the endings of these novels in conventional marriages seemingly negate. Glaspell's novels allow her heroines to continue the quest for self-reliance, with marriage as a means toward self-knowledge, not an end in itself. Third, the novels that Baym describes end with "a new woman and, by extension, the reformation of the world immediately around her as this new person calls out different relations and responses to her environment" (20). The reformed "world" of these novels is based upon, if not limited to, the domestic or private, but Glaspell's novels stress the future in that such domestic reformation can lead to a better world for all humanity. Further, Glaspell's novels are less optimistic than those Baym discusses: the heroine's success is marked by her ability to continue to hope for a better world, not the achievement of that world.

Glaspell's novels divide into three sets of three. The first group consists of the novels written before she began her career as a playwright for the Provincetown Players: *The Glory of the Conquered* (1909), *The Visioning* (1911), and *Fidelity* (1915). Glaspell only resumed her career as a novelist after her break with the Provincetown Players, her sojourn in Greece with her husband, George Cram Cook, and Cook's death in January 1924. She then published *Brook Evans* (1928), *Fugitive's Return* (1929), and *Ambrose Holt and Family* (1931). The theater once more interrupted the flow of her fiction, as her play *Alison's House* won the 1931 Pulitzer Prize and she directed the Midwestern Federal Theater Project in the mid-1930s. She again returned to fiction and, before her death in 1948, produced *The Morning Is near Us* (1939), *Norma Ashe* (1942), and *Judd Rankin's Daughter* (1945). In each of these periods Glaspell's basic plot remains that of the heroine achieving self-reliance while retaining her hope for the future. The confidence of that conclusion, though, varies with Glaspell's personal circumstances and those of the era, as I will show through the discussion of one novel from each period: *Fidelity, Fugitive's Return,* and *Norma Ashe.*

The imagery of circumferences and edges as the boundary of the social circle permeates *Fidelity,* as it would many of Glaspell's plays such as *The*

Outside (1920) and *The Verge* (1922). A local doctor meditates about "how hard it was for women whose experiences had all fallen within the circle of things as they should be to understand a thing that was— disrupting" (*F* 15). Ruth Holland, as the well-to-do offspring of one of Freeport's most respected families, begins her life firmly entrenched behind these barricades of ignorance for women (Noe 76). Ruth is not satisfied by banal comfort but longs for something beyond the sphere of domesticity. She wants to go to college, but her father will not allow it, since he believes women should simply marry and raise children. Although thwarted here, her need would find expression elsewhere, since, "with Ruth, the desire to go to college had been less a definite craving for knowledge than a diffused longing for an enlarged experience" (*F* 41), one she believes she has found through her love for a married man, Stuart Williams, with whom she eventually leaves Freeport for life in Colorado.

If the story ended here, the title would mean that, while Ruth and Stuart are committing an act of infidelity, adultery, they remain faithful to a higher law, that of true love. Glaspell provides an ironic twist because Ruth and Stuart do not live happily ever after; their relationship outside society becomes as constricting as society's conventions. The mountains that encircle their ranch represent both their isolation from society and the barriers that they have erected between them. Because Stuart's wife vengefully persists in refusing a divorce, Ruth does not bear the children she so badly wants. The gregarious Stuart is cut off from the camaraderie and competition of the business world. A hand-to-mouth life-style further cramps their attempt to be free spirits. Meaningful communication between them ceases, for they fear to exacerbate each other's hurts and losses. Ruth understands what has happened to them when she concludes that "love should be able to be a part of the rest of life; the big relationship, but one among others; the most intense interest, but one with other interests. Unrooted, detached, it might for the time be the more intense, but it had less ways of saving itself" (*F* 276).

Glaspell again confounds our expectations when, eleven years after Ruth left Freeport, she returns to visit her dying father. Although I have related these events chronologically in order to show how Glaspell subverts the conventional romance, Ruth's return to Freeport is the start of the novel, a beginning in the middle in order that Ruth might spiral backward, as well as outward, in her quest for self-knowledge. Consequently, instead of experiencing a hackneyed, unambivalent vindication of true love, Ruth is stricken "dumb in this new realization of how terrible it had been for them all" to remain in town in the scandal's aftermath while Ruth and her lover had left for a new life (*F* 197). The Hollands needed the support of society; they were incapable of self-reliance, so their retreat to their domestic circle was not warm and nurturing but, instead, bleak and blighting. Ruth's mother died brokenhearted, her father became bitter, and the lives of her siblings were warped in various ways. Glaspell is certainly an idealistic writer, but she does not wear rose-colored glasses and clearly delineates the price paid for maintaining an ideal in the face of society's opposition.

Ruth's response to her family's disintegration is placed in context by Glaspell's use of two foils, Mildred Woodbury and Annie Morris Herman. Mildred is a young woman in love with a married man. She seeks out Ruth, whom she idealizes, to affirm her decision to flaunt convention. In the light of her stultified relationship with Stuart and the plight of her family, Ruth is unfaithful to her belief in love and advises Mildred to take a trip to Europe with a local society matron. Mildred is sorely disillusioned but takes Ruth's advice, and her last appearance in the novel shows how she has profited from it: upon her return from Europe she is putting on airs about redecorating the family house and dating a rich man.

Annie Morris Herman shows Ruth how it is possible to remain alive spiritually despite poverty and a less-than-ideal marriage. Annie, a poor girl, had admired the socialite Ruth in high school and followed her life with interest. In order to give Ruth time to recuperate from the knowledge of what she had done to her family, Annie shelters Ruth at her farm, which she, an enormously hard worker, runs while she raises her children. Unlike Ruth, Annie has managed to sustain her spirit through reading of the greater world outside of Freeport. For Ruth, "a whole new world seemed to open from these things that were vital to Annie":

There was promise in them—a quiet road out from the hard things of self. There were new poets in the world; there were bold new thinkers; there was an amazing new art; science was reinterpreting the world and workers and women were setting themselves free. (*F* 269)

Heartened by the sense that she could have spiritual comrades in her challenging of convention and an intellectual context for her rebellious feelings, Ruth returns to Colorado.

Stuart learns that his wife has had a change of heart and will grant a divorce, but Glaspell will not allow us the conventional happy ending here either. Ruth offers a new definition of fidelity when she decides to end her relationship with Stuart because "it isn't unfaithful to turn from a person you have nothing more to offer, for whom you no longer make life a living thing. It's more faithful to go" (*F* 419). Ruth will join the free spirits in New York, but she does not believe her union with Stuart was a mistake, since "love could not fail if it left one richer than it had found one" (422) and, in leaving her richer, had contributed to life's progress. The last lines of the novel are enthusiastically optimistic: "Life was wonderful, limitless, a great adventure for which one must have great courage, glad faith. Let come what would come!—she was moving on!" (420).

As the ending indicates, Glaspell wrote *Fidelity* in a period of personal and cultural growth. Her flouting of convention with the married George Cram Cook had ended happily with his divorce and their marriage in 1913. They moved to Provincetown, Massachusetts, and New York City's Greenwich Village, centers of artistic ferment and socialist and feminist fervor, where they would begin the work of founding the highly experimental and successful Provincetown Players. When Glaspell returned to writing fiction in the late 1920s, her novels, such as *Fugitive's Return*, also reflect her changed life and times.

Fugitive's Return begins with what seems like the end of its heroine, since Irma Lee Shraeder is preparing to take her own life. Three years ago her husband left her for another woman, and her only child, her small daughter Bertha, or "Birdie," recently died. Irma looks at her mature body in a mirror and sees it as "less desirable now, breasts, hips, fuller" (2). Since Irma really sees no self beyond her roles as wife, mother, or sex object, her plan of suicide seems a logical extension of that lack of self; if no gaze validates her existence, she really does not exist. Irma is saved by the timely arrival of a sister figure, her cousin Janet, who sees Irma as an individual with desires of her own, not merely a supplier of the wants of others. In the remainder of the novel Glaspell takes us backward and forward in Irma's life to discover the source of her negligible self-image and what she will experience to become a person in her own right.

In her youth Irma had an incessant sense of failing to be what she should be. Her family had once owned most of the west side of town, but only the land around the homestead remained theirs. Irma's father was a foreman over day laborers and her mother a well-intentioned but slatternly housekeeper. If Irma had not known any other life, she might have simply accepted her life as it was, but she was constantly reminded of an ostensibly better way of life through her wealthy cousin Janet, who kept trying to include Irma in her social set. These attempts were doomed to failure, for, aside from Janet, these girls were snobs who were more interested in the fact that Irma lacked an indoor toilet than that Irma lacked self-confidence. Glaspell is not indicting Irma for acquiescing to superficial values but is demonstrating, instead, how hard it is to form a self from an impoverished life outside a social order. She writes of Irma's longing for Janet's way of life: "She wanted these things in common, and in the security of them she could more freely have been herself" (*FR* 113).

Irma does not become more herself but less so. She deadens herself without and within because she believes she is so vulnerable to the opinions of others. She keeps her countenance "impassive," a "mask" (*FR* 125, 6), and so appears "haughty" to others (3), who, repelled by her armor, simply reinforce her sense of herself as not worth knowing. She becomes attracted to a young farmer, who "was unlike anyone she had known, and Irma came to the conclusion the difference was in his acting upon what went on within him" (135). Horace does not wear a mask and is not afraid to risk showing his feelings to Irma. Despite, or perhaps because of, the way he makes her feel "a fulness, richness, beauty in which there was also pain" (137), she rejects him, since she believes marrying a farmer would only confirm her family's fallen status.

Irma then compounds her betrayal of her true self by marrying Dan Shraeder, a man from Janet's set with a "careless, worldly sort of gaiety" (*FR* 160). She does not love Dan but, rather, the image of herself that he sees. "She was excited by being desired" (159). In addition, she believes marriage to Dan will keep her safe from deeply feeling or truly living: "Her love for Horace opened her to it all, and her love for Dan enclosed her with itself" (164). A caged, limited woman is not good company, so Irma gradually alienates Dan by her inability to let herself go and authentically respond to him, either by participating in his life or letting him into hers.

Instead, Irma constructs two defenses against life. The first is the remodeling and tending of her house on Cape Cod, which she uses as a fortress to keep her away from others and often from Dan, whose work is in Boston. Her second defense is vicariously living through her daughter. She had wanted a son because "life seemed too complex for a girl; it seemed her own difficulties would be more likely to reappear in the life of a daughter, and that a son might free himself of them" (*FR* 174). Had Birdie survived, the pressure of her mother's hopes may have caused "difficulties" enough, since Irma was refusing Birdie her individuality, her self, by believing that, "in seeing pleasures, opportunities, come to her little girl, it would be as if she herself had had them when she had not had them" (191). Irma is also denying herself by attempting to rewrite the past that was part of her.

Her cousin Janet not only prevents Irma's suicide but also sets her on the road to recovery by presenting her with the passport of a friend, Myra Freeman, who could not use it. The identity of Myra is the first role Irma tries in her attempt to escape herself and her memories. If the letter *i* is exchanged for *y*, then Myra is an anagram of Irma; *Freeman* foreshadows the way this transformed name will lead to Irma's transformation and liberation. Initially, though, Irma remains without a real identity, since on her travels she allows others to believe she is unable to speak. Because she does not speak, she listens, and others "could say to her what they could not say to one another" (38). If Irma Shraeder no longer exists, she does not have to be defended, and the receptivity of "Myra" allows her to learn.

Irma's travels as Myra eventually take her to Delphi, where she rents the only house on the ruins of the temple. Here she takes on another role, the dignified and enigmatic "Kyria of the Archai" (*FR* 50). Some of the villagers believe she is "the prophetess of the temple, and that she did not speak because the temple had fallen" (51). Sheltered by her silence and her role and nurtured by the elusive beauty of Delphi, Irma begins to feel. As if people remain too threatening, she starts with animals, such as pet lambs about to be butchered and birds threatened by the slingshots of small boys. Finally, as she sees the villagers sadistically about to hang a stray dog, she speaks: "Was it for this Jesus died?" (89). Although these words represent progress, Irma is still playing a role, that of Christ, for she believes that "out of those mists had he come—out of his silence, compelled to raise voice because they were cruel to one another, driven to speech because the beasts could not speak" (91).

Irma's path toward an identity is furthered not only by the roles that she plays but also by four women of Delphi, who serve as foils. Vascelo, an angry young widow whom no one will marry because of her crippled son, represents a self-destructive way to deal with solitude. Her sister, Stamula, is the traditional wife and mother, well integrated into her subservient place in society and seemingly happy in it, the role Irma believed she was playing as Dan's wife and Birdie's mother. Theodora, an attractive dancing and laughing refugee, uses her charms on men but is willing to tease and torment another woman, much like the snobbish girls of Irma's childhood. Her victim is Constantina, a dwarfed shepherd girl rejected by her father because she was not a son and raped by the man who would become Theodora's betrothed because she would not relinquish her rights to her flock. Constantina is the deformed and abused woman who represents Irma's image of her inner self.

Since these four women are all defined by their relations with men, Glaspell implies that the true test of Irma's recovering self is her next relationship with a man, the archaeologist John Knight, who becomes her lover. Irma is perfectly aware that Knight is not her knight; he will not rescue her, nor does she need rescuing. He clings to a decade-long unrequited love for another woman, but Irma is not devastated by this. She can "leave him what he was, loving him for it, even though it withheld from her, and dwelling with him where it was hers to dwell" (*FR* 294). She does not dwell with him long, for she leaves him and Delphi in order to help another woman, Constantina, who has killed her rapist. Irma and Stamula help Constantina escape over the mountain; the new woman and the traditional woman unite to help an abused woman, who is a part of their identity as women in a male-dominated society. Since Irma knows the villagers' anger would prevent her from living in Delphi, she decides to return to the United States, where, in the novel's last lines, "she would labor in her vineyard. In her own vineyard would she labor" (324).

Although this ending seems to affirm Irma's love of humanity, demonstrated by her rescue of Constantina, and her increasing self-reliance, manifested in her resolution to labor independently, it is different from Ruth Holland's spirited march into the future at the conclusion of *Fidelity*. Like Voltaire's Candide, who resolves to cultivate his own garden, Irma may be making a retreat, if only a temporary one, from a troubled world. The tentativeness of this conclusion, and the difference between Ruth and Irma, lies in Glaspell's personal loss by the death of a loved one, George Cram Cook, in 1924 and her prior professional loss of a career as a playwright by Cook and Glaspell's removal to Greece in 1922. When Glaspell returned to the United States in 1924 she, like Irma, faced the difficulties of reconstructing an identity in middle age, and thus the optimism of *Fugitive's Return* is tempered by the fourteen years that had passed since *Fidelity*. In *Norma Ashe,* a novel written late in life, after the Depression and amid World War II, Glaspell presents us with a heroine whose difficulties are even greater and hopes even more tenuous.

If Irma Lee Shraeder is pathetic at the beginning of *Fugitive's Return,* the woman we see in the opening section of *Norma Ashe* is grotesque. Mrs. Utterbach is the shrill and shabby proprietor of a boardinghouse in a once genteel, now run-down neighborhood in Iroquois City, Illinois. She treats her boarders like "riffraff" (56) and tries to prevent her daughter, Lorna, from associating with them because she wants Lorna to be a part of the town's high society, to which they no longer can afford to belong. As she screams at the coal man, who will not deliver the coal without cash in advance, she fails to notice a well-dressed visitor in her parlor. Her closest college friend, Rosie, has sought Norma Ashe to reinspire her youthful idealism, but she cannot see Norma in the enviously materialistic Mrs. Utterbach. Nor can Norma Ashe Utterbach herself, who, jolted from her rut by Rosie's visit, begins her search for her lost self: "She was trying to find out what became of Norma Ashe. She really did not know, and for some reason she could not have given, she had to know" (66).

In an extended flashback Glaspell traces the trajectory that led Norma to become a woman her earlier self would have abhorred. At Pioneer College she and Rosie had belonged to a small group of disciples who clustered around a charismatic philosophy teacher, Joseph Langley. His brand of idealism is difficult to identify from the novel, as if by this point Glaspell were disappointed by too many *isms* to delineate the specifics of one more, but it involves a belief that, like the creatures that made a great leap from the water to the land, human beings were about to make an evolutionary leap in spiritual progress. Under his tutelage Norma apparently experienced some sort of mystical vision of this future. Although Langley died before the disciples graduated from college, he believed he had prepared them to promote and benefit from the evolutionary leap. Norma was to do so by attending graduate school at the University of Chicago on scholarship and becoming a college teacher who would inspire others as Langley had inspired her.

Norma loses her ideals and identity not through selfishness or evil but, instead, through chance, compassion, and love, all of which Glaspell believes are genuine parts of life that can be denied only by denying life itself. On her train away from Pioneer College Norma meets Max Utterbach, when their train is delayed and rerouted because of a wreck on the line. Her life becomes rerouted as she feels compassion for Max, who is accompanying the coffin of his mother and is stricken by guilt for neglecting her at the end of her life. Eventually, Norma loves Max:

> The passion that grew between them . . . all sweeping into the passion of man for woman, woman for man, the hot sharp need to weld into one that frightened them both, making them so nearly one it was almost the same, almost as if already they had merged their lives and there could be no drawing back before what was and had to be. (*NA* 119)

As this description indicates, Glaspell is not denying that passion is a necessary part of life but, rather, is suggesting the threat to individual identity if this merging is mistaken for all of life.

Norma sacrifices her identity as scholar and becomes a wife and mother. As a newlywed in Texas, it "still seemed strange when she and Max were referred to as the Utterbachs" (*NA* 136), but, because of his need for her and her love for him, she eventually becomes resigned to the fact that "I can't be myself and be his wife" (165). She even seems to accept Max's relegation of her ideals to domestic trivia, when he tells her,

"You keep the dream and let me make the money" (166). His shady dealings in Texas cause them to move suddenly to Illinois, where his obsessive need for money causes him to make risky speculations. When Max is killed, impatiently trying to fix a piece of equipment in his plant, as if money could not be produced fast enough, Norma is left a bankrupt widow with two small children and begins her decline into the haglike keeper of the boardinghouse.

Norma seems to hit bottom when she must travel to Chicago to sell the diamond Max had given her, her last keepsake, to free her son, Fred, from jail on a bootlegging charge. She vows never to return to Iroquois City, taking a job, instead, as the hired "girl" at a Chicago boardinghouse. Although she has fallen even farther in social status, she begins her spiritual ascent. When she hears one of Langley's disciples, Austin Wurthen, lecture at the University of Chicago, she recognizes that this factory owner has twisted Langley's words to use them in support of paternalistic capitalism, a honeyed-over exploitation of workers. She rises in the lecture hall and denounces this perversion of Langley's teachings. When she does so, she regains the jewel, her idealistic vision, which she had traded for Max's diamond: "Not as that which has faded did she see it now, but like a diamond, imperishable, forever lighted from within itself" (*NA* 236).

Norma feels her children have failed her, since Fred is a criminal and Lorna has married a sleazy charlatan, "Doc" Staunton, and is running the boardinghouse with him. After her ejection from Wurthen's lecture Norma is approached by a student, Scott Neubolt, who is genuinely curious about the wisdom beneath the appearance of an impoverished washerwoman. He is inspired by her ideals and helps her find a better position and place to live. Norma comes to regard him as her spiritual son, who will carry her and Langley's ideals into the future. Although Norma once more loses her faith, when she receives the false information that Langley mocked his disciples behind their backs, she leaves Chicago and returns to Iroquois City rather than disillusion Scott. Her refusal to tell Scott what she now believes to be the truth suggests that she does not really believe that Langley was a fraud but, rather, feels too old and warped to maintain his ideals.

Near the end of the novel Norma works like a servant in her daughter and Doc's boardinghouse, despite her failing health, and moves like a zombie through one wretched day after another. When Doc Staunton, with rough kindness, finds a box of Norma's college books and notebooks and brings them to her, she believes he is mocking her, and her anger at him snaps her out of her lethargy. She vows that "this time [she] will see *all the way*. And it was not herself, after an hour, raised her head from the place it had come to rest" (*NA* 349). This ending can be interpreted in two ways. If Norma has died and someone else has raised her head, she has died trying to reclaim her vision and, in that sense, has reclaimed her identity. If the power of that vision has allowed her to raise her head, she has also triumphed spiritually. In either case, however, she remains sick and old, surrounded by uncongenial companions. Her idealism has changed her attitude, but it has not changed the world, not even her own circumstances. Only through Scott Neubolt, the new bolt of light, does the hope of future change remain alive.

With this relatively bleak ending Glaspell seems to be suggesting that idealism as yet has no power over the external world but that the belief in such ideals keeps us human and makes life seem worth living. A woman can choose to be the shrewish automaton Mrs. Utterbach or the inwardly happy idealist Norma Ashe. The extreme tentativeness of this "happy" ending reflects Glaspell's own life at this time. In the 1930s her lover, the novelist Norman Matson, left her for a nineteen-year-old girl. She faced financial difficulties, intermittent writer's block, a drinking problem, and deteriorating health. Around her she saw first the Depression and then the start of World War II, as if to reinforce the fact that the ideals of her youth had changed nothing.

Throughout Glaspell's novels, however, even her less optimistic later ones, she maintains her belief in a woman's power to choose her identity, despite male domination, social conventions, or economic hardships. These novels deserve to be read today for their sensitive yet realistic depictions of women's lives and for the pleasure they give as well-crafted work. Glaspell's fiction should return to print so that new generations of women and men can learn from this compassionate, perceptive, and highly skilled novelist. Despite our canonical presuppositions, something significant did occur in the American novel between Henry James and Ernest Hemingway.

NOTE

Works by Susan Glaspell discussed in the text are abbreviated as follows: *Fidelity* (*F*), *Fugitive's Return* (*FR*), *and Norma Ashe* (*NA*).

WORKS CITED

Ammons, Elizabeth. *Conflicting Stories: American Women Writers at the Turn into the Twentieth Century*. New York: Oxford University Press, 1991.

Baym, Nina. *Woman's Fiction: A Guide to Novels by and about Women*. Ithaca: Cornell University Press, 1978.

Glaspell, Susan. *Fidelity*. Boston: Small, Maynard, 1915.

———. *Fugitive's Return*. New York: Stokes, 1929.

———. *Norma Ashe*. Philadelphia: Lippincott, 1942.

Harris, Susan K. *Nineteenth-Century American Women's Novels: Interpretive Strategies*. Cambridge: Cambridge University Press, 1990.

Noe, Marcia. "A Critical Biography of Susan Glaspell." Ph.D. diss., University of Iowa, 1976. (I am also indebted to this work for biographical information.)

Susan Glaspell Chronology

1876	Born July 1, in Davenport, Iowa, the middle child and only daughter of Elmer and Alice Feeney Keating Glaspell. [In later years Glaspell gave her birthdate as 1882.] Her paternal grandparents, Susan—for whom she was named—and Silas, were early settlers of Davenport. The family lived in a rented house at 502 Cedar Street and moved nine years later to 317 E. 12th Street, which remained in the family throughout Glaspell's life and is standing today.
1890–94	Attended Central High School. Unlike her brothers Frank and Charles (known as Ray), who were not good students and left school after one year, Glaspell excelled, taking the most difficult Latin track program. She gave a commencement speech entitled "Songs That Live."
1894	Began newspaper work, first as a reporter for the *Davenport Morning Republican* and then as society editor for *The Weekly Outlook,* under the name Susie Keating Glaspell. Met Cook family for first time.
September 1897–June 1899	Attended Drake University, graduating with a Ph.B. degree in Philosophy. Known for her oratory skills, she represented Drake in a state debate, giving a talk entitled "Bismark and European Politics." Wrote feature articles for the Drake paper, the *Delphic.* At class exercises presented the only short story.

June 1899	Began to work for the *Des Moines News* the day after graduation, covering the State House and the Legislature; also wrote a human interest column under byline "The Newsgirl."
December 1900– April 1901	Covered the Hossack murder investigation and trial for the *News;* articles became the basis for *Trifles* and "A Jury of Her Peers."
Spring 1901– Spring 1902	Returned to family home in Davenport; wrote short stories, many of which were based on newspaper experiences. In contest of February 26, 1902, won $150 prize from *Black Cat* magazine for her story "The Work of the Unloved Libby"; in October 1904 won $500 *Black Cat* first prize for the story "For the Love of the Hills."
1902–4	In Chicago. Enrolled for summer session 1902 in the graduate program in English at the University of Chicago (nonmatriculating). Worked as a free-lance reporter for Chicago newspapers, including the *Chicago Daily Review.*
1904–7	Returned to Davenport. Publication of work in national magazines such as *Harper's, Leslie's,* and *Munsey's* made her a local celebrity, often featured in newspaper interviews about her developing career. Continued to write and work on first novel, *The Glory of the Conquered,* based on her Chicago experiences. Traveled to Chicago and New York.
1907	Attended meetings of the newly formed Monist Society, a group of free thinkers in Davenport, headed by George Cram "Jig" Cook and Floyd Dell. In November Cook and Dell visited Glaspell, and Cook began a friendship with her, while awaiting divorce from his first wife, Sarah, so he could marry his fiancé, Molly Price. Details of the friendship appear in Cook's letters to Price.
1908	Price and Cook married. Glaspell left Davenport

and traveled to Europe, spending eight months in Paris, with Drake college friend Lucy Huffaker.

1909 *The Glory of the Conquered* published. Returned to Davenport, planning to go once more to Europe. Instead, after visiting Cook and Price, immediately left for Colorado to stay with family friend.

1910 Marriage between Cook and Price ended, after the birth of two children, Harl and Nilla. Glaspell returned to Davenport and continued relationship with Cook. She spearheaded the "Library Controversy," against censorship at the Davenport Library.

1911 *The Visioning* (novel) published.

1911–13 Published short stories and traveled between Davenport, Chicago, New York, and Provincetown, during the two-year period required for Cook to receive his divorce.

1912 Short story collection *Lifted Masks* published.

1913 April 14, Glaspell and Cook married in Weehawken, New Jersey. Soon after Glaspell had a miscarriage, which prevented her from having any children, although she became an active stepmother to Harl and Nilla.

1913–15 Along with friends, including John Reed, Mabel Dodge, Sinclair Lewis, Wilber Daniel Steele, and Mary Heaton Vorse, Glaspell and Cook became active in New York literary and political life, spending winters in Greenwich Village and summers in Provincetown.

1915 *Fidelity* (novel) published. July 15 (?), performed *Suppressed Desires,* written with Cook, in the Provincetown home of Neith Boyce and Hutchins Hapgood, on a double bill with Boyce's *Constancy* (first unofficial production of the Provincetown Players), Glaspell playing Henrietta; Cook playing Stephen.

Summer 1916	The Provincetown Players officially named and organized. Eugene O'Neill joined the group, and his play *Bound East for Cardiff* was performed in the Wharf Theatre, July 24–28. *Trifles* was performed on August 8.
1916	In fall, at urging of Cook, the Provincetown Players moved to Greenwich Village, establishing the Playwrights' Theatre, first at 139 MacDougal Street and, after 1918, at 133 MacDougal. Glaspell became a member of the board, a position she held for the six years the Provincetown Players existed.
1917–18	Opening of *The People* (Mar. 9–14), Glaspell as the Woman from Idaho; *Close the Book* (Nov. 2–6), Glaspell as Mrs. Root; and *The Outside* (Dec. 28–Jan. 3, 1918), Glaspell as Allie Mayo. "A Jury of Her Peers" published in *Everyweek,* March 5.
1918	*Woman's Honor* (Apr. 26–May 2), Glaspell as the Cheated One; *Tickless Time,* written with George Cram Cook (Dec. 20–26).
1919	*Bernice,* Glaspell's first full-length play (Mar. 21–27), Glaspell as Abbie.
1919–20	Sabbatical from Provincetown Players, traveled to Davenport; in Provincetown wrote *Inheritors* and *The Verge. Plays* published.
1921	*Inheritors* (Mar. 21–Apr. 10). *The Verge* (Nov. 14–Dec. 1).
1922	*Chains of Dew* (Apr. 27–May 15). Provincetown Players voted on February 2 to close theater for year. Glaspell and Cook sailed March 2 for indefinite stay in Greece, fulfilling Cook's lifelong dream.
1922–24	Lived in Athens, Delphi, and summered on slopes of Mount Parnassus. Glaspell returned to Davenport in late 1922 when her father died but returned quickly to Greece, accompanied by Nilla.

1924	January 14, Cook died from glanders, a disease contracted from a pet dog, and was buried in Delphi. Glaspell returned to the United States in February and took up residence in Provincetown. Met writer Norman Matson, with whom she lived for the next eight years.
1925	Edited *Greek Coins,* a dual English/Greek edition of Cook's poems. Began work on biography of Cook.
1926	Publication of *Trifles and Six Other Short Plays.*
1927	*The Road to the Temple* (Cook biography) published. Participated in demonstrations and letter writing in support of Sacco and Vanzetti. *The Comic Artist,* written in collaboration with Norman Matson, published.
1928	*The Comic Artist* premiered in London (Strand), June 24; (official run began at the Players' Theatre November 22, 1929; produced in New York, April 19, 1933. *Brook Evans* (novel) published, marking Glaspell's return to fiction after thirteen years.
1929	*Fugitive's Return* (novel), based on experiences in Greece, published.
1930	*Alison's House,* produced by Eva LeGallienne's Civic Repertory Company at the Civic Repertory Theatre in New York, December 1.
1931	Won Pulitzer Prize for *Alison's House,* the second woman to be so honored. *Ambrose Holt and Family* (novel) published, a variation of plot used in *Chains of Dew.*
1932	Matson left her to marry Anna Walling, nineteen-year-old daughter of Glaspell's friend, Anna, Sr.
1936–38	Named director of Midwest Play Bureau of Federal Theatre Project; oversaw productions of numerous plays, including Arnold Sundgaard's *Spirochete* and Theodore Ward's *Big White Fog.*

1938	Resigned position and returned to Provincetown, to her home at 564 Commercial Street.
1939	*The Morning Is Near Us* (novel) published.
1940	*The Morning Is Near Us* chosen as Literary Guild selection. Honored by J. B. Lippincott. *Cherished and Shared of Old* (children's story) published.
1942	*Norma Ashe* (novel) published.
1945	*Judd Rankin's Daughter* (novel) published. *Springs Eternal* (unpublished and unproduced play).
1948	Died on July 27 of pulmonary embolism, after struggling with cancer. She was cremated, a commemorative headstone laid in Truro at the Snow cemetery.

Susan Glaspell Bibliography

Original Publications

The following list of publications by Susan Glaspell is restricted to book publications in English and translation. For short stories, essays, and unpublished works see *Susan Glaspell: A Research and Production Sourcebook,* edited by Mary Papke.

Alison's House: A Play in Three Acts. New York: Samuel French, 1930.

Ambrose Holt and Family (novel). New York: Frederick A. Stokes, 1931. London: Victor Gollancz Ltd., 1931. Reprint, Hamburg, Paris, and Bologna: The Albatross, 1932; New York: A. L. Burt, 1933.

Bernice: A Play in Three Acts. In *Plays* (1920). Reprinted in *Three Plays by Susan Glaspell* (1924); and in *Contemporary American Dramatists,* vol. 3, no. 3. London: Ernest Benn Ltd., 1924.

Brook Evans (novel). New York: Frederick A. Stokes, 1928. London: Victor Gollancz Ltd., 1928. Translated as *Narzissa,* by Georg Schwartz. Vienna: TAL, 1929. Reprint, New York: A. L. Burt, 1930 (photoplay edition with title *The Right to Love*); reprinted as *The Right to Love.* London: Readers Library Publishing Co., 1932. Translated as *Dreptul La Iubire,* by Elena Fotescu. Iaşi, Rumania: Albina Româneasca, 1936.

Cherished and Shared of Old (children's story), illus. Alice Harvey. New York: Julian Messner, Inc., 1940. Reprinted in *Fireside Book of Yuletide Tales,* ed. E. C. Wagenknecht. Indianapolis: Bobbs Merrill, 1940.

Close the Book. In *Plays* (1920).

The Comic Artist: A Play in Three Acts (with Norman Matson). New York: Frederick A. Stokes, 1927. Reprinted in *Contemporary American Dramatists,* vol. 6. London: Ernest Benn Ltd., 1927.

The Complete Edition of the Plays of Susan Glaspell, ed. and intro. Linda Ben-Zvi and J. Ellen Gainor, forthcoming.

Fidelity: A Novel. Boston: Small, Maynard, 1915. London: Jarrolds Pub. Ltd., 1924. Translated as *Treue,* by Rudolf Nutt and Hans Beppo Wagenseil. Wiesbaden: Limes-Verlag, 1947.

Fugitive's Return (novel). New York: Frederick A. Stokes, 1929. London: Victor Gollancz Ltd., 1929. Reprint, New York: A. L. Burt, 1931.

The Glory of the Conquered: The Story of a Great Love (novel), New York: Frederick A. Stokes, 1909. London: Sir Isaac Pitman and Sons, 1909. Reprint, Philadelphia: Library Company of Philadelphia, 1910; New York: A. L. Burt, 1912; London: Jarrolds Pub. Ltd., 1925. Translated as *Magluparin Zaferi*, by Sofi Huri. Istanbul: Amerikan Bord Nesriyat Daimesi, 1954. *Greek Coins: Poems*, by George Cram Cooke. Ed. Susan Glaspell. New York: George Doran, 1925.

Inheritors: A Play in Three Acts. Boston: Small, Maynard, 1921. Reprinted in *Contemporary American Dramatists*, vol. 2. London: Ernest Benn Ltd., 1924; and in *Three Plays by Susan Glaspell* (1924). Reprint, New York: Dodd, Mead, 1928. Reprinted in *Plays by Susan Glaspell* (1987).

Judd Rankin's Daughter (novel). Philadelphia: J. B. Lippincott, 1945. Published as *Prodigal Giver*. London: Victor Gollancz Ltd., 1946. *Judd Rankin's Daughter*. Books of Distinction. New York: Grosset and Dunlap, 1947.

"*A Jury of Her Peers*." In *Best Short Stories of 1917*, ed. Edward J. O'Brien. Boston: Small, Maynard, 1918. Reprinted in *A Jury of Her Peers*. London: Ernest Benn Ltd., 1927; Translated in *Ai Là Thù-pham* (an anthology containing works by Washington Irving, Louis Bromfield, Frank R. Stockton, Mary E. Wilkins Freeman, Susan Glaspell, and Bret Harte), trans. Anh Thu, Kim Dĩnh et al. Saigon: Tho'i-Dai, 1959. (For contemporary listings, see Papke, 125.)

Lifted Masks: Stories. New York: Frederick A. Stokes, 1912. Reprinted in "*Lifted Masks*" *and Other Works*, ed. and intro. Eric S. Rabkin. Ann Arbor: University of Michigan Press, 1993.

Looking after Clara (a contest selection, arranged by L. H. Strack). Boston: Walter H. Baker, 1926.

The Morning Is Near Us: A Novel. New York: Frederick A. Stokes, 1940. London: Victor Gollancz Ltd., 1940. Reprint, New York: Literary Guild of America, Inc., 1940. Translated as *A Madrugada Se Aproxima*, by Maluh de Ouro Prêto. Rio de Janeiro: Olympio, 1943.

Norma Ashe: A Novel. Philadelphia: J. B. Lippincott, 1942. Reprint, London: Victor Gollancz Ltd., 1943.

The Outside: A Play in One Act. In *Plays* (1920). Reprinted in *Sea Plays*, ed. Colin Campbell Clement. Boston: Small, Maynard, 1925; and in *A Century of Plays by American Women*, ed. Rachel France. New York: Richards Rosen Press, 1979. Reprinted in *Plays by Susan Glaspell* (1987).

"*The People*" *and* "*Close to the Book*": *Two One-Act Plays*. New York: Frank Shay, 1918. *The People* and *Close to the Book*, both reprinted in *Plays* (1920).

Plays. Boston: Small, Maynard, 1920. New York: Dodd, Mead, 1920.

Plays by Susan Glaspell, ed. and intro. C. W. E. Bigsby. Cambridge: Cambridge University Press, 1987.

The Pulitzer Prize Plays, ed. K. H. C. Cordell and W. H. Cordell. New York: Random House, 1935.

The Road to the Temple: A Biography of George Cram Cook. London: Ernest
Benn Ltd., 1926. Reprint (with four illustrations from photographs); New
York: Frederick A. Stokes, 1927; and without illustrations and with a new
foreword by the author. New York: Frederick A. Stokes, 1941.

Suppressed Desires: A Comedy in Two Scenes (with George Cram Cook). New
York: Frank Shay, 1916. (The book's cover reads: *The Provincetown Plays
II: Supressed Desires: A Freudian Comedy in One Act,* by George Cram
Cook and Susan Glaspell.) Reprinted in *Representative One Act Plays by
American Authors,* ed. Margaret G. Mayorga. Boston: Little, Brown, 1920;
in *The Provincetown Plays,* ed. George Cram Cook and Frank Shay. Cincin-
nati: Stewart Kidd, 1921. Reprint, New York and London: Samuel French,
Inc., 1932. Reprinted in *Trifles and Six Other Short Plays* (1926). Reprint,
Boston: Walter H. Baker, 1934. (For contemporary listings, see Papke, 101.)

Three Plays (*The Verge, Inheritors,* and *Bernice*). In *Contemporary American
Dramatists,* vols. 1–3. London: Ernest Benn Ltd., 1924.

Tickless Time: A Comedy in One Act (in collaboration with George Cram Cook).
In *Plays* (1920). Reprinted in *Contemporary One-Act Plays of 1921* (Ameri-
can), sel. and ed. Frank Shay. Cincinnati: Stewart Kidd, 1922. Reprinted in
Baker's Royalty Plays. Boston: Walter H. Baker, 1925.

Trifles. New York: Frank Shay / The Washington Square Players, 1916. Reprinted
in *Plays* (1920); and in *Trifles and Six Other Short Plays* (two of them
written in collaboration with George Cram Cook) (1926). Reprint, New
York: Samuel French, 1932. Reprinted in *Plays by Susan Glaspell* (1987).
(There are over thirty anthologies of drama that include *Trifles.* For contemporary listings, see Papke, 102–3.)

Trifles and Six Other Short Plays (with George Cram Cook). London: Ernest
Benn Ltd., 1926.

The Verge: A Play in Three Acts. Boston: Small, Maynard, 1922. New York:
Dodd, Mead, 1922. Reprinted in *Contemporary American Dramatists,* vol.
1. London: Ernest Benn Ltd., 1924; and in *Three Plays* (1924), and *Plays by
Susan Glaspell* (1987).

The Visioning: A Novel. New York: Frederick A. Stokes, 1911. Reprint, London:
John Murray, 1912; New York: A. L. Burt, 1913.

Whom Mince Pie Hath Joined Together (contest selection by L. H. Strack). Boston: Walter H. Baker, 1926.

Woman's Honor. In *Plays* (1920).

Selected Critical Works

For an annotated, chronological study of reviews and critical articles about Glaspell, American women playwrights, and the Provincetown Players, see Mary
Papke.

Aarons, Victoria. "A Community of Women: Surviving Marriage in the Wilderness." *Rendezvous: Idaho State University Journal of the Arts and Letters* 21 (1986): 3–11.

Alkalay-Gut, Karen. " 'A Jury of Her Peers': The Importance of Trifles." *Studies in Short Fiction* 21 (Winter 1984): 1–9.

Andrews, Clarence. "Parnassus on the Prairie." *A Literary History of Iowa.* Iowa City: University of Iowa Press, 1972, 165–85.

Andrews, Clarence, and Marcia Noe. "Susan Glaspell of Davenport." *The Iowan* 25 (Summer 1977): 46–53.

Atlas, Marilyn. "Creating Women's Myth: Emily Dickinson's Legacy to Susan Glaspell." *Focus: Teaching English Language Arts* 8 (Fall 1981): 55–61.

Bach, Gerhard. "Susan Glaspell: A Bibliography of Dramatic Criticism." *The Great Lakes Review* 3 (1977): 1–34.

———. "Susan Glaspell: Provincetown Playwright." *Great Lakes Review* 4 (1978): 31–43.

———. *Susan Glaspell und die Provincetown Players: Die Anfänge des modernen amerikanischen Dramas und Theaters.* Frankfort: Peter Lang, 1979.

Barlow, Judith. "Introduction." *Plays by American Women: The Early Years.* 1981. Reprint. New York: Applause Book Pub., 1985: ix–xxxiii.

Ben-Zvi, Linda. " 'Murder, She Wrote': The Genesis of *Trifles.*" *Theatre Journal* 44 (1992): 141–62. Reprinted in this volume.

———. "Susan Glaspell: A Biographical Essay." In *Notable Women in American Theatre,* ed. Vera Roberts et al. Westport, Conn.: Greenwood Pennsylvania, 1990: 341–46.

———. "Susan Glaspell and Eugene O'Neill." *Eugene O'Neill Newsletter* 6 (1982): 21–29.

———. "Susan Glaspell, Eugene O'Neill, and the Imagery of Gender." *Eugene O'Neill Newsletter* 10 (1986): 22–27.

———. "Susan Glaspell's Contributions to Modern Women Playwrights." In *Feminine Focus,* ed. Enoch Brater. New York: Oxford University Press, 1989: 147–66.

Bigsby, C. W. E. "Introduction." *Susan Glaspell: Plays.* Cambridge: Cambridge University Press, 1987: 1–31.

———. "Provincetown: The Birth of Twentieth-Century American Drama." In *A Critical Introduction to Twentieth Century American Drama: Vol. 1, 1900–1940.* Cambridge: Cambridge University Press, 1982: 1–35.

Bongas, Pamela Joan. "The Woman's Woman on the American Stage in the 1930s." Ph.D. diss., University of Missouri–Columbia, 1980. *Diss. Abstracts Intl.,* no. 42 (1981): 456A.

Carroll, Kathleen. *Centering Women Onstage: Susan Glaspell's Dialogic Strategy of Resistance.* Ph.D. diss., University of Maryland, College Park, 1990. *Diss. Abstracts Intl.* 52, no. 3 (Sept. 1991): 914A.

Chinoy, Helen Krich. "Suppressed Desires: Women in the Theater." In *Women, the Arts, and the 1920s in Paris and New York,* ed. Kenneth W. Wheeler and Virginia Lee Lussier. New Brunswick: Transaction Books, 1982: 126–32.

Corey, Anne. *Susan Glaspell: Playwright of Social Consciousness.* Ph.D. diss., New York University, 1990. *Diss. Abstracts Intl.* 51, no. 12 (June 1991): 4119A–20A.

Dymkowski, Christine. "On the Edge: The Plays of Susan Glaspell." *Modern Drama* 31 (March 1988): 91–105.

Fetterley, Judith. "Reading about Reading: 'A Jury of Her Peers,' 'Murder in the Rue Morgue,' and 'The Yellow Wallpaper.' " In *Gender and Reading: Essays on Readers. Texts and Contexts,* ed. Elizabeth A. Flynn and Patrocinio P. Schweickart. Baltimore: Johns Hopkins University Press, 1986: 147–64.

Flavin, Louise. " 'A Jury of Her Peers' Needs a Jury of Its Peers." *Teaching English in the Two-Year College* 10 (Spring 1984): 259–60.

France, Rachel. "Apropos of Women and the Folk Play." In *Women in American Theatre,* ed. Helen Krich Chinoy and Linda Walsh Jenkins. New York: Crown, 1981. Rev. ed. New York: TCC, Inc., 1987: 145–52.

Friedman, Sharon. "Feminism as Theme in Twentieth Century American Women's Drama." *American Studies* 25 (Spring 1984): 69–89.

———. "Feminist Concerns in the Works of Four Twentieth-Century American Women Dramatists: Susan Glaspell, Rachel Crothers, Lillian Hellman, and Lorraine Hansberry." Ph.D. diss., New York University, 1977. *Diss. Abstracts Intl.,* no. 39 (1978): 858A.

Gainor, J. Ellen. "A Stage of Her Own: Susan Glaspell's *The Verge* and Women's Dramaturgy." *Journal of American Drama and Theatre* 1 (Spring 1989): 79–99.

Gilbert, Sandra M., and Susan Gubar. *No Man's Land: The Place of the Woman Writer in the Twentieth Century,* vol. 1: *The War of the Words.* New Haven, Conn.: Yale University Press, 1988.

Goldman, Michael. "Review of *Plays by Susan Glaspell,* ed. C. W. E. Bigsby. *Times Literary Supplement* 5 (February 1988): 139.

Gould, Jean. "Susan Glaspell and the Provincetown Players." *Modern American Playwrights.* New York: Dodd, Mead, 1966: 26–49.

Gubar, Susan, and Anne Hedin. " '*A Jury of Her Peers*': Teaching and Learning in the Indiana Women's Prison." *College English* 43 (1981): 779–89.

Hedges, Elaine. "Small Things Reconsidered: Susan Glaspell's 'A Jury of Her Peers.' "*Women Studies* 12 (1986): 89–110. Reprinted in this volume.

Helle, Anita Plath. "Re-presenting Women Writers Onstage: A Retrospective to the Present." In *Making a Spectacle: Feminist Essays on Contemporary Women's Theatre,* ed. Lynda Hart. Ann Arbor: University of Michigan Press, 1989: 195–208.

Ingle, Patricia. "Departures from Realism on the New York Stage, 1919–1930."

Ph.D. diss., University of Arkansas, 1965. *Diss. Abstracts Intl.*, no. 26 (1965): 1043.

Jenkins, Linda Walsh. "Locating the Language of Gender Experience." *Women and Performance: A Journal of Feminist Theatre* 2 (1984): 5–20.

Kazmark, Mary Ellen. "The Portrayal of Women in American Theatre, 1925–1930." Ph.D. diss., University of California, Los Angeles, 1979. *Diss. Abstracts Intl.*, no.40 (1980): 3633A.

Keyssar, Helene. *Feminist Theatre: An Introduction to Plays of Contemporary British and American Women.* New York: Grove Press, 1985.

Kolin, Philip. "Therapists in Susan Glaspell's *Suppressed Desires* and David Rabe's *In the Boom Boom Room.*" *Notes on Contemporary Literature* 18 (1988): 2–3.

Kolodny, Annette. "A Map for Rereading: Or, Gender and the Interpretation of Literary Texts." *New Literary History* 11 (Spring 1980): 451–67. Reprinted in *The New Feminist Criticism: Essays on Women, Literature, and Theory,* ed. Elaine Showalter. New York: Pantheon Books, 1985: 46–62.

Larabee, Ann E. "Death in Delphi: Susan Glaspell and the Companionate Marriage." *Mid American Review* 2 (1987): 93–106.

———. "Meeting the Outside Face to Face: Susan Glaspell, Djuna Barnes, and O'Neill's *The Emperor Jones.*" In *Modern American Drama: The Female Canon,* ed. June Schlueter. Rutherford, N.J.: Fairleigh Dickinson University Press, 1990: 77–85.

Maddock, Mary Denise. "Private Scripts, Public Roles: American Women's Drama, 1900–1937." Ph.D. diss., Indiana University, 1987. *Diss. Abstracts Intl.*, no. 49 (1988): 819A.

Mael, Phyllis. "*Trifles:* The Path to Sisterhood." *Literature/Film Quarterly* 17, no. 4 (1989): 281–84.

Makowsky, Veronica. *Susan Glaspell's Century of American Women.* New York: Oxford University Press, 1993.

Malpede, Karen. *Women in Theatre: Compassion and Hope.* New York: Drama Book Pub., 1983.

Mustazza, Leonard. "Gender and Justice in Susan Glaspell's 'A Jury of Her Peers.' " *Law and Semiotics* 2 (1988): 271–76.

———. "Generic Translation and Thematic Shift in Susan Glaspell's *Trifles* and 'A Jury of Her Peers.' " *Studies in Short Fiction* 26, no. 4 (Fall 1989): 489–96.

Newman, Kathy. "Susan Glaspell and *Trifles:* 'Nothing Here but Kitchen Things.' " *Trivia: A Journal of Ideas* (Fall 1983): 88–94.

Noe, Marcia. *A Critical Biography of Susan Glaspell.* Ph.D. diss., University of Iowa, 1976. *Diss. Abstracts Intl.* 37 (1977): 7753A.

———. "A Romantic and Miraculous City." *Western Illinois Regional Studies* 1 (Fall 1978): 176–98.

———. "Region as Metaphor in the Plays of Susan Glaspell." *Western Illinois Regional Studies* 4 (Spring 1981): 77–85.

————. "Susan Glaspell's Analysis of the Midwestern Character," with a Susan Glaspell checklist. *Books at Iowa* no. 27 (1977): 3–20.

————. *Voice from the Heartland.* Macomb: Western Illinois University Press, 1983.

Ozieblo, Barbara. "Rebellion and Rejection: The Plays of Susan Glaspell." In *Modern American Drama: The Female Canon,* ed. June Schlueter. Rutherford: Fairleigh Dickinson University Press, 1990.

Papke, Mary. *Susan Glaspell: A Research and Production Sourcebook.* Westport, Conn.: Greenwood Press, 1993.

Payerle, Margaret Jane. " 'A Little Like Outlaws': The Metaphorical Use of Restricted Space in the Works of Certain American Women Realistic Writers." Ph.D. diss., Case Western Reserve University, 1984. *Diss. Abstracts Intl.,* no. 45 (1985): 2876A.

Radel, Nicholas F., "Provincetown Plays: Women Writers and O'Neill's American Intertext." *Essays in Theatre* 9 (November 1990): 31–43.

Rudnick, Lois. "The New Woman." In *1915, the Cultural Moment: The New Politics, the New Woman, the New Psychology, the New Art and the New Theatre in America,* ed. Adele Heller and Lois Rudnick. New Brunswick: Rutgers University Press, 1991: 69–81.

Sarlós, Robert K. *Jig Cook and the Provincetown Players: Theatre in Ferment.* Amherst: University of Massachusetts Press, 1982.

Shafer, Yvonne. "Susan Glaspell: German Influence, American Playwright." *Zeitschrift für Anglistik und Amerikanistik* 36 (1988): 333–38.

Sheaffer, Louis. "Glaspell, Susan Keating." In *Dictionary of American Biography: Supplement Four, 1946–50,* ed. John A. Garraty and Edward T. James. New York: Charles Scribner's Sons, 1974: 329–30.

Showalter, Elaine. "Common Threads." *Sister's Choice: Tradition and Change in American Women's Writing.* Oxford: Clarendon Press, 1991.

Sievers, W. David. *Freud on Broadway.* New York: Hermitage House, 1955.

Smith, Beverly. "Women's Work—Trifles? The Skill and Insights of Playwright Susan Glaspell." *International Journal of Women's Studies* 5 (March/April 1982): 172–84.

Sochen, June. *Movers and Shakers: American Women Thinkers and Activists, 1900–1970.* New York: Quadrangle/The *New York Times* Book Co., 1973.

————. *The New Woman: Feminism in Greenwich Village.* New York: Quadrangle/New York Times Book Co., 1972.

Stein, Karen. "The Women's World of Glaspell's *Trifles.*" In *Women in American Theatre,* ed. Helen Krich Chinoy and Linda Walsh Jenkins. Rev. ed. New York: TCC, Inc., 1987: 253–56.

Stephens, Judith. "Gender, Ideology, and Dramatic Convention in Progressive Era Plays, 1890–1920." In *Performing Feminisms: Feminist Critical Theory and Theater,* ed. Sue-Ellen Case. Baltimore: Johns Hopkins University Press, 1990: 283–93.

Sutherland, Cynthia. "American Women Playwrights as Mediators of the 'Woman's Problem.' " *Modern Drama* 21 (1978): 319–36.

Tanselle, Thomas. "George Cram Cook and the Poetry of Living, with a Checklist." *Books at Iowa* 24 (April 1976): 3–31, 35–37.

Toohey, John L. "1930–31: *Alison's House.*" *A History of the Pulitzer Prize Plays.* New York: The Citadel Press, 1967: 89–93.

Trimberger, Ellen Kay. "Feminism, Men, and Modern Love: Greenwich Village, 1900–1922. In *Forms of Desire: The Politics of Sexuality,* ed. Ann Snitow et al. New York: Monthly Review Press, 1983: 131–52.

Waterman, Arthur. *Susan Glaspell.* Boston: Twayne, 1966.

———. "Susan Glaspell and the Provincetown." *Modern Drama* 7 (1964): 174–84.

———. "Susan Glaspell's *The Verge:* An Experiment in Feminism." *Great Lakes Review* 6 (1979): 17–23.

Weisbrod, Carol. "Images of the Woman Juror." *Harvard Women's Law Journal* 9 (Spring 1986): 59–82.

Williams, Linda. "*A Jury of Their Peers:* Marlene Gorris's *A Question of Silence.*" In *Postmodernism and Its Discontents,* ed. E. Ann Kaplan. London: Verso Press, 1988: 107–15.

Contributors

Karen Alkalay-Gut teaches at Tel Aviv University. Her publications include *Alone in the Dawn: The Life of Adelaide Crapsey* (1988) and seven books of poetry. Numerous articles related to women writers have appeared in the following journals: *American Literature, Journal of Modern Literature, World Literature Today, Studies in Short Fiction, Poesis*, and *American Book Review*. She is presently working on murder.

Gerhard Bach is Professor of American Studies at the Pädagogische Hochschule in Heidelberg, Germany. In 1985–86 he was a Fulbright Senior Lecturer at West Virginia University and from 1990 to 1992 he was Visiting Professor of English at Brigham Young University. He is author of *Susan Glaspell und die Provincetown Players* (1979). His articles on Glaspell have appeared in *American Literary Realism* and *Great Lakes Review*. He is also editor of *Saul Bellow at 75: A Collection of Critical Essays* (1991) and has published on contemporary Jewish writers in *Saul Bellow Journal* and *Studies in American Jewish Literature*.

Judith E. Barlow is Associate Professor of English and Women's Studies at the State University of New York at Albany. She has published *Final Acts: The Creation of Three Late O'Neill Plays* (1985) and edited *Plays by American Women: The Early Years* (1981; rpt., 1985). She has written on Eugene O'Neill, Tina Howe, and Rachel Crothers in the books *Feminine Focus, International Dictionary of the Theatre, Eugene O'Neill in China*, and *Eugene Dramatists* and in such journals as *Studies in American Drama* and *Modern Drama*. She has recently published a second volume of *American Women Playwrights, 1930–1960*.

Linda Ben-Zvi is Professor of English and Theater at Colorado State University. Her publications include the following: *Samuel Beckett* (1986) and *Women in Beckett: Performance and Critical Perspectives* (1990), and numerous articles on modern drama have appeared in journals including *PMLA, Contemporary Drama, Modern Drama,* and *Theatre Journal.* She is currently editing *Vital Voices: An Anthology of Plays by American Women Playwrights,* a collection of essays entitled *Theater in Israel,* co-editing the plays of Susan Glaspell, and completing the authorized biography of Glaspell.

Jackie Czerepinski received a Ph.D. in Theory and Criticism from the University of Colorado at Boulder, where she taught performance of literature and fundamentals of acting in the Theater Department. She has also served as dramaturg for the Colorado Shakespeare Festival and the University of Colorado Theater Department. She has also taught in the Theater Department at Idaho State University in Pocatello.

Sharon Friedman is on the faculty of the Gallatin Division at New York University. Her publications related to women and theater include "Feminism as Theme in Twentieth Century American Women's Drama," in *American Studies,* and a bibliographical essay on Lorraine Hansberry, in *Contemporary Authors Bibliographic Series: American Dramatists.* She is also coauthor of *Writing and Thinking in the Social Sciences.*

J. Ellen Gainor is Assistant Professor of Theater at Cornell University. Her books include *Shaw's Daughters: Discourses of Gender and Female Identity in the Work of George Bernard Shaw* (1992), and she has published on Shaw, Sam Shepard, and Glaspell in *Themes of Drama, The Performance of Power: Theatrical Discourse and Politics,* and *New England Theatre Journal, Vol. 1.* She is presently co-editing the plays of Susan Glaspell.

Elaine Hedges is Professor of American Literature and Coordinator of Women's Studies at Towson State University. She is editor of Charlotte Perkins Gilman's *The Yellow Wallpaper* (1973) and of a critical biographical study of Meridel LeSueur, *Ripening* (1981). Her other publications include *In Her Own Image: Women Working in the Arts* (with Ingrid Wendt, 1980) and *Land and Imagination: The Rural Dream in America* (with William L. Hedges, 1980).

Karen Laughlin is Associate Professor of English at Florida State University, where she teaches drama, film, and critical theory. Her articles on dramatic theory and on the work of Beckett, Brecht, Gambaro, Henley, and other modern playwrights have appeared in numerous anthologies and in journals including *Modern Drama, Latin American Theatre Review,* and *Women & Performance*. She is currently editing a collection of essays on *Theatre and Feminist Aesthetics*.

Colette Lindroth is Professor of English at Caldwell College. She has published on Jean Rhys; on film and literature, in *Film and Literature Quarterly;* and on the work of Milan Kundera, in *Modern Fiction*.

Veronica Makowsky is Professor of English at the University of Connecticut. She has edited *Henry Adams* and *Studies in Henry James* by R. P. Blackmur and has published essays on F. Scott Fitzgerald, Walker Percy, Stark Young, and Caroline Gordon. Her most recent book is *Susan Glaspell's Century of Amerian Women* (1993).

Karen Malpede is a playwright, critic, and teacher. She has written three books on theater: *People's Theatre in Amerika,* a study of radical theater movements in the United States; *Three Works by the Open Theatre,* an analysis of works by this avant-garde repertory group; and *Women in Theatre: Compassion and Hope,* edited and with an introduction by Malpede. Among her many plays are *A Lament for Three Women, The End of the War,* and *Sappho and Aphrodite,* published under the title *A Monster Has Stolen the Sun and Other Plays*. Her articles on theater appear in the *New York Times,* the *Village Voice, Theatre Journal,* and other newspapers and periodicals.

Liza Maeve Nelligan is completing a Ph.D. in Women's Studies at the University of California, San Diego. She is a founding member of a Colorado chapter of "Ladies against Women" and has performed her character "Mrs. Phyllis Leschaft" at the Graduate Women's Studies Conference, in Ann Arbor, Michigan, and at the Colorado Women's Studies Association, in Boulder.

Marcia Noe is Professor of English at the University of Tennessee at Chattanooga. Her book *Voice from the Heartland* (1983) was the first extensive biographical study of the life of Susan Glaspell. She has also published articles on Glaspell in several periodicals, including *Western*

Illinois Regional Studies, which published her biography in their monograph series.

Barbara Ozieblo is Professor Titular in the Department of English at the University of Malaga, Spain. She has also held a Research Fellowship at the University of Sheffield, England. She has published on Susan Glaspell in *Modern American Drama: The Female Canon* (1990). She is presently working on a biographical study of Glaspell.

Katharine Rodier is currently a doctoral student at the University of Connecticut. She has contributed reviews to *American Literature* and *Review* and published poems in several journals. Her essay "Glaspell and Dickinson: Surveying the Premises of *Alison's House*" received the Kathleen Gibson McPeek Critical Essay Award at the University of Connecticut.

Megan Terry is playwright and codirector of the Omaha Magic Theatre. A leading American writer, with over forty plays to her credit, she was a founding member of the Open Theatre. Her plays include *Calm Down Mother, Viet Rock,* and *Approaching Simone,* for which she won the Obie Award in 1970 for Best Play, and numerous productions at the Magic Theatre, including *Mollie Bailey's Travelling Family Circus: Featuring Scenes from the Life of Mother Jones, American King's English for Queens,* and *Babes in the Bighouse.*

Index

273, 289. *See also* Hossack, Margaret; "Jury of Her Peers, A"
absence of main character, 34–35
and cult of domesticity, 87–88
differences from Hossack case, 34–35
and female bonding, 86–87
and feminism, 41–42
first production, 86
kitchen setting of, 35
meaning of Minnie Wright's name, 72
men's attitudes toward clues, 76–77, 88
Minnie's position in the bed, 74–75
mode of killing, 74
motives for violence in, 35, 38–39
and quilting, 73, 79–80
real story behind, 21–33
relation of characters to Hossack case, 35–36
reviews of, 245
role of men in, 36
role of women in, 37–38
significance of knotting, 79–80
symbolism and feminine significance of the kitchen, 72–73
synopsis of, 33–34
women sticking together, 75–77, 78–80, 89–90
and women's legal status, 71–72, 77
women's reaction to clues, 88–89
writing of, 21, 210–11
Trimberger, Ellen Kay, 274–75
Tuesday Club, 105
Two Slatterns and a King, 261, 290
Two Sons, The, 280

Utterbach, Max (in Norma Ashe), 327

Van Doren, Mark, 199–200, 205
Verge, The, 6, 8–9, 10, 112, 115,
116–17, 127, 131, 152, 156, 241, 245, 246, 248, 249–50, 268, 280, 290
binary oppositions in, 136
and contemporary French feminist theory, 132–33
contrasted with *Trifles,* 90, 92, 93, 98
dialog from, 125, 129, 134–35, 137, 138, 139, 140, 253–54
and feminine individualism, 91
first production, 90, 129
and loss of language, 140, 252–53
madness of Claire Archer, 91, 97, 115–16, 123, 152, 254
and 1920s feminism, 90–91, 126
nonverbal expression of meaning, 251–52
questioning of companionate marriage, 96–97
reviews, 97, 99, 129, 131–32, 133, 138, 245–46, 250–51
and romantic love, 124–26
tension between sisterhood and individualism, 93–94
and transformation of women, 98–99
Vienna School, 105
"Vine, The," 60
Visioning, The, 319
Vollmer, Lulu, 155
Vorse, Mary Heaton, 41, 206–9, 213, 242, 260, 277, 287, 292
as New Woman, 208
as source of information on Emily Dickinson for Glaspell, 207–9

Ware, Caroline, 185
Warren, Mercy Otis, 7
Warren, Samuel, 223–24
Washington Square Players, 108, 109, 112, 168